Families as
Learning Environments
for Children

Families as Learning Environments for Children

Edited by

LUIS M. LAOSA

and

IRVING E. SIGEL

Educational Testing Service
Princeton, New Jersey

PLENUM PRESS • NEW YORK AND LONDON

Library of Congress Cataloging in Publication Data

Main entry under title:

Families as learning environments for children.

  (Families—research and practice; v. 1)
  Includes bibliographical references and index.
  1. Child development. 2. Family. 3. Learning, Psychology of. 4. Intellect. I. Laosa,
Luis M., 1946–   . II. Sigel, Irving E. III. Series.
QH767.9.F35 1982   649′.1   82-18062
ISBN 0-306-40939-9

© 1982 Plenum Press, New York
A Division of Plenum Publishing Corporation
233 Spring Street, New York, N.Y. 10013

Printed in the United States of America

Contributors

Barbara J. Anderson, University of Michigan, Ann Arbor, Michigan

Richard D. Ashmore, Rutgers—The State University, New Brunswick, New Jersey

Margaret K. Bacon, Rutgers—The State University, New Brunswick, New Jersey

Richard L. Cain, Jr., National Institute of Child Health and Human Development, Bethesda, Maryland

W. Partick Dickson, University of Wisconsin, Madison, Wisconsin

Candice Feiring, Rutgers Medical School—UMDNJ, Medical Educational Building, New Brunswick, New Jersey

Steven Fosburg, Abt Associates, Inc., Cambridge, Massachusetts

Robert D. Hess, Stanford University, Stanford, California

Susan Holloway, Stanford University, Stanford, California

Michael E. Lamb, Departments of Psychology, Psychiatry, and Pediatrics, University of Utah, Salt Lake City, Utah

Luis M. Laosa, Educational Testing Service, Princeton, New Jersey

Michael Lewis, Rutgers Medical School—UMDNJ, Medical Educational Building, New Brunswick, New Jersey

Ann V. McGillicuddy-DeLisi, Educational Testing Service, Princeton, New Jersey

Ross D. Parke, Department of Psychology, University of Illinois, Urbana-Champaign, Illinois

Frank A. Pedersen, National Institute of Child Health and Human Development, Bethesda, Maryland

James L. Peterson, Child Trends, Inc., Washington, D.C.

Thomas G. Power, Department of Psychology, University of Houston, Houston, Texas

Gary G. Price, University of Wisconsin, Madison, Wisconsin

Irving E. Sigel, Educationial Testing Service, Princeton, New Jersey

Martha J. Zaslow, National Institute of Child Health and Human Development, Bethesda, Maryland

Nicholas Zill, Child Trends, Inc., Washington, D.C.

Preface

The chapters in this volume reflect the work and thoughts of a group of researchers interested in studying families as learning environments for children. As we proceed in our quest to identify and understand with some specificity the familial factors associated with the intellectual and social development of children, the time is ripe for the reintroduction of families as units of study in psychological and educational research. With the increasing focus on the changing organization of the modern family, it is of more than academic interest to identify those variables that play a significant role in the child's development. Such knowledge certainly should help in the planning and design of appropriate and credible applications.

These chapters, representing a broad spectrum of research, derive from papers presented and discussed at a working conference on families as learning environments sponsored by Educational Testing Service in Princeton, New Jersey. Following the conference, the papers were revised and edited for inclusion in this volume. We are indebted to a number of people whose contributions helped make the conference a success: Samuel J. Messick and Winton H. Manning for their support; Jan Flaugher, Jessie Cryer, Linda Kozelski, and Betty Clausen for assistance with local arrangements; and William Nemceff, Kathleen Lingle, and Kalina Gonska for help with the audio-recording of the proceedings.

LUIS M. LAOSA
IRVING E. SIGEL

vii

Contents

Introduction

LUIS M. LAOSA

Recent secular trends in the United States and other industrialized countries have given rise to a great deal of speculation and concern about the current status and the future of families. The interest in families has become so widespread and the topic has reached such national significance that in 1980 Americans witnessed, for the first time in history, a series of White House Conferences on Families. With the increased attention being paid to families, new data have emerged as well as new issues and questions, bringing renewed vigor to the field of family research. This book deals with one area of research within this broad field: *families as learning environments for children.*

In considering children's learning and development, one can readily see that the family is not only the first but possibly, for many, the most significant influence. Indeed, even in totalitarian societies the influence of the family endures despite systematic attempts to minimize its role in the development of individuals. Perhaps the most important aspect of the topic addressed in this volume lies in the view that a society's future can be predicted to a large extent by examining what and how its children learn.

Typically, children's learning and development is studied in the laboratory or in schools and child care centers. Thus, the vast research literature available on children's learning is based for the most part on studies that do not take into account families as learning environments. Given the growing interest in families and the increased disillusionment with the imbalanced focus on research in child development that ignores the role of families as learning environments, a volume such as this should make an important contribution to the research literature on children's learning, child and family development, and education.

In editing the eleven chapters of this volume, my coeditor and I invited contributions from a number of colleagues who are currently conducting what we consider to be among the most advanced research on families as learning environments for children. Therefore, the chapters have been prepared by individuals who are the research producers themselves. The chapters are based upon the current research of the authors and include enough particulars about the doing of their research to give the readers an appreciation of their varied research strategies.

In Chapter 1, I deal with what is perhaps the most critical conceptual and methodological issue in research on families as learning environments—the issue of *causal inferences*. Practical and ethical considerations in family research make it extremely difficult to assess causation. Advances in causal-inference methodology now make it possible, however, to test theoretical models that involve complex networks of causation. Taking advantage of these technical advances, I elaborated and empirically tested a causal model of families as facilitators of their pre-school-age children's intellectual development. To this end, I employed a measurement strategy that included both process and status variables and that obtained assessments by a combination of direct observations in the home, interviews, and psychometric tests. The intent was to construct a reasonably comprehensive causal model incorporating a number of variables that, based on prior research claims, should play an indirect or direct causal role in shaping young children's intellectual development. I accomplished this by means of an approach to path analysis that—unlike other path-analytic techniques with their problems in attenuation from measurement error— allows for the use of hypothetical, error-free unmeasured variables, takes errors of measurement into consideration, and relies on the simultaneous estimation of parameters in the model.

In Chapter 2 my coeditor for this volume, Irving E. Sigel, presents data that describe parents' teaching strategies observed in the laboratory. The basic interest in his research centers on different types of parental teaching strategies and their consequences for children's intellectual development. Specifically, the basic question is: What kinds of strategies do parents employ as they teach their children particular types of tasks? A related question is: What effects do these strategies have for the child's cognitive development? Sigel's conceptualization reflects a constructivist perspective with strong overtones of Piagetian influence. He conceptualizes teaching strategies in the context of *distancing*, a construct used as a metaphor to denote the psychological separation of the person from the ongoing present. He views the process of distancing as critical in the development of representational thinking.

In Chapter 3, Robert D. Hess, Susan Holloway, Gary G. Price, and W. Patrick Dickson examine children's development of *literacy* in the context of the family. Literacy is considered in most families in western societies to be perhaps the single most important skill that children must acquire.

Nevertheless, as fields of inquiry, research on the cognitive processes involved in reading and studies of family influences on reading have proceeded along quite different lines. Research on reading, which has produced relatively differentiated models of the act of reading, has not examined, in the family setting, the specific origins of the various component skills involved in the act of reading. Conversely, studies of family influences on children's development of reading have, for the most part, used global measures of reading skill rather than differentiated measures of the specific components of the act of reading. Hess and his co-workers set out to bridge these two fields of inquiry and hence to increase our knowledge of the role of families as facilitators of children's development of literacy. To this end, they try to identify some of the reading-relevant elements found in family environments. They then provide an analysis and description of the processes through which children may utilize such family resources in learning to read.

In Chapter 4, Michael Lewis and Candice Feiring elaborate a definition of families as *social systems* and describe their efforts to conceptualize a measurement procedure that might afford an opportunity to capture several levels of family functioning at the same time. Certainly, in moving toward more accurate conceptualizations of the family, researchers must include multiple networks of relationships. But such inclusive conceptualizations, however accurate and superior, are perhaps impossible to use for measurement and analysis. Lewis's and Feiring's procedure yields analyses that are still at the dyadic level, but it permits an examination of the distribution of the various dyadic interactions. Using this procedure, Lewis and Feiring describe and analyze family interactions during dinner.

Play is the focus of the research that Thomas G. Power and Ross D. Parke describe in Chapter 5. Play involving parents and their infants is increasingly being recognized as a context in which infants may learn and develop a number of social and cognitive skills. However, our understanding of the nature of parent–infant interactions during play is still quite limited. To narrow this gap in our knowledge, Power and Parke provide descriptive data regarding the predominant kinds of parent–infant play interactions that occur during the second half-year of life. Their analysis, in addition to providing descriptions, led to the generation of hypotheses concerning the ways through which different types of parent–infant play interactions may facilitate the development of social and cognitive skills. That is, by examining the structure of various kinds of play interactions, it was possible to speculate about the effects that these interactions may have on the infant's development. A primary purpose of the study was to develop an observational system that would permit codification of molar units of parent–infant play interactions and also

provide a detailed description of the content and structure of the interactions. Another significant feature of this work is that it was carried out in
two different settings—laboratory and homes—thus permitting an examination of the extent to which patterns of family interaction identified in
the laboratory are generalizable to more naturalistic settings.

The notion that intrafamilial relationships have an enormous impact
on psychosocial development has never been seriously challenged. There
remains, however, a good deal of disagreement about the nature of their
influences, the mechanisms whereby these influences are mediated, and the
ways in which these processes can profitably be studied. Noting these
disagreements, Michael E. Lamb outlines in Chapter 6 a perspective for the
examination of family influences on infant development, underscoring the
diverse issues that he believes should occupy the collective attention of
researchers who seek a clearer and more complete understanding of the
nature and process of early personality development. Lamb bases his
interpretive framework on the ethological attachment theory of Mary
Ainsworth and John Bowlby, giving central importance to the concept of
parental sensitivity. He considers two related questions: (1) What factors
influence individual differences in parental sensitivity? (2) What implications do variations in the security of parent–infant attachment have for
later development? Finally, Lamb discusses the possibility that mothers,
fathers, and siblings have distinctive influences on infant development by
virtue of the fact that they represent characteristically different types of
experiences for young infants.

The next two chapters reflect research concerns regarding secular
trends toward the increased participation of mothers of young children in
the labor force. In Chapter 7, Frank A. Pedersen, Richard L. Cain, Jr.,
Martha J. Zaslow, and Barbara J. Anderson remind us that research
conceptualizations of parent–infant relationships generally assume a
traditional family-role organization in which the mother characteristically
is the infant's primary caregiver and the father fulfills the wage-earner role.
This assumption stands in contrast to the clear secular trend, observable in
industrialized nations, toward families more typically having two wage
earners. Indeed, the rate of increase in employment rates for mothers is
greatest for families with pre-school-age children. Despite the increasing
prevalence of *dual-wage-earner families*, little is known about whether
families with two wage earners have different styles of interacting with and
caring for the young infant than that characteristically found in single-
wage-earner families. To shed light on this issue, Pedersen and his co-
workers observed and analyzed mother–infant and father–infant interaction at age 5 months in the homes of single-wage-earner families and in
homes where both the mother and the father were employed.

The increased participation of mothers of young children in the labor force has made day care—the care of a child by someone other than a member of the nuclear family—a growing and important social and economic support for families. Furthermore, the relative youth of the children entering day care has recently brought greater attention to *family day care*, Steven Fosburg's focus in Chapter 8. A *family day care home* is generally defined to be a private home in which care is given to several children—sometimes including the caregiver's own—for any part of a 24-hour day. Family day care constitutes the single largest system of out-of-home care in the United States, both in terms of the number of families using day care and in the number of children. Despite the widespread use of family day care and its increased role in federally supported care, little has been known about the nature of the home environments that characterize family day care. Until recently, research has focused almost exclusively on day care centers, which are visible community facilities with relatively easy access for researchers. The National Day Care Home Study, which Fosburg designed and directed, is the first national study of family day care and the first attempt to describe the ecology of family day care as a complex and culturally diverse social system. Fosburg presents data from this large-scale study, focusing on analyses designed to increase our understanding of family day care homes as learning environments for children.

Whereas the chapters discussed thus far deal primarily with observed behaviors, the next two chapters deal with the implicit theories and *beliefs* that family members may have about children's behavior and development. A great deal of research on families has focused on parental behavior, but a few investigators have become interested in the role that parental beliefs might play as mediators of the observed behaviors. Do parents' beliefs about child development have important consequences for how the parents behave toward their children? In Chapter 9, Ann V. McGillicuddy-DeLisi attempts to answer this question. She hypothesizes that parents' beliefs about child development are open to change as new information is provided in the course of the parents' interactions with their children. Her analyses were designed to test the hypothesis that there is a link between the parents' beliefs about child development and the number of children in the family, the children's ordinal position and sex, and the family's socioeconomic status. For example, the number of children in the family might be an important factor because the potential for disconfirming previously held beliefs could increase as the parent has the opportunity to compare different children in the family. Socioeconomic status of the parents also might affect the content of parents' beliefs about child development. That is, if one considers socioeconomic status as a descriptive variable reflecting individual differences in life experience, one can see that the information upon which parents construct their beliefs about children might be related to such differences in life experience. To test these hypotheses, McGillicuddy-DeLisi, who collaborates closely with Irving Sigel, presents data and analyses derived from the larger investigation that also forms the basis of Sigel's chapter.

In Chapter 10, Margaret K. Bacon and Richard D. Ashmore report their attempts to uncover the implicit theories of child behavior held by parents and older siblings. Their research was prompted by a concern over the fact that typically the data collected in studies of child socialization follow an organization imposed by the investigator. Bacon and Ashmore contend that such methods of data collection do not provide answers to the following questions: What aspects of ongoing child activity do parents and siblings notice? How do they segment the behavioral stream into meaningful units? What labels do they apply to these units? How do they organize them into categories and along dimensions consistent with the implicit theories of child behavior that they "carry in their heads?" How do they decide what is the proper socializing response? These processes are seen to mediate parental response to child behavior, yet very little is known about the nature of these processes or the factors that influence them. Bacon's and Ashmore's research is intended to narrow this gap in our knowledge. To this end, they analyze their data by means of multidimensional scaling and hierarchical clustering, two useful techniques seldom applied by other investigators who study children and families.

Learning in children encompasses far more than academic and intellectual skills. An important aspect of children's learning in families involves the development of *practical skills*, the topic covered by Nicholas Zill and James L. Peterson in the final chapter. Practical skills include such domestic skills as shopping, making beds, and cooking; mechanical skills—how to use tools, how to operate household appliances, how to build and repair things: and such social skills as dealing with peers and taking care of younger children. Until recently, we have not had much systematic data on how children from different family backgrounds vary in their ability to perform specific practical tasks at different ages. Zill and Peterson present data measuring practical skills in a national sample of elementary-school children and describe the relationship of a number of family background characteristics to levels of practical skill in children.

Although every chapter in this book is focused upon a common theme—families as learning environments for children—the reader no doubt will be struck by the astounding diversity among the various studies. There is rich and creative diversity not only with regard to the specific research questions asked by the various investigators but also in the variables we choose to measure, the behaviors and processes we focus upon, the methods we employ to collect our data, the techniques we use for analysis, and the explicit or implicit theoretical orientations that guide and buttress our research. This diversity, which defies facile integration, is indeed representative of the creative energy, richness, diversity, and flux that currently characterizes this challenging and exciting field of research.

CHAPTER 1

Families as Facilitators of Children's Intellectual Development at 3 Years of Age

A Causal Analysis

LUIS M. LAOSA

Introduction

The intellectual development of the young child and the factors that influence its course are concerns that have long occupied the minds of psychologists, educators, and parents. The recent history of research on families as learning environments spans a broad range: from the clinical investigations of the 1930s on the grim effects of institutionalization to the studies that compared groups of children whose child-rearing experiences had differed on some single, presumably central dimension such as feeding practices or toilet training to the current approach that began in the 1950s and seeks to quantify and measure many aspects of the home environment and to relate these to the child's behavior and development (Clarke-Stewart, 1977). Much useful information has been derived from this research, but a limitation of many of the studies is that typically each has examined a narrow set of variables rather than models based on more complex patterns of relationships that might reflect with greater accuracy the child's experiences in the family. Moreover, even those studies that have examined large numbers of variables simultaneously have not been designed to yield conclusions about cause-and-effect relationships. Although the literature is replete with reports of studies that examine the effects of environmental contingencies upon the developing child, by and large the manner in which such research has been designed does not permit us to address adequately the key issue that underlies the main concerns: How do we test

LUIS M. LAOSA ● Educational Testing Service, Princeton, New Jersey 08541.

hypotheses about organism–environment interactions through scientific models that will allow us to postulate cause-and-effect relationships involving complex patterns of variables?

Part of the reason for the dearth of research that directly addresses issues of causation in children's development is that most of the phenomena of interest to the scientist who investigates teaching and learning in families are beyond manipulative control. Whereas for, say, the educational psychologist it is within the realm of possibility to manipulate systematically what occurs in a classroom or in a microteaching situation and to introduce experimental controls under such conditions, most of what takes place within the family is clearly beyond experimental manipulation. Furthermore, difficulties appear because complex data and analysis are needed to examine a causal relationship embedded in a network of other causal relationships. Nontrivial questions about families usually involve many different kinds of events, determined by a number of different causes, each affecting a number of other variables. The elaboration of networks of causation in which many variables are linked with one another makes causality difficult to study. At the same time, it is a feature that makes causality more fascinating. Hence, the question of causation what events within families lead to what outcomes in children—certainly has been of theoretical interest; but the implicit understanding in almost all the scientific work on families as learning environments has been that one could never hope to answer the question directly.

Advances in causal-inference methodology now make it possible, however, to test theoretical models that involve complex networks of causation. These developments have yielded analytic procedures that broaden the range of possible approaches to the problem of causation. The procedures, based on ideas originally developed in biology (Wright, 1934) and economics (Wold & Jureen, 1953), enable the social scientist to evaluate causal models in a parsimonious and intuitively appealing manner. The purpose of the study reported here is to elaborate and empirically test a causal model of families as facilitators of their pre-school-age children's intellectual development. The intent is to construct a reasonably comprehensive model incorporating a number of variables that, based on prior research claims, should play an indirect or direct causal role in shaping young children's intellectual development. This is to be accomplished by means of an approach to path analysis that—unlike other path-analytic techniques with their problems in attenuation from measurement errors— allows for the use of hypothetical, error-free unmeasured variables, takes errors of measurement into consideration, and relies on the simultaneous estimation of parameters in the model. As far as I know, this will be the first time that this particular approach to path analysis is applied to a complex model of family influences on the pre-school-age child's intellectual development. Before I proceed, it may be useful to discuss several assumptions underlying causal analysis in this type of research.

Causality in Research on Families

In scientific research we conceive of causality in terms of simplified hypothetical "models" of the real world. Such models include a finite number of specified variables and relations out of the universe of psychological and social reality. Certainly, a good deal of thought and research precedes the decision as to exactly which variables to include in the system. Using the results of past research and current theory, the investigator writes the causal model as a set of structural equations that represent the causal processes assumed to operate among the variables under consideration. The structural equations, in turn, lead to parameter estimation procedures and evaluation of the model (Land, 1969). The outcome of the empirical evaluation process is either the corroboration or reformulation of the causal model.

To take care of the effects of variables that have not been included in the model, one may introduce error terms. If a variable is not included, the assumption is that either "it is not an influence on the dependent variable or, if it is an influence, it is uncorrelated with all the independent variables in the equation" (Werts & Linn, 1970, p. 18). Failure to include relevant influences could result in biased estimates for the variables studied. One must admit that had another set of variables been selected, the model might have looked different. A fundamental difficulty is that there seems to be no systematic way of ascertaining whether one has located all the relevant variables, nor are there any foolproof procedures for deciding which variables to use. In other words, there is nothing absolute about any particular model. Nor is it true that if two models make use of different variables, either one or the other must in some sense be "wrong" (Blalock, 1964). But one can proceed by eliminating or modifying inadequate models, that is, models that give predictions inconsistent with the data. The inadequacies of the model should precipitate a reconstruction of the substantive theory that generated the causal model at the outset. In this manner the scientist discovers new variables and formulates revised causal laws that predict with greater precision to a broader range of phenomena. Causal models thus offer a promising strategy for increasing the interaction between theory and data.

In this view, causal thinking belongs on the theoretical level. Causal laws can never be proven empirically beyond all doubt. This is true even with well-designed experiments, although one can reduce the uncertainty inherent in causal inferences by using experimental data. Because it is nonexperimental for both practical and ethical reasons, most research on families can only establish covariations and temporal sequences. Nevertheless, it is helpful to think causally and to develop causal models that are indirectly testable, although in working with these models it will be necessary to make use of untestable simplifying assumptions (cf. Frank, 1961). Unless we permit ourselves to make such assumptions, we shall never be able to generalize beyond the single and unique event (Blalock, 1964). Perhaps our best justification for dealing with this difficult problem is that, when we examine research on families, we find so many social scientists attempting to make causal inferences even when the underlying rationale is not at all clear.

As indicated earlier, in formulating a causal model, considerable thought and research must be devoted to the choice of variables and to making decisions about their hypothesized relationships. These choices and decisions are based on the results of previous research and on current theory. Let us now turn to a brief summary and discussion of past research on the possible determinants of young children's intellectual development.

Research on Young Children's Intellectual Development

Individual differences in intellectual ability have been attributed to many sources, some of which are hereditary, others primarily environmental. The various correlates that have so far been found with intellectual abilities are impressive indicators of the rich complexity, still largely unexplored, of this topic (Bayley, 1970). Research on the role of the family experience in children's intellectual development point to several characteristics of families and to particular child-rearing practices as possible determinants of children's performance on tests of intellectual ability. Below are what appear to be the strongest or most important correlates of the pre-school-age child's intellectual development. The purpose here is not to present an exhaustive review of this body of research, which is exceedingly rich, but rather to identify broad categories of seemingly important correlates of young children's intellectual development.

Socioeconomic Status

Studies of differences related to the socioeconomic status and schooling level of parents reveal significant variation in young children's intellectual development, parents' behavior, family size and structure, and the physical environment of the home (Deutsch, 1973; Hess, 1970; Laosa, 1978, 1980a, 1981a). Differences in children's test performance gradually increase with age, children in middle-class families becoming increasingly more advanced than those from less affluent and less educated families.

Maternal Behavior

A large number of researchers have related measures of children's intellectual competence to various aspects of maternal behavior. Their findings suggest that the child's most valuable intellectual experiences during early childhood occur in interactions with another person who explains, teaches, reasons with, helps, entertains, converses with, praises, shares, and expands the child's activities. These kinds of maternal behaviors as well as maternal warmth seem to be more beneficial for intellectual development than are child-rearing practices characterized by strict control, coaxing, commands, threats, and punishment (Clarke-Stewart, 1977). Of course, maternal behavior is not likely to be the only determinant of children's intellectual ability. That ability is probably also related, through genetic inheritance, to parental intelligence (Bouchard & McGue, 1981). Hence, if there is a substantial effect of maternal behavior on children's intellectual development, it must be demonstrated after genetic components of variance have been eliminated. When genetic variation cannot be controlled, studies can be made more interpretable by controlling for parents' intelligence (Scarr-Salapatek, 1975).

Paternal Behavior

As yet there is relatively little unequivocal evidence on the effects of paternal behavior on children's intellectual development (Clarke-Stewart, 1977; Lamb, 1976; Radin, 1976). Some evidence suggests that in families where there is a high degree of father–child interaction, children exhibit less anxiety when confronted with a stranger and perform better on tests of intellectual development (Clarke-Stewart, 1977). Paternal nurturance appears to be closely associated with the intellectual competence of boys but not that of girls (Radin, 1976). Some data also suggest that paternal teaching strategies that involve demands to symbolize are beneficial for the child's intellectual development (Sigel, McGillicuddy-De Lisi, & Johnson, 1980).

Parental Expectations and Intellectual Activities in the Home

In addition to those already discussed, certain environmental processes in the home have been found to correlate with children's intellectual development (Dave, 1963; Henderson, Bergan, & Hurt, 1972; Hess & Holloway, 1979; Shipman, McKee, & Bridgeman, 1976; Wolf, 1964). Process variables concern attitudes and dispositions as well as patterns of interactions among family members. The most important of these seem to be participation with the child in intellectual activities such as reading and expectations for the child's educational attainment.

Reciprocity

It has been claimed that the child's given characteristics shape parental action (Bell & Harper, 1977; Lerner & Spanier, 1978). This new perspective has been challenged by a strongly argued reassertion of the view that "parent shapes child." These two antithetical positions have led to a synthesis to the effect that parent and child influence each other's ongoing behavior by reciprocal interaction. The critical question of how the equation of influence may be balanced as a function of specific characteristics and situational constraints is a difficult one and has been left unanswered. Nevertheless, it seems obvious that at least in some instances the child's behavior vis-à-vis parental actions would influence the nature of the interaction between parent and child.

Family Size and Birth Order

The effects of the parents on the child's development seem to be further complicated by the structure of the family. Family size and birth order are structural variables that appear to play a role in the child's intellectual development. Several studies have reported an inverse relationship between the number of siblings and the child's intellectual achievement. There is evidence, however, of an interaction with social class, so that the correlation of family size and ability is higher in samples of lower socioeconomic status (Anastasi, 1956; Marjoribanks, Walberg, & Bargen, 1975). Although reviews of the literature on the effects of birth order are beset with equivocal findings (Schooler, 1972), there is some evidence that when other factors are taken into account, ordinal position may have an influence on family interaction and on the child's intellectual development (Cicirelli, 1978; Laosa & Brophy, 1972; Marjoribanks, 1979; Sigel *et al.*, 1980; Zajonc & Markus, 1975.)

Television

The potential impact of television on children's intellectual development has been widely discussed in recent years. Although early studies of commercial television indicated that relatively little learning occured, more recent research shows that modeling and other televised techniques can teach a wide variety of cognitive skills (Stein & Friedrich, 1975).

Preschool Programs

After the detrimental effects of extreme environmental deprivation were first reported (Dennis, 1960; Spitz, 1946), a number of studies examined the effects of educational programs for young children. Such interventions can effect significant increments in measured intellectual ability, although the magnitude and duration of the gains vary in different studies depending on the kinds of interventions (Bronfenbrenner, 1974). Activities of the sort typically experienced by children in nursery school have been shown to improve intellectual achievement (Brown, 1978; Fowler, 1962).

Maternal Employment

With the increasing trend for mothers of young children to work outside the home, maternal employment has become an important variable in research on families. The available research reveals no consistent effects of maternal employment on children's development. But because of the rapidly changing social values and family roles associated with maternal employment, this is an area of research that warrants further examination.

Research Questions and Hypotheses

Although the very brief summary of previous findings presented above is not intended to reflect the great richness and complexity of past research on the subject, it is clear that impressive strides have been made toward uncovering the seemingly important correlates of children's intellectual development. Nevertheless, our understanding of the meaning of the observed relationships between variables is not at all clear. Specifically, there remain two fundamental questions:

1. How are these various variables organized in a structure of causal relationships as each variable exerts its influence upon others and ultimately upon the child's intellectual development?
2. What is the magnitude of each variable's direct and indirect influence when considered in the context of a structural network of multiple causation?

I sought to answer these questions by elaborating a hypothetical model, evaluating its adequacy, and estimating the magnitude of the hypothesized effects of its components. The conceptual model is shown in schematic form in Figure 1, in which the conventional notation for drawing path diagrams is used. Here, the postulated causal relations among the variables are portrayed by unidirectional arrows extending from each determining variable to each variable dependent on it. Double-headed arrows represent unanalyzed correlations; in this case the linkage is left ambiguous: the covariation may be causal or spurious and the direction of causation may be from A to B, from B to A, or reciprocal. Residual variables, introduced to account for variance not accounted for by variables in the system, are symbolized by unidirectional arrows leading from an invisible variable to the dependent variable. The absence of any arrow connecting two variables represents no covariation between them.

I should explain at this point the omission of certain specific variables from the conceptual model and mention some of the implications of this omission. Certain paternal variables that might be considered as important as their maternal counterparts were not included in the model. Specifically, paternal intelligence and paternal teaching strategies, which hypothetically might contribute to the child's intellectual development as much as might maternal intelligence and maternal teaching strategies, were excluded because practical considerations prevented the collection of such data. However, because of assortative mating, these maternal and paternal variables are likely to be correlated. Therefore, for purposes of the present analytic approach, which takes into account the intercorrelations among variables, this omission does not present a critical problem insofar as maternal intelligence and maternal teaching strategies may be viewed as proxies of more encompassing parental variables that include their respective paternal counterparts. Nevertheless, the issue of whether these maternal and paternal variables indeed have similar effects remains a hypothesis that should be tested in future research.

To study the various family influences postulated in the conceptual model, data were gathered on a sample of 50 families. A home interview, direct observations of mother–child interactions, and standardized tests were used for obtaining measures of the variables in the model. Data processing and analyses proceeded in five major steps. First, the distributions of the variables whose shape might have distorted the results of the analyses were suitably transformed. Then, estimates of reliability were obtained. Next bivariate analyses were performed to describe the interrelationships among all the measured variables. The fourth step involved the construction of unmeasured variables and represents an attempt both to test whether variables that appear to be conceptually related are indeed related statistically and to reduce the large number of measured variables into a smaller but conceptually and statistically meaningful set of constructs. The last step, an attempt to gain insights into the causal

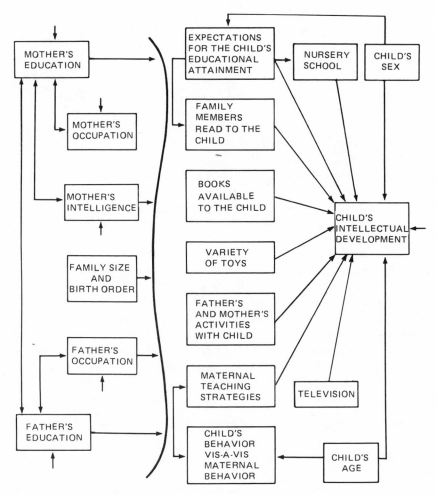

Figure 1. Schematic diagram of conceptual model of family influences on pre-school-age children's intellectual development.

structure underlying the complex relationships among the variables, involved the use of path models to estimate the adequacy of the conceptual model of family influences formulated here.

Method

Sample

The sample consisted of 50 families, each with a child approximately 3 years of age (25 boys, 25 girls). All the families were white English-speaking residents of a large metropolitan area in the southwestern United States.

The age of the study children was in the range of 37 to 55 months, with a mean of 45.4 and a standard deviation of 4.4. The fathers' occupational status ranged from service workers in other than private households to professional and technical workers (see FOCC in Table 1). Sixty-eight percent of the mothers had occupations other than housewife; their occupational status ranged from service workers in other than private households to professional and technical workers (see MOCC in Table 1). The number of years of schooling completed by the fathers ranged from 10 to 22, $M = 15.00$, $SD = 2.96$. Mothers' years of schooling ranged from 9 to 18, $M = 13.30$, $SD = 1.93$. Of the study children, 68% had attended some form of preschool education program. Twenty percent had no siblings and none had more than four. The mothers' ages were in the range of 19 to 41, $M = 28.2$, $SD = 4.5$. The fathers' ages were in the range of 20 to 45, $M = 31.1$, $SD = 5.7$. Additional information descriptive of the participant families can be found in Table 1.

The sample was selected to be as representative as possible of white English-speaking families in the United States with respect to socio-economic status characteristics. It was selected from a pool of volunteers who responded to announcements disseminated through the mass media (newspapers, radio) and in such places as supermarkets, churches, and nursery and public schools. In order to include fathers in the study, an effort was made to select only intact families; thus all but three of the families were intact. Only children with no known physical or mental abnormalities were included in the study. The families were informed that the focus of the study was on how children learn.

Procedures

The data were collected in the participants' homes by 8 data collectors (2 men, 6 women) in 1977. Each family was visited at a prearranged time by a team of two data collectors. Families were randomly assigned to pairs of data collectors. After establishing rapport, one of the data collectors individually administered a 30-minute structured interview and the Cattell Culture Fair Intelligence Scale to the mother while the other data collector individual administered the Preschool Inventory to the child in another room. Then one of the data collectors administered the mother–child interaction tasks to both mother and child while the other data collector sat in a different room with any other persons present in the home. Care was taken to provide a distraction-free atmosphere to the participants during the administration of the procedures.

Mother's Interview

The structured interview administered to the mothers focused on factual information about family characteristics and processes. Variables 1 through 23 in Table 1 were derived from the interview.

Mother–Child Interaction Tasks

Development of the procedures used in this study to assess mother–child interactions was an extension and elaboration of the Maternal Teaching Observation Technique, a set of procedures I developed earlier to assess maternal teaching strategies (Laosa, 1980b). To assess in this study the mothers' teaching strategies and the children's behaviors vis-à-vis their mothers' teaching behaviors, each mother–child dyad was observed during two interaction tasks. Each task was as follows. The mother was given an assembled Big Tinkertoy model (Questor Education Products Company, Bronx, N.Y.) and all the disassembled parts needed to build an identical model. (The parts of the assembled model were glued together to prevent their being taken apart, and the disassembled parts were "worked" in and out prior to using them with the participants until none was unusually difficult for a child to fit into any other part.) The mother was asked to teach her child how to make a model like the one already assembled. The "man" shown in the manual that accompanies the Big Tinkertoy kit was used for the first task (task 1). A "swingseat" composed of 34 parts was used for the second task (task 2). Both Big Tinkertoy models are of approximately equal difficulty. These tasks were chosen in order to elicit a broad range of behaviors from both mother and 3-year-old child around materials sufficiently engaging and appealing in terms of difficulty level and ability to elicit and maintain the attention of all participants.

For each task the observer manually recorded on a protocol the frequency of behaviors in the categories corresponding to variables 26 through 40 in Table 1. Operational definitions of the basic behavior categories are presented in Appendix A. A review of the literature, together with the experience of observing mothers teach their own young children, provided the basis for ascertaining what categories of behavior would be considered for inclusion. An attempt was made to include among the categories assessed a sample of the instructional processes emphasized by diverse views of the psychology of teaching. Practical considerations also guided the selection: categories were chosen so that the observation procedure could yield data on a set of behaviors (1) that would occur with sufficiently high frequency for the type of analysis called for by the research plan and (2) that would be amenable to manual recording and reliable

Table 1. Descriptions, Abbreviated Labels, Means, and Standard Deviations of Measured Variables

	Description	Abbreviated label	Mean	SD
1.	Child's sex (1 = boy, 2 = girl).	CSEX	1.50	.50
2.	Child's chronological age (in months).	CAGE	45.44	4.40
3.	Child's birth order (1 = first-born or only child, 2 = second-born, etc.).	BORD	1.86	1.01
4.	Is child an only child? (1 = no, 2 = yes).	ONLY	1.20	.40
5.	How many brothers and sisters does child have?	SIBS	1.22	.93
6.	Since child was born, has mother not been employed outside the home since child was born.	MEMP	2.56	1.66
	1 = No, mother has not been employed outside the home since child was born.			
	2 = Yes, part time, but not most of the time since child was born.			
	3 = Yes, full time, but not most of the time since child was born.			
	4 = Yes, part time most of the time since child was born.			
	5 = Yes, full time most of the time since child was born.			
7.	Is mother now employed outside the home? (1 = employed, 2 = not employed).	MNEM	1.54	.50
8.	Mother's usual occupation.	MOCC	5.98	1.60
	(Scale adapted from that used by the U.S. Bureau of the Census)			
	1 = Private household workers			
	2 = Service workers except private household			
	3 = Laborers and farmers			
	4 = Equipment operator			
	5 = Craftsmen, foremen, and kindred workers			
	6 = Sales, clerical, and kindred workers			
	7 = Small business owners or managers, or administrators			
	8 = Professional and technical			
	9 = Large business owners or managers			

Note. Mothers with no occupation outside the home were assigned the mean scale value obtained for the mothers with an occupation outside the home. A comparison of the correlation results using this variable to the results obtained using a variable that assigned a zero value to the mothers with no occupation outside the home yielded similar results. Sixty-eight percent of the mothers had an occupation outside the home; the mean scale value for these mothers was 6.

9. MED Mother's education (years of schooling completed). 13.34 1.93
10. FED Father's education (years of schooling completed). 15.00 2.96
11. FOCC Father's usual occupation. 6.45 1.92
    (Same scale as that used for MOCC above.)
12. MEXR How much education mother thinks child will receive, realistically. 5.28 1.14
    1 = Complete elementary school
    2 = Complete junior high school
    3 = High school graduate
    4 = Technical or vocational school
    5 = Some college
    6 = College graduate
    7 = Master's degree
    8 = Professional degree (M.D., Ph.D., LL.D.)
13. MEXI Ideally, how much education mother would like child to receive. 6.41 1.17
    (Same scale as MEXR above.)
14. MIED Minimum amount of education mother thinks child should receive. 4.00 1.38
    (Same scale as MEXR above.)
15. MREA Does mother ever read to child? How much? 3.42 1.01
    0 = Never
    1 = About once a month or less
    2 = About twice a month
    3 = About once a week
    4 = More than once a week
16. FREA Does father ever read to child? How much? 2.12 1.60
    (Same scale as MREA above.)

Continued

Table 1. (Continued)

Description	Abbreviated label	Mean	SD
17. Do others in the household ever read to child? How much? (Same scale as MREA above.)	OREA	1.24	1.73
18. Number of hours per week (including weekends) child typically spends with mother.	TWM	52.00	20.44
19. Number of hours per week (including weekends) child typically spends with father in some activity.	TWF	22.87	12.00
20. Number of books and comic books child has of his or her own or that he or she shares with others.	BKS	43.86	32.31
21. Number of different toys in the house that child can play with.	TOYS	35.86	25.33
22. Number of hours per week (including weekends) child typically watches television during school year.	TV	16.88	9.18
23. Number of months child has attended preschool education program.	PS	10.48	10.74
24. Mother's raw score on the Cattell Culture Fair Intelligence Scale (Scale 2, Form A).			
Test 1	CCF_1	9.62	1.51
Test 2	CCF_2	7.50	2.10
Test 3	CCF_3	9.20	1.83
Test 4	CCF_4	5.58	1.47
Scale total	CCF	31.90	4.99
25. Child's score (number of correct responses) on the Preschool Inventory.	PSI	35.92	12.23
26. Mother's use of inquiry as a teaching strategy.			
Task 1	$MINQ_1$	3.42	1.06
Task 2	$MINQ_2$	3.09	.90
Average	MINQ	3.29	.89
27. Mother's use of directive as a teaching strategy.			

Task 1	MDIR$_1$	3.66	.95
Task 2	MDIR$_2$	3.65	.92
Average	MDIR	3.67	.88
28. Mother's use of praise following child's independent act, as a teaching strategy.			
Task 1	MPRF$_1$	1.75	.60
Task 2	MPRF$_2$	1.84	.65
Average	MPRF	1.84	.54
29. Mother's use of praise not following child's independent act, as a teaching strategy.			
Task 1	MPRN$_1$	2.28	.89
Task 2	MPRN$_2$	2.11	.80
Average	MPRN	2.24	.76
30. Mother's use of verbal disapproval with no specific feedback, as a teaching strategy.			
Task 1	MVDN$_1$	1.70	.42
Task 2	MVDN$_2$	1.58	.44
Average	MVDN	1.67	.35
31. Mother's use of verbal disapproval with specific feedback, as a teaching strategy.			
Task 1	MVDF$_1$	1.69	.56
Task 2	MVDF$_2$	1.62	.57
Average	MVDF	1.70	.49
32. Mother's use of physical affection following child's independent act, as a teaching strategy.			
Task 1	MPAF$_1$	1.00	.00
Task 2	MPAF$_2$	1.02	.15
Average	MPAF	1.01	.10
33. Mother's use of physical affection not following child's independent act, as a teaching strategy.			
Task 1	MPAN$_1$	1.01	.08

Continued

Table 1. (Continued)

Description	Abbreviated label	Mean	SD
Task 2	$MPAN_2$	1.00	.00
Average	MPAN	1.01	.05
34. Mother's use of visual cue following child's request for assistance, as a teaching strategy.			
Task 1	$MVCF_1$	1.00	.00
Task 2	$MVCF_2$	1.00	.00
Average	MVCF	1.00	.00
35. Mother's use of visual cue not following child's request for assistance, as a teaching strategy.			
Task 1	$MVCN_1$	2.51	.79
Task 2	$MVCN_2$	2.57	.63
Average	MVCN	2.56	.64
36. Mother's use of modeling following child's request for assistance, as a teaching strategy.			
Task 1	$MMOF_1$	1.04	.16
Task 2	$MMOF_2$	1.09	.32
Average	MMOF	1.09	.23
37. Mother's use of modeling not following child's request for assistance, as a teaching strategy.			
Task 1	$MMON_1$	2.58	1.03
Task 2	$MMON_2$	2.46	1.03
Average	MMON	2.56	.95

38.	Child requests mother's assistance during the teaching tasks.			
	Task 1	$CASK_1$	1.70	.62
	Task 2	$CASK_2$	1.84	.60
	Average	CASK	1.81	.55
39.	Child rejects mother's assistance during the teaching tasks.			
	Task 1	$CREJ_1$	1.24	.39
	Task 2	$CREJ_2$	1.35	.47
	Average	CREJ	1.34	.37
40.	Child acts independently of the mother during the teaching tasks.			
	Task 1	$CIND_1$	2.60	.83
	Task 2	$CIND_2$	2.71	.82
	Average	CIND	2.69	.72

Note. Variables corresponding to descriptions 26 through 40 are based on the mother–child interaction tasks and are expressed as rate-per-minute scores transformed to $\sqrt{x} + \sqrt{x+1}$. These variables are defined in greater detail in Appendix A. Subsequent analyses excluded the variables corresponding to descriptions 32 through 34 because of zero and near-zero frequencies.

coding by a trained human observer during the conduct of an ongoing mother–child interaction around the types of tasks employed.

For each task the observation was discontinued 5 minutes after the mother was signaled to begin teaching or when the task was completed, whichever occurred first. The duration of the observation was recorded in seconds. The interval between tasks was approximately 10 minutes. The frequencies obtained for each variable for each task were divided by duration of observation and multiplied by 60 to obtain rate-per-minute scores for each mother–child dyad. The respective means and standard deviations for each variable were quite similar across tasks (Table 1), and in general the cross-task correlations were of at least moderate magnitude (Appendix B). These results indicate that the two tasks may be considered parallel forms of the assessment technique and the measures derived from them parallel measures. Therefore for some analyses, the rate-per-minute scores were summed across tasks and divided by 2 to obtain an average rate-per-minute score on each variable. To improve linearity of regression, to improve normality of distribution, and to stabilize the variances approximately, each rate-per-minute score and each average rate-per-minute score was transformed to $\sqrt{x} + \sqrt{x + 1}$ (Freeman & Tukey, 1950). A visual comparison of the transformed and untransformed distributions revealed substantial improvements resulting from this transformation. The purpose of the transformation was to decrease as much as possible the probability of serious violations of assumptions underlying the parametric analyses.

The observers began collecting the present data after achieving exact interobserver agreement within one frequency point on every variable. Estimates of reliability during data collection also were obtained: consistency of scores across tasks (Appendix B) and interobserver reliability during data collection (Appendix C). These estimates indicate that in general the observations yielded at least adequately reliable and moderately consistent measures of maternal teaching strategies and child behaviors. As evidence of the validity of measures such as these, it should be noted that Stallings and Porter (1980) recently found a correspondence between maternal behaviors measured in structured situations such as these and the behaviors that mothers exhibit in observed everyday interactions in the home.

Preschool Inventory

The Preschool Inventory was used to measure children's general intellectual development. The Preschool Inventory, developed by Bettye Caldwell as a general achievement test for preschool children, taps a range of verbal, quantitative, and perceptual–motor skills defined by teachers as expected of children in kindergarten (Cooperative Tests and Services, 1970b). The 64-item 1970 revised version was used in this study (Caldwell, 1970; Cooperative Tests and Services, 1970a). The available evidence indicates that the Preschool Inventory is a reliable and valid measure of children's general intellectual development (Caldwell & Freund, 1980; Cooperative Tests and Services, 1970b; Gilbert & Shipman, 1972; Laosa, 1981b).

Culture Fair Intelligence Scale

The Cattell Culture Fair Intelligence Scale was used to measure mothers' general intelligence. The Cattell Culture Fair Intelligence Scales measure individual intelligence in a manner designed to reduce as much as possible the influence of verbal fluency, cultural climate, and educational level. Each scale contains four tests involving different perceptual tasks. The test manual (Institute for Personality and Ability Testing, 1973) provides reliability and validity estimates that are at least adequate. Scale 2, Form A, was used in this study. Based on the available evidence, each scale appears to be a good measure of the general intelligence factor "g" as the early intelligence theorists identified it.

Table 1 presents a description of the variables used in the analyses. The means and standard deviations for each variable are shown in the same table.

Results

Bivariate Analyses

To examine the bivariate relationships among the measured variables, the complete matrix of Pearson product–moment correlations was computed. These zero-order correlation coefficients are displayed in Tables 2, 3, and 4.[1]

---

[1] In computing the correlations displayed in Tables 2 through 4, missing data were handled by pairwise deletion of cases, a procedure that maximizes the use of the available information by excluding from the computation of a given coefficient only those cases with missing data on one or both of the variables that go into computing the coefficient at hand. For purposes of the structural analyses, the entire correlation matrix was recomputed, this time using a listwise deletion procedure, which achieves uniformity of sample size by excluding from the computation of every coefficient all cases with missing data on any variable in the matrix. Listwise deletion yielded a matrix based on 46 cases. The two matrices were, however, practically identical.

Table 2. Zero-Order Intercorrelations of Demographic, Home Process, and Test Variables

	CAGE	BORD	ONLY	SIBS	MEMP	MNEM	MOCC	MED	FED	FOCC	MEXR
CSEX	-01	.06	.10	.06	.02	.04	.02	.01	-.13	.05	-.11
CAGE		.03	.10	.01	.02	-.09	.20	.07	-.07	.04	.23
BORD			-.43^a	.84^a	.27^c	-.17	.01	.02	-.11	.06	.04
ONLY				-.66^a	.07	.06	-.12	-.09	-.18	-.06	.05
SIBS					.12	-.04	.01	.03	-.09	.02	.02
MEMP						-.79^a	-.03	-.04	-.09	.28^c	-.08
MNEM							.15	.02	.06	-.22	.09
MOCC								.37^b	.34^b	.21	.22
MED									.57^a	.46^a	.37^b
FED										.71^a	.31^c
FOCC											.33^b
MEXR											
MEXI											
MIED											
MREA											
FREA											
OREA											
TWM											
TWF											
BKS											
TOYS											
TV											
PS											
CCF											

Note: Pairwise deletion of missing data yielded n's in the range of 46 to 50. Names of variables are as follows:

CSEX = Child's sex
CAGE = Child's age (months)
BORD = Child's birth order
ONLY = Only child
SIBS = Number of siblings
MEMP = Maternal employment since child was born
MNEM = Mother now employed

MOCC = Mother's occupational status
MED = Mother's education
FED = Father's education
FOCC = Father's occupational status
MEXR = Mother's "realistic" expectations for child's educational attainment
MEXI = Mother's "ideal" expectations for child's educational attainment

$^a p < .001.$
$^b p < .01.$
$^c p < .05$; one-tailed tests.

From these essentially descriptive analyses many things become clear about the relationships among the variables. For those variables that have been examined also in previous studies, the present results are consistent with previous research (for example: Clarke-Stewart, 1977; Dave, 1963; Deutsch, 1973; Hess, 1970; Holtzman, Díaz-Guerrero, & Swartz, 1975; Shipman *et al.*, 1976; Wolf, 1964). Furthermore, considering all the variables included in the present analyses, the pattern and magnitude of these zero-order correlations tend to complement prior research findings.

Table 2. (Continued)

MEXI	MIED	MREA	FREA	OREA	TWM	TWF	BKS	TOYS	TV	PS	CCF	PSI
-.01	-.03	-.02	-.05	-.19	-.01	-.11	.11	-.12	-.05	.17	.12	.25[c]
.10	.19	-.21	-.13	.06	-.28[c]	-.16	.06	.01	-.09	.26[c]	-.28[c]	.44[a]
.10	.18	-.04	.00	.56[a]	-.21	-.10	.10	-.01	-.18	.10	.15	.04
.26[c]	-.04	.09	-.25[c]	-.35[b]	.28[c]	.09	-.13	.07	.16	.07	-.08	.06
-.10	.06	.01	.11	.40[b]	-.23[c]	-.16	.08	-.02	-.18	.02	.06	-.02
.19	.22	-.14	.09	.08	-.26[c]	.21	-.08	-.09	-.17	.55[a]	.07	-.06
-.13	-.20	.19	-.03	-.09	.33[b]	-.22	.13	.08	.24[c]	-.43[a]	-.07	-.01
.08	.13	.23	.25[c]	.08	-.02	.12	.12	.10	.17	.00	.00	.32[c]
.32[b]	.20	.35[b]	.19	.23	-.04	.19	.36[b]	.22	-.33[b]	.06	.33[b]	.48[a]
.15	.21	.16	.29[c]	.20	-.06	.22	.20	-.03	-.12	-.12	.24[c]	.28[c]
.36[b]	.29[c]	.25[c]	.20	.13	.04	.30[c]	.27[c]	.13	-.37[b]	.18	.22	.24[c]
.49[a]	.40[b]	.11	.02	-.03	-.04	.12	.22	.06	-.30[c]	.21	.05	.16
	.38[b]	.22	-.06	-.13	.00	.08	.15	.16	-.28[c]	.30[c]	.33[b]	.03
		-.02	.06	.07	-.01	.15	.41[b]	.07	-.23[c]	.38[b]	.16	.03
			.32[c]	.03	.25[c]	.07	.24[c]	.31[c]	-.08	-.03	.32[b]	.15
			-.08	-.13	.41[b]	.05	-.02	-.01	.33[b]	.13	.09
				-.06	-.02	.28[c]	-.07	-.21	-.26[c]	.13	.33[b]
					.12	.26[c]	.05	-.04	-.24[c]	.17	-.01
						.23	.25[c]	-.05	.19	.01	.16
							.09	-.18	.05	.25[c]	.27[c]
								-.03	.08	.11	-.03
									-.32[b]	-.11	-.24[c]
										.02	.11
											.11

MIED = Minimum amount of education mother thinks child should receive
MREA = How much mother reads to child
FREA = How much father reads to child
OREA = How much others in household read to child
TWM = Time child spends with mother
TWF = Time child spends with father in some activity

BKS = Number of books
TOYS = Variety of toys
TV = Television viewing time
PS = Preschool program attendance
CCF = Mother's score on the Cattell Culture Fair Intelligence Scale
PSI = Preschool Inventory score

This consistency adds to our confidence in these data in general and in the choice of variables in particular. Yet, as is also the case with the results of previous studies, the interpretation of relationships such as these becomes ambiguous once we attempt to go beyond a mere description of the direction and magnitude of the associations. Although useful, this type of analysis does not allow us to answer the questions posed in this study. Therefore, to add more precise understanding of the inferential conclusions that can be drawn from zero-order correlations and stepwise

Table 3. Zero-Order Intercorrelations among Measures of Observed Mother–Child Interactions ($n = 50$)

	MDIR	MPRF	MPRN	MVDN	MVDF	MVCN	MMOF	MMON	CASK	CREJ	CIND
MINQ	-.03	.34[b]	.01	.03	-.28[c]	-.19	.19	-.24[c]	.03	-.15	.16
MDIR		-.20	.48[a]	.16	.41[b]	.31[b]	-.17	-.20	.00	.07	-.28[c]
MPRF			-.26[c]	.11	-.12	-.08	.31[b]	-.28[c]	.13	-.04	.68[a]
MPRN				.09	.30[c]	-.04	-.33[b]	-.28[c]	-.01	.05	-.48[a]
MVDN					.21	.09	.04	.06	.07	-.01	.18
MVDF						.15	-.27[c]	-.13	.11	.11	-.17
MVCN							.01	-.07	.05	-.19	.15
MMOF								-.17	.10	.07	.33[b]
MMON									-.21	.01	-.19
CASK										-.03	.07
CREJ											-.07

Names of variables are abbreviated as follows:

MINQ = Mother's use of inquiry
MDIR = Mother's use of directive
MPRF = Mother's use of praise following child's independent act
MPRN = Mother's use of praise not following child's independent act
MVDN = Mother's use of verbal disapproval with no specific feedback
MVDF = Mother's use of verbal disapproval with specific feedback

MVCN = Mother's use of visual cue not following child's request for assistance
MMOF = Mother's use of modeling following child's request for assistance
MMON = Mother's use of modeling not following child's request for assistance
CASK = Child asks mother for assistance
CREJ = Child rejects mother's assistance
CIND = Child acts independently

[a] $p < .001$.
[b] $p < .01$.
[c] $p < .05$; one-tailed tests.

multiple regressions, I turned to the use of path-analytic models that provide estimates of complex causal effects.

Structural Analyses

I was interested in a particular solution to the path-analysis model: a solution that (1) takes into consideration errors in variables, (2) allows for the use of "error-free" unmeasured variables (constructs, latent variables), and (3) relies on a simultaneous estimation procedure. The errors resulting from the use of estimated factor scores are avoided when one directly estimates the relationships among unmeasured constructs. One can think of path coefficients that estimate the causal effects between such constructs as being corrected for many types of measurement error (e.g., observer bias, instrument error, imprecise or poorly operationalized concepts). Thus it is possible to minimize the distorting effects of measurement error through the use of unmeasured variables. The simultaneous estimation of relationships between constructs based on multiple indicators minimizes the problem of unstable regression coefficients that in the traditional regression approach results from including as independent variables several measures of the same construct. All of this increases the chances of accurately estimating the "true" path coefficients.

A maximum-likelihood estimation procedure developed by Sörbom and Jöreskog (1976) can be used to obtain the type of solution called for in my analysis plan. The procedure estimates unknown coefficients in a set of linear structural equations. The variables in the equation system may be unmeasured hypothetical constructs, and there may be several measured or multiple indicators for each unmeasured variable. Any values may be specified in advance for any of the parameters in the model. The method of estimation allows for both errors in equations (residuals, disturbances) and errors in the observed variables (errors of measurement, observational errors). A preliminary interpretation of the hypothesized structure can be successively modified to determine a final solution that is acceptable from the point of view of both goodness of fit and psychological interpretation. By means of this procedure, three successive analyses were performed, each yielding a better solution. The decisions concerning the rejection of hypotheses were made on both logical and statistical grounds on the basis of three sources of evidence: the chi-square goodness-of-fit measure, the matrix of residuals between observed and reproduced correlations, and the magnitude of the parameter estimates.

The first analysis (Structural Model I) was essentially a test of hypotheses regarding the presence of unmeasured constructs in the model. Each hypothesis centered on whether the influence exerted by a given set of measured variables (indicators) on Preschool Inventory scores emanates from a construct underlying the variables rather than from each separate variable. Table 5 shows the hypothetical structure tested in this analysis.

The solution to Structural Model I revealed that, as hypothesized, father's education and occupational status form a clear-cut construct (factor), with loadings (λ) of .88 for education and .81 for occupational status. Similarly, mother's education and occupational status form a clear and well-defined factor, $\lambda = .74$ for education and $\lambda = .44$ for occupational status. Probably because of assortative mating, these two "socioeducational" factors were highly correlated; estimated true correlation = .84.

The three variables measuring time spent reading to the child (by mother, father, and others) failed to form a clear factor, suggesting that these three variables are not indicators of a single underlying construct. This interpretation was suggested by two findings. First, the loadings were low ($\lambda = .42$ for MREA, $\lambda = .26$ for FREA, and $\lambda = .35$ for OREA), none corresponding to a reliability greater than .20 as a measure of the construct. Second, the factor failed to account for the intercorrelations among these

Table 4. Zero-Order Correlations of Observed Mother–Child Interactions with Demographic, Home Process, and Test Variables

	MINQ	MDIR	MPRF	MPRN	MVDN	MVDF	MVCN	MMOF	MMON	CASK	CREJ	CIND
CSEX	-.07	.06	.12	-.08	.20	.18	.23	-.16	-.20	.07	-.11	-.03
CAGE	-.16	-.38^b	.28^c	-.52^a	-.16	-.37^b	-.04	.23^c	.08	-.04	-.07	.42^a
BORD	.20	.03	.12	-.04	-.02	-.14	-.11	.18	.21	.05	.25^c	.01
ONLY	.03	-.06	.20	-.04	-.01	.17	-.05	-.03	.06	.17	.00	.00
SIBS	.12	.02	.01	-.07	.04	-.17	-.04	.08	-.12	-.08	.12	-.08
MEMP	.05	.16	.04	.05	.05	.19	-.15	.13	-.07	.10	.27^c	.03
MNEM	-.08	-.20	.00	.03	.09	-.05	-.03	-.20	-.03	-.11	-.24^c	-.11
MOCC	.10	.04	-.05	.17	-.05	.07	-.01	.05	-.29^c	.01	-.14	-.10
MED	.27^c	-.08	.14	.18	-.32^b	-.31^b	-.07	.13	-.27^c	-.06	-.06	.05
FED	.06	.04	-.03	.36^b	-.17	-.14	-.13	.07	-.20	-.06	-.09	-.13
FOCC	.20	-.03	.04	.22	-.04	-.11	-.02	.15	-.30^c	-.07	-.02	.04
MEXR	-.05	-.14	.05	.00	-.03	-.32^b	.15	.05	.12	.07	-.01	.00
MEXI	.04	.09	.03	.18	-.06	-.11	.19	.06	-.11	-.08	.17	.00
MIED	.04	.08	.11	.01	.17	-.05	.07	.06	-.05	.14	.02	.37^b
MREA	.34^b	.11	.06	.29^c	.02	-.02	.16	-.09	-.26^c	-.22	-.15	-.01
FREA	.18	.26^c	-.03	.20	.14	-.06	-.05	-.10	-.15	-.05	-.15	-.07
OREA	.21	.01	.32^b	.15	-.18	-.17	-.23^c	.21	-.41^b	.15	.19	.20
TWM	.10	.00	.06	.14	-.05	.40^b	.07	-.06	-.30^c	.29^c	.06	.02
TWF	.28^c	.10	-.05	.06	-.02	-.08	.11	.23	-.01	.26^c	-.12	-.12
BKS	.11	-.14	.10	.13	-.19	-.28^c	-.09	-.04	-.37^b	-.01	.00	.15
TOYS	.21	-.28^c	-.01	-.14	.02	-.18	.12	.03	.06	-.07	-.11	.23

TV	-.07	-.01	-.27[c]	-.05	-.02	.29[c]	-.10	-.26[c]	.01	.00	.05	-.27[c]
PS	.00	-.11	.01	-.11	.12	-.12	.02	.02	.21	.09	.05	.14
CCF	.24[c]	.28[c]	.11	.31[b]	-.13	.11	.14	-.13	-.48[a]	-.04	.08	.05
PSI	.16	-.18	.35[b]	-.16	-.21	-.28[c]	.00	.29[c]	-.25[c]	.01	-.16	.22

Note. Pairwise deletion of missing data yielded n's in the range of 46 to 50. Names of variables are abbreviated as follows:

CSEX = Child's sex
CAGE = Child's age (months)
BORD = Child's birth order
ONLY = Only child
SIBS = Number of siblings
MEMP = Maternal employment since child was born.
MNEM = Mother now employed
MOCC = Mother's occupational status
MED = Mother's education
FED = Father's education
FOCC = Father's occupational status
MEXR = Mother's "realistic" expectations for child's educational attainment
MEXI = Mother's "ideal" expectations for child's educational attainment
MIED = Minimum amount of education mother thinks child should receive
MREA = How much mother reads to child

FREA = How much father reads to child
OREA = How much others in household read to child
TWM = Time child spends with mother
TWF = Time child spends with father in some activity
BKS = Number of books
TOYS = Variety of toys
TV = Television viewing time
PS = Preschool program attendance
CCF = Mother's score on the Cattell Culture Fair Intelligence Scale
PSI = Preschool Inventory Score
MINQ = Mother's use of inquiry
MDIR = Mother' use of directive
MPRF = Mother's use of praise following child's independent act
MPRN = Mother's use of praise not following child's independent act

MVDN = Mother's use of verbal disapproval with no specific feedback
MVDF = Mother's use of verbal disapproval with specific feedback
MVCN = Mother's use of visual cue not following child's request for assistance
MMOF = Mother's use of modeling following child's request for assistance
MMON = Mother's use of modeling not following child's request for assistance
CASK = Child asks mother for assistance
CREJ = Child rejects mother's assistance
CIND = Child acts independently

[a] $p < .001$.
[b] $p < .01$.
[c] $p < .05$; one-tailed tests.

Table 5. Structural Model I

Measured and unmeasured variables

Indicators	I	II	III	IV	V	VI	VII	VIII	IX	X	XI	XII	XIII	XIV	XV	XVI	XVII	XVIII	XIX	XX	XXI	XXII	XXIII	XXIV
CSEX	X																							
CAGE		X																						
PS			X																					
TV				X																				
BKS					X																			
TWF					X	X																		
PSI						X	X	X	X	X	X	X	X	X	X	X	X	X	X	X	X	X	X	X
MOCC								X																
MED								X																
FOCC									X															
FED									X															
MEXR										X														
MEXI										X														
MIED										X														
MREA											X													
FREA											X													
OREA											X													
CCF$_1$												X												
CCF$_2$												X												
CCF$_3$												X												
CCF$_4$												X												
MINQ$_1$													X											
MDIR$_1$														X										
MPRF$_1$															X									
MPRN$_1$																X								
MVDN$_1$																	X							
MVDF$_1$																		X						
MVCN$_1$																			X					

MMOF$_1$
MMON$_1$
CASK$_1$
CREJ$_1$
CIND$_1$
MINQ$_2$
MDIR$_2$
MPRF$_2$
MPRN$_2$
MVDN$_2$
MVDF$_2$
MVCN$_2$
MMOF$_2$
MMON$_2$
CASK$_2$
CREJ$_2$
CIND$_2$

Indicators:

CSEX = Child's sex
CAGE = Child's age (months)
PS = Preschool program attendance
TV = Television viewing time
BKS = Number of books
TWF = Time child spends with father in some activity
PSI = Preschool Inventory scores
MOCC = Mother's occupational status
MED = Mother's education
FOCC = Father's occupational status
FED = Father's education
MEXR = Mother's "realistic" expectations for child's educational attainment
MEXI = Mother's "ideal" expectations for child's educational attainment

MIED = Minimum amount of education mother thinks child should receive
MREA = How much mother reads to child
FREA = How much father reads to child
OREA = How much others in household read to child
CCF = Mother's score on the Cattell Culture Fair Intelligence Tests
MINQ = Mother's use of inquiry
MDIR = Mother's use of directive
MPRF = Mother's use of praise following child's independent act
MPRN = Mother's use of praise not following child's independent act
MVDN = Mother's use of verbal disapproval with no specific feedback

MVDF = Mother's use of verbal disapproval with specific feedback
MVCN = Mother's use of visual cue not following child's request for assistance
MMOF = Mother's use of modeling following child's request for assistance
MMON = Mother's use of modeling not following child's request for assistance
CASK = Child asks mother for assistance
CREJ = Child rejects mother's assistance
CIND = Child acts independently

variables, as reflected in a mean discrepancy of .16 between the observed and reproduced intercorrelations. Although poorly defined, this factor showed a perfect correlation with the factor defined by mother's education and occupational status. This suggested that at least one of the reading variables might be an indicator of the mother's socioeducational factor described above. This hypothesis was tested in the second analysis.

As hypothesized, the three variables measuring mother's expectations for the child's educational attainment clearly defined a single construct. The λ values were .64 for the mother's "realistic" aspirations (MEXR), .53 for her "ideal" aspirations (MEXI), and .70 for the minimum amount of education she thought her child should receive (MIED).

Also in line with the hypotheses, maternal scores on the four tests of the Cattell Culture Fair Intelligence Scale were found to reflect a single underlying factor, λ = .82, .44, .63, and .55. This finding suggests that this is indeed a single-factor test.

Finally, the constructs postulated to underlie every pair of repeated measures that were derived from the mother–child interaction tasks emerged as generally clear factors. This constitutes additional evidence of the reliability of the variables measuring observed mother–child interactions. Not surprisingly, a strong correlation was found between two of these factors—mother's praise of the child's independent acts and child's independent acts; estimated true correlation = .92. This correlation suggests that there is not enough independent variance in these two factors to justify their inclusion as separate constructs; therefore, in the next analysis they were treated as a single construct.

In the second analysis I tested two hypotheses suggested by the solution to Structural Model I and the observed correlations. One hypothesis was that the amount of time fathers spent reading to their children was an indicator of the construct defined by father's education and occupational status. The other hypothesis was that the time mothers and others (except the father) spent reading to the children were indicators of the construct underlying the mother's education and occupational status. Structural Models I and II differed in another respect: because the results of Model I revealed that several variables did not make an independent contribution to the explanation of variability in Preschool Inventory scores, in Model II the parameters estimating the contribution of these variables to the Preschool Inventory scores were specified to be zero. These variables are those corresponding to IX, X, XVI, and XX in Model I (Table 5).

The results of Structural Model II partly confirmed one hypothesis and led to the rejection of the other. The amount of time the mother spent reading to her child appears to be an indicator of the construct underlying the mother's education and occupational status; however, the amount of time others spent reading to the child is not an indicator of the construct. Interestingly, the amount of time the father spent reading to his child is not an adequate indicator ($\lambda = .32$) of the construct underlying the father's education and occupational status.

The results of the two previous analyses led me to postulate the hypothetical structure depicted in Table 6 (Structural Model III). The solution to this model revealed a good fit of the model to the data. The

Table 6. Structural Model III

Indicators	Measured and unmeasured variables												
	I	II	III	IV	V	VI	VII	VIII	IX	X	XI	XII	XIII
CSEX	X												
CAGE		X											
PS			X										
TV				X									
PSI	X	X	X	X	X	X	X	X	X	X	X	X	X
MOCC				X									
MED				X									
MREA				X									
OREA					X								
MDIR$_1$							X						
MPRF$_1$								X					
MVDN$_1$									X				
MVDF$_1$										X			
MVCN$_1$											X		
MMON$_1$												X	
CASK$_1$													X
MDIR$_2$							X						
MPRF$_2$								X					
MVDN$_2$									X				
MVDF$_2$										X			
MVCN$_2$											X		
MMON$_2$												X	
CASK$_2$													X

Indicators:
CSEX = Child's sex
CAGE = Child's age (months)
PS = Preschool program attendance
TV = Television viewing time
PSI = Preschool Inventory score
MOCC = Mother's occupational status
MED = Mother's education
MREA = How much mother reads to child
OREA = How much others in household read to child
MDIR = Mother's use of directive

MPRF = Mother's use of praise following child's independent act
MVDN = Mother's use of verbal disapproval with no specific feedback
MVDF = Mother's use of verbal disapproval with specific feedback
MVCN = Mother's use of visual cue not following child's request for assistance
MMON = Mother's use of modeling not following child's request for assistance
CASK = Child asks mother for assistance

Table 7. Chi-Square Goodness-of-Fit Values for Three
Successive Structural Models

Model	χ^2	df
I	1599.92[a]	682
II	1658.56[a]	731
III	184.16[b]	150

[a] $p < .0001$.
[b] $p > .01$.

chi-square goodness-of-fit measure yielded a value of 184.16 with 150 degrees of freedom, which was not significantly different from zero at the .01 level. Typically, a chi-square value of up to twice the number of degrees of freedom suggests a reasonably good fit of the model to the data. An inspection of the residuals matrix provided additional evidence of a good fit. The residuals were in the range of .00 and .32; the mean of the absolute value of the residuals was .06. As can be seen in Table 7, the fit of Structural Model III is much better than that of the two previous models. The reader

Table 8. Zero-Order Intercorrelations (Unanalyzed) among Predictor Variables in Structural Model III

	I	II	III	IV	V	VI	VII	VIII	IX	X	XI	XII	XIII
I.	1.00	.00	.18	-.12	-.03	-.19	.05	.08	.22	.22	.26	-.31	.00
II.		1.00	.21	-.06	.03	.06	-.20	.26	-.01	-.37	-.13	.02	.04
III.			1.00	-.32	.02	-.26	-.15	.08	.07	-.07	.06	.12	.02
IV.				1.00	-.35	-.21	-.07	-.34	.02	.32	-.13	.02	.00
V.					1.00	.25	.08	.30	-.47	-.41	.03	-.34	.01
VI.						1.00	.26	.36	-.11	-.29	-.21	-.24	-.02
VII.							1.00	-.11	-.03	.23	.28	-.22	-.04
VIII.								1.00	.15	-.15	.01	-.01	.03
IX.									1.00	.13	.10	.21	.03
X.										1.00	.21	-.12	-.05
XI.											1.00	-.15	.01
XII.												1.00	-.02
XIII.													1.00

Variable labels:
I. Child's sex
II. Child's age (months)
III. Preschool program attendance
IV. Television viewing time
V. Mother's socioeducational values
VI. How much persons in household other than parents read to child
VII. Mother's use of directive
VIII. Mother's use of praise following child's independent act
IX. Mother's use of verbal disapproval with no specific feedback
X. Mother's use of verbal disapproval with specific feedback
XI. Mother's use of visual cue not following child's request for assistance
XII. Mother's use of modeling not following child's request for assistance
XIII. Child asks mother for assistance

should examine also Table 8 and note that the intercorrelations among the independent variables in the model are not sufficiently high to yield statistically significant colinearity which, if present, could result in spurious path coefficients.

Figure 2 presents in conventional pictorial fashion the results of solving the structural equations underlying Model III. Only the variables that appear to have an influence (either directly or indirectly) on Preschool Inventory scores are represented in this diagram. The circles represent unmeasured or "true" variables (constructs) and the rectangles portray

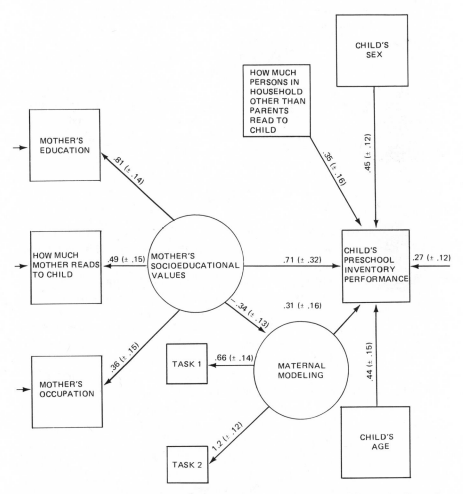

Figure 2. Causal model of family influences on pre-school age children's intellectual development.

measured variables. Standard errors are shown in parentheses next to each standardized path coefficient. The very high reliability obtained with the Preschool Inventory makes it unnecessary to correct the parameter estimates for the minute attenuation resulting from the slight unreliability of this measure (the Kuder-Richardson Formula 20 reliability coefficient obtained with these data was .93).

Considering the overall effects first, it can be seen that in this model all but about one-fourth of the variation in Preschool Inventory scores is accounted for by the other variables in the model. This finding, based on the magnitude of the squared multiple correlation ($r^2 = 1 - .274 = .726$), indicates that the model has strikingly substantial explanatory power. The influence labeled for easy reference "mother's socioeducational values" is the most important determinant of the child's performance on the Preschool Inventory. Indeed, this influence is at least 0.6 times more important than any other source. Also strong, though less powerful, is the influence exerted on Preschool Inventory performance by four other variables: the amount of time that persons in the household other than the parents spent reading to the child, the mother's use of modeling as a teaching strategy, whether the child is a boy or a girl, and his or her chronological age.

Discussion

The consistency of the present findings with the correlational results of previous studies adds to our confidence in the causal model postulated in Figure 2. The finding that mothers' socioeducational values exert a strong influence on their young children's intellectual development as measured by Preschool Inventory performance is harmonious with previous research showing a correlation between family socioeconomic status and children's performance on mental tests (Deutsch, 1973; Hess, 1970). The influence of chronological age may seem surprising considering the fact that the study's sampling design restricted the range of this variable in order to control for its effect; however, this result, too, is consistent with previous data (Gilbert & Shipman, 1972; Laosa, 1981b), indicating that performance level on the Preschool Inventory improves noticeably over the developmental period of 3 to 4½ years of age and hence contributing evidence of the construct validity of this measure.

The significant influence of child's sex indicates that girls obtained higher Preschool Inventory scores than did boys. This result, too, is harmonious with previous findings (Gilbert & Shipman, 1972). Such a sex difference has been attributed to differential instruction in the home, resulting in parents involving girls more than boys on school-relevant activities. In the present analysis, the sex difference was obtained even after the environmental influences measured in the study were held constant. Thus, to obtain an adequate explanation of the sex difference in young children's intellectual performance, the influence of variables other than those included here should be examined in future research.

One of the important findings in this study centers on the influence that people other than the parents have on the young child's intellectual development. Specifically, the findings revealed that the amount of time that people in the household other than the parents spent reading to the child has a significant influence on the child's intellectual development. Who are these other people? The evidence indicates that they are older siblings. The source of this answer lies in the bivariate analyses (Table 2), as follows. Significant correlations occurred between OREA and variables that measure the number of siblings, that is, BORD, ONLY, and SIBS. However, the correlation is particularly strong between OREA and the number of older siblings (i.e., BORD). In addition, people other than the child's parents and siblings resided in only two households and the correlation between the number of these others and the child's intellectual development is near zero ($r = -.09; n = 50$). Also important to note in this regard are the near-zero correlations of BORD, ONLY, and SIBS with the child's intellectual development. In sum, the evidence indicates that older siblings may influence the intellectual development of their pre-school-age brothers and sisters, and that this influence is mediated at least in part by the older sibling's reading to the young child.

Another important discovery in this study is the *positive* influence that maternal modeling—that is, the mother's use of physical demonstration as a teaching strategy—appears to have on the child's intellectual development. That this influence is positive may come as a surprise for three reasons. First, it contradicts the generally held view that, for purposes of fostering young children's intellectual development, teaching strategies that are verbal in nature are superior to those that are nonverbal. Second, it stands in marked contrast to what one would expect on the basis of the obtained zero-order correlation. Whereas the zero-order correlation between maternal modeling (MMON) and the child's intellectual development is negative, the path coefficient between these two variables shows a positive influence. Third, this positive influence of maternal modeling on the child's intellectual development appears quasi-paradoxical in light of two other influences also revealed by the path analysis. Namely that, just as one would expect on the basis of previous research (e.g., Deutsch, 1973; Hess, 1970; Laosa, 1981a), the variable labeled *mother's socioeducational values*, a social class index, is shown to have an inverse influence on maternal modeling but a positive influence on the child's intellectual development.

Although the results described in the preceding paragraph may be in part surprising and seemingly paradoxical, they can be unambiguously understood, indeed, on the basis of both statistically and psychologically plausible explanations. Statistically, they can be understood in light of our knowledge of and experience with suppressor variables in multiple regression analysis. Of particular relevance here is a rather infrequent type of suppression called negative suppression. It occurs when a predictor variable has a partial regression weight (i.e., path coefficient) opposite in sign to its zero-order correlation with the criterion (Conger, 1974; Darlington, 1968; Nunnally, 1967). It occurs because one or more of the predictor variables in the multiple regression equation operate by removing ("suppressing") some irrelevant variance. Thus, by controlling (partialing) the effects of certain variables, the true relationship emerges, as revealed in the partial regression weights. Unless the irrelevant (confounding) variance is suitably controlled by such techniques as the inclusion of suppressors, the investigator can be misled into drawing incorrect conclusions from the data. In the present study, the difference in sign between the zero-order correlation and the path coefficient to which I have been alluding suggests the presence of confounding variance and indicates that suppression may have operated to remove such variance, showing that the relationship between maternal modeling and children's intellectual development is a positive one. Let us turn now to a plausible psychological explanation of this finding.

Perhaps because of previous findings showing that maternal modeling—that is, the mother's use of physical demonstration as a teaching strategy—has inverse zero-order correlations with both her schooling level (Laosa, 1978, 1981a) and with her child's performance on intellectual tests (Deutsch, 1973; Hess, 1970), it has been implicitly assumed, reasonably, that modeling, or physical demonstration, is not a particularly effective teaching strategy for enhancing the child's intellectual development. Other strategies (i.e., verbal strategies in general and inquiry in particular) are typically considered more important in this regard (e.g., Sigel, 1979; Sigel & Saunders, 1979). Cognitive modeling and observational learning have been either ignored or their status denigrated. However, the results of the present study suggest that this assumption may be unwarranted, at least with regard to pre-school-age children. That is, as we have seen in the foregoing, it appears that the variance that social class as a variable (i.e., mothers' socioeducational values) shares with both maternal teaching strategies and children's test performance confounds the zero-order correlation between maternal teaching strategies and children's test performance. Therefore, unless mother's socioeducational values or some other appropriate social class index is suitably partialed out, one is likely to obtain a negative correlation between maternal modeling and children's intellectual development such as I obtained in the bivariate analyses. However, when social class is suitably held constant, as I did in Structural Model III, one can see that maternal modeling, that is, physical demonstration as a teaching strategy, appears to have a positive influence on children's intellectual development. The latter finding is harmonious with the results of experimental research demonstrating the potency of adult modeling on children's behavior and indicating that intellectual development can take place simply on the basis of observational learning (Bandura, 1977; Rosenthal & Zimmerman, 1978).

The absence of a relationship between variables is often as important, from a psychological perspective, as is a statistically significant association. One such absence of a relationship is particularly intriguing because of its direct relevance to the foregoing discussion and because it, too, has important implications for psychological and educational theory and practice. I refer here specifically to mothers' use of inquiry as a teaching strategy. Mothers' use of inquiry was found to have a positive but weak and nonsignificant zero-order correlation with children's intellectual development; however, in the structural analyses it was found to exert *no* significant influence on the child's intellectual development. This finding is important because it serves to clarify and qualify a generally accepted notion among some psychologists and early childhood educators. I refer here to the view that inquiry, that is, question asking, as a teaching strategy exerts a positive influence on the pre-school-age child's intellectual development because of the cognitive "demand" that such mode of interaction makes on the child (e.g., Sigel, 1979; Sigel & Saunders, 1979). In this regard, inquiry has been considered superior to modeling. The results of the present study suggest that this view requires critical scrutiny. Specifically, the present results suggest that, at least during preschool age, teaching strategies that involve modeling, that is, physical demonstration, are more effective in fostering children's intellectual development than are teaching strategies that involve inquiry. From a developmental perspective that takes into account the relative limitations on the young child's information-processing facility, this finding makes sense. That is, it is plausible that certain information-processing skills are prerequisite to enabling the child to benefit intellectually from teaching strategies that involve inquiry. It very well could be that, at an early age, children have yet to acquire the cognitive structures necessary for adequately processing, assimilating, or accommodating certain forms of discourse that involve inquiry. On the other hand, even at this early age, children probably already possess the psychological wherewithal necessary for cognitive acquisition on the basis of observational learning (Bandura, 1977; Rosenthal & Zimmerman, 1978). If cognitive development means some analogous and dependent "layering" of skills, then there would be little grounds for dispute that this is a plausible hypothesis that warrants urgent investigation.

Now, whether inquiry teaching strategies applied during the preschool-age years have a "sleeper" effect that does not emerge until later by virtue of a lag between this type of specific environmental experience and intellectual manifestation is yet another question, one that would require longitudinal investigation. Also of particular value would be studies that specify and differentiate among different types of teaching strategies that involve inquiry, since different types of inquiry strategies may vary in the level and type of cognitive "demand" they place on the child. In this regard, it may be necessary also to specify and differentiate among different aspects of intellectual performance, since different strategies might differentially influence different aspects of intellectual development. Also important would be methodological investigations that examine different types of parent–child interaction tasks, since widely different types of tasks are likely to elicit different types of teaching strategies, and each type of task or situation probably elicits only a subset of all the teaching strategies available in the parent's repertoire.

In addition to the substantive findings of this study, which have important implications for both theory and practice—implications that are of sufficient importance to warrant urgent attempts at replication of the findings—perhaps one of the most salient contributions of the study is methodological in nature. First, a complex model of family influences on young children's intellectual development was elaborated. The aim was to produce a testable hypothetical model of family influences on children's development, a model in which many variables that previous studies have shown to be important are linked with one another in a fairly complex and comprehensive network of causation. Second, a measurement strategy that included both process and status variables and that obtained assessments by a combination of direct observations in the home, interviews, and psychometric tests was employed. The aim here was to achieve a greater specification of early family influences and their relationships to the child's intellectual development. Third, the model was tested using a particular approach to path analysis that, unlike other path-analytic approaches with their problems in attenuation from measurement errors, allows for the use of hypothetical, error-free unmeasured variables, takes errors of measurement into consideration, and relies on the simultaneous estimation of parameters in the model. Using this research method, I found that certain aspects of the family environment, which heretofore have been considered unimportant and uninfluential aspects of the family as a learning environment for children, were more strongly related to the child's intellectual development than were other aspects of the family environment upon which researchers and educators have traditionally focused.

ACKNOWLEDGMENTS

Grateful appreciation is expressed to Dr. Gloria Zamora for assistance in coordinating data collection and to Dr. Charles E. Werts for statistical advice and computational assistance. Appreciation is expressed also to the following individuals for assistance in collecting and processing data: Carmen Cortez, Amalia Garcia, Robert Hernandez, Ilyana Jacobson, Judy Liskin-Gasparro, Gilbert Lopez, Judy Morgan, William Nemceff, Rosemary Perez, Cornelia Salas, and Lucy Villarreal.

Appendix A

Operational Definitions of Basic Categories of Maternal Teaching Strategies and Child Behaviors Assessed in the Mother–Child Interaction Tasks[2]

Maternal Teaching Strategies

Inquiry. The mother asks the child a question or makes an interrogative suggestion to the child. Examples:

- "Now, where does the blue one go?"
- "What can you do with that part?"
- "Would you put that there?"

Directive. The mother verbally commands/tells/makes a declarative suggestion to the child to pursue a given course of action. Examples:

- "Put the blue one right there."
- "Now tighten it up a little more."
- "I would look for a larger part."

---

[2] Types of physical contact that generally would be considered as physical punishment or physical control or restraint were not included among the categories of maternal behavior assessed in this study. The reason for this exclusion is that in previous research using a similar sample of participants and similar tasks and interaction situations, such contact occurred very infrequently (Laosa, 1980a,b).

Praise. The mother praises, or otherwise verbally expresses approval of, the child or the child's activity or product. (The observer makes note of whether or not the praise [immediately] follows an *independent act* by the child.) Examples:

- "That's good."
- "Yes, that's the way."
- "Mm hum."
- "Good boy (girl)."
- "How nice."
- "O.K."
- "Fine."

Verbal Disapproval. The mother verbally indicates to the child that a given course of action taken by the child is incorrect or that she is displeased with the child or with the child's activity or product. (The observer makes note of whether or not the disapproval involves or is accompanied by *specific feedback. Specific feedback* is defined as giving a reason for the disapproval or making reference to at least one property of the Tinkertoy parts that is specific to the accomplishment of the task.)
Examples of verbal disapproval with *no* specific feedback:

- "That's wrong."
- "Don't use that part."
- "No."
- "Dummy."
- "Don't put that one there."
- "No, put that one in the other hole." (This example would be coded both as verbal disapproval with no specific feedback and as directive.)

Examples of verbal disapproval *with* specific feedback:

- "That's wrong, it's too big."
- "No, that goes in the head." (That is, the head of the Tinkertoy "man.")
- "Don't use a blue part there."
- "No, does one that size go there?" (This example would be coded both as verbal disapproval with specific feedback and as inquiry.)

Physical Affection. The mother makes physical contact with the child as an expression of a favorable feeling toward the child or toward the child's activity or product. (The observer makes note of whether or not the physical affection [immediately] follows an *independent act* by the child.) Examples:

- Patting the child on the head or arm.
- Kissing the child.
- Gently squeezing the child's shoulder.

Visual Cue. The mother attempts to attract the child's attention toward a given aspect of the task by providing a visual cue. This category is limited to attempts to attract the child's attention by sliding, pushing, or lifting a Tinkertoy part or portion of the Tinkertoy model being assembled (but short of fastening or unfastening parts). The behavior unit is considered complete (and a frequency point is recorded) when the mother releases the part or portion of the model or otherwise moves her hand away from it. (The observer makes note of whether or not the visual cue [immediately] follows the child's *asking for help, information, or advice*.) (More subtle visual cues, such as pointing to or touching a Tinkertoy part, were not included among the behavior categories assessed in this study. The reason for this exclusion is that in previous research using similar tasks and interaction situations, attempts to manually record such behaviors yielded only moderate reliabilities [Laosa, 1980b].) Examples:

- Moving a Tinkertoy part in the direction of the child.
- Handing the child a part.
- Taking two parts and placing them next to each other (but not fastening them) as an indication that they should go together.

Modeling. The mother physically demonstrates, or models for the child, how to accomplish the task. More specifically, the mother works on the construction of the Tinkertoy model and the child observes. A behavior unit is considered complete (and a frequency point is recorded) every time the mother fastens or unfastens two parts. (The observer makes note of whether or not the mother's modeling behavior [immediately] follows the child's *request for help, information, or advice*.)

Child's Behaviors

Asks for Help, Information, or Advice. The child verbally asks the mother for help in accomplishing the task or for information or advice regarding the task or its accomplishment. Examples:

- "Here, Mommy, you help me do it."
- "I can't do it, it's too hard" (handing the parts to the mother).
- "Where does this part go?"
- "Is this right?"

Rejects Help, Information, or Advice. The child (verbally or nonverbally) actively rejects the mother's help, information, or advice or the mother's attempt or offer to help, inform, or advise. Examples:

- Mother is demonstrating how to assemble a portion of the Tinkertoy model. Child says, "No, let me do it."
- Mother says, "Here, let me show you how to do it." Child takes the parts away from the mother and attempts to do it himself or herself.
- Mother says, "Put the blue one there now." Child responds, "I want to do it this way."

Independent Act. The child exhibits independence or initiative toward accomplishing the task. A behavior unit is considered complete (and a frequency point is recorded) every time that the child, on his or her own initiative rather than in compliance to the mother's suggestion, hint, directive, or cue, fastens or attempts to fasten two Tinkertoy parts. Examples:

- Child fastens (or attempts to fasten) two parts in the absence of mother's suggestions, hints, directives, or cues to do this.
- Child fastens (or attempts to fasten) two parts contrary to (or in spite of) mother's directives, suggestions, hints, or cues to do something else.

Appendix B

Cross-Task Correlations of Mother–Child Interaction Variables

Variables	Correlations	
	Rank-order	Product-moment
Maternal teaching strategies		
Inquiry	.72[a]	.70[a]
Directive	.75[a]	.79[a]
Praise:		
Following child's independent act	.56[a]	.55[a]
Not following child's independent act	.72[a]	.68[a]
Verbal disapproval:		
With specific feedback	.57[a]	.53[a]
With no specific feedback	.36[b]	.42[a]
Physical affection:		
Following child's independent act	—	—
Not following child's independent act	—	—
Visual cue:		
Following child's request for assistance	—	—
Not following child's request for assistance	.56[a]	.69[a]
Modeling:		
Following child's request for assistance	—	—
Not following child's request for assistance	.74[a]	.78[a]
Child behaviors		
Asks mother for help, information, or advice	.66[a]	.68[a]
Rejects mother's help, information, or advice	.27[c]	.27[c]
Independent act	.59[a]	.62[a]

Note. Coefficients in the first column are Spearman rank-order correlations based on (untransformed) rate-per-minute scores. Coefficients in the second column are Pearson product-moment correlations based on rate-per-minute scores transformed to $\sqrt{x} + \sqrt{x+1}$. Dashes indicate where coefficients were not computed because of very low frequency.
$n = 50$.
[a]$p < .001$.
[b]$p < .01$.
[c]$p < .05$; one-tailed tests.

Appendix C

Interobserver Reliability during Data Collection

Interobserver reliability for the variables derived from the mother–child interaction tasks was assessed as follows. A 4×2 factorial design was constructed using observer and sex of child as independent classifications. Analyses of variance were performed on this factorial design, using (transformed) average rate-per-minute scores as dependent variables. The F ratios of the observer main effect and of the observer $\times$ sex-of-child interaction were used to estimate interobserver reliability during data collection. As shown below, the four observers obtained generally similar means, and none but one of the F ratios was significant beyond the .05 level. These results provide evidence that in general the interobserver reliability for these variables is at least adequate.

| | Means | | | | $F(3, 42)$ | |
Variables	Observer 1 ($n = 16$)	Observer 2 ($n = 16$)	Observer 3 ($n = 7$)	Observer 4 ($n = 11$)	Observer	Observer $\times$ sex
Maternal teaching strategies						
Inquiry	3.31	3.19	3.81	3.07	1.24	1.66
Directive	3.37	3.62	4.16	3.87	1.65	.81
Praise	2.43	2.89	2.99	2.73	2.18	1.61
Verbal disapproval	2.08	1.96	2.41	2.15	1.68	2.60
Visual cue	2.82	2.44	2.21	2.58	1.93	2.57
Modeling	2.79	2.59	1.92	2.74	1.61	.89
Child's behaviors						
Asks for help	1.79	1.63	2.00	1.97	1.25	1.43
Rejects help	1.18	1.35	1.56	1.44	2.12	1.03
Independent act	3.06	2.61	2.86	2.17	4.31[a]	.22

Note. Physical affection was excluded from the analysis because of very low frequency.
[a] $p < .01$.

References

Anastasi, A. Intelligence and family size. *Psychological Bulletin*, 1956, *53*, 187–209.

Bandura, A. *Social learning theory*. Englewood Cliffs, N.J.: Prentice Hall, 1977.

Bayley, N. Development of mental abilities. In P.H. Mussen (Ed.), *Carmichael's manual of child psychology* (Vol. 1). New York: Wiley, 1970.

Bell, R. Q., & Harper, L. V. *Child effects on adults*. New York: Wiley, 1977.

Blalock, H. M., Jr. *Causal inferences in nonexperimental research*. New York: Norton, 1964.

Bouchard, T. J., Jr., & McGue, M. Familial studies of intelligence: A review. *Science*, 1981, *212*, 1055–1059.

Bronfenbrenner, U. *A report on longitudinal evaluations of preschool programs* (Vol. 2). *Is early intervention effective?* (DHEW Publication No. OHD 76-30025). Washington, D.C.: U.S. Department of Health, Education, and Welfare, 1974.

Brown, B. (Ed.). *Found: Long-term gains from early intervention*. Boulder, Colo.: Westview Press, 1978.

Caldwell, B. M. *Cooperative Preschool Inventory: Revised edition—1970*. Princeton, N.J.: Educational Testing Service, 1970. (Distributed by Addison-Wesley Publishing Co., Menlo Park, Calif.)

Caldwell, B. M., & Freund, J. H. *The Preschool Inventory*. Little Rock, Ark.: Center for Child Development and Education, University of Arkansas, 1980 (Distributed by Addison-Wesley Publishing Co., Menlo Park, Calif.)

Cicirelli, V. G. The relationship of sibling structure to intellectual abilities and achievement. *Review of Educational Research*, 1978, *48*, 365–379.

Clarke-Stewart, A. *Child care in the family: A review of research and some propositions for policy*. New York: Academic Press, 1977.

Conger, A. J. A revised definition for suppressor variables: A guide to their identification and interpretation. *Educational and Psychological Measurement*, 1974, *34*, 35–46.

Cooperative Tests and Services. *Preschool Inventory: Revised edition—1970: Directions for administering and scoring*. Princeton, N.J.: Educational Testing Service, 1970. (Distributed by Addison-Wesley Publishing Co., Menlo Park, Calif.) (a)

Cooperative Tests and Services. *Preschool Inventory: Revised edition—1970: Handbook*. Princeton, N.J.: Educational Testing Service, 1970. (Distributed by Addison-Wesley Publishing Co., Menlo Park, Calif.) (b)

Darlington, R. B. Multiple regression in psychological research and practice. *Psychological Bulletin*, 1968, *69*, 161–182.

Dave, R. H. *The identification and measurement of environmental process variables that are related to educational achievement*. Unpublished doctoral dissertation, University of Chicago, 1963.

Dennis, W. Causes of retardation among institutional children: Iran. *Journal of Genetic Psychology*, 1960, *96*, 47–59.

Deutsch, C. P. Social class and child development. In B.M. Caldwell & H. N. Ricciuti (Eds.), *Review of child development research* (Vol. 3). Chicago: The University of Chicago Press, 1973.

Fowler, W. Cognitive learning in infancy and early childhood. *Psychological Bulletin*, 1962, *59*, 116–152.

Frank, P. *Modern science and its philosophy*. New York: Collier, 1961.

Freeman, M.F., & Tukey, J. W. Transformations related to the angular and the square root. *Annals of Mathematical Statistics*, 1950, *21*, 607–611.

Gilbert, L. E., & Shipman, V. C. Preschool inventory. In V. C. Shipman (Ed.), *Disadvantaged children and their first school experiences*: *Technical report series* (ETS PR 72-27). Princeton, N.J.: Educational Testing Service, 1972.

Henderson, R. W., Bergan, J. R., & Hurt, M., Jr. Development and validation of the Henderson Environmental Learning Process Scale. *Journal of Social Psychology*, 1972, *88*, 185–196.

Hess, R. D. Social class and ethnic influences on socialization. In P. H. Mussen (Ed.), *Carmichael's manual of child psychology* (Vol. 2). New York: Wiley, 1970.

Hess, R. D., & Holloway, S. *The intergenerational transmission of literacy*. Report prepared for the Department of Health, Education and Welfare, National Institute of Education. Stanford University, June 1979.

Holtzman, W. H., Díaz-Guerrero, R., & Swartz, J. D. in collaboration with Lara-Tapia, L., Laosa, L. M., Morales, M. L., Lagunes, I. R., & Witzke, D. B. *Personality development in two cultures: A cross-cultural longitudinal study of school children in Mexico and the United States*. Austin, Texas: University of Texas Press, 1975.

Institute for Personality and Ability Testing. *Measuring intelligence with the Culture Fair Tests*. Champaign, Ill.: Institute for Personality and Ability Testing, 1973.

Lamb, M. E. The role of the father: An overview. In M. E. Lamb (Ed.), *The role of the father in child development*. New York: Wiley, 1976.

Land, K. C. Principles of path analysis. In E. F. Borgatta (Ed.), *Sociological methodology 1969*. San Francisco: Jossey-Bass, 1969.

Laosa, L. M. Maternal teaching strategies in Chicano families of varied educational and socioeconomic levels. *Child Development*, 1978, *49*, 1129–1135.

Laosa, L. M. Maternal teaching strategies in Chicano and Anglo-American families: The influence of culture and education on maternal behavior. *Child Development*, 1980, *51*, 759–765 (a)

Laosa, L. M. Measures for the study of maternal teaching strategies. *Applied Psychological Measurement*, 1980, *4*, 355–366. (b)

Laosa, L. M. Maternal behavior: Sociocultural diversity in modes of family interaction. In R. W. Henderson (Ed.), *Parent–child interaction: Theory, research, and prospects*. New York: Academic Press, 1981. (a)

Laosa, L. M. *Psychometric characteristics of Chicano and non-Hispanic white children's performance on the Preschool Inventory* (ETS RR 81-56). Princeton, N.J.: Educational Testing Service, 1981 (b).

Laosa, L. M., & Brophy, J. E. Effects of sex and birth order on sex-role development and intelligence among kindergarten children. *Developmental Psychology*, 1972, *6*, 409–415.

Lerner, R. M., & Spanier, G. B. *Child influences on marital and family interaction: A life-span perspective*. New York: Academic Press, 1978.

Marjoribanks, K. *Families and their learning environments: An empirical analysis*. London: Routledge & Kegan Paul, 1979.

Marjoribanks, K., Walberg, H. J., & Bargen, M. Mental abilities: Sibling constellation and social class correlates. *British Journal of Social and Clinical Psychology*, 1975, *14*, 109–116.

Nunnally, J. C. *Psychometric theory*. New York: McGraw-Hill, 1967.

Radin, N. The role of the father in cognitive, academic, and intellectual development. In M. E. Lamb (Ed.), *The role of the father in child development*. New York: Wiley, 1976.

Rosenthal, T.L., & Zimmerman, B. J. *Social learning and cognition*. New York: Academic Press, 1978.

Scarr-Salapatek, S. Genetics and the development of intelligence. In F. D. Horowitz (Ed.), *Review of child development research* (Vol. 4). Chicago: University of Chicago Press, 1975.

Schooler, C. Birth order effects: Not here, not now! *Psychological Bulletin*, 1972, *78*, 161–175.

Shipman, V. C., McKee, J. D., & Bridgeman, B. *Disadvantaged children and their first school experiences: Stability and change in family status, situational, and process variables and their relationship to children's cognitive performance* (ETS PR 75-28). Princeton, N.J.: Educational Testing Service, 1976.

Sigel, I. E. On becoming a thinker: A psychoeducational model. *Educational Psychologist*, 1979, *14*, 70–78.

Sigel, I. E., & Saunders, R. An inquiry into inquiry: Question asking as an instructional model. In L. Katz (Ed.), *Current topics in early childhood education* (Vol. 2). Norwood, N.J.: Ablex, 1979.

Sigel, I. E., McGillicuddy-DeLisi, A. V., & Johnson, J. E. *Parental distancing, beliefs, and children's representational competence within the family context* (ETS RR 80-21). Princeton, N.J.: Educational Testing Service, 1980.

Sörbom, D., & Jöreskog, K.G. *COFAMM—confirmatory factor analysis with model modification: A Fortran IV program.* Chicago, Ill.: National Educational Resources, 1976.

Spitz, R. A. Hospitalism: A follow-up report. *Psychoanalytic Study of the Child*, 1946, *2*, 113–117.

Stallings, J., & Porter, A. *National day care home study: Final report* (Vol. 3). *Observation componet.* Menlo Park, Calif.: SRI International, June 1980.

Stein, A. H., & Friedrich, L. K. Impact of television on children and youth. In E. M. Hetherington (Ed.), *Review of child development research* (Vol. 5). Chicago: University of Chicago Press, 1975.

Werts, C. E., & Linn, R. L. A general linear model for studying growth. *Psychological Bulletin*, 1970, *73*, 17–22.

Wold, H., & Jureen, L. *Demand analysis: A study in econometrics.* New York: Wiley, 1953.

Wolf, R. M. *The identification and measurement of environmental process variables related to intelligence.* Unpublished doctoral dissertation, University of Chicago, 1964.

Wright, S. The method of path coefficients. *Annals of Mathematical Statistics*, 1934, *5*, 161–215.

Zajonc, R. B., & Markus, G. B. Birth order and intellectual development. *Psychological Review*, 1975, *82*, 74–88.

CHAPTER 2

The Relationship between Parental Distancing Strategies and the Child's Cognitive Behavior

IRVING E. SIGEL

Introduction

To map the terrain of the family as a functioning system is a complex task. Nevertheless, there has been a resurgence of interest in family dynamics, with current advocates espousing a multicausal, multidisciplinary, multi-everything approach. The recognition that the family is a complex organization and that it cannot be understood from the conceptualization or methodology of any one discipline may not be new. Nevertheless, it is only recently that the family has been the unit of study for psychologists (e.g., Cochran & Brassard, 1979; Hetherington, 1979; Lamb, 1978; Lewis & Lee-Painter, 1974; Parke & O'Leary, 1975). Recent discoveries of family networks (Cochran & Brassard, 1979; Lewis & Feiring, 1979) and of child effects on the family (Bell & Harper, 1977)—in addition to the traditional studies—are, in my estimation, signs of a rapprochement between the idealized world of the psychologist's view of human behavior and the realities of family interaction. In spite of this increased convergence between the reality and the idealized image of the social scientist's conception of the family, there is still a considerable gap between our sophisticated awareness of the complexities and the methodological competence we now have to cope with this complex phenomenon. Consequently, we modify our conceptualization in practice to conform to the practical methods we have for data analysis. In an excellent volume edited by Lerner and Spanier (1978), the continual problem between "the

IRVING E. SIGEL ● Educational Testing Service, Princeton, New Jersey 08541. Research reported in this chapter was supported by NIH Grant R01 HD10686.

tyranny of data" and the final outcome is clearly shown. Various authors in that volume have presented elaborate conceptual systems that map onto the family reality in exciting and provocative ways. However, the dilemma persists between the volume of data that must be gathered for so complex an interaction system as the family and our current knowledge of how to deal with the data.

One solution, a temperate and somewhat restrained approach, is to acknowledge the complexity of the task and to realize our limits while also beginning to conceptualize some domains of interaction; in a sense, this is a "chunking" approach, similar to the way in which one reads a sentence (one tends to "chunk" elements of a sentence, realizing that each chunk contributes to the whole but that the whole cannot be assimilated and accommodated in its totality). To be sure, this sounds contrary to the old gestalt statement that the whole is greater than the sum of its parts. It is, in fact, this very awareness that may account for the caution that is generally displayed when the complexities of the family environment are discussed. Nevertheless, we proceed and cautiously define areas that appear to have conceptual quasi-independence which can be treated as a subsystem of the whole. Ultimately the hope is that—as the research continues—the subsystem can be embedded into a large system. It is with this perspective that we conceptualized the family as a *learning environment*, where the roles of the parent are those of teacher and provider of human (e.g., affection) and material resources. The parents function in these roles, since as adults they possess power to control and to dispense material and psychological goods and services. Further, they represent the intersect between the child/family group and the broader society. The parental role can be identified and fractionated into various other roles (Emmerich, 1969). Essentially, one notion that can readily be accepted is that a parent functions as a teacher, using the concept of teacher in its broadest sense. This is not a new insight, but its presence is a relatively recent acquisition for psychological research and is acknowledged more specifically (Hess & Shipman, 1965).

Another traditional approach has been to view parental behavior as transcending context, as though parental behaviors were traits. Yet, investigations of parental interactions with children revealed that parental behaviors were not consistent and that consistency was not so desirable. Rather, parent behaviors are contingent on the particular contexts in which they interact with children. This new discovery regarding the role of ecological factors influencing parent behavior is a fortunate reiteration of the old Lewinian notions of field forces (Lewin, 1936).

The report that I wish to present comes to terms with some ecological issues, particularly those related to the context in which the behavior is observed and evaluated.

The parental role featured in this report is that of teacher, which essentially involves efforts to instruct another, be it a child or an adult, by imparting information. Teaching occurs in many subtle and direct ways in the course of parental interactions with children. It need not necessarily be a self-conscious, deliberate activity but can be embedded within the daily routines of existence. Consequently, there are times when parents may not be aware of teaching. Nevertheless, the parent is a teacher, since he or she engages the child as a teacher might. Even when the teaching is informal, nonstructured, and not within the parent's awareness, I assume that a teaching function exists.

This chapter will not focus on the antecedents or preconditions for defining the teaching role. Rather, it will present observational data describing parent–child interactions as they occurred in a laboratory context where parents were instructed to teach their children a predefined task (see Chapter 9).

Teaching, irrespective of its definition and context, does necessarily involve techniques or strategies. It involves communicative acts that, at some level, are employed to achieve some educational objective. Types of teaching strategies and their consequences for the child's intellectual development form the basic interest of the research reported herein. Specifically, the basic question is: What kinds of strategies do parents employ as they teach their children particular types of tasks? A related question is: What effects do these strategies have for the child's cognitive development? Since the parent has choices as to what techniques to use, my argument is that the strategies "selected" are those most compatible with the parent's belief systems and style of interaction.

Conceptualization of Distancing

The domain of teaching strategies has been explored and catalogued by various educators attempting to create classifications for the behaviors of teachers. Various systems are available, each of which purports to focus on particular classes of behavior which are considered essential (e.g., Hess & Shipman, 1965; Laosa, 1980a,b). The formulation presented here is no exception to that proposition since the conceptualization reflects a constructivist perspective with strong overtones of Piagetian influence. The basic conceptual argument is that presentations of communication from one person to another activate or energize the response system of the other. Different classes of presentations have different effects. Thus, presenting a lecture has a different cognitive impact than asking a question. Presenting a joke has a different impact than presenting a serious statement. The instigation of the behavior of another through some channel of communication provides the respondent with the material that must be construed or interpreted in some way. The response that is presented to the speaker provides a new set of stimuli and can evoke additional verbalizations. This kind of reciprocal feedback system in communication is the critical unit of analysis.

We have conceptualized communication strategies in the context of *distancing*, a construct that is used as a metaphor to denote the psychological separation of the person from the immediate, ongoing present. The distancing metaphor suggests that individuals can project themselves into the past or into the future or can transcend the immediate present. This process of distancing is conceptualized as critical in the development of representational thinking. Representational thinking, representation, or re-presentation are the mental products of that psychological distancing interaction. For example, the mother says to the child, "Where have you been?" The child responds, "I have been to school." The mother asks, "What did you do in school today?" The child responds by describing an array of activities. The mother's query prompts the child to reconstruct previous experience and, in the process of this reconstruction, the child re-presents the experiences to himself or herself. At this stage, it is not relevant to discuss how or what the mental contents of this re-presentation are, since this raises questions of imagery and other symbol systems which are not germane to our discussion. What is of particular relevance for us is that parental distancing strategies are hypothesized as activating the child's cognitive process or processes in the form of some kind of representation. Some distancing strategies can activate the child's anticipatory schema; others may focus on reconstructive schema. There are varieties of strategies that target different temporal perspectives, contents, and communication structures.[1] Of interest to us is the documentation of the types of distancing strategies parents use and how these strategies contribute to the ontogeny of representational thought.

Distancing strategies are social events. For the young child, these social experiences occur in the course of interaction with one or more significant individuals. Over time, these experiences are assumed to contribute to the development of verbal thinking skills, which may be conceptualized as internalized speech akin to Vygotsky's notion of inner speech, since "Inner Speech is to a large extent thinking in pure meanings" (Vygotsky, 1962).[2] For example, in decision making, individuals may engage in internal questioning strategies as though they were addressing others. These types of internal dialogues are, I contend, internalizations of earlier social experiences involving distancing encounters.

[1] Although these strategies are not limited to parent–child interactions, they are present potentially in any dyadic or probably more complex interaction.
[2] Elaboration of this point is left to other places.

Although distancing strategies vary in structure (see Table 1), our hypothesis is that those which are in an inquiry form will be particularly influential in the ontogenesis of representational thought because open-ended inquiry in particular places a mental operational demand on the hearer to respond. Once the hearer becomes engaged in the distancing interaction, he or she can respond only by employing some form of

Table 1. Examples of Mental Operational Demands on Child through Parent Distancing Strategies[a]

Demand on child to:

Observe	Getting the child to be attentive using any senses: hearing, seeing, smelling; asking the child to examine, e.g., parental demonstration that calls on the child to observe. *Examples*: "Look at the book." (statement) "Do you see No. 1?" (inquiry)
Label	Naming a singular object or event or action; naming a place, appropriate designation of something, locating; identifying, a single discrimination; *no elaboration*; ownership, possessives. Labeling is discrete and does not involve inference. *Examples*: "The name of this book is *Little Rock*. (statement) "Do you know the name of what we're going to make?" (inquiry)
Describe	Providing elaborated information of a single instance, e.g., "appears like," "looks like." A statement may be definitional. Actions or inner states of self—such as feelings, fantasies, ideas—are classes of parent verbalization coded in this category. *Examples*: "There are many flowers hiding the rainbow." (statement) "What is the boy doing?" (inquiry)
Interpret	To attribute or to explain meaning; more personal than a definition. *Examples*: "The reason Johnny is sad is because he broke his toy." (statement) "What does it mean to make believe?" (inquiry)
Infer similarities	Identifying nonobservational commonalities. Conceptual analysis—instances not present for sensory comparison; analogies, part–whole relationships. *Examples*: "This looks more like a hat than a boat." (statement) "Does it look like a mirror to you?" (inquiry)
Sequence	Temporal ordering of events, as in a story or carrying out a task; steps articulated. Types of key words are *last*, *next*, *afterwards*, *start*, and *begin*.

Continued

Table 1. (Continued)

Examples:
"First we'll do No. 1, then we'll do No. 2." (statement)
"What do we do next?" (inquiry)

Reproduce Reconstructing previous experiences; dynamic interaction of events, interdependence, functional; open ended; child's organization of previous experience.

Examples:
"Remember, you made one of these with Daddy." (statement)
"Have you flown on a plane?" (inquiry)

Propose alternatives Different options, different ways of performing the task; no negative aspect. Possible key words are *other, another, different from before*.

Examples:
"You could fold it another way, like this." (statement)
"Do you know another way to make a boat?" (inquiry)

Resolve conflict Presentation of contradictory or conflicting information with a resolution; problem solving; negative condition exists with focus on an alternative solution—one situation which is an impossibility needs to be resolved in another way; does include inferences of cause–effect relationships but includes an additional element of identifying the central element in one situation that can be transferred to another situation.

Examples:
"If there were only one piece of paper left, you could still make an airplane." (statement)
"If there is no light in here, how could we see to read?" (inquiry)

Transform Changing the nature, function, appearance of instances; focusing on the process of change of state of materials, persons, or events. Inferring is a part of this—the prediction of what will happen relating to a change of state.

Examples:
"Look and see how the color changes when I add another color." (statement)
"What do you need to do to a rock to change it into sand?" (inquiry)

[a]Complete observational system available on request from the author.

representation. This may involve transforming information from one symbol system to another; organizing previous experience by using classifications, sequencing, and so on; or anticipating outcomes (predictions). It is assumed that the responder has to generate some response. If, on the other hand, the inquiry is closed or highly constrained in its demand or if the distancing content is in a declarative statement, it would probably present minimal demands for complex reflective activity. The hearer can almost respond nonreflectively, virtually automatically. This type of automated response is hypothesized as not conducive to the development of representational thinking (Sigel & Saunders, 1979).

The outcome or the response to a distancing strategy is a representation. The capacity to employ representations is termed *representational competence*. The term *representation* has been increasingly evident in the research literature among cognitive theorists, ranging from those with an information processing persuasion to those who are committed Piagetians. The term is ambiguous through no fault of the psychologist. The English language does not provide sufficient synonyms or sufficient definitional specificity for the word *representation*. *Representation* can be defined in two ways (Piaget, 1962). It can be said to refer to all thought, because all thinking is internal and in a form that is discrepant from and not isomorphic to its referent. Mental activities are representations because they are abstractions from an experienced whole. Thus, we think in abstractions simply because we cannot assimilate the totality of an experience and hence cannot deal with the totality. If I experience a dog, for example, I certainly do not experience that animal in all its complexity. There is a selectivity, a reductionism, that perforce is required and necessary if I am to adapt to that experience. All thinking can be viewed as representational. On the other hand, there is a more specific definition of representation, to the effect that a given sign or symbol represents or stands for something else; something is substitutable for something else. Thus, the flag represents the nation; the word represents the object. This type of representation is closer to the everyday use of symbols or signs. For our purposes, I see no reason to get involved in these rather fine-grained distinctions. What is necessary here is to think of representation as essentially dealing with the awareness and the comprehension of signs or symbols as indicators or representations of their referents. Understanding that a map is a representation of physical locations and distances is, to me, dealing with a representation. The competence to comprehend these representations is what I refer to as *representational competence*, which means that the child comprehends and hence can deal with transformations of generate transformations of information from one domain to another. This type of transformation is exemplified by information represented in pictures which is transformed into words, or words transformed to pictures, or written words transformed to verbal utterances. These are all representational transformations. The understanding of equivalence among these systems is a developmental achievement which comes with time and considerable effort. Unfortunately, research efforts in this direction are relatively sparse and little attention has been paid to the social ontogenesis of representational competence. Most of the research efforts have dealt with the decontextualized child (i.e., the development of representational competence with minimal attention paid to the specifics of social experience), who is seen as an individual evolving competence to think in symbolic terms, to deal with symbol systems, and so on. Piaget's work—along with the thousands of studies that have flowed from it—is the best example of this decontextualization. There are, of course, exceptions, but these exceptions—such as Murray (1972) and others—have dealt with the social context in which the child evolves or comes to become a conserver. These are not studies that deal with a fine-grained analysis of environmental features which engage the child and which hypothetically can be argued to be the ingredients influencing representational competence. The basic hypothesis in this study is that representational competence in the child emerges to the degree that the parents use distancing strategies. The study to be reported was designed to test this hypothesis.

Sample

The study involved 120 families, two spacing patterns, and two socioeconomic levels (middle and working class). The age of the target child was, on the average, 4 years. The family configurations were single-child and three-child families where the first two siblings were of the same sex and no more than 3 years apart or three-child families where the first two siblings were of the same sex and more than 3 years apart. Equal numbers of the same-sex pairs were selected. In this report, we shall present the analyses of the data on the 4-year-old child.

Methods and Procedure

Data collection required two contact sessions with each family at the Educational Testing Service Research Laboratory. Families had the option of coming together as a family for both sessions or having the mother come with the children for one session and the father come with the children for the other. Once the selected family made this decision, the family was assigned to one of 12 schedules that serve to balance the order of task administration both within and between families.

Parent–Child Observation

Each father and mother performed two teaching tasks with their child—a storytelling task and an origami task (paper folding). A different story and a different origami task was used by each parent. Stringent controls for order of task presentation between and within families were maintained. For each family, if the mother performed the story task first and then the origami task in the observation situation, the father taught the origami first and then the story. (Note that there were two story tasks and two origami tasks for each child, so that the tasks were new for both parent and child.)

The parent–child interactions were videotaped through a one-way mirror. Administration of interviews and questionnaires was part of the procedure (see McGillicuddy-DeLisi, Chapter 9).

Each interaction was coded separately, yielding two sets of scores for each parent–child dyad—one for the structured teaching (origami) task and one for the semistructured (story) task. The coding system focuses on child and parent behaviors. Those aspects that deal with child behaviors are (1) degree of engagement in the interaction (e.g., the child is actively engaged in the interaction, is actively engaged in some other activity, is passively engaged in the interaction such as listening to the parent, or is passively unengaged in any activity), (2) evaluations of the child's success in completing each step of the origami task, and (3) points at which the child is the initiator and parental behaviors are responses rather than vice versa.

Five aspects of parental behaviors are coded: (1) teaching/management demands placed upon the child, (2) verbal emotional support systems, (3) nonverbal parental behaviors that provide task facilitation or serve as emotional support systems, (4) form of utterances, and (5) cohesion of the interaction. For coding purposes, one utterance and all five aspects listed above are considered for each coding unit. Many variables comprise each of the five aspects, and these are defined in the Parent–Child Interaction (PCI) Manual (Sigel, Flaugher, Johnson, & Schauer, 1977). Several examples of variables that are included in the coding system are presented in Table 1.

Six coders were necessary for scoring observations, as the coding system is quite complex and a total of 800 parent–child observations were collected (2 parents × 120 target children × 2 tasks + 2 parents × 80 older siblings × 2 tasks).

Estimates of reliability between observational data coders have been computed at different points of the coding process, yielding agreement rates for 20% of the videotapes from 72 to 99% with an average agreement of 86.5%. Reports of these efforts are available in a published paper describing the project (McGillicuddy-DeLisi, Sigel, & Johnson, 1979).

Child Assessments

Seven tasks are used to assess the child's representational abilities and problem-solving competence. Four of these are related to knowledge of the physical world. Three of these "physical cognition" tasks are directly derived from the work of Piaget (Conservation, Kinetic Anticipatory Imagery (KAI), Static Reproductive Imagery [SRI], 1952, 1971), and the fourth is a classification task called the Object Categorization Test (Classification) (Sigel, Anderson, & Shapiro, 1966). The other three tasks are related to knowledge of the social world and are administered with a semiclinical interview technique. These tasks deal with the child's conception of friendship (derived from Volpe, 1976), understanding the rules and conventions, and strategies in solving interpersonal problems (a modification of the PIPS; Spivak & Shure, 1974). A brief description is in the Appendix.

Results

Descriptive Analysis of Parental Behaviors

In this section, attention will be directed initially to a description of the parent behaviors employed in each of the two teaching situations (storytelling and paper folding). The first results to be reported were obtained from descriptive and exploratory correlational analyses of parental behavior during the two observation tasks. Following presentation of these results, the relationship between parental behaviors and children's representational competence will be discussed.

Comparison of Parental Behaviors across Demographic Groups and Tasks

Factors that may influence parental behaviors during interactions with a child include family constellation, socioeconomic status (SES), sex of the parent, sex of the child, and the task to be accomplished during the course of the interaction. There is evidence that parental behaviors are in fact influenced by all the above factors, including the context in which the behavior occurs, that is, the task the parent and child are involved in (Grusec & Kuczynski, 1980; Bell, Johnson, McGillicuddy-DeLisi, & Sigel, 1981). In order to investigate the influence of these factors with the current sample of parents, a series of $3 \times 2 \times 2 \times 2 \times 2$ (family constellation $\times$ SES $\times$ sex of parent $\times$ sex of child $\times$ task) analyses of variance with a repeated measure on the last factor were conducted on parent behavior scores. A variety of significant main and interaction effects were obtained; these are listed in Table 2.

As indicated in Table 2, main effects for family constellation were, contrary to predictions, significant for only two distancing variables. Parents of an only child used low-level mental operational demands more

Table 2. Observation Data Repeated Measures ANOVAs[a]

Dependent variable	F	p Value
No mental operational demands		
SES	5.74	.02
Configuration × sex of parent	3.16	.04
Low-level statements		
Sex of child	4.05	.05
Sex of child × sex of parent	12.72	.01
Sex of child × SES × sex of parent	9.01	.01
SES × configuration × sex of parent	3.52	.03
Task	181.35	.01
Task × sex of child × sex of parent	3.92	.05
Low-level questions		
Sex of child × sex of parent	4.36	.04
SES × configuration × sex of parent	5.31	.01
Task	16.24	.01
Intermediate-level statements		
Task × sex of parent	5.92	.02
Intermediate-level questions		
SES × configuration	3.56	.03
Task × SES × configuration	3.20	.04
High-level statements		
Configuration × sex of parent	4.90	.01
Task	28.07	.01
Task × SES	4.87	.03
High-level questions		
Configuration	3.78	.02
Sex of child × sex of parent	6.32	.01
Sex of child × configuration × sex of parent	3.33	.04
Task	6.12	.01
Number of statements		
SES	4.10	.04
Task	432.54	.01
Task × sex of child × sex of parent	6.69	.01
Task × SES × sex of parent	4.30	.04
Task × sex of child × SES × configuration	4.91	.01
Number of questions		
Sex of parent	3.86	.05
Task	26.19	.01
Number of low-level mental operational demands		
Sex of child	3.89	.05
Configuration	4.46	.01
Sex of child × sex of parent	14.80	.01
Sex of child × SES × sex of parent	4.75	.03
Sex of child × configuration × sex of parent	3.27	.04
Task	107.81	.01
Task × SES	4.80	.03
Number of intermediate-level mental operational demands		
SES × configuration	4.63	.01

Continued

Table 2. (Continued)

Dependent variable	F	p Value
Number of high-level mental operational demands		
Sex of child X sex of parent	4.07	.04
Task	19.12	.01
Task X configuration	3.20	.04

[a]Sex of child X SES X configuration X sex of parent X task.

often and high-level questions less often than parents of three children (both near- and far-spacing). Means of the distancing behavior variables are presented in Tables 3 through 6 by task, sex of parent, family constellation, SES, and sex of child.

Main effects for SES were obtained for frequency of no mental operational demands and number of statements. Middle-class parents evidenced higher frequencies of no mental operational demands than working-class parents. Main effects for sex of parent were obtained for number of questions. Means of fathers were higher than those of mothers for all these variables. Number of low-level statements and number of low-level mental operational demands varied with sex of the child, and frequencies were higher for male children than for female children on each variable.

A main effect for task was obtained for 7 of the 12 analyzed variables (see Table 2). Scores for low-level statements, low-level questions, high-level statements, high-level questions, number of questions, and low-level mental operational demands were higher for the story task than for the paper task.

Although task was clearly the major factor along which parent behaviors varied, many interaction effects involving family constellation, SES, and sex of parents and children were obtained. With regard to the distancing variables, family constellation was involved in an interaction for low-level statements (SES X family constellation X sex of parent), low-level questions (SES X family constellation X sex of parent), intermediate-level questions (task X SES X family constellation), high-level statements (family constellation X sex of parent) and high-level questions (family constellation X sex of parent X sex of child). Middle-class mothers with near spacing and middle-class fathers with far spacing used fewer low-level statements than other parents. Working-class fathers of an only child evidenced more low-level questions than working-class fathers with far spacing and middle-class mothers with far spacing. Working-class parents of an only child used fewer intermediate-level questions than other parents and fathers of an only child used fewer high-level statements than other parents. Mothers of an only child who was female used fewer high-level

Table 3. Mean Number of Maternal Responses on Selected Variables[a]

	One-child family						Three-child family with near spacing						Three-child family with far spacing					
	Working class (WC)			Middle class (MC)			Working class (WC)			Middle class (MC)			Working class (WC)			Middle class (MC)		
Variable	Girl	Boy	WC	Girl	Boy	MC	Girl	Boy	WC	Girl	Boy	MC	Girl	Boy	WC	Girl	Boy	MC
Low-level statements	2.50	2.00	2.25	2.00	1.60	1.85	2.30	1.50	1.90	1.70	1.50	1.60	2.20	1.60	1.90	1.60	2.50	2.05
Low-level questions	5.10	3.60	4.35	3.60	3.60	3.90	3.40	3.50	3.45	3.90	4.20	4.05	4.20	5.00	4.60	2.60	2.60	2.60
Intermediate-level statements	.60	.80	.70	.80	.50	.55	.80	.50	.65	.80	.30	.55	.50	.10	.30	.40	.60	.50
Intermediate-level questions	1.20	1.40	1.30	1.40	1.30	1.40	1.20	1.90	1.55	1.80	.80	1.30	1.10	.90	1.00	1.60	2.00	1.80
High-level statements	1.10	1.40	1.25	1.40	1.00	1.05	1.40	.70	1.05	1.70	1.30	1.50	.50	.40	.45	.90	.80	.85
High-level questions	2.90	3.20	3.05	3.20	3.90	3.60	3.40	4.50	3.95	2.90	5.10	4.00	4.00	4.30	4.15	4.00	4.50	4.25
Number of statements	5.20	4.60	4.90	4.60	4.20	4.45	5.30	3.06	4.45	5.20	4.20	4.70	4.80	3.40	4.10	4.20	5.00	4.43
Number of questions	9.20	6.20	8.70	8.20	8.80	8.90	8.00	9.90	8.95	8.60	10.10	9.35	9.30	10.20	9.75	8.20	9.10	9.45
Number of low-level mental operational demands	7.60	5.60	6.60	6.30	5.20	5.75	5.70	5.00	5.35	5.60	5.70	5.65	6.40	6.60	6.50	4.20	5.10	5.00

Continued

Table 3. (Continued)

Variable	One-child family						Three-child family with near spacing						Three-child family with far spacing					
	Working class (WC)			Middle class (MC)			Working class (WC)			Middle class (MC)			Working class (WC)			Middle class (MC)		
	Girl	Boy	WC	Girl	Boy	MC	Girl	Boy	WC	Girl	Boy	MC	Girl	Boy	WC	Girl	Boy	MC
Number of intermediate level mental operational demands	1.80	2.20	2.00	2.10	1.80	1.95	2.00	2.40	2.20	2.60	1.10	1.85	1.60	1.00	1.30	2.00	2.60	2.15
Number of high-level mental operational demands	4.00	4.60	4.30	4.40	4.90	4.65	4.80	5.20	5.00	4.60	6.40	5.50	4.50	4.70	4.60	4.90	5.30	5.78

[a]From observations of the Child Storytelling Task by family configuration, SES, and sex of child.

Table 4. Mean Number of Paternal Responses on Selected Variables[a]

Variable	One-child family						Three-child family with near spacing						Three-child family with far spacing					
	Working class (WC)			Middle class (MC)			Working class (WC)			Middle class (MC)			Working class (WC)			Middle class (MC)		
	Girl	Boy	WC	Girl	Boy	MC	Girl	Boy	WC	Girl	Boy	MC	Girl	Boy	WC	Girl	Boy	MC
Low-level statements	1.40	3.30	2.35	2.30	2.60	2.45	1.50	3.40	2.45	1.50	2.20	1.85	2.20	3.10	2.65	1.40	1.50	1.45
Low-level questions	4.80	6.30	5.55	4.20	4.60	4.40	3.50	5.00	4.25	3.80	3.90	3.85	3.60	2.90	3.25	3.80	4.00	3.90
Intermediate-level statements	.50	1.00	.75	1.10	1.20	1.15	.60	.80	.70	.60	.40	.50	.80	.80	.80	.60	.40	.50
Intermediate-level questions	.90	.90	.90	2.10	1.20	1.65	.80	1.30	1.05	1.10	1.40	1.25	1.60	.70	1.15	1.50	1.50	1.50
High-level statements	.90	.90	.90	.50	.90	.70	.70	.60	.65	1.20	1.40	1.30	1.40	.70	1.05	1.60	1.60	1.60
High-level questions	4.50	2.70	3.60	3.00	2.50	2.75	5.30	4.00	4.65	4.70	3.90	4.30	3.70	4.20	3.90	4.90	4.80	4.85
Number of statements	3.80	6.00	4.90	4.40	5.50	4.95	3.60	5.30	4.45	4.10	4.90	4.50	5.80	5.50	5.65	4.50	4.00	4.25
Number of questions	10.20	9.90	10.05	9.30	8.30	8.80	9.60	10.30	9.95	9.60	9.20	9.40	8.90	7.80	8.35	10.20	10.30	10.25
Number of low-level mental operational demands	6.20	9.60	7.90	6.50	7.20	6.85	5.00	8.40	6.70	5.30	6.10	5.70	5.80	6.00	5.90	5.20	5.50	5.35
Number of intermediate-level mental operational demands	1.40	1.90	1.65	3.20	2.40	2.80	1.40	2.10	1.75	1.70	1.80	1.75	2.40	1.50	1.95	2.10	1.90	2.00
Number of high-level mental operational demands	5.40	3.60	4.50	3.50	3.40	3.45	6.00	4.60	5.30	5.90	5.30	5.60	5.10	4.90	5.00	6.50	6.40	6.45

[a]From observations of the Child Storytelling Task by family configuration, SES, and sex of child.

Table 5. Mean Number of Paternal Responses on Selected Variables[a]

Variable	One-child family						Three-child family with near spacing						Three-child family with far spacing					
	Working class (WC)			Middle class (MC)			Working class (WC)			Middle class (MC)			Working class (WC)			Middle class (MC)		
	Girl	Boy	WC	Girl	Boy	MC	Girl	Boy	WC	Girl	Boy	MC	Girl	Boy	WC	Girl	Boy	MC
Low-level statements	.60	1.00	.80	.30	1.40	.85	.30	.40	.35	.70	.90	.80	.40	.60	.50	.40	.30	.35
Low-level questions	3.00	4.10	3.55	2.80	2.50	2.65	2.30	4.90	3.60	3.10	3.50	3.30	2.90	2.50	2.70	3.10	4.00	3.55
Intermediate-level statements	.10	.60	.35	.90	.50	.70	.70	.40	.55	.40	.80	.60	.40	.60	.50	.50	.70	.60
Intermediate-level questions	1.10	.80	.95	1.90	1.20	1.55	2.00	2.40	2.20	1.30	.70	1.00	1.70	1.60	1.65	1.30	.90	1.10
High-level statements	.90	.30	.60	.50	.50	.50	.20	.50	.35	.20	.50	.35	.70	.50	.60	.60	.80	.70
High-level questions	3.80	3.10	3.45	3.30	4.00	3.65	3.00	3.10	3.05	4.90	3.20	4.05	3.40	4.50	3.95	3.60	4.40	4.00
Number of statements	9.50	9.10	9.30	10.00	9.70	9.85	10.20	7.60	8.90	8.20	9.10	8.65	9.40	10.00	9.70	10.00	8.10	9.05
Number of questions	7.90	8.00	7.95	8.00	7.70	7.85	7.30	10.40	8.85	9.30	7.40	8.35	8.00	8.60	8.30	8.00	9.30	8.65
Number of low-level mental operational demands	3.60	5.10	4.35	3.10	3.90	3.50	2.60	5.30	3.95	3.80	4.40	4.10	3.30	3.10	3.20	3.50	4.30	3.90
Number of intermediate-level mental operational demands	1.20	1.40	1.30	2.80	1.70	2.25	2.70	2.80	2.75	1.70	1.50	1.60	2.10	2.20	2.15	1.80	1.60	1.70
Number of high-level mental operational demands	4.70	3.40	4.05	3.80	4.50	4.15	3.20	3.60	3.40	5.10	3.70	4.40	4.10	5.00	4.55	4.20	5.20	4.70

[a]From observation of the Child Paper-Folding Task by family configuration, SES, and sex of child.

Table 6. Mean Number of Maternal Responses on Selected Variables[a]

Variable	One-child family						Three-child family with near spacing						Three-child family with far spacing					
	Working class (WC)			Middle class (MC)			Working class (WC)			Middle class (MC)			Working class (WC)			Middle class (MC)		
	Girl	Boy	WC	Girl	Boy	MC	Girl	Boy	WC	Girl	Boy	MC	Girl	Boy	WC	Girl	Boy	MC
Low-level statements	.80	.50	.65	.40	.80	.60	1.30	.30	.80	.20	.50	.35	.40	.10	.25	.40	.90	.65
Low-level questions	2.70	3.70	3.20	3.90	3.50	3.70	3.10	2.80	2.95	3.80	2.60	3.20	3.70	2.80	3.25	3.20	3.30	3.25
Intermediate-level statements	.60	.70	.65	.40	1.60	1.00	.80	.60	.70	.80	.60	.70	.80	.40	.60	.60	.60	.60
Intermediate-level questions	.50	1.00	.75	1.70	1.60	1.65	1.10	1.40	1.25	1.90	.80	1.35	1.30	1.60	1.45	.80	1.30	1.05
High-level statements	.80	.80	.80	.80	.70	.75	.80	.70	.75	.50	.20	.35	.70	.60	.65	.40	.60	.50
High-level questions	2.20	3.60	2.90	2.70	4.10	3.40	2.80	3.90	3.35	3.20	3.20	3.20	2.30	2.80	2.55	4.30	3.60	3.95
Number of statements	11.90	9.20	10.55	7.60	8.90	8.25	10.50	10.30	10.40	8.00	10.80	9.40	9.80	10.40	10.10	9.40	8.60	9.00
Number of questions	5.40	8.30	6.85	8.30	9.20	8.75	7.00	8.10	7.55	8.90	6.60	7.75	7.30	7.20	7.25	8.30	8.20	8.25
Number of low-level mental operational demands	3.50	4.20	3.85	4.30	4.30	4.30	4.40	3.10	3.75	4.00	3.10	3.55	4.10	2.90	3.50	3.60	4.20	3.90
Number of intermediate-level mental operational demands	1.10	1.70	1.40	2.10	3.20	2.65	1.90	2.00	1.95	2.70	1.40	2.05	2.10	2.00	2.05	1.40	1.90	1.65
Number of high-level mental operational demands	3.00	4.40	3.70	3.50	4.80	4.15	3.60	4.60	4.10	3.70	3.40	3.55	3.00	3.40	3.20	4.70	4.20	4.45

[a]From observation of the Child Paper-Folding Task by family configuration, SES, and sex of child.

questions than other parents. Thus, variation in parental teaching strategies with family constellation factors appears to occur when other factors such as SES and sex of parent are included.

What, in effect, these results demonstrate is that the frequency of distancing strategies, and probably many other classes of behavior, is influenced by ecological and personal–social variables. This will be addressed in some detail in the discussion section.

Nevertheless, it would behoove the reader to examine the tables carefully, thereby noting the differences in mean frequencies. Identifying the frequency of distancing behaviors and the conditions under which they appear is but the initial step in trying to identify the significance of such behaviors for the child's intellectual growth. We turn now to an examination of parental consistency between the paper-folding and storytelling tasks.

Consistency of Parental Behaviors between Paper-Folding and Storytelling Tasks

The task in which the parent and child were engaged appeared to be the most salient dimension along which parental behaviors varied. Correlations between behavior scores on the two tasks were computed to assess whether parents evidenced any consistent pattern across the two tasks. Although the magnitude of relationships was generally low (ranging from .15 to .40; $r \geqslant .15 = p \leqslant .05$), the pattern of relationships obtained for fathers and for mothers was somewhat different. Behavior variables that were correlated across the two tasks for mothers and fathers are presented in Table 7.

Approximately equal numbers of behavior variables correlated across tasks for fathers and for mothers. However, the types of behaviors that were correlated across the two tasks were different for fathers and for mothers. Fathers were relatively more consistent than mothers in their use of distancing strategies across tasks (intermediate-level questions, high-level statements, number of questions, intermediate-level mental operational demands). Significant correlations between mothers' behaviors on the two tasks tended to occur for emotional-support-system variables (approvals, negative physical affect, takeover intrusions, structuring). Thus, when parents did evidence consistency in teaching style across tasks, the nature of that consistency appeared to be dependent on the sex of the parent. Consistent maternal styles involved emotional tone in both verbal and nonverbal modes; for fathers consistency lay in the form and content through which information was conveyed to the child (form of utterance and mental demand).

To summarize thus far, parental behaviors appear to be influenced by

Table 7. Behavior Variables Significantly Correlated across Tasks

Fathers' behaviors	r	Mothers' behaviors	r
Length of interactions	.26	Length of interactions	.40
Number of interaction units	.29	Number of interaction units	.38
No mental operational demands	.25	No mental operational demands	.18
Intermediate-level questions	.28	—	
High-level statements	.16	—	
Number of questions	.18	—	
Number of intermediate-level mental operational demands	.30	—	
Feedback	.35	Feedback	.22
Correction	.18	Correction	.15
Attention getting	.17	Attention getting	.28
—		Structuring	.21
—		Approval	.15
—		Negative physical affect	.23
—		Takeover intrusions	.18
Not time for child response	.19	No time for child response	.17

Child Behaviors			
With father		With mother	
Actively engaged in interaction	.21	Actively engaged in interaction	.19
Passively engaged in interaction	.20	Passively engaged in interaction	.22
Passively not engaged in interaction	.15	—	

a variety of factors. The task in which the parent and the child are engaged is an important determinant of the types of behaviors parents are likely to exhibit. This may, in fact, be a positive attribute of parental teaching styles, and consistency in parental practice may not be as advantageous to child outcomes as flexibility and the ability to adopt alternative strategies. That is, parents may modify their strategy in accordance with the particular demands of the tasks and may do so appropriately. Perhaps inquiry is a good way to stimulate a child to think about a story, but demonstration is the best way to get a child to make a paper boat. In the following section, the relationships between parental behaviors during each of the teaching situations and children's performance on representational thinking tasks will be reported.

Relationships between Mothers' and Fathers' Teaching Strategies with Story Task and Child Outcomes

Results reported in prior sections indicate that both parental teaching behaviors and children's representational ability scores varied with demographic characteristics such as SES and family constellation. These findings are consistent with those of previous studies reporting that middle-class mothers evidence higher levels of questioning in problem-solving tasks with their children (cf. Bee, Van Egeren, Streissguth, Nyman, & Leckie, 1969) and that middle-class children evidence higher levels of representational competence than children from lower SES backgrounds (cf. Sigel & Olmsted, 1971). In addition, parental behaviors appear to vary with task and sex of parent. To determine the degree to which relationships between distancing and child outcomes may be due to demographic characteristics such as family constellation and SES, a set of regression analyses was undertaken. Regressions were conducted separately for behaviors of mothers and fathers and for the paper and the story task. These regression analyses were similar to those used to establish relationships between parental beliefs and parental behaviors (see McGillicuddy-DeLisi, Chapter 9). In this way, the relationship between parental distancing strategies and children's representational competence could be determined while also controlling for the confounding effects of SES and family constellation.

In Table 8 we can see the regression coefficients for mothers' teaching strategies on each of the two tasks. It will be noted that significant relationships occur for the control variables (i.e., social class and family configuration) that were used as covariates in subsequent analyses. Building on these variables, the subsequent variables were stepped into the analysis of parent behavior, yielding significant relationships between an array of teaching strategies and child outcomes.

Teaching strategies employed in the story condition predict children's performance on tasks involving conservation predictions and anticipatory imagery. In the former case, the less the mothers intrude and the less the children are passively engaged the better children predict what would happen in the task. Children's performance on a task involving anticipatory imagery was related positively to the mother's use of high-level questions when the child was not passively involved ($R = .37, p < .05$).

High-level mental demands on the story task were found to relate to two dependent variables on the object categorization task: the creation of logical groupings ($R = .33, p < .05$) and rational descriptions ($R = .35, p < .05$).

In sum, mothers' use of "distancing strategies" did relate to the children's performance on tasks requiring logical reasoning, anticipatory imagery, and transformation.

Turning to the fathers' behavior on the story task, with the same class of variables as described with mothers, we find that more of the fathers' teaching strategies related significantly to the children's performance on the memory task. Further, little that the fathers did seemed to contribute to the children's performance on the classification task.

Table 8. Multiple Correlation Coefficients for Mothers' Storytelling and
Paper-Folding Behaviors and Selected Child Assessment Variables

Mothers' behaviors on storytelling task		Mothers' behaviors on paper-folding task	
		Time to reconstruct array (SRI)	
		Social class	.20[a]
		Family configuration	.34[a]
		Interaction terms	.36
—		Takeover intrusions	.49
		Number of interaction units	.54
		High-level questions	$(-)$[b].58
		Low-level statements	$(-)$.60
		Recognition (SRI)	
		Social class	.13
		Family configuration	.20
		Interaction terms	.30[a]
Helping intrusions	.37	Diverting	.35
Number of high-level mental operational demands	.41		
		Correct sequence pairs reconstructed (SRI)	
		Social class	.15
		Family configuration	.21
		Interaction terms	.24
—		Attention getting	$(-)$.37
		Child passively engaged in other activity	.43
		Correct items reconstructed (SRI)	
		Social class	.01
		Family configuration	.13
		Interaction terms	.13
—		Attention getting	$(-)$.27
		Takeover intrusions	$(-)$.32
		Prediction of transformation (conservation)	
		Social class	.11
		Family configuration	.21
		Interaction terms	.31[a]
Takeover Intrusions	$(-)$.39	No time for child response	.39
Child passively engaged with parent	$(-)$.43	Number of statements	.45
		Verbal disapprovals	.49
Reading	.47	Intermediate-level statements	.53
		Anticipation of rotation (KAI)	
		Social class	.08
		Family configuration	.10
		Interaction terms	.22

Continued

Table 8. (Continued)

Mothers' behaviors on storytelling task		Mothers' behaviors on paper-folding task	
Child passively engaged in other activity	$(-).31$	—	
High-level questions	.37		
Child actively engaged with parent	$(-).44$		
Out of contact	$(-).48$		
Verbal approvals	$(-).51$		

Logical classification groupings
Social class	$.18^{a}$		
Family configuration	.22		
Interaction terms	.22		

| Number of high-level mental operational demands | .33 | — | |

Groupings based on descriptive characteristics
Social class	.19	
Family configuration	.27	
Interaction terms	.30	

| Number of high-level mental operational demands | .35 | No time for child response | .35 |

Groupings based on logical classes
Social class	.01	
Family configuration	.11	
Interaction terms	.17	

Low-level statements	.25	Diverting	.40
Number of questions	.32		
Time of interaction	$(-).37$		

Note. All R's for relationship between parent behaviors and child outcomes are significant at $p < .05$.
[a]Indicates p of .05 or less for demographic variables.
[b](−) Indicates direction of zero-order correlation.

In general, the father's behavior as expressed in the storytelling task seems to be of less moment than the mother's in influencing the child's mnemonic, anticipatory, and classificatory performance.

How will these results hold up when we examine the relationships between mothers' and fathers' strategies on the paper-folding task? Theoretically, we would expect that the relationships between distancing strategies employed on this task will be similar to those obtained with the story task.

We shall follow the same format—presenting results for mothers alone and fathers alone.

Relationships between Fathers' and Mothers' Teaching Strategies and Children's Performance on the Paper-Folding Task

It will be recalled that the parent–child interactions observed with the paper-folding task were different from those found on the story task (see Table 2). Inspection of Table 8 indicates that for the paper task no significant relationships were obtained between the mothers' distancing strategies and the children's performance on memory tasks, anticipatory imagery, and classification. However, strong associations were found between the mothers' behavior and the children's understanding of transformations in a conservation task. The particular mother behaviors are use of statements to the child indicating disapproval and accompanying statements pointing out various relationships among elements in the task ($R = .53$, $p < .05$). This is the only set of mother behaviors in the paper-folding task that related to the child's response on the conservation task (see Table 8).

The results for the fathers are quite different. Fathers' behaviors are related to the children's performance on memory tasks and prediction of transformation. Specifically, the fathers' use of high-level mental demands relates to sequential memory ($R = .39$, $p < .05$), and reconstructive memory $R = .35$, $p < .05$). However, when the fathers make strong demands on the children to respond through the use of high-level questions, negative results are obtained ($R = .47$, $p < .05$). Solutions to the problems involving prediction of transformations relate positively to the positive supports in conjunction with structuring the task (see Table 9).

No significant relationships are obtained between "distancing strategies" and other physical cognitive tasks.

Relationships between Parental Behaviors and Child Outcomes for the Story and Paper-Folding Tasks

When fathers' and mothers' teaching behavior scores were worked into the regression equation to ascertain the relative contribution of each to child outcomes, the following results emerged with the story task: when the mothers' and fathers' scores are stepped into the regression analysis for the anticipatory imagery task, the level of involvement of fathers and mothers

Table 9. Multiple Correlation Coefficients for Fathers' Storytelling and Paper-Folding Behaviors and Selected Child Assessment Variables

Fathers' behaviors on storytelling task		Fathers' behaviors on paper-folding task	

Time to reconstruct array (SRI)
- Social class $.20^{a}$
- Family configuration $.34^{a}$
- Interaction terms   .36

Attention getting	$(-)^{b}.40$	Takeover intrusions	.54
		Helping intrusions	(-).58
		High-level statements	(-).61
		Time of interaction	.64

Recognition (SRI)
- Social class   .13
- Family configuration   .20
- Interaction terms $.30^{a}$

Diverting	(-).35	Child actively engaged in other activity	.36
		Intermediate-level statements	(-).40
		Verbal disapprovals	(-).45

Correct sequence pairs reconstructed (SRI)
- Social class   .15
- Family configuration   .21
- Interaction terms   .24

| Out of contact | .35 | Number of high-level mental operational demands | .39 |

Correct items reconstructed (SRI)
- Social class   .01
- Family configuration   .13
- Interaction terms   .13

Number of interaction units	(-).28	Number of high-level mental operational demands	.35
		No time for child response	.40
		Out of contact	(-).44

Prediction of transformation (Conservation)
- Social class   .11
- Family configuration   .21
- Interaction terms   .31

No mental operational demands	.38	Child passively engaged with parent	(-).36
Child management	.43	Positive nonverbal supports	.40
Diverting	(-).46	Structuring task	.44

Table 9. (Continued)

Fathers' behaviors on storytelling task		Fathers' behaviors on paper-folding task	
	Anticipation of rotation (KAI)		
	Social class	.08	
	Family configuration	.10	
	Interaction terms	.22	
Child passively engaged in other activity	Takeover intrusions		(-).29
(-).36	Attention getting		.34
	Logical classification groupings		
	Social class	.18^a	
	Family configuration	.22	
	Interaction terms	.22	
—			—
	Groupings based on descriptive characteristics		
	Social class	.19^a	
	Family configuration	.27	
	Interaction terms	.30	
Intermediate-level statements	(-).36		
Reading	.40		
Verbal approvals	.43		
	Groupings based on logical classes		
	Social class	.01	
	Family configuration	.11	
	Interaction terms	.17	
—	No mental operational demands		.28

Note. All R's for relationship between parent behaviors and child outcomes are significant at $p < .05$.
^{a}Indicates p of .05 or less for demographic variables.
^{b}(-) Indicates direction of zero-order correlation.

sets the stage for the import of high-level questions ($R = .49, p < .05$). To illustrate the value of this type of analysis, let me digress to point out that when we analyzed the relationships for mothers alone, a significant but much lower R was obtained (.35, $p < .05$). Stepping in the fathers' behaviors indicates that their behaviors do aid and abet the mothers' actions (see Table 10).

Turning now to the relationship between parents' behaviors and the children's performance on the classification task, our results are mixed. The mothers continued to be more influential than the fathers, since their

Table 10. Multiple Correlation Coefficients for Parental Storytelling and Paper-Folding Behaviors and Selected Child Assessment Variables

Parental behaviors on storytelling task		Parental behaviors on paper-folding task	
Time to reconstruct array (SRI)			
Social class		$.20^a$	
Family configuration		$.34^a$	
Interaction terms		.36	
Attention getting (fathers)	$(-)^b.40$	Takeover intrusions (fathers)	.54
Interaction units (mothers)	.44	Takeover intrusions (mothers)	.59
No mental operational demands (mothers)	.47	Number of interaction units (mothers)	.65
		Helping intrusions (fathers)	$(-).69$
		Low-level statements (mothers)	$(-).69$
		High-level questions (mothers)	$(-).71$
		Child management (fathers)	.71
		High-level statements (fathers)	$(-).72$
Recognition (SRI)			
Social class		.13	
Family configuration		.20	
Interaction terms		$.30^a$	
Helping intrusions (mothers)	.37	Intermediate-level statements (fathers)	$(-).40$
Number of high-level mental operational demands (mothers)	.41	Diverting (mothers)	.46
		Verbal disapprovals (fathers)	$(-).47$
Correct sequence pairs reconstructed (SRI)			
Social class		.15	
Family configuration		.21	
Interaction terms		.24	
Out of contact (fathers)	.35	Number of high-level mental operational demands (fathers)	.39
		Attention getting (mothers)	$(-).46$
		Child passively engaged with parent (mothers)	.50
Correct items reconstructed (SRI)			
Social class		.01	
Family configuration		.13	
Interaction terms		.13	

Table 10. (Continued)

Parental behaviors on storytelling task		Parental behaviors on paper-folding task	
Number of interaction units (fathers)	(-).28	Number of high-level mental operational demands (fathers)	.35
		Attention getting (mothers)	(-).40
		No time for child response (fathers)	.45
		Takeover intrusions (mothers)	(-).49

Prediction of transformation (conservation)
Social class .11
Family configuration .21
Interaction terms .31[a]

Takeover intrusions (mothers)	.39	No time for child response (mothers)	.39
Child management (fathers)	.44	Number of statements (mothers)	.45
No mental operational demands (fathers)	.48	Positive nonverbal supports (fathers)	.50
Number of statements (mothers)	(-).52	Child passively engaged with parent (fathers)	(-).54
No mental operational demands (mothers)	(-).55	Low-level questions (mothers)	.56
		Out of contact (mothers)	(-).59
		Number of interaction units (fathers)	.62
		Number of questions (fathers)	(-).64

Anticipation of rotation (KAI)
Social class .08
Family configuration .10
Interaction terms .22

Child passively engaged in other activity (fathers)	(-).36	Takeover intrusions (fathers)	(-).29
Child passively engaged in other activity (mothers)	(-).41	Attention getting (fathers)	.34
Child actively engaged with parent (mothers)	(-).45		
High-level questions (mothers)	.49		
Out of contact (mothers)	(-).52		

Logical classification groupings
Social class .18[a]
Family configuration .22
Interaction terms .22

Continued

Table 10. (Continued)

Parental behaviors on storytelling task		Parental behaviors on paper-folding task	
Number of high-level mental operational demands (mothers)	.33	—	
Groupings based on descriptive characteristics			
Social class	.19[a]		
Family configuration	.27		
Interaction terms	.30		
Intermediate-level statements (fathers)	(–).36	Reading (fathers)	.39
Number of high-level mental operational demands (mothers)	.42	No time for child response (mothers)	.43
Groupings based on logical classes			
Social class	.01		
Family configuration	.11		
Interaction terms	.17		
—		Diverting (mothers)	.40
		No mental operational demands (fathers)	.44
		Child actively engaged in other activity (fathers)	(–).47

Note. All R's for relationship between parent behaviors and child outcomes are significant at $p < .05$.
[a]Indicates p of .05 or less for demographic variables.
[b](–) Indicates direction of zero-order correlation.

use of high-level mental demands does relate positively to the child's creation of logical groupings ($R = .33$, $p < .05$). However, the quality of the grouping seems to be associated with the degree to which the father uses lower-level statements, which enhances the significance of the mothers' behavior (mother alone was $R = .33$, $p < .05$, with the mothers and fathers $R = .42$, $p < .05$).

None of the strategies parents used in the story task related to the child's creation of logical classifications (see Table 10).

Distancing strategies as expressed in statements and questions on the story task are associated with children's memory, anticipatory imagery, and classification behavior.

Turning now to a review of major findings for the paper-folding task, we note that—as with the storytelling tasks—the results obtained from scores of both mothers and fathers yield different patterns than those for each set of parents separately (see Table 10).

Recognition memory performance is associated with low use of intermediate statements from the fathers, diverting the child's attention from a non-task related activity to the task at hand. This constellation of relationships yields an R of .47, $p < .05$.

Reconstructive sequential memory performance is associated with high-level mental operational demands from fathers ($R = .39$, $p < .05$), low attention getting from mothers, and the child quietly engaged with the mother. These combinations of dimensions result in a multiple R of .50, $p < .05$.

Building in this stepped up fashion, we find that reconstructive memory is associated with the fathers' use of high-level mental operational demands ($R = .35$, $p < .05$). Low attention-getting techniques of the mother enhance the correlation to .40; if the father demands that the child respond and the mother does not intrude, this constellation yields a multiple R of .49, $p < .05$.

Children's level of predicting of transformation is another case where fathers' and mothers' performance yields higher levels of associations than either one alone. The mother's use of low-level questions emerges as a significant factor built upon positive support by the father and mother's actively speaking to the child.

The final task we shall discuss is the object-sorting classification. This is another instance where each parent contributes, the mother in getting the child on target and the father in placing no pressure on the child to distance yields an R of .44, $p < .05$. This suggests that the children have to be encouraged to engage in the task and the fathers have to keep a low profile. It is as though the children, not requiring parental support, do their own exploration and organization.

Discussion and Conclusions

Distancing behaviors are hypothesized to serve as activators of representational thinking, since they impose a cognitive demand on the receiver which requires the individual to re-present and transform experience into some form of symbol system. Irrespective of the source of the distancing strategy—whether it be a teacher, a parent, or a peer—the psychological function of distancing behaviors is similar. For example, inquiry is one type of distancing strategy. It matters little whether the inquiry is from teacher, parent, or peer, since the psychological demands of such a response is similar—namely, the respondent has to discern the message and engage in the appropriate representational mental operations in order to formulate a response. Thus, the contention is that distancing strategies by their very nature function as activators of representational thinking. This assertion, however, is too global, since our results indicate that distancing strategies vary in level and type of cognitive demand as a function of various demographic and contextual factors (see Table 2). Therefore, while the assertion that distancing strategies *in toto* serve as cognitive activators appears reasonable, little is learned about the significance of distancing strategies from such global analyses. It is necessary to specify and differentiate among the strategies to identify the particular role of the various types in their psychosocial context. For example, inquiry in general may, to be sure, have positive outcomes for children's cognitive growth. With preschoolers, however, we learned that parental use of low-level questions related differently to children's representational thinking than high-level questions. The multiple regression analyses demonstrate relationships among demographic, contextual, and distancing factors relative to children's representational thinking.

The fact that the results of this study point to a set of complex relationships should not be surprising, since distancing strategies by their very nature occur in a social context, with focus on some activity. There is reason to expect that events embedded in a social context would be influenced, among other things, by the context itself. For example, opportunities to initiate and follow up a set of inquiries will depend on the understanding of the task by the adult, his or her ability to communicate to the child, and both participants' freedom from distraction.

The findings of these analyses do demonstrate that distancing strategies relate significantly to child outcome measures and thus support the basic hypothesis. The further finding that obtained relationships are contingent on other interpersonal and contextual characteristics does not vitiate the significance of the obtained results. Rather, these relationships provide a taste of social reality in which most interactions occur. Research in this area tends often to employ an experimental paradigm, ignoring many sources of experimental error. The findings obtained in experimental contexts, while having a validity in their own right, still have to identify the constraints of such findings for explanatory purposes. It is necessary to study experimentally isolated and manipulated variables in a naturalistic environment as the final test. This study moves in the direction of increasingly approximating a natural setting and including a broad spectrum of relevant variables.

Although distancing strategies in general play a significant role, the results of this study demonstrate which factors set the stage for identifying conditions that facilitate or enhance their impact.

The regression analysis reported here moves us toward studying effects of each parent not as they are isolated one from the other but as a conjoint influence. Psychological research tends to examine parent–child relationships in terms of single dyads, mother–child or father–child, rather than as a triad. Valuable as this may be, such studies negate the reality that children are subject to the influence of each parent. How the child integrates experiences with each parent is a research question in its own right, and that is still to be explored. This study at least demonstrates how various kinds of interactional parental behaviors support each other. In other words, various constellations of behaviors from mothers and fathers relate to particular children's cognitive performance. For example, as noted, mothers' use of low level questions emerges as a significant factor relating to children's predicting of performance when built upon positive support by the father.

The message from these results is twofold. Distancing strategies serve a significant function of children's problem-solving competence; their importance, however, resides not only in the significance of a particular strategy but also in their association with other parent behaviors.

Do these findings negate those reported in other studies, where only one parent was the focus of study? Not at all. The significant role of mothers, for example, as important socialization agents in their children's development is not challenged, since significant outcomes were found for mothers' and for fathers' teaching strategies. However, a new set of results emerges with appropriate analyses of mothers' and fathers' behaviors not as summed aggregates, as is often done, but rather as discrete variables, each potentially influencing others.

Finally, the study also demonstrates sharply that parental teaching strategies are task-dependent. Correlations of mothers' and fathers' distancing strategies on the paper and story tasks yields few significant and low correlations. For all intents and purposes, the parents' strategies are particular to the tasks. This raises an important issue: significant as the distancing construct may be, there is reason to hold that its potency is influenced by a number of ecological factors in addition to the social ones described previously. Of particular interest is the fact that each task elicits only some of the possible teaching strategies and that parents are not consistent across tasks. Thus, generalizations about parent distancing strategies have to be tempered, constrained by the activity involved (as well as the other social factors). Yet distancing behaviors when identified and irrespective of task seem to be of some import. Thus, we can conclude that the basic hypothesis that distancing strategies do in fact relate to children's cognitive functioning was verified. The frequency and types of distancing strategies that occur, however, will vary as a function of social and ecological factors.

In conclusion, we have certainly not included all the social or psychological factors that influence the child's intellectual development, but I feel our attempts at including parent × family configuration × spacing as demographic factors of influence moves us in the direction the model builders describe. To return to the geographical metaphor, the terrain is being mapped more accurately than has been the case. What we have also discovered in our mapping efforts is that there is a considerable gap between the models of family functioning and the methods by which to study the models. I believe our conceptualizations, by *our* I mean "collective," are quite sophisticated, as in the work of Hill (1973), Lewis and Lee-Painter (1974), Becker (1964), and Lerner and Spanier (1978). Nevertheless, few of these investigators have created a methodological and, to date, an analytical procedure to encompass the model. After our years of work, I am less likely to be critical of the model builders for not using the model as a template to impress upon their experimental design and data collection. To date, all of us are engaged in procedural efforts, but the pieces are getting larger. Yet, when it is clear that four or five factors interact, then we are faced with interpretation problems in spite of the fact that more variables are functioning in various temporal relationships. In short, I feel our methods are increasingly in step with conceptualization. Who knows, we may yet come to generate steps toward further understanding of family dynamics.

Appendix

Data Gathering Procedures

Parent Teaching Tasks—Storytelling and Paper Folding

Materials. The materials for the storytelling tasks used in this study were edited versions of popular children's books. Each book had a comparable theme, which involved all the possible ways some object could be used. The stories were edited to eliminate sex bias and to attain approximately equal length between the story the mother would read and the one the father would read. A total of four stories were used, one for each parent to use with preschool children and one for each parent to use with the oldest child in multiple-child families. The stories for the 3- to 4-year-old children and the ones for the older children were selected with their age levels in mind. The stories used with preschool children were edited versions of *Hello Rock* (1965) by Roger Bradfield and *A Rainbow of My Own* (1966) by Don Freeman. The oldest sibling's stories were edited versions of *A Big Ball of String* (1958) by Marion Holland and *Christina Katerina and the Box* (1971) by Patricia Lee Gauch.

The materials for the paper-folding tasks involved a 40 × 30 in. rectangular board. Each step of the folding process was represented on this board by a piece of 8½ × 8½ in. white paper folded in the appropriate

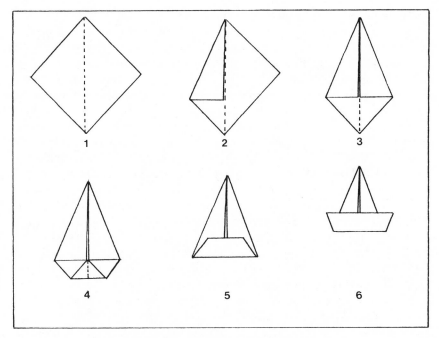

Figure 1. Diagram of paper-folding task display board.

manner. Each step was presented in sequence and each step was numbered. This procedure was adapted from the work of Croft, Stern, Siegelbaum, and Goodman (1976). A stack of 8½ × 8½ in. paper was also provided. Four paper-folding tasks were used, one for each parent to use with each child included in the study. Preschool children constructed a boat with one parent and a plane with the other parent. These two tasks were equated for difficulty and length. That is, each task had the same number of steps and the same number of horizontal and vertical versus diagonal folds. Oldest siblings performed on tasks involving a bird and a whale. These two tasks were also equated for difficulty and length. All paper-folding tasks were adapted versions of those presented in *Origami* (1960) by Harry Helfman. The order of administration of tasks was counterbalanced for story–paper, oldest–preschool child, and mother–father pairs within and between families.

These two tasks were selected on the basis of the extent to which they demand teaching on the part of the parents and the extent to which the task is structured. The paper-folding task has inherent structure in that a number of specific steps are presented to the parent–child dyad. In addition, a specific product—the boat, for example—is specified, which makes a clearer demand on the parent to teach the child something. The storytelling task, on the other hand, has fewer structure and teaching demands inherent in the task. With two such tasks, a comparison of parental strategies across two different types of tasks was possible.

Administration. The parent was seated at a low table facing a one-way mirror. If the storytelling task was administered first, the book was placed on the table. If the paper-folding task was administered first, the stack of paper was placed on the table to the upper left of the parent and the display board of the task placed on an easel in front and a little to the left of the parent. Instructions for the appropriate task were then read to the parent. The instuctions are essentially the same for observations with both preschool and older children, but the child's name and age are included in the instructions. The child is then brought to the room, sits to the right of the parent behind the table, and the door is closed as the experimenter exits. After the first task is completed, the child and the materials for the first task are taken out of the room. The experimenter brings the materials for the second task into the room, reads to the parent the instructions for that task, and then the child returns. Thus, the second task is administered immediately upon completion of the first task.

In addition to the materials needed to complete each task, a toy telephone is placed on the table in the upper-right corner. We decided to include the telephone as a prop to distract the child in order to obtain spontaneous measures of parental management and structuring of the task when a child becomes distracted. A telephone was chosen because it is relatively unloaded with respect to sex bias as a plaything and most preschool children are immediately drawn to it.

Child Assessments

Static Reproductive Imagery (SRI)

Materials. The apparatus consists of a large standing mirror, two sets of blocks that vary in shape and color, an opaque screen, and a 26 × 27 in. board upon which five rows of seven blocks have been mounted. A stopwatch is also used.

Administration. The task consists of three phases: (1) imitation, (2) reproduction and perspective taking, and (3) recognition. The experimenter and the child sit opposite each other at a low table for the duration of the assessment. In Phase 1, the child is given one set of blocks and is requested to build a row of blocks that exactly matches the experimenter's row, which remains in plain view.

For Phase 2, a screen is set up between the child and the experimenter. The child is asked to build a row of blocks exactly like the row that was built during Phase 1. At the same time, the child is required to tell the experimenter how to build a row on the experimenter's side of the screen, so that when they are done both rows will look exactly the same. The screen is removed after the rows are completed; the child is asked to explain any discrepancies between the two rows.

For the final testing phase, all materials are removed from view and the board displaying five rows of seven blocks is presented to the child. The child is asked to point to the row that is just like the one the experimenter first constructed when the child entered the room. The child is then asked how he or she knew which one to choose.

Scoring. For Phase 1 of the task, the time in seconds that it takes the child to copy the experimenter's array of blocks is the only score given.

For Phase 2, the time that elapses as the child constructs his or her row and instructs the experimenter is noted in seconds. The child's explanation of discrepancies between his or her own row of blocks and that of the experimenter is also coded. This code discriminates between children who feel they did not provide adequate descriptions of how they were building the row, those who attribute the errors to the experimenter, and those who attribute the error to some external or irrelevant source. The order in which the child places each block in the row is recorded, as is the final form of the row of blocks. These are, respectively, indications of the child's strategy (beginning at left or right for example) and success.

For the final phase of the assessment, the child's selection from the recognition board is recorded and coded as correct or incorrect. The reason given when asked how he or she knew which row to choose is coded into a type of memory category (e.g., recognitory, "I knew it when I saw it," versus reconstructive, "That's the way I built it first").

Kinetic Anticipatory Imagery (KAI)

Materials. The materials for this task consist of a clear 14-in.-square plexiglass board. A 2-in. blue square is firmly affixed to the center of the board and a 2-in. red square is attached to the lower right corner of the blue square by a pivot screw. Movement of a handle projecting from the red square causes the red square to rotate while the blue square remains stationary. A rectangular choice board with the two squares forming various configurations is also used as stimulus material.

Administration. This task consists of three phases: (1) a training phase used to familiarize the child with the way the board works, (2) four tests of anticipation of rotation of the red square, and (3) a perspective-taking phase. The experimenter and the child sit on opposite sides of a narrow table with the plexiglass board between them for duration of the task.

First the child receives feedback predictions of the results of two rotations. This is the training phase.

During Phase 2, the actual rotations stipulated by the experimenter are performed and the child receives no feedback about performance. The child is asked to point to the pair of squares on the choice board that represents what the squares would look like after four discrete rotations—90, 180, 225, and 360 degrees.

Phase 3 consists of the same rotations but with the experimenter and the child seated on opposite sides of the board. The child is asked whether he or she sees more red or more blue and is asked to predict whether the experimenter sees more red or more blue.

Scoring. The training session is not scored. Each rotation during phase two is coded in two ways: (1) the child's selection on the choice board (used to indicate success or failure for that trial) and (2) the time in seconds taken by the child to make the selection. Each rotation during Phase 3 is coded in two ways: (1) how much red or blue is seen by the child from his or her side of the plexiglass (to make sure the child is referring to the colors correctly) and (2) how much red and blue the child predicts the experimenter sees from the rear of the plexiglass.

Conservation of Continuous Quantity

Materials. The materials include a large flask half filled with colored water, two 500-ml beakers, and a 75-ml cylinder.

Administration. The experimenter pours 50 ml of liquid into one beaker and 100 ml into the second beaker from the flask. The experimenter adjusts the level of the liquid in the second beaker until the child agrees there is the same amount in both containers.

The empty cylinder is then placed in front of the child. The child is first asked to predict the liquid's level if it were to be poured from one of the beakers into the cylinder. He is then asked why the liquid would be at that level in the cylinder. The experimenter then pours the liquid from one of the beakers into the cylinder. The child is asked if his or her prediction was correct and why or why not. Then he or she is asked whether there is the same amount to drink in the cylinder as there is in the beaker with 50 ml of liquid in it and why.

Next, the experimenter tells the child that he is going to pour the liquid from the cylinder back into the empty beaker. The child is asked to predict the level the liquid will reach in the beaker and why. The experimenter pours the liquid back into the beaker. The child is asked whether there is as much to drink in the beaker as there was in the cylinder and why. Then he or she is asked whether the two beakers have the same amount to drink. Then the child is asked whether the two beakers had the same amount to drink when the experimenter adjusted the two liquid levels at the beginning of the testing session. Finally, the child is asked what happened to the liquid during all this time.

Scoring. The child's performance on each transformation of liquid that is performed is coded in three ways: (1) the child's prediction of the liquid level (coded in milliliters) that will be attained after the transformation; (2) the child's performance is summarized as (*a*) nonconservation, (*b*) intermediate, or (*c*) conservation based on answers concerning the amount to drink after the transformation; and (3) the type of argument given for the transformation (compensation, identity, reversibility). This scoring system is based on Piaget's original conceptualization of the task (1952) and

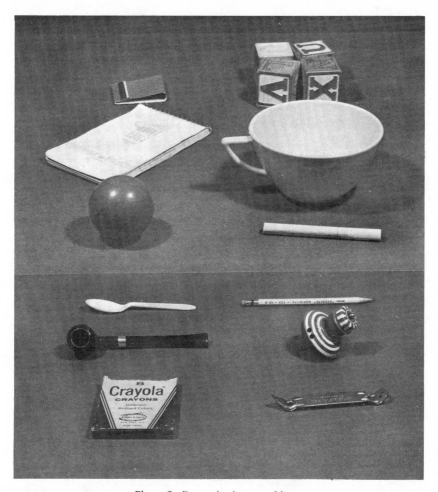

Figure 2. Categorization test objects.

subsequent researchers who have used this task (cf. Peterson, Hooper, Wanska, & DeFrain, 1976).

Object Categorization Task

Materials. The materials include a blue matchbook, four multicolored blocks glued together on a small platform; a white spoon; a yellow pencil; a red, blue, and white metallic top; a brown and black pipe; a yellow cup; a white notebook; a blue ball; a white cigarette; a box of crayons; and a metal bottle opener.

The child and the experimenter sit side by side at a table. The experimenter introduces the objects one at a time in the above order and asks the child what each object is called. The objects are placed into a 4 × 3 in. matrix as the child labels them (see Figure 2). Testing is divided into two phases: (1) the active sort and (2) the passive sort. During phase 1, the experimenter first removes the pencil from the matrix and puts it on the table near the child. The child is asked to get all the other things that are the same or like the one the experimenter has placed aside. After the child groups the items he or she is asked how the objects chosen are the same or alike. The objects are then returned to their place in the matrix. This procedure is repeated for five other trials—the ball, then the bottle opener, the notebook, the blocks, and the spoon.

The passive sort consists of four trials. The experimenter first removes all the objects from view. He then places the pipe, cigarette, and matches in front of the child. The child is then asked how these items are the same or alike. These objects are removed from view. The same procedure is followed for the remaining trials. Trial 2 objects are the cup, bottle opener, and spoon. The notebook, pencil, and crayons are used for Trial 3, and Trial 4 consists of the ball, the blocks, and the top.

Scoring. Each response made by the subject will be scored for two aspects, the verbal level of the response and the type of classification used.

References

Becker, W. C. Consequences of different kinds of parental discipline. In M. L. Hoffman & L. W. Hoffman (Eds.), *Review of child development research* (Vol. 1). New York: Russell Sage Foundation, 1964.

Bee, H. L., Van Egeren, L. F., Streissguth, A. P., Nyman, B. A., & Leckie, M. S. Social class differences in maternal teaching strategies and speech patterns. *Developmental Psychology*, 1969, *1*(6), 726–734.

Bell, C. S., Johnson, J. E., McGillicuddy-DeLisi, A. V., & Sigel, I. E. The effects of family constellation and child gender on parental use of evaluative feedback. *Child Development*, 1981, *53*, 701–704.

Bell, R. Q., & Harper, L. V. *Child effects on adults*. Hillsdale, N.J.: Lawrence Erlbaum, 1977.

Bradfield, R. *Hello rock*. Racine, Wis.: Whitman, 1965.

Cochran, M. M., & Brassard, J. A. Child development and personal social networks. *Child Development*, 1979, *50*, 601-616.

Croft, R., Stern, S., Siegelbaum, H., & Goodman, D. *Manual for description and functional analysis of continuous didactic interactions*. Rochester, N.Y.: University of Rochester, 1976.

Emmerich, W. The parental role: A functional-cognitive approach. *Monographs of the Society for Research in Child Development*, 1969, *34* (8, Serial No. 132).

Freeman, D. *A rainbow of my own*. New York: Viking Press, 1966.

Gauch, P. L. *Christina Katerina and the box*. New York: Coward, McCann & Geoghegan, 1971.

Grusec, J. E., & Kuczynski, L. Direction of effect in socialization: A comparison of the parent versus the child's behavior as determinants of disciplinary techniques. *Developmental Psychology*, 1980, *16*, 1-9.

Helfman, H. *Origami*. New York: Child Guidance Press, 1960.

Hess, R. D., & Shipman, V. C. Early experience and the socialization of cognitive modes in children. *Child Development*, 1965, *36*, 869-886.

Hetherington, E. M. Divorce: A child's perspective. *American Psychologist*, 1979, *34*, 851-858.

Hill, R. Modern systems theory and the family: A confrontation. *Social Science Information*, 1973, *10*, 7-26.

Holland, M. *A big ball of string*. New York: Random House, 1958.

Lamb, M. E. The influence of the child on marital quality and family interaction during prenatal, paranatal and infancy periods. In R. M. Lerner & G. B. Spanier (Eds.) *Child influences on marital and family interaction*. New York: Academic Press, 1978.

Laosa, L. M. Maternal teaching strategies in Chicano and Anglo-American families: The influence of culture and education on maternal behavior. *Child Development*, 1980, *51*, 759-765. (a)

Laosa, L. M. *The impact of schooling on interactions between parents and children*. Paper presented at the Conference on Changing Families, Educational Testing Service, Princeton, N.J., November 1980. (b)

Lerner, R. M., & Spanier, G. B. A dynamic interactional view of the child and family development. In R. M. Lerner & G. B. Spanier (Eds.), *Child influences on marital and family interaction*. New York: Academic Press, 1978.

Lewin, K. *Principles of topological psychology*. New York: McGraw-Hill, 1936.

Lewis, M., & Feiring, C. The child's social network: Social object, social functions, and their relationship. In M. Lewis & L. Rosenblum (Eds.), *The child and its family: The genesis of behavior* (Vol. 2). New York: Plenum Press, 1979.

Lewis, M., & Lee-Painter, S. An interactional approach to the mother-infant dyad. In M. Lewis & L. A. Rosenblum (Eds.), *The effects of the infant on its caregiver*. New York: Wiley, 1974.

McGillicuddy-DeLisi, A. V., Sigel, I. E., & Johnson, J. E. The family as a system of mutual influences: Parental beliefs, distancing behaviors, and children's representational thinking. In M. Lewis & L. A. Rosenblum, *The child and its family*. New York: Plenum Press, 1979.

Murray, F. B., The acquisition of conservation through social interation. *Developmental Psychology*, 1972, *6*, 1-6.

Parke, R. D., & O'Leary, S. Father-mother-infant interaction in the newborn period: Some findings, some observations, and some unresolved issues. In K. F. Riegel & J. Meacham (Eds.), *The developing individual in a changing world* (Vol. 2). *Social and environmental issues*. The Hague: Mouton, 1975.

Peterson, G. W., Hooper, F. H., Wanska, S. K., & DeFrain, J. *An investigation of instructional transfer effects for conservation, transitive inference and class inclusion reasoning in kindergarten and first grade children.* Madison, Wis.: Wisconsin Research and Development Center, 1976.

Piaget, J. *The child's conception of number.* New York: Humanities Press, 1952.

Piaget, J. *Play, dreams and imitation in childhood.* New York: Norton, 1962.

Piaget, J. *Biology and knowledge.* Chicago: University of Chicago Press, 1971.

Sigel, I. E., Anderson, L. M., & Shapiro, H. Categorization behavior of lower- and middle-class Negro preschool children: Differences in dealing with representation of familiar objects. *Journal of Negro Education,* 1966, Summer, 218–229.

Sigel, I. E., & Olmsted, P. The development of classification and representational competence. In I. J. Gordon (Ed.), *Readings in research in developmental psychology.* Glenview, Ill.: Scott, Foresman, 1971.

Sigel, I. E., Flaugher, J., Johnson, J., & Schauer, A. *Parent–Child Interactions Observation Schedule (PCI).* Unpublished manual, 1977. (Available from authors, Educational Testing Service, Princeton, N.J. 08541.)

Sigel, I. E., & Saunders, R. An inquiry into inquiry: Question asking as an instructional model. In L. Katz (Ed.), *Current topics in early childhood education* (Vol. II). Norwood, N.J.: Ablex Publishing Corp., 1979.

Spivak, G., & Shure, M. B. *The PIPS Test Manual: A cognitive measure of interpersonal problem solving ability.* Philadelphia; Community Mental Health/Mental Retardation. Center, 1974.

Volpe, J. *Children's concepts of friendship.* Paper presented at the annual meeting of the American Psychological Association, Washington, D.C., 1976.

Vygotsky, L. S. *Thought and language.* Cambridge, Mass.: M.I.T. Press, 1962.

CHAPTER 3

Family Environments and the Acquisition of Reading Skills

Toward a More Precise Analysis

ROBERT D. HESS, SUSAN HOLLOWAY, GARY G. PRICE, and W. PATRICK DICKSON

As fields of inquiry, studies of family influences on reading and research on cognitive processes involved in reading have developed along quite different lines. Several researchers have constructed relatively differentiated models of the act of reading. By identifying independent components, these differentiated models make it possible to describe more precisely the steps through which reading is learned, to diagnose reading problems, and to plan interventions directed at particular difficulties. Taking a different approach, researchers on the effects of family variables on reading have attempted to identify aspects of the family environment that are correlated with global measures of reading skill. Studies of family effects have not often taken advantage of the differentiated analysis of reading to specify how particular features of family experience map onto the components of this skill. Conversely, research on reading has not examined the specific origins of component skills in the family setting.

In this chapter we try to identify some of the reading-relevant elements

ROBERT D. HESS ● Stanford University, Stanford, California 94305.   SUSAN HOLLOWAY ● Stanford University, Stanford, California 94305.   GARY G. PRICE ● University of Wisconsin, Madison, Wisconsin 53706.   W. PATRICK DICKSON ● University of Wisconsin, Madison, Wisconsin 53706. The data presented here are a part of a larger cross-cultural study of the effects of home environments upon the development of school-related cognitive skills in the United States and Japan which is directed by Robert D. Hess of Stanford University and Hiroshi Azuma of the University of Tokyo. This collaborative research effort by research teams in the two countries is funded by a grant from the Spencer Foundation through the Social Science Research Council and the Japanese Science Foundation.

found in family environments and attempt to describe the processes through which the child utilizes such resources in learning to read. The usefulness of this approach is then examined by a reanalysis of data from a study of family influences upon school readiness.

A brief summary of research on reading is provided as a context for this discussion.

Research on the Act of Reading

In the past decade, research and theory on reading as a cognitive act have identified a number of specific elements that are now believed to be essential parts of reading English. Although specialists in the field do not agree about how reading as a total skill is acquired, there is strong support for the view that the beginning reader decodes the visual stimuli (letters), matches the letters to phonemes, and then applies knowledge of vocabulary, syntax, and more general information about the world in order to comprehend the meaning of the sentence or phrase. An inquiry into the effects of family experience on the acquisition of reading skill would thus reasonably include an attempt to identify specific facets of family environments that contribute to acquisition of these component skills.

The Component Skills of Reading

Attention

Attention is a general process involved in all aspects of reading. One important function of attention is the ability to focus one's mental capacity on the task (Piontkowski & Calfee, 1979). Another crucial aspect is the selection of relevant features from the stimulus field; the reader must learn to make decisions efficiently by selectively scanning the visual stimuli for patterns that are salient. A mental set that defines what is relevant seems to be characteristic of the skilled reader. Although beginning readers may be encouraged to use such mental sets, this skill probably cannot be taught directly (Gibson & Levin, 1975).

Memory

Several components of memory are important in the reading process (Calfee, 1975). These include at least the following:

1. Perceptual memory: a sizeable capacity for undecoded information (stimulus material) but extremely rapid loss of information.

2. Short-term memory: this has a limited capacity of about five to nine chunks of information; rate of loss is rapid unless the information is transferred to long-term memory.
3. Long-term memory: unlimited capacity; little if any loss of information except by overwriting; retrieval of information is highly dependent on the way sets of information are organized for storage.
4. Control processes: these link memory-system components with one another and with other cognitive processes. Subsumed in this category are the potentially conscious strategies that people may employ to aid in information storage and recall.
5. Metamemory: the individual's knowledge of and awareness of memory or of anything pertinent to information storage and retrieval (Flavell & Wellman, 1977). An example of metamemory is knowing that one is a good memorizer or that information that one is trying to recall is on "the tip of the tongue."

The basic operations and processes of memory, as delineated in categories 1 through 3, emerge during late infancy; further development is governed largely by maturational factors. Control processes and meta-memory continue to develop through early childhood and may be more susceptible to environmental influences, especially those of parents and teachers. Nonrehearsers, for example, can be induced to rehearse by instruction and practice, although some soon abandon the strategy if they are not reminded of it (Keeney, Canizzo, & Flavell, 1967). Other studies show that children often fail to realize that "chunking" and other forms of conceptual organization are effective strategies for remembering.

Decoding

The decoding process can be divided into a number of components (Carroll, 1976).

1. Dissect spoken words into component sounds. The ability to recognize the sounds composing a word and the temporal order in which they are spoken, as well as to recombine the sounds into words, is essential for mastery of the speech system and for decoding written symbols. Primary-grade children generally lack the ability to abstract and use the phoneme in a task situation (Calfee & Drum, 1978; Gibson & Levin, 1975), even though they make use of minimal contrasts like *pit* versus *bit* in spoken language (Weir, 1962). Readers must also be able to segment sentences into words and words into syllables. This ability seems to be easier to develop than phonemic dissection; by age 4 many children are proficient at it (Liberman, 1973).

2. Recognize and discriminate letters of the alphabet in their various forms (capitals, lowercase, printed, and cursive). By age 3, children are able to distinguish graphic displays of objects from those containing letters (Gibson & Levin, 1975; Hiebert, 1978). They use criteria of linear arrangement, variety (non-repetitiveness of units), number of units, and internal contrastive features. They learn the features first, then the letters, and not vice versa. This early ability develops spontaneously, simply by "having plenty of graphic displays around to look at" (Gibson & Levin, 1975, p. 239). Children from cultural settings where graphic displays are not common show less knowledge about writing (Downing & Ollila, 1975).

3. Learn the left-to-right principle. This is an aspect of learning to read that is assumed but seldom discussed or studied in detail. It is incorporated into the curriculum of *Sesame Street* (Gibbon, Palmer, & Fowles, 1975) and reinforced in contact with printed material. It may be one of the first conceptioins of reading English that children acquire.

4. Learn that there are patterns of highly probable correspondence between letters and sounds. Evidence for the hypothesis that letters are converted to sound, then meaning, is provided by children's ability to recognize written words that are in their spoken vocabulary but new to them in printed form (Rozin & Gleitman, 1977). Adults, too, are able to handle the unfamiliar words they occasionally encounter in a text. On the other hand, experimental studies have shown that a sentence whose words are spelled "wrong" but are phonologically correct (as in "Chute hymn inn the haul") are harder to decipher than if they were spelled correctly ("Shoot him in the hall"). Clearly, regularities in the written code are not ignored entirely. Readers evolve from a purely phonological approach to a direct-meaning encoding with growth of fluency.

5. Learn to recognize printed words from whatever cues can be used. Once readers have attained some degree of fluency, they no longer need to attend to every letter and word but rather to sample the text, making use of redundant information from the topic of the text, meaning of the sentence, and syntax as well as from letter arrangements. Two mechanisms may be involved (Hochberg, 1970). *Peripheral search* guides the reader's glance to the most informative part of the page by using information from peripheral vision. Evidence for this mechanism is found in the fact that the number of eye fixations drops as reading skills develop. The second mechanism, *cognitive search guidance*, is used when the reader scans the page, picks up some information, constructs the remainder, and then tests tentative hypotheses. Evidence for high-level cognitive guidance includes the finding that oral errors are usually syntactically and semantically appropriate, even in first-grade readers. "He lost his cap" may be read as "He lost his hat."

In summary, the efficient reader is able to make use of information from a variety of cues, including the configuration of a word, the letters composing it, the sounds represented by the letters, and the meaning suggested by the context.

Vocabulary

A number of skills are subsumed by the general category of word knowledge. Readers must be able to locate one or more definitions for each word, to state definitions, and to recognize the appropriate common usage of words (Calfee, Spector, & Piontkowski, 1979).

Syntax

Syntax indicates the grammatical category to which words belong and so allows the reader to enter the semantic network with directed commands of the form "find the noun which corresponds to *constituent*" (Juel, 1977). A study of reading errors (Weber, 1970) indicates that even first-grade children anticipate syntactic structure. Ninety percent of their oral reading errors showed a tendency to grasp the syntax correctly but select the wrong word. Results from several studies indicate the importance of syntactical knowledge in early reading (Ruddell, 1976).

Comprehension

In the comprehension aspect of reading, the reader synthesizes the accumulated information in the passage based on explicit cues in the text and knowledge of language and the world (Juel, 1977). Calfee and Drum (1978) hypothesize that one important part of reading is *role-playing*— being able to put oneself in the position of the message sender. The child must create a plausible context for the text, fleshing out and making concrete the otherwise barren symbols. Comprehension thus involves applying one's personal experiences and knowledge of the world to the surface structures of sentences to yield meaning. The "meaning" of a passage comes from activation and organization of information the reader brings to the reading act.

Family Experiences That Facilitate Reading: A Summary of the Evidence

Over the past thirty years or so, many studies have shown an association between various types of home resources and skill in reading. This literature is reviewed here to illustrate the research approach that is often used to describe the areas of the environment that are correlated with reading proficiency.

Promoting Verbal Skills

The types of verbal interaction that parents engage in with their children influence the acquisition of linguistic cognitive skills important to reading. The modifications parents make in their speech to toddlers are related to the children's vocabulary and syntactic ability. Vocabulary may be enhanced by parents' tendency to repeat and elaborate their children's utterances. The range of semantic relations expressed in parents' speech, as well as the intelligibility and fluency with which these linquistic features are communicated, may also have an impact on children's use of words (Nelson, Carskaddon, & Bonvillian, 1973; Newport, Gleitman, & Gleitman, 1975). Grammatical acquisition may be aided by parents' tendency to use simple sentence structures and to elaborate the structures used by children (Cross, 1977, 1978).

Although the linguistic interactions children have with parents are undoubtedly related to mastery of syntactic structure, some studies have suggested that parents' verbal input to children is not as fine-tuned (Newport, Gleitman, & Gleitman, 1977) or as uniform across cultures (Harkness, 1977; Heath, in press) as earlier investigators had hypothesized. Variety in the features of parents' language may result in differences in the rate of acquisition of syntactic knowledge or in the routes that are taken, but all children achieve fluency in their native language. Focus has shifted from the acquisition of syntactic structure to the growth of communicative competence. Numerous studies have suggested that success in school is dependent on mastery of conventions for answering questions, reporting factual material, participating in group discussion, and the like (Philips, 1972; Boggs, 1972). In reading, for example, children with more exposure to "why" questions will be more skilled in drawing inferences from the text (Heath, in press). When the conventions employed by parents do not match those used in the classroom, children's ability to demonstrate their knowledge is impaired.

Other studies of parent–child verbal interaction have examined the extent to which parents encourage verbal expression from their children. Several investigators have found that mothers' use of questions is positively related to certain aspects of language acquisition (Snow, Arlman-Rupp, Hassing, Jobse, Joosten, & Vorster, 1976; Furrow, 1979; Ringler, 1978). Mothers' tendency to elicit verbal rather than nonverbal responses from their preschool children and to ask questions requiring the children to generate responses in their own terms is correlated with letter knowledge and math ability in kindergarten and first grade (Price & Hess, 1979). Finally, the tendency of mothers to accept their children's interests and intentions in a conversation, continuing the dialogue until discrepancies of meaning are resolved, has been related to subsequent performance in reading (Wells, 1976). A number of explanatory mechanisms could be cited to account for these findings. One possibility is that giving children the opportunity to initiate and actively influence the verbal interchange fosters perceptions of efficacy in the children, which, in turn, stimulate the child to persist in attempts to develop communicative skills.

A number of studies report that the amount of time parent and child spend together is correlated with reading achievement. Presumably, a significant aspect of this experience is the verbal interaction that occurs between the two (Durkin, 1966). Children who regularly spend long periods of time alone or in company of peers, unsupervised by the mother, tend to perform poorly on tests of reading readiness and achievement (Miller, 1970).

Reading Habits of Parents

Children's reading performance is correlated with the amount of reading done by their parents, the quality of parents' reading material, and the value placed on reading by parents. Parents of early readers tended to read more than those of children who were not early readers (Durkin, 1966) and to characterize themselves as frequent readers and as enjoying a variety of books (Clark, 1976). Parental reading practices are also correlated with reading performance of later readers (Hansen, 1969).

Reading to the Child

The tendency of parents to read to their children is correlated with performance on measures of reading proficiency (Briggs & Elkind, 1977; Clark, 1976; Durkin, 1966; King & Friesen, 1972). Reading aloud also correlates with performance on reading tests (Almy, 1949; Hansen, 1969; Miller, 1969; Milner, 1951). Verbal aspects of the interaction may be mechanisms through which these results are achieved. Flood (1977) found that the total number of words spoken, the number of questions asked and/or answered by the child, the number of pre- and poststory questions asked by the parent, and the amount of positive reinforcement given by the parent were all related to test performance.

Availability of Reading and Writing Materials

Children who have access to reading and writing materials tend to become more proficient readers than children lacking such opportunity (Callaway, 1968; Flood, 1975; Hansen, 1969; Milner, 1951). Parents of early readers were more likely than parents of later readers to buy picture dictionaries, alphabet books, and basal readers as well as to provide paper, pencils, and blackboards (Briggs & Elkind, 1977; Clark, 1976; Durkin, 1966). Early readers are frequently taken to the library by their parents (Berry, Fischer, Parker, & Zwier, 1971; Briggs & Elkind, 1977; Clark, 1976; King & Friesen, 1972).

Exposure to a Variety of Activities

Some evidence suggests that children's reading skills profit from prior exposure to varied experiences. Children who are superior readers in primary school attend more cultural activities than average readers (Berry *et al.*, 1971), participate in a wider variety of activities, and go on more family trips (Miller, 1969, 1970). In studies addressing the role of varied experience, alternative hypotheses may easily be suggested, especially the possibility that the social class and educational level of parents may affect both reading readiness and exposure to a variety of experiences.

Help with Reading

Although many professionals in the field of reading advise parents to leave reading instruction to the teacher, studies of early readers show that they usually received some form of direct tutoring from their parents. Some parents set out deliberately to teach their children reading only because the children persisted in asking for help in identifying words and letters (Clark, 1976; Durkin, 1966). Parents of early readers may identify letters, words, and numbers; help with spelling and printing; define words; and demonstrate the sounds of letters (Briggs & Elkind, 1977; Hansen, 1969; King & Friesen, 1972). In a few cases, children also received tutoring directly from siblings.

Regulation and Use of Television

The major contributions in this are are the evaluations of *Sesame Street* by Ball and Bogatz (Ball & Bogatz, 1970; Bogatz & Ball, 1971) and the reanalysis of relevant data by Cook, Appleton, Conner, Shaffer, Tamkin, and Weber (1975). The conclusions are not simple and not entirely beyond dispute. There appears to be evidence that viewing *Sesame Street* was correlated with gains in certain prereading skills and that amount of time spent viewing affects the magnitude of gains.

Levels of Specificity in Family Research

There is thus an impressive accumulation of studies that show an association between academic achievement and family environment. The list of studies actually stretches back to 1910, when Decroly and Degand reported that children from dissimilar occupational backgrounds performed at different levels on the scale that Binet had recently constructed (Binet & Simon, 1916). For a number of reasons, however, our knowledge of the processes that link family experience to success in the classroom is still limited. One of the most obvious limitations of most of these studies is the lack of specificity in the variables used to represent both environmental features and academic performance. The attempt to bring greater specificity and precision to studies of family influences has been a prominent theme in research during the past two decades.

Variables used in studies of family influence on school performance range from molar constructs to more specific behavior, but they are most often global surrogate variables. Familiar examples of molar variables are culture, ethnicity, and socioeconomic status. Some studies include mid-level variables such as nurturance, authoritarian control, and verbal environment of the home. A few investigators have used more specific measures, such as the frequency of a particular act in an interaction sequence between parent and child (e.g., the proportion of parental verbal messages that are questions).

Molar and mid-level variables are relatively efficient predictors of academic achievement in samples drawn from a reasonably wide range of backgrounds. Occupational status, education of parents, and aspirations for the child's success in school, for example, are effective predictors of performance on scholastic tests, grades in school, and years of schooling.

The research now available thus has substantial predictive power. If prediction of academic outcomes on the basis of family variables is a goal, the existing research designs and family variables do quite well. Indeed, the limits of efficiency may have been approached. Given constraints of research time and expense, there seems to be little point to designing studies intended to increase the size of R^2 coefficients.

Although studies of links between family variables and reading skill have predictive efficiency, they lack explanatory power. A deeper under-

96 Robert D. Hess *et al.*

standing of the processes involved requires more specificity in defining variables. The obvious strategy for designing studies with more specificity is to define global variables in terms of their separate components, which can then be selected for more focused analysis. Several previous efforts to analyze processes through which family influence is mediated have attempted to "unpack" molar constructs to identify more specific elements of relevant family variables (Hess & Shipman, 1965; Wolf, 1964; Yarrow, Rubenstein, & Pedersen, 1975). However, these studies often used relatively global measures of mental ability (IQ) or school achievement (grades, test scores) as child outcomes. For example, a particular aspect of social class, such as verbal environment of the home or a characteristic of maternal speech, may be correlated with IQ or grades in school. The global nature of such outcome variables limits the usefulness of such findings for understanding the processes involved.

It may be more effective to select specific elements of both family and school-achievement variables. Global achievement measures may be subdivided into performance in a given area—reading, for example—and the separate components of this skill identified. These may be related to specific elements of the verbal environment of the home or a feature of parental speech. Each step of this subdividing process requires a judgment as to which variable is the most promising; this decision is based on both empirical and theoretical grounds. The progression from molar to specific variables on both home and school sides of the family–achievement linkage is illustrated in Figure 1.

Although knowledge of component skills involved in reading may help identify relevant elements of the family environment, we recognize that this type of environment–skill matching covers only a part of the total process by which a child learns to read. Such matching occurs within a larger matrix of exchanges between family and school and between the child and the family. If one were to construct a more comprehensive model, it might include (1) the availability of essential preparatory experiences provided by the home, (2) the child's cognitive processes that organize and interpret the relevant information, (3) other child aptitudes (e.g., curiosity, cognitive style) that help regulate such cognitive processes, (4) facilitating behavior by an adult in helping the child learn from the environment, (5) factors that influence the motivation of the child to learn to read, and (6) conditions external to the family (e.g., social support systems, economic deprivation) and internal to the family (e.g., divorce, availability of parents) that affect its capability to offer preparatory experiences and support.

A brief enumeration of the features that might be included in a more comprehensive model does not describe the processes involved in learning

INCREASING LEVEL OF SPECIFICITY

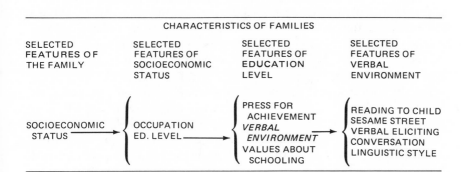

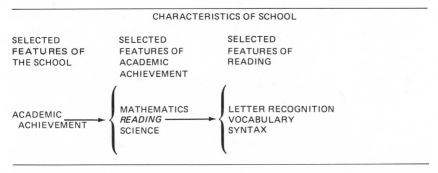

Figure 1. Progression of specificity in selection of variables in research on family effects on reading.

to read. It may, however, indicate the variety and complexity of family influence upon achievement in scholastic tasks. Any one study of family influence can incorporate only a selected feature of the total process, but specificity in findings may eventually contribute to the development of more general models.

Analysis of Family Environments and Child Outcomes

To illustrate the utility of a matching-components approach, an analysis of available data on the effects of family environments on cognitive development was carried out. The data were gathered as part of a cross-national study of families in Japan and the United States. Only data from the research group in the United States were used, the families who participated in the study being recruited through preschools and child care centers in the San Francisco Bay area. Sixty-six mothers and their first born children participated in the study. All were Caucasian; 14 were single parents at the time the study began. The mothers ranged in age from 20 to 36 years, with a median of 27. Families were selected to ensure a wide range of socioeconomic backgrounds. For example, the average education of the parents in 20 of the families was high school graduation or less; however, the parents in 19 of the families had completed an average of 4 or more years of college. The mothers' median years of schooling was 13.

Data were gathered from mothers through interviews, questionnaires, and structured interaction with children. Data from children were gathered through these interaction tasks, standardized tests, and several techniques devised or adapted for this study.

Four types of analysis are presented here: (1) the *availability* of elements of the home environment and the child's ability to recognize letters, (2) *verbal eliciting* techniques by the mother and their effects upon letter recognition, (3) a comparison of the effects of *availability and maternal press for achievement* on letter recognition, and (4) a comparison of the effects of *verbal eliciting* techniques and *press for achievement* on recognition.

Availability of Essential Preparatory Experience

The initial analysis of data from the study included a composite variable that represented the "verbal environment" of the home. This was made up of several items from the mother interview, including number of magazines read by the parent, quality (relevance for school) of magazines read, how long mother reads to the child, availability of a record player, and number of educationally relevant records owned by the child. This composite measure correlated at a significant level with several measures of school-relevant abilities of children (knowledge of letters and numbers, WISC full IQ at age 6, and simple measures of concepts of quantity).

The reanalysis was designed to investigate the differential impact of more specific features of the home experience. The component skill of reading selected was *decoding*, measured by the child's ability to identify verbally 22 letters of the alphabet. The decoding measure was administered when the child was 5 years old.

Recognition of letters and naming of letters presented visually are efficient predictors of later skill in reading (Chall, 1967; de Hirsch, Jansky, & Langford, 1966). The reason for the salience of these skills has been debated in the literature on reading acquisition. Attempts to raise achievement scores in reading by teaching letters names have generally been unsuccessful (Venezky, 1978), leading some investigators to suggest that letter naming is a *symptom* of a child's interest in language and reading rather than a crucial skill. Others have suggested that knowledge of letter names may provide children with a verbal label that helps them differentiate letter forms and to identify or remember sounds of letters (Mason, 1982). In any case, this measure is apparently tied to important aspects of the skills that help a child learn to read. Children who cannot recognize the letters of the alphabet will encounter difficulties in their intitial attempts to learn to read. Failure at this early stage may initiate a chain of problems in educability and competence in school.

Our strategy was to identify children whose knowledge of letters was relatively high compared with their knowledge of other reading-relevant skills. We selected a measure of word meaning—the vocabulary subtest of the WISC—that required the child to encode a definition of words without assistance from visual cues. A differentiation between visual decoding and oral encoding was made by computing double median splits on the decoding (letters) and encoding (vocabulary) variables. This procedure produced four groups, each representing one of the cells generated by the median split. Our interest lay primarily in two of the four groups: children who were low on decoding and high on vocabulary and children skilled in decoding but deficient in vocabulary knowledge. We expected that children in the second category would have been exposed to experiences directly pertinent to letter recognition (decoding).

In order to identify the family variables that were associated with relatively high ability to recognize letters, the items describing family activities and resources were divided on *a priori* gounds into three categories: (1) those that involve direct contact between the child and reading materials or that encourage the child to name letters; (2) items that represent attempts by the mother to tutor the child in nonreading skills— counting, recognizing colors, learning the names of shapes; and (3) items that indicate the mother's interest in reading books, magazines, and newspapers. These three groups thus indicate experiences that should have differential effects on skill in letter recognition and naming. Environmental specificity may be indicated if the child's ability to decode letters is more closely related to the first of these three categories than to the other two types of parental activities.

As the data in Table 1 show, the children who are skilled in both letter naming and vocabulary received the most assistance from their families in all three categories. Children lacking skills in letter recognition but high in vocabulary received the least assistance in all three categories. The contrast between the low letter recognition–high vocabulary group and high letter

Table 1. Mean Scores and Standard Deviations on Home Environment Composites [a]

Home variables	Low letter recognition–low vocabulary ($n = 16$)	Low–high ($n = 14$)	High–low ($n = 13$)	High–high ($n = 21$)
Experience relevant to:				
Letter awareness				
(9 items)	23.13	22.64	26.92	27.10
	(5.18)	(5.37)	(4.54)	(4.08)
General tutoring				
(5 items)	13.13	12.77	13.15	15.05
	(3.30)	(2.09)	(1.72)	(2.50)
Parent's reading practices				
(5 items)	11.08	10.56	10.62	10.71
	(3.12)	(1.74)	(2.60)	(2.02)

Note: Standard deviation in parentheses.
[a] For groups formed by median splits on letter recognition and WISC-R vocabulary subtest ($n = 64$).

recognition–low vocabulary group is particularly interesting. Children in the latter group received more experience in letter recognition but differed little from the other group in nonreading assistance or parental reading. A two-way analysis of variance was performed with the letter awareness composite, revealing a main effect for letter recognition [F (1.58) = 11.57, $p < .001$] and not for vocabulary (Table 2). These findings reinforce the notion that the ability to recognize and name letters is associated with elements of the home environment that offer direct experience with visual and verbal forms essential to this component reading skill.

These data were gathered originally to answer other questions. A study of family environments which was designed to collect more differentiated information about the child's contact with letters and letter names could explore more precisely how these specific elements of the home environment are related to recognition of letters and letter names.

Table 2. Analysis of Variance on a Letter Awareness Composite Variable

Source	df	MS	F
Vocabulary (A)	1	.31	.01
Letter recognition (B)	1	261.95	11.57[a]
A $\times$ B	1	1.68	.07
Residual	58	22.65	—

[a] $p < .001$.

Table 3. Background Characteristics of Mothers and Children[a]

Groups		Mother's IQ	Child's IQ	Social class	Marital status
Low letter recognition	Mean	111.19	104.00	8.69	6 single
Low vocabulary	Median	106.50	105.50	7.83	10 married
(n = 16)	SD	9.33	9.68	3.40	
Low letter recognition	Mean	108.79	115.14	8.79	6 single
High vocabulary	Median	109.50	112.50	7.50	8 married
(n = 14)	SD	12.99	11.73	3.85	
High letter recognition	Mean	114.85	108.69	9.08	2 single
Low vocabulary	Median	114.00	105.75	8.33	11 married
(n = 13)	SD	10.15	10.21	3.01	
High letter recognition	Mean	118.00	124.76	10.91	2 single
High vocabulary	Median	118.00	123.00	11.00	19 married
(n = 21)	SD	10.82	9.32	2.30	

[a]Groups formed by median splits on letter recognition and WISC-R vocabulary subtest.

These results appear to support our general point, but an alternative interpretation of the data must be explored. One possibility is that both maternal behavior and child scores are affected by intelligence of mother and/or child. The high-decode group may simply be a group of children who absorb elements from the environment because they are brighter or more alert.

This explanation can be examined by reference to the data in Table 3. The measure of maternal IQ is the verbal score on the WAIS; the measure for the child is the full IQ score on the WISC. Two additional family variables are included in the table for their general interest: socioeconomic status (SES)—measured by a composite of father's occupation, father's education, and mother's education— and marital status of the mother. Marital status is included because of the accumulating evidence that children from single-parent homes do less well on scholastic measures than children from two-parent families (Shinn, 1978).

The comparison of the two target cells (high decode–low vocabulary, low decode–high vocabulary) is best done in the context of differences among the four groups. The possibility that the high-decode group represents children of higher intelligence is clearly not supported; the high-decode group scores below the low-decode group (108.69 to 115.14). Mothers of the high-decode group have slightly higher IQ means, but since this advantage is not matched by their children's scores (relative to the low-decode group), the results do not seem to be a function of a difference in general intelligence.

The other background measures offer some supplementary information. The mothers of the high-decode group have a slightly higher SES mean, and there are more single mothers in the low-decode cell. The picture that emerges of the low-decode–high-vocabulary group is one of children who are bright but whose mothers do not or cannot provide them with as much experience with reading and reading materials as the mothers of the high-decode–low-vocabulary children.

Facilitating Behavior: The Mother's Elicitation of Verbal Responses

Children's ability to utilize relevant environmental experience may be facilitated by the actions of the adults with whom they interact. This aspect of the model is concerned with the way in which essential home experiences are presented to children.

Certain kinds of language experiences (which are now more available in some environments than in others) are widely believed to influence the formation of various school-relevant abilities, including reading. Little is known about how the elements of the linguistic environment are related to the child's cognitive operations. Traditionally, the link between verbal environment and the child's ability to read has been attributed to an underlying and irreducible verbal–educational ability hypothesized to contribute in a diffuse way to the development of academic skills.

In contrast to a search for environmental correlates of underlying general abilities, we propose a model in which specific components of the abilities to be measured in the child's performance are fostered by discrete aspects of the environment. In addition to being available, the information provided by the environment must be appropriate to the child's abilities. Therefore, the child's mental operations must also be understood, for they specify behavior of adults that might facilitiate the formative process.

There are thus two types of correspondence: the elements in the environment must map onto the specific skills to be displayed, and the facilitating behavior of the adult must correspond to the mental operations that the child undertakes to utilize the materials that are available. An implication of this view is that these correspondences between child skill and facilitation/environment are developmentally tuned. The effects of particular aspects of the context interact with aptitudes (including developmental features) of the child (Parke, 1978).

Opportunity for Verbal Expression

The opportunity for verbal expression, particularly in communication with a more experienced speaker, is an aspect of language experience that varies across environments. In the presence of a more experienced speaker (adult, mother, father), the child's opportunity for verbal expression will be determined in part by the style of adult–child interaction. These styles include such features as frequency of interchange, vocabulary, imbalance in contribution of the members of the communicating dyad, and accuracy of referential communication. For example, questions, requests, and commands (directives) differ, according to how they are phrased, in the likelihood that they will elicit a verbal response. Commands like "Tell me . . ." more consistently trigger a verbal response than commands like "Show me . . ." Thus the input from the adult—that is, actions over which the adult may have control—can substantially affect the extent to which young children participate verbally and the style of their verbal communication.

Even those directives from an adult that call for an oral response can differ in the verbalization requirements that they place on children and in the cognitive processes involved in producing the utterance (Price & Hess,

1979). Directives that can be answered with a yes or no or with terms supplied by the adults (e.g., "is the ball *red* or *blue?*") do not require children to generate terms of their own. Such directives or invitations can place demands on children that are cognitively complex, but the actual responses require less verbal encoding and different cognitive processing than do responses to questions requiring children to generate an original response.

The cognitive-linguistic process exercised as children verbally and orally encode their thoughts deserves more careful analysis. Oleron (1977, p. 81) has suggested that the use of language habituates children to the interposition of cognitive processing between perception or impulse, on the one hand, and action on the other—developing a sort of extended pathway. Studies of memory suggest that information can be held in short-term or "shallow" memory long enough to carry out a task and then be lost (Craik, 1979). This may happen more easily if the information is supplied by an external source—a parent, for example—rather than drawn from deeper memory.

This section of the chapter examines mother–child interaction from the perspective of the linguistic and cognitive demands made by the form of the mother's verbal message. It draws from the data set described earlier, but the interaction task deserves more specific description.

Observation Context

Mother–child interaction was videotaped in a room at a research center when the children were 4 years old plus or minus 1 month. This report concerns verbal aspects of the interaction that took place as the mother taught her child how to perform a block-sorting task developed by Hess and Shipman (1965) and used in their study. The task requires children to ignore the varying color and cross-sectional shapes of blocks while placing them into groups defined conjointly as having the same *height* (tall or short) and the same *mark* on the end of the block (X or O). The children were also asked to justify their placements by explaining the similarity of height and mark that serves as the sorting principle. Mothers were given 20 minutes to teach their children how to perform this task; each was free to end the session ahead of time if she believed her child had learned to perform the task. Before this task was introduced, each pair played together with pegboard games for 10 minutes while becoming familiar with the room.

Measures

One aspect of the mother's verbal behavior is described here—her tendency to phrase directives to her child so as to make verbal responding likely. This measure was generated from typewritten transcripts of mother–child interaction. A person watching a videotape of the interaction verified and annotated the transcript, also recording nonverbal events (pointing, patting, restraining). Transcripts were segmented into message units according to a procedure adapted from Loban's (1963) system. An account of the coding procedures is available elsewhere (Price, 1977). Coders agree in their categorization 97% of the time.

Control variables included a measure of SES, maternal verbal IQ (WAIS), and three measures of child ability. The three child measures were the Concept Familiarity Index, a test of such concepts as color, number, size, and relationship developed by Palmer (1970). It was administered individually when children were 44 months old. At the same session, children were given the Block Design portion of the Wechsler Preschool–Primary Scale of Intelligence. Near their fourth birthday, children were given the Peabody Picture Vocabulary Test. The dependent variable for this analysis was a measure of letter recognition, described earlier.

Results

The correlation between requests for verbal rather than nonverbal feedback and recognition of letters was .36 ($p < .001$). This remained significant (.32; $p < .05$) when maternal IQ, SES, and the three measures of child ability were partialed out, thus confirming that knowledge of letters was influenced by environmental factors other than the ability of the child, the social-class background of the family, or verbal intelligence of the mother.

Comparable findings have been reported from analysis of maternal behavior in the block-sort task in a different population (Hess, Shipman, Brophy, & Bear, 1969) where the tendency for mothers to request block placement (rather than verbalization) correlated negatively with reading readiness scores (Lee-Clark Primer) and grades in reading during the first 2 years of school. This measure is the complement of the one used in this analysis. These correlations were at roughly the same level for a subsample of working-class children as for a wide range of SES backgrounds. The magnitude of these correlations was remarkably similar to those reported here ($-.36$ for full SES sample, $p < .001$; $-.27$ for working class only, $p < .001$).

Motivational Components in the Acquisition of Reading Skills

The analysis thus far has attended to the availability of experiences in the home that are essential to the development of component skills in reading. It is not obvious that availability necessarily leads to acquisition of the skill; some motivational aspect must almost certainly play an important role. The motivation may come from the children, as studies of early readers suggest (Durkin, 1966), but parents also influence acquisition throught various motivational strategies—imitation, rewards, punishment, and the like. These strategies themselves deserve study and comment, but our data do not permit an analysis of this aspect of parental behavior.

Measure of Maternal Press

The motivational features of the home environment that were available were represented by a composite that we call *press for achievement*. It was made up of five subscores. One was a score on an instrument devised to indicate the mother's expectations about the age at which her child would master each of 38 developmental skills (Hess, Kashiwagi, Azuma, Price, & Dickson, 1980). The mean score on this developmental expectations instrument was supplemented by two subscores: those items of the instrument that dealt with school achievement and those that asked about verbal initiative and assertiveness on the part of the child. In addition to these three measures of developmental press, three scales from the maternal interview were used: *parental concern* over the child's (hypothetical) progress in school, *prediction* of the child's occupational and educational achievement, and the *importance* that the mother assigned to language learning activities in the preschool that her child attended. In a general sense, then, the composite indicated the mother's attempt to motivate the child to achieve in school.

Maternal Press and Elements of the Home Environment

A composite variable was created using five items that had been identified as providing direct experience relevant to decoding. The variables included the following: (1) hours spent watching *Sesame Street*, (2) hours parent coviews *Sesame Street*, (3) whether parent checks out books from the library for the child, (4) how often the child listens to educational records, and (5) the amount of time the parent spends reading to the child. A double median split on the home environment composite and the maternal press composite was performed to identify four groups: high availability–high press, low availability–low press, high availability–low press, low availability–high press. Means for each cell were computed on the decoding variable (letter naming).

Examination of the four means reveals that children whose parents do not push them to succeed do not perform as well on letter recognition as

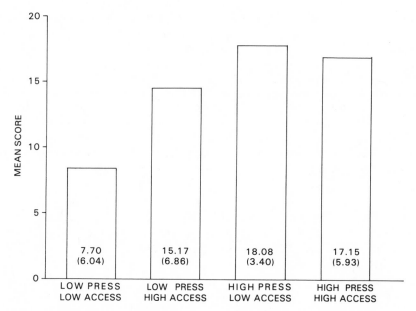

Figure 2. Mean score and standard deviation (in parentheses) on letter recognition for groups formed by median splits on maternal press and availability of reading-relevant home experiences ($n = 66$).

those from homes where there is considerable press for performance. Additionally, level of access to reading-relevant home experiences seems less important for children in high-press homes than it does for children in low-press homes. It may be that in high-press homes a minimal level of access is needed and that increments beyond that level do not greatly influence performance (Figure 2). An analysis of variance (Table 4) produced main effects for both press [F (1,61) = 18.36, $p < .001$] and access to relevant experiences [F (1,61) = 4.66, $p < .05$] as well as a significant

Table 4. Analysis of Variance: Effects of Maternal Press and Elements of the Home Environment on Letter Recognition

Source	df	MS	F
Press (A)	1	607.19	18.36[b]
Home (B)	1	154.20	4.66[a]
A X B	1	270.70	8.19[a]
Residual	61	33.07	—

[a] $p < .05$.
[b] $p < .001$.

interaction effect [F (1,61) = 8.19, $p < .05$]. The main effect for access seems to be primarily due to the difference between low and high access for those children whose parents do not pressure them to succeed.

Maternal Press and Eliciting Behavior

The relative effect of maternal eliciting behavior and motivational components (expressed by the composite measure of *press*, described earlier) was analyzed in a comparable manner. A double median split of *press* versus *request verb* was performed and means for letter recognition were computed. The mothers' tendency to pressure the children to achieve appears to have a very important influence, but their tendency to request verbal statements from the children is also of significance in both the high-press and low-press groups (Figure 3). The analysis of variance bears out these findings; significant main effects were found for both press [F (1,62) = 21.16, $p < .001$] and for elicing verbalization [F (1,62) = 8.80, $p < .05$]: see Table 5.

Discussion

These results are consistent with a growing literature on the role of the social and verbal context in memory processes in young children. The gist

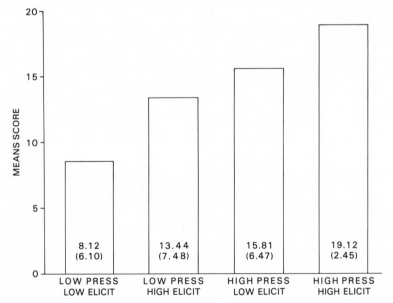

Figure 3. Mean score and standard deviation (in parentheses) on letter recognition for groups formed by median splits on maternal press and verbal elicitation ($n = 66$).

Table 5. Analysis of Variance: Effects of Maternal Press and Verbal Elicitation on Letter Recognition

Source	df	MS	F
Press (A)	1	737.25	21.16[b]
Elicit (B)	1	306.58	8.80[a]
A × B	1	16.73	.48
Residual	62	34.84	—

[a] $p < .05$.
[b] $p < .001$.

of this literature is that when persons (including young children) verbalize informational content, they are more likely to remember it. Several studies suggest that preschool children remember less efficiently than older children because they do not rehearse material (Flavell & Wellman, 1977; Hagen & Stanovich, 1977; Ornstein & Naus, 1978). Mothers or other adults can, however, help the child remember by externally sustaining rehearsal by asking questions, making requests for verbal feedback, and asking the child to generate ideas (Price, Hess, & Dickson, 1981) or solve problems. There is also the possibility that the child who is asked to verbalize an original response may store it in memory in a way that is compatible with concepts already available. Concepts stored in this way may be more accessible than a label or term provided by the adult.

The data discussed here also suggest that the role of motivation in early school-related learning is relatively powerful. Our data do not permit a fine-grained analysis of the effectiveness of maternal press at different levels of environmental availability. It seems possible, however, that there is a threshold—a minimal level of information that a child needs in order to learn—regardless of the impetus provided by the family's reward system or the child's own interest.

More specific measures of motivational elements are needed. If information were available about the pressure from parents on the child to acquire a particular reading-relevant skill (vocabulary, syntax, etc.), the role of focused motivation and of more general pressure to achieve (if such a global push does indeed exist) could be indicated in greater detail. It seems possible that press for performance is specific to some degree. This sort of more detailed analysis, incidentally, may be particularly appropriate for school-related skills because they can be defined more precisely than can competence in many other areas.

The most general implication that may, tentatively be drawn from these results is that analyses of the family as a learning environment may usefully be designed with the specific requirements of the outcome in mind. If these can be identified (and it is assumed that this is sometimes possible), the investigation of the environment can be guided by both empirical work and theory. As such specific information is accumulated, we may be able to identify more exactly the relative contribution of the several components of the family as a learning environment.

ACKNOWLEDGMENTS

Special acknowledgment should be given to Eleanor B. Worden for her key role in administering the interaction instruments to the mothers and teachers.

References

Almy, M. C. *Children's experiences prior to first grade and success in beginning reading.* Contributions to Education, No. 954. New York: Teachers College, Columbia University, 1949.

Ball, S., & Bogatz, G. A. *The first year of Sesame Street: An evaluation.* Princeton, N.J.: Educational Testing Service, 1970.

Berry, M. T., Fischer, S. L., Parker, F. S., & Zwier, M. D. Average and superior readers in lab school. *Reading Teacher,* 1971, *25,* 271-275.

Binet, A., & Simon, T. *The development of intelligence in children.* Translated by Elizabeth S. Kite. Baltimore: Williams & Wilkins, 1916.

Bogatz, G. A., & Ball, S. *The second year of Sesame Street: A continuing evaluation.* (2 vols.). Princeton, N.J.: Educational Testing Service, 1971.

Boggs, S.T. The meaning of questions and narratives to Hawaiian children. In C. B. Cazden, V. P. John, & D. Hymes (Eds.), *Functions of language in the classroom.* New York: Teachers College Press, 1972.

Briggs, C., & Elkind, D. Characteristics of early readers. *Perceptual and Motor Skills,* 1977, *44,* 1231-1237.

Calfee, R. C. Memory and cognitive skills in reading acquisition. In M. Duane & M. Rawson (Eds.), *Reading, perception and language.* Baltimore, Md.: York Press, 1975.

Calfee, R. C., & Drum, P. A. Learning to read: Theory, research, and practice. *Curriculum Inquiry,* 1978, *8,* 183-249.

Calfee, R. C., Spector, J., & Piontkowski, D. An interactive system for assessing reading and language skills, *Bulletin,* Towson, Md.: The Orton Society, Inc., 1979.

Callaway, B. Relationship of specific factors to reading. From *Proceedings of the Thirteenth Annual Convention of the International Reading Association, Part 1,* (Vol. 13). Newark, Delaware: International Reading Association, Inc., 1968.

Carroll, J. B. The nature of the reading process. In H. Singer & R. B. Ruddell (Eds.), *Theoretical models and processes of reading.* Newark, Del.: International Reading Association, 1976.

Chall, J. S. *Learning to read: The great debate.* New York: McGraw-Hill, 1967.

Clark, M. M. *Young fluent readers: What can they teach us?* London: Heinemann Educational Books, 1976.

Cook, T. D., Appleton, H., Conner, R. F., Shaffer A., Tamkin, C., & Weber, S. J. *"Sesame Street" revisited.* New York: Russell Sage Foundation, 1975.

Craik, F. I. M. Human memory. *Annual Review of Psychology*, 1979, *30*, 63–102.

Cross, T. G. Mothers' speech adjustments: The contributions of selected child listener variables. In C. E. Snow & C. A. Ferguson (Eds.), *Talking to children: Language input and acquisition*. Cambridge: Cambridge University Press, 1977.

Cross, T. G. Mother's speech and its association with rate of linguistic development in young children. In N. Waterson & C. E. Snow (Eds.), *The Development of communication*. New York: Wiley, 1978.

de Hirsch, K., Jansky, J. J., & Langford, W. S. *Predicting reading failure: A preliminary study of reading, writing, and spelling disabilities in preschool children*. New York: Harper & Row, 1966.

Downing, J., & Ollila, L. Cultural differences in children's concepts of reading and writing. *British Journal of Educational Psychology*, 1975, *45*, 312–316.

Durkin, D. *Children who read early*. New York: Teachers College Press, 1966.

Flavell, J. H., & Wellman, H. M. Metamemory. In R. V. Kail, Jr., & J. W. Hagen (Eds.), *Perspectives on the development of memory and cognition*. Hillsdale, N.J.: Lawrence Erlbaum, 1977.

Flood, J. E. *Predictors of reading achievement. An investigation of selected antecedents to reading*. Unpublished doctoral dissertation, Stanford University, 1975.

Flood J. E. Parental styles in reading episodes with young children. *Reading Teacher*, 1977, *30*, 864–867.

Furrow, D. *The benefits of motherese*. Paper presented to the Society of Research in Child Development, San Francisco, March 1979.

Gibbon S. Y., Jr., Palmer, E. L., & Fowles, B. R. "Sesame Street," "The Electric Company," and reading. In J. B. Carroll & J. S. Chall (Eds.), *Toward a literate society*. New York: McGraw-Hill, 1975.

Gibson, E. J., & Levin, H. *The psychology of reading*. Cambridge, Mass.: M.I.T. Press, 1975.

Hagen, J. W., & Stanovich, K. G. Memory: Strategies of acquisition. In R. V. Kail, Jr., & J. W. Hagen (Eds.), *Perspectives on the development of memory and cognition*. Hillsdale, N.J.: Lawrence Erlbaum, 1977.

Hansen, H. S. The impact of the home literacy environment on reading attitude. *Elementary English*, 1969, 46, 17–24.

Harkness, S. Aspects of social environment and first language acquisition in rural Africa. In C. E. Snow & C. A. Ferguson (Eds.), *Talking to children: Language input and acquisition*. Cambridge: Cambridge University Press, 1977.

Heath, S. B. Questioning at home and school: A comparative study. In G. Spindler (Ed.), *The ethnography of schooling: Educational anthropology in action*, in press.

Hess, R. D., & Shipman, V. Early blocks to children's learning. *Children*, 1965, *12*, 189–194.

Hess, R. D., Shipman, V. C., Brophy, J. E., & Bear, R. M. *The cognitive environments of urban preschool children: Follow-up phase*. Unpublished manuscript, The Graduate School of Education, The University of Chicago, 1969.

Hess, R. D., Kashiwagi, K., Azuma, H., Price, G. G., & Dickson, W. P. Maternal expectations for early mastery and the development of cognitive and social competence of preschool children in Japan and the United States. *International Journal of Psychology*, 1980, *15*, 259–271.

Hiebert, E. H. Preschool children's understanding of written language. *Child Development*, 1978, 49, 1231–1234.

Hochberg, J. Components of literacy: Speculations and exploratory research. In H. Levin & J. P. Williams (Eds.), *Basic studies on reading*. New York: Basic Books, 1970.

Juel, C. L. *An independent-process model of reading for beginning readers*. Unpublished doctoral dissertation, Stanford University, 1977.

Keeney, T. J., Canizzo, S. R., & Flavell, J. H. Spontaneous and induced verbal rehearsal in a recall task. *Child Development*, 1967, *38*, 953-966.

King, E. M., & Friesen, D. T. Children who read in kindergarten. *Alberta Journal of Educational Research*, 1972, *18*(3), 147-161.

Liberman, I. Y. *Segmentation of the spoken word and reading acquisition*. Paper presented to the Society for Research in Child Development, Philadelphia, March 1973.

Loban, W. D. *The language of elementary school children: A study of the use and control of language and the relations among speaking, reading, writing and listening*. Champaign, Ill.: National Council of Teachers of English, 1963. (NCTE Research Report, No. 1.)

Mason, J. Meta-cognitive skills: Prereading. In P. D. Pearson (Ed.), *Handbook of reading research*. New York: Longman, 1982.

Miller, W. H. Home prereading experiences and first-grade reading achievement. *Reading Teacher*,1969, *22*, 641-645.

Miller, W. H. An examination of children's daily schedules in three social classes and their relation to first-grade reading achievement. *California Journal of Education Research*, 1970, *21*, 100-110.

Milner, E. A study of the relationship between reading readiness in grade one school children and patterns of parent–child interaction. *Child Development*, 1951, *22*, 95-112.

Nelson, K. E., Carskaddon, G., & Bonvillian, J. D. Syntax acquisition: Impact of environmental assistance in adult verbal interaction with the child. *Child Development*, 1973, *44*, 497-504.

Newport, E. L., Gleitman, L. R., & Gleitman, H. A study of mothers' speech and child language acquisition. *Papers and Reports on Child Language Development* (No. 10). Stanford, Calif: Stanford University, 1975.

Newport, E. L., Gleitman, H., & Gleitman, L. R. Mother, I'd rather do it myself: Some effects and non-effects of maternal speech style. In C. E. Snow & C. A. Ferguson (Eds.), *Talking to children: Language input and acquisition*. Cambridge, England: Cambridge University Press, 1977.

Oleron, P. *Language and mental development*. Translated by R. P. Lorion. Hillsdale, N.J.: Lawrence Erlbaum, 1977.

Ornstein, P. A., & Naus, M. J. Rehearsal process in children's memory. In P. A. Ornstein (Ed.), *Memory development in children*. Hillsdale, N.J.: Lawrence Erlbaum, 1978.

Palmer, F. H. Socioeconomic status and intellectual performance among Negro preschool boys. *Developmental Psychology*, 1970, *3*, 1-9.

Parke, R. D. Children's home environments: Social and cognitive effects. In I. Altman & J. F. Wohlwill (Eds.), *Children and the environment*. New York: Plenum Press, 1978.

Philips, S. V. Participant structures and communicative competence: Warm Springs children in community and classroom. In C. B. Cazden, V. P. John,& D. Hymes (Eds.), *Functions of language in the classroom*. New York: Teacher's College Press, 1972.

Piontkowski, D., & Calfee, R. C. Attention in the classroom In G. Hale & M. Lewis (Eds.), *Attention and the development of cognitive skills*. New York: Plenum Press, 1979.

Price, G. G. How cognitive abilities of preschool children are influenced by maternal teaching behavior: A causal model analysis. Doctoral dissertation, Stanford University, 1976. *Dissertation Abstracts International*, 1977, *37*, 6377A. (University Microfilms No. 77-7149, 135.)

Price, G. G., & Hess, R. D. *Aspects of mothers' verbal behavior when interacting with their preschool children: Relations to different cognitive abilities*. Paper presented to the Society for Research in Child Development, San Francisco, March 1979.

Price, G. G., Hess, R. D., & Dickson, W. P. Processes by which verbal-educational abilities are affected when mothers encourage preschool children to verbalize. *Developmental Psychology*, 1981, *17*, 554-564.

Ringler, N. A. A longitudinal study of mothers' language. In N. Waterson & C. E. Snow (Eds.), *The development of communication*. New York: Wiley, 1978.

Rozin, P., & Gleitman, L. R. The structure and acquisition of reading II: The reading process and the acquisition of the alphabetic principle. In A. S. Reber & D. L. Scarborough (Eds.), *Toward a psychology of reading: The proceedings of the CUNY Conferences*. Hillsdale, N.J.: Lawrence Erlbaum, 1977.

Ruddell, R. B. Language acquisition and the reading process. In H. Singer & R. B. Ruddell (Eds.), *Theoretical models and processes of reading* (2nd ed.). Newark, Dela.: International Reading Association, 1976.

Shinn, M. Father absence and children's cognitive development. *Psychological Bulletin*, 1978, *85*, 295–324.

Snow, C. E., Arlman-Rupp, A., Hassing, Y., Jobse, J., Joosten, J., & Vorster, J. Mothers' speech in three social classes. *Journal of Psycholinguistic Research*, 1976, 5, 1–19.

Venezky, R. Reading acquisition: The occult and the obscure. In F. Murray & John Pikulski (Eds.), *The acquisition of reading: Cognitive, linguistic, and perceptual prerequisites*. Baltimore, Md.: University Park Press, 1978.

Weber, R. M. First-graders' use of grammatical context in reading. In H. Levin & J. P. Williams (Eds.), *Basic studies in reading*. New York: Basic Books, 1970.

Weir, R. H. *Language in the crib*. The Hague: Mouton, 1962.

Wells, G. *Describing children's communicative competence*. Paper given to SSRC Seminar on Collecting, Using and Reporting Talk for Educational Research, Reading, England, March 1976.

Wolf, R. M. *The identification and measurement of environmental process variables related to intelligence*. Unpublished doctoral dissertation, University of Chicago, 1964.

Yarrow, L. J., Rubenstein, J. L. & Pedersen, F. A. *Infant and environment: Early cognitive and motivational development*. New York: Wiley, 1975

CHAPTER 4

Some American Families at Dinner

MICHAEL LEWIS and CANDICE FEIRING

Socialization theories in the past have stressed the role, at least in early childhood, of the mother. Only recently has there been much work on the role of fathers (Lamb, 1981), and research on siblings during the infancy/early-childhood period is almost nonexistent (Cicirelli, 1975; Dunn & Kendrick, 1979). Although a growing number of studies bear witness to the recognition that other social objects play an important role in the early development of children, there are relatively few theoretical perspectives that can be used to anchor any empirical findings. Bronfenbrenner (1977) and Lewis (Lewis, 1982; Lewis & Feiring, 1978, 1979; Lewis, Feiring, & Weinraub, 1981; Lewis & Weinraub, 1976; Weinraub, Brooks, & Lewis, 1977) have begun to lay out a more theoretical perspective. In each of these views, the child's place in the social network, rather than specific dyadic relationships, becomes the primary focus. Lewis (1982), in describing the social network of young children, has suggested that the role of any dyadic relationship cannot be fully appreciated without a broader perspective of placing that dyad into the larger framework of the child's life. In particular, for example, when discussing the role of the father, it becomes obvious that part of the father's role is his indirect influence, that is, those effects of the father's behavior, values, and goals that are experienced by the child through the father's behavior to others, who, in turn, act on the child (Lewis & Feiring, 1981).

By refocusing interest on the social system and on the complex nature

MICHAEL LEWIS and CANDICE FEIRING ● Rutgers Medical School—UMDNJ, Medical Educational Building, New Brunswick, New Jersey, 08903. Preparation of this chapter was supported by NICHD Grant N01-HD-82849.

of this system, two important features of current research interest are addressed. The first is the extension of our concern from the mother–infant relationship as the singularly important dyad to other relationships. In particular, research on relationships with fathers, siblings, and peers has now begun in earnest but should be extended to other family members such as grandparents, uncles, and aunts—important people for some children— and teachers and adult friends such as day care teachers, baby sitters, parents' friends, and others. Such an extension will provide information on the entire array of people that inhabit the child's life and probably play an important role in socialization.

In all the families that we have studied ($n = 117$), we found that 3-year-old children, the targets of our inquiry, are described by their mothers as seeing an average of 3.20 different relatives besides the nuclear family members on a weekly basis (see Table 1). These 3-year-old children also come in weekly contact with an average of 4.43 friends and 4.38 adults, usually the mother's friends and/or the child's teachers. Our data suggest that the number of different people seen by the child per week other than the immediate family is approximately 12. Thus, there is strong support for our belief that the child's social network involves family members other than siblings, fathers, and mothers and also includes many friends: the child's friends, the child's siblings' friends, and the child's parents' friends.

While awareness grows for the study of relationships other than that of mother–child, the emphasis in psychological studies has been for the most part in examining other dyadic relationships, that is, sibling–child (Cicirelli, 1975; Dunn & Kendrick, 1979, 1980) or father–child dyads (Lamb, 1981; Lewis, Feiring, & Weinraub, 1981; Lynn & Cross, 1974; Parke & O'Leary, 1975; Pedersen, 1975). Although information on such dyads is important, such a perspective still restricts our conceptualization to dyads and avoids the need to focus on a systems approach. Outside the psychological literature, viewing the family as a system is not new, since various sociologists and therapists have applied such models for the last two decades (Bowen, 1972; Hill, 1973; Parsons & Bales, 1955; Slater, 1974).

Table 1. The 3-Year-Old Child's Social Network

	$\overline{X}$	SD	Range
Number of relatives other than parents seen at least once a week	3.20	2.85	0–15
Number of child's friends seen at least once a week	4.43	2.87	0–13
Number of adults seen at least once a week	4.38	3.87	0–24

Systems are not only made up of various elements but are defined by the kinds of connections between these elements. Dyadic analysis needs to give way to other, more complicated ways of dealing with the description of total systems. Work on the effects of the triad on the dyad (Clarke-Stewart, 1978; Lamb, 1977) and on the different kinds of influence processes that operate on systems larger than a dyad the work on direct and indirect effects (Lewis & Feiring, 1981; Lewis, Feiring, & Weinraub, 1981; Parke, Power, & Gottman, 1979) has begun, but these efforts are still tentative.

The issues of (1) the various people (besides the mother) in the child's social system and (2) the various kinds of processes that connect and influence the child and the members of its social system are, in our conceptualization, the two central aspects in the study of families. These two issues can be used as defining characteristics for the focus of family research. Thus, we hold as a working definition that family research has as its major features the study of multiple relationships among people who live together and the process of how these relationships affect one another. The people traditionally defined as the family members may be mother, father, child, and siblings, but the definition may also include extended family such as grandparents, aunts, and so on or, in a less traditional way, two adults of the same sex (as in a homosexual family). Definition of which people constitute a family is open to debate, although—for our present discussion—we shall focus on the traditional nuclear family of mother, father, child, and siblings. To understand how the child functions as a member of a social system, rather than as a member of a mother–child dyad, it is useful to define the family as a social system.

The Family as a Social System

A system is a set of interrelated elements (Monane, 1967; Von Bertalanffy, 1967). The assumption is made that each element influences and is influenced by each other element. Structurally, a system is usually composed of an interdependent network of subsystems. For example, within a family consisting of mother, father, child, and sibling, the parent-parent, parent–child, child–sibling, and parent–sibling dyads can be conceptualized as subsystems. Pedersen (1975) conducted a study that demonstrates the ways in which parent-parent and parent–child subsystems-influence each other. This research indicated high interrelationships for the families of boys between the child's alertness, motor maturity, and irritability; the mother's feeding competence; father–infant play; the effect of the father's esteem for the mother as "mother"; and the amount of tension and conflict in marriage. Research conducted by Cicirelli (1975) indicates the interdependent nature of the child–parent and sibling–child subsystems. It was found that for children with an older sister, the help of a mother or sister led to improvement on a problem-solving task. For children with older brothers, however, the help of a mother or brother led to no improvement in problem solving by comparison with children who worked alone. The findings of this study are of interest in that they demonstrated the influence of siblings on the mother–child relationship.

The research of Dunn, Wooding, and Hermann (1977) indicates that the birth of a sibling can affect the amount of time the mother has available for interacting with the first-born child. The birth of the second child was associated with a decrease in the frequency of the mother's initiation of periods of joint play, attention, and conversational episodes and with an increase in the frequency of prohibitive commands. The behavior of the first born also changed with the addition of a new child to the family, showing increases in autonomy, demanding behavior, negative behavior directed at the mother, and in sleeping, toileting and feeding problems. This study indicates how changes in the family environment influences the behavior of subsystems (e.g., the mother–child dyad) and the interdependent nature of the mother–child and mother–sibling subsystems. In a similar fashion Lewis and Kreitzberg's (1979) demonstration of mother–infant and father–infant differences in interaction as a function of the infants' birth order point out how the mother–father–infant interaction is affected by family structure as reflected in birth-order, family-size, and birth-spacing variables.

Social systems also possess the quality of nonadditivity; that is, knowing everything about the subsystems that comprise a system will not tell you everything about the system as it operates as a whole. Any subsystem behaves quite differently within the system from the way it does in isolation. Lamb (1976) reported that infants interact more with either parent in isolated dyads than when the parent–child dyads are embedded in the entire family system of two parents and child. In addition, the parent is far less interactive with the child when the spouse is present. Clarke-Stewart (1978) observed mothers, fathers, and children in dyadic (parent–child) and triadic (mother–father–child) subsystems. This research indicated that the quantity and quality of behavior in the mother–child subsystem in isolation was changed when the mother–child subsystem was embedded in the mother–father–child subsystem. The mother initiated less talk and play with the child (quantity) and was also less engaging, reinforcing, directive, and responsive in her child-directed interactions (quality) when the father was present than when she was alone with the child. Pedersen, Anderson, and Cain (1977) report that although the father/husband frequently divides his behavior between child and spouse in a three-person setting, the mother/wife spends much more time in dyacid interaction with the child. A study by Parke and O'Leary (1975) illustrates both the qualities of interdependence and nonadditivity in the family system. When mothers were with their husbands, they were more likely to explore the child and smile at the child than when they were alone. In addition, when mothers were with fathers they tended to touch their male children more than their female children; this difference was not evident when the mother and child were alone. Still other research demonstrates the influence of the child on the parent subsystem. Rosenblatt (1974) found that the presence of one or more children reduced the adult–adult touching, talking, and smiling in selected public places such as the zoo, park, and shopping centers.

Another important aspect of social systems including the family is that they are characterized by steady states. The term *steady state* describes the process whereby a system maintains itself while always changing to some degree. A steady state is characterized by the interplay of flexibility and stability by which a system endeavors to maintain a viable relationship between its elements and its environment. Social systems are defined as goal-oriented and steady-state processes are directed toward goal achievement. However, as the system changes to adapt to its environment, the same general goal may be served by different patterns of behavior. For example, when the 3-year-old first-born child acquires a new brother, the structure of the family system is changed. However, the child's goal of learning to adapt to its environment (e.g., learning to read, ride a bike, etc.) remains the same even though its actual activities may alter. Research indicates that the child's functioning in its family system is described both by adaptation (steady state) and the development of new behavior patterns (flexibility) in the service of prior goals (stability). For example, Dunn and Kendrick (1979) found that first-born children's independent behavior increased upon the birth of a sibling. Although independent behavior occurred and was encouraged by the mother prior to the birth of the second child and was a developmental goal, the amount, kind, and opportunity for independent behavior changed as the family system changed to include a new member.

Social systems are also characterized by their purposeful quality. The family system is generally said to exist to perform certain functions or goal-oriented activities necessary to the survival of its members, the species, as well as to the perpetuation of the specific culture and society. Family functions are often enumerated as procreation and child rearing, suggesting that the family is the principal agent of these societal goals. Beyond this level of generality, there are numerous ways of describing and defining family functions(Lewis & Feiring, 1978; Parsons & Bales, 1955). In the study of the child's early social relationships, apart from restricting the nature of those relationships by focusing more or less exclusively on the mother, a careful analysis of the types of activities engaged in by family members has not been undertaken. If only caregiving functions are considered, then the mother as the most important (and only) element to be studied makes some sense. However, other functions exist as needs in the child's life, including, for example, play and teaching, which may involve members other than the mother.

In any analysis of the family, it is necessary to consider the range of functions. Although different family members may be characterized by particular social functions. Although different family members may be characterized by particular social functions, it is often the case that persons and functions are only partially related (Lewis & Feiring, 1978, 1979; Lewis & Weinraub, 1976; Lewis, Feiring, & Weinraub, 1981). Consequently, the identity of the family member does not necessarily define the type or range of its social functions. Whereas caregiving (a function) and mother (a person) have been considered to be highly related, recent work indicates that fathers are equally adequate in performing this caregiving function. Play, another function, appears to be engaged in more by siblings and fathers than by mothers (Ban & Lewis, 1974; Clarke-Stewart, 1978; Lamb, 1976, 1981).

As indicated previously, a family member may perform several functions within the context of the family system. Different family members may be characterized more by certain functions than by others. Thus, parents may do more caregiving and teaching, while children do more playing. The relative amount of interaction time spent in different functions would certainly be expected to influence the child's development. For example, a child in a family where teaching was the most frequent activity (regardless of to whom the teaching was being directed—child, sibling, or parent) would be expected to be different than a child in a family where caregiving was the most frequent activity. In addition, the relative amount of activity directed by the same individual to the child might influence the child's development. For example, a child whose mother engaged in more caregiving activity than play would be expected to be different from a child whose mother engaged in both equally.

There are almost no data on the distribution of persons and functions within the family nor on how this may affect the child's development. Edwards and Lewis (1979) looked directly at the person–function relationship by exploring how young children perceive the distribution of functions and persons. Persons were represented by dolls of infants, peers, older children, and parent-aged adults. Social functions were created for the child in the form of a story. In both studies to be discussed, the children, who varied in age from 3 to 5 years, were asked to choose which person they wanted to interact with for a specific social function. In all the studies, the functions were (1) being helped, (2) teaching about a toy, (3) sharing, and (4) play. For *help*, the adults were selected, while for someone to *play* with, children choose adults and infants last and peers and older children first. For *teaching* how to use a toy, older children were selected, while for *sharing* there was no differentiation among social objects. In a second study, photographs including the faces and upper torsos of infants, peers, older children, adults (parent-aged), and grandparents were used. The results indicated that older persons were chosen for *help*. The *teaching* function supported the results of the first study in that older peers rather than adults were chosen. For *play*, peers and older children were preferred, but there was again no difference in the social object for *share*. This constitutes a replication of the earlier findings. Interestingly, the data on grandparent-aged adults are most similar to those for parent-aged adults.

The Edwards and Lewis (1979) study also suggests that the persons and functions that describe a child's social system will be influenced by the situation in which the person performs the functions. An important aspect of a social system is the environment in which the system exists. Consequently the family system, its members, and the functions performed by its members may be different depending on the situation or environment in which the family is interacting.

In any study that focuses on multiple family members and their relationship within a context larger than a dyad, both situational and methodological constraints must be considered. The issue of situational constraints will be addressed first before turning to the problem of measurement.

Situational Determinants or Traits

In the study of interpersonal relations, the issue of situational determinants versus trait qualities has rarely been discussed. Unlike personality research, where the controversy of situational versus trait theories has received wide discussion (see Mischel, 1970, or Pervin & Lewis, 1978, for reviews), the study of interpersonal relations is dominated by the belief that parenting and the nature of a dyadic relationship can be characterized in a unitary fashion, much like a trait that is constant across any condition. Such a notion has wide appeal; for example, a dyad can be characterized as securely attached, a relationship may be described as reciprocal, or a mother and father can be said to be responsive to their baby. Such a tendency to describe relationships or interactions without regard to situation probably grows out of the personality-theory orientation. This orientation stresses traits that are enduring characteristics, that persist over multiple situations, and that reside within the organism rather than within situations or the interactions of people in situations. Another reason for the predominance of the trait notion stems from the main thrust of genetic epistemology, in which theory focuses on the emergence of similar structures in different contexts. Riegel (Riegel, 1976; Riegel & Meacham, 1978), in reflecting on this problem, saw that for most developmental theories, the major determinant of behavior, although immersed in an interaction between organism and environment, is the genetic unfolding of invariate sequences and structures; lacking was the situational or contextual concern in such theories. The focus on genetic factors favors a trait theory. Given this perspective, the extension of an individual trait-like notion to parent–child relations was easy.

While some progress has been made in increasing the level of complexity in the analysis of behavior (Gottman & Bakeman, 1979; Lamb, Suomi, & Stephenson, 1979; Lewis & Lee-Painter, 1974; Sackett, 1978), relatively less attention and almost no systematic effort have been directed toward the study of the context in which the behavior flow is emitted. This lack of interest and information was acceptable as long as the situations in which behavior was observed remained few (chiefly laboratory observation) and the behavior or relationship observed was assumed to be invariant in regard to situational constraints. In fact, such studies were thought to be aspects of the relationship, not aspects of the situation. Unfortunately, not enough work has been done to either defend or refute such a view, although several studies have demonstrated differences as a function of different situations. One of the best examples in terms of parent–child relationship research is in the area of attachment. Attachment relationships are experimentally determined in a singular situation—reunion after the mother leaves and then returns to her child. However, this situation and its accompanying behavior are not related to other situations of mother–child interaction—for example, situations of free play or departure and separation-(Weinraub & Lewis, 1977). In addition, Clarke-Stewart (1973) has shown differences in attachment behavior as a function of whether the Ainsworth and Wittig (1969) experimental procedure is conducted in the home or in a laboratory situation.

Mother–infant interaction patterns are also highly influenced by context or situation (Lewis & Freedle, 1973, 1977; Parke & O'Leary, 1975). For example, Lewis and Freedle (1973, 1977) found that the interactions between 3-month-old infants and their mothers were influenced by situation or context. When infants are on their mothers' laps, mothers and infants exchange vocalizations in a conversation-like fashion five times more often than when the infant and the mother are together but the infant is not on the mother's lap. It is fair to assume that situations not only affect the level of individual interaction patterns but also may be nonlinear, so that mother A may be more responsive in situation X than mother B, but mother B may be more responsive in situation Y than mother A. Unfortunately, answers to these types of issues are not yet available, but they have important implications for our study of relationships. For example, studies of attachment past the first 18 months or so of life are limited, since attachment has been restricted to a set of behaviors in a particular situation. Although attachment may be important past this time period, the study of the phenomenon awaits a conceptualization of an attachment that can be measured in contexts other than separation from or reunion with the mother.

The discussion of a situation when it does occur is often restricted to considering the differences between laboratory and field contexts (*field* for human infants usually referring to home, although doctor's office, playground, or even day care center have been considered). The laboratory versus field research controversy centers around the belief in the importance of obtaining ecological validity in observation of *natural* situations of the organism, where one can observe the *natural* behaviors of the subject. However, this belief ignores the basic assumption that behavior is influenced by context and that there is no one situation in which all behaviors can be observed. In a sense, the issue of laboratory versus field study is only a limited case of the broader question of the role of situation. The question is not which situation is *natural* or *real* but rather the nature of the situation. What is important in situational analysis is (1) the differences in behavior across situations and the possible cause and (2) the stability within a situation rather than the generalization across all situations—in general, a less than likely occurrence (Lewis, 1978).

The analysis of situations calls for the selection of situations that characterize the phenomenon under study. The ethologist's selection of situations meets this need by looking at situations in relation to responses. It matters little whether such situations are laboratory-or home based, real or fictitious. What must be of concern is the nature of the situation in relation to the phemomena under study.

Although it still needs to be demonstrated, it is difficult to imagine that any single situation would provide the opportunity to explore all aspects of a relationship. In our analysis of family systems and social network theory, we have stressed the role of functions (or needs) and the people that inhabit the child's world (Lewis, 1982). Such an analysis provides the framework for a situational consideration, since certain situations are more likely to be associated with some functions than others; for example, a bedtime story may be more likely to be associated with nurturance, whereas a play situation during the day may be more likely to be associated with teaching.

Situational considerations and family studies may interface around functions. Thus, one is probably more likely to observe certain family members interacting around certain functions more than others (Edwards & Lewis, 1979; Lewis & Feiring, 1981), and these functions may be more likely to occur in some situations than others. Thus, the selection of functions influences the observation of people and situations and the selection of situations affects the observation of functions and people who perform them.

In the child development research on families, members are often brought together in a single room, either laboratory or home, and the function of the exchange is left somewhat vague; for example, "We want to observe the child's play with you both present" (or "you present and your spouse absent" or the reverse). The situation is usually constructed as a play situation (there are many toys available); however, it may be that most parents perceive this as an educational rather than a play situation. The determinants of the parents' perception of a laboratory "free play" setting are many but may have to do in part with the parental belief—often fostered by psychologists, news media, and so on—that the parental function of education is the most important of all. In this example, the family—or part of it, since siblings are usually omitted—is brought together when they might not normally be together, the nature of the situation is left vague, and the functions to be carried out are left undefined. Because of these situational features of a laboratory observation, the nature of interactions between parents is unclear. A playroom situation may not constitute one in which parents or children perform functions that relate to daily or even less frequent family activities. Thus, for the family, there may be little precedent for family patterns of interaction as defined by the laboratory situation. Finally, from a systems point of view, many studies concentrate on each parent–child interaction, leaving parent–parent interactions out of their data analysis. The need to include these other non-child-focused exchanges in order to understand a particular child–family member interaction has been made clear by several investigators (Feiring, 1975; Lewis & Feiring, 1978, 1981; Lewis, Feiring, & Weinraub, 1981; Pedersen, Yarrow, Anderson, & Cain, 1979) although little empirical work on this problem has been done.

These considerations point to the importance, in studying family interaction, of choosing a situation in which (1) all members of the family are usually present during the situation, (2) interactions between all members is the common experience, (3) the situation has important function(s), and (4) the situation occurs with some frequency in the family's life (not a single or once-a-year phenomenon).

Interestingly, few situations meeting all these requirements are available for study. One such situation is the family dinner, and it is this situation that was chosen for study (Dreyer & Dreyer, 1973a,b). In general, (1) all the family members are usually present, although—as will be apparent—there are exceptions; (2) interaction between all members is the common experience; (3) the situation has the important function of eating, although—as we shall see—the function of information exchange is the most salient activity of the members; and (4) a family meal occurs with a very high frequency, usually daily.

Because the dinner meal represents a situation that merits observation for several reasons, as enumerated above, it is by its nature unusual; however, it remains to be determined whether results of its interactions can be generalized to other situations or contexts. Moreover, because a family dinner usually requires that all members sit facing each other and eat, certain functions are either precluded or should occur with varying frequencies. For example, one would expect, in general, greater amounts of caregiving and nurturance functions and less play functions at the dinner table. Individual family differences in the functions performed might reflect important socialization practices. Thus, for example, families that engage in more control or education functions and less play may be quite different in terms of values, beliefs, and goals than families that engage in more play than education. To our knowledge, no analysis of functions and their distribution in families has been undertaken. To anticipate one of the more interesting findings, we discovered that information exchange—rather than either control, caregiving, or nurturance functions—is predominant at the table. This has led us to conclude that one important function of the dinner meal for families is maintaining the familiy system through the exchange of information between members (elements of that system). This function of information exchange may be an example of a steady-state process whereby family members maintain continuity in their family relationships. Eating, though an important biological function, is only one of the functions being fulfilled by all family members sitting down to dinner together.

Measuring Family Interactions

Having settled on a situation (or situations) in which to study the family, the issue of measurement becomes of critical importance. The measurement of interaction (rather than relationship) has received consideration since earlier work on interaction (Lewis, 1972; Lewis & Freedle, 1973; Lewis & Goldberg, 1969; Lewis & Lee-Painter, 1974). Several new methods for measuring interaction have been suggested (see books edited by Cairns, 1979; Lamb, Suomi, & Stephenson, 1979; and Sackett, 1978, for a more complete review). In most cases, the methods refer to interactions with dyads, although some work has focused on families (Patterson, 1979; Patterson & Moore, 1979). Even in the family research, empirical results usually focus on frequency of occurrence of selected behaviors for each parent and child and on these frequencies compared or related in some manner, as in comparing behavior frequencies when the other parent is or is not present. Although some theoretical attempt has been made to apply sequential analysis to family data, the increase in number of participants when one is examining a family of three members or more so complicates the data analysis that such techniques do not seem easy to use (Gottman & Bakeman, 1979). The analysis of direct interactions is further complicated by what we have called *indirect effects* (Lewis & Feiring, 1981; Lewis, Feiring, & Weinraub, 1981). Recently, Lewis and Feiring (1981) have suggested ways in which both direct and indirect effects interact in the ongoing interactions of members of any group greater than two—in particular, the relationship within a family or between mother, stranger, and child.

Without question, research on families and on interactions remains limited by the data recording and analysis techniques available. The unit of measurement remains open to consideration and, as suggested by Cairns (1979), should be determined by the theoretical position governing the research. What has emerged after a decade of intense research effort is that (1) no scoring method can capture all occurring events and (2) no analytical technique(s) is available to capture all aspects of interactions. Whether one uses molar scaling or molecular sequential analysis, the choice of data collection and analytic techniques must be governed by the problem studied. Perhaps this is no different than any observation by any observer in which what and how to observe is selected in part by the hypothesis governing the observation. The lesson to be learned is simple: there is too much behavior to be observed and all of it cannot be captured by any method. It is evident that the method of observation and analysis will affect what is found (Lewis, 1980). This assertion is made obvious from the findings of twentieth-century quantum mechanics. For example, the particle-like and wave-like behavior of light are both supported by observations of light, yet these two views of the property of light are not compatible. The conclusion of quantum mechanics is that these properties of light are only properties we assign it; in 1934 Neils Bohr wrote, "an independent reality in the ordinary physical sense can be ascribed neither to the phenomena nor to the agencies of observation," *agencies of observation* referring to instruments of measurement (Zukav, 1979, p. 335).

Using our systems approach as a guide, it would seem necessary at least to specify interactions in the family subsystem (e.g., parent–child, parent–

parent, parent–sibling, and child–sibling) at the dyad level as well as at levels that go beyond direct person–person interactions (indirect effects) that may characterize the family as a group. As part of our interest in family systems we have tried to conceptualize a measurement system that might afford an opportunity to capture several levels of family functioning at the same time. The procedure that we have employed details examining all possible dyadic interactions and looking at the distribution of these interactions, ranking them in order between most and least interactive. Such an analysis, though at a dyadic level, does not attempt to deal with the individual value for any dyad but rather looks at the distribution of these dyadic interactions. Moreover, by observing variables that might affect the distribution of these dyads, we can observe the dynamic flow or change in family interactions. Whereas in dyadic interactions each member is the unit of analysis, in family interactions each of the dyads becomes the unit of analysis. Admittedly such an analytic technique, while representing some aspects of a family system, does not capture the flow of interaction. It is apparent that no single measurement system can capture all the features of family interactions. The procedure used here limits itself to a static structural analysis of family life; that is, changes in distribution of dyadic interaction were not examined as a function of time during the meal. However, our analyses do attempt to go beyond a unidirectional dyadic description of parent–child interaction to a broader description of the family given a particular set of demographic characteristics.

Family Characteristics and Observational Procedures

The dinner-time interaction of 33 families was examined in our study. All the families were nuclear in structure, consisting of mother, father, and child(ren). Each family contained a 3-year-old target child who was the focus of the study. All the families had previously participated in a longitudinal study (Lewis, 1980) in which the social and cognitive characteristics of children at 3, 12, and 24 months of age were examined.

Twenty-two families were from the upper middle socioeconomic group and 11 were from the middle socioeconomic group (as determined by both parents' education and occupation, using a modified Hollingshead category system; Feiring & Lewis, 1982). The families were distributed by family size: family size 3, $n = 5$; family size 4, $n = 14$; family size 5, $n = 9$; family size 6, $n = 5$. Thirty-three 3-year-old target children were studied. Of these, 10 were first borns, 11 were second borns, 9 were third borns, and 3 were fourth borns. There were 16 female target children and 17 males.

Before the child's third birthday, the parents were contacted by phone and asked to participate in a study of families at dinner. Parents were told that we wished to gather information about the behavior of the target child (whom we had observed previously at 3 months at home and at 12 and 24 months in the laboratory) in its family environment. Permission was given by the majority of families contacted to videotape a mealtime interaction during which all nuclear family members were present. The majority of families indicated that all family members did not always eat dinner together but that a meal with all members took place at least twice a week. If permission for making a videotape of a mealtime was obtained from the parents, a convenient date for filming was arranged within a 2-week period. Upon entering the home, the camera crew set up the video equipment so that all family members were in view of the camera, turned on the equipment, and then left the home. The videotapes ran for an hour or until the family finished dinner and turned it off. Families were told that we were interested in recording the kinds of things they did at mealtime and were asked to try as much as possible to go about their "normal" business, as if the camera were not present. After the film crew returned, many families showed interest in watching themselves on the video recorder.

In capturing a segment of family interaction, we chose to use videotape rather than trained observers for several reasons. First and perhaps most important, we wished to obtain the most complete sample of ongoing behavior of the family members. In our effort to conduct a study of the family at mealtime, we used videotape because it is a technique that does not impose a predetermined observation system on the recording of the data (Willems, 1969). Another advantage in using videotape is that it makes it easy to pick up interaction between all family members. The number of observers necessary to code all interactions between three to six family members would have been equally if not more intrusive than the presence of a video camera. Of course, the disadvantages of videotape is that the family members knew the were being taped and thus may have altered their behavior. This problem would have existed as well if we had used observers. However, since the camera was not run by a person, its presence may have been more readily forgotten than an observer's would have been. Interviews with the families following the taping sessions indicated that they became less aware of the camera as the meal progressed; nevertheless, the adults and older siblings were more obviously aware that they were being filmed. For example, one father became quite angry when his son took a long time eating and was fooling around with his food. The father raised his voice and said, "Stop messing with your food!" and then after a pause during which it appeared he recalled the camera, he began speaking again, "And the reasons why you should not, etc.. . ." Younger children perhaps were somewhat less affected by the presence of the camera. For example, one 3-year-old target child announced in the middle of the meal,

"Daddy, I have to go make." The mother said, "I knew this would happen" while the father was obliged to take his son to the bathroom.

Once the family interaction had been recorded, the tapes were scored for the duration of time each family member spent talking to every other family member during the meal and when all family members were present. Thus, we obtained the amount of time each family member spoke to and received vocal input from every other family member. For family sizes larger than 3, this required watching the videotape at least twice. At first, the coders found it difficult to watch the families larger than size 4 because of the great amount of speaker overlap and general chaos. However, after training on pilot tapes, coders became quite proficient at coding the verbal behavior of family members. Interrater reliability on 10 families (2 families from each family size 3 and 4, and 3 families from family size 5 and 6) was calculated by correlating the observations of two independent raters for each speaker-to-recipient unit for a 10-minute portion of family interaction. Interrater reliabilities were adequate and often quite high, ranging from .67 to .99 with a mean of .88.

Because the families did not all spend the same amount of time in mealtime interaction, it was necessary to use proportion scores in analyzing the data. (Dreyer & Dreyer, 1973a,b, in their analysis of family interaction, also found the use of proportion scores necessary for the same reason.) Our unit of analysis was thus the total duration of time a family member spoke to each family member divided by the total amount of time spent in talk by all family members. Our data, therefore, consist of the proportion of time one family member spent talking to another family member relative to the total amount of time spent in conversation by all family members. Because a good deal of time was spent not talking but eating, we decided to use as our denominator the total time coded in order to enable us to consider larger proportions.

Family Verbal Interactions

All Families

The first level of analysis is to look at all possible dyadic exchanges over all families. Recall that the values to be used represent the proportion of time a dyad spoke divided by the total time each family was engaged in talking. In addition, when considering the data for all families together, it must be remembered that our families are of different sizes; thus, the target child may have older siblings, younger siblings, or both older and younger. In the first analysis to be considered, all data are combined in order to address the general question of who does the most talking and to whom the most conversation is addressed at the dinner table. In this analysis, all possible family members are included. Given that the target child is 3 years old, it was possible to have more than one younger sibling (YS), but no target child did. Either none, one, two, or three older siblings were possible; however, in the first analysis we will consider the average of all older siblings. For the first analysis of all families, the family configuration will consist of five possible role identities: mother (M), father (F), target child (TC), older sibling(s) (OS), and youngest sibling (YS).

Table 2 presents the duration of vocalization as a proportion of the

Table 2. Percentage of Vocalization and Rank Order of the Possible Dyads

Dyad	Percentage of time	Rank
Unidirectional		
M → F	14.04	1
M → T	13.36	2
F → T	9.09	4
F → M	9.76	3
T → F	4.84	12
T → M	8.57	5
M → YS	5.33	8
F → YS	5.12	11
T → YS	0.13	20
YS → M	3.59	13
YS → F	2.20	14
YS → T	0.30	19
M → OS	5.77	7
F → OS	5.29	9
T → OS	0.55	18
OS → T	1.06	15
OS → M	8.11	6
OS → F	5.19	10
OS → YS	0.58	17
YS → OS	0.86	16
Reciprocal		
M ↔ F	23.80	1
M ↔ T	21.93	2
M ↔ OS	13.98	4
M ↔ YS	8.92	6
F ↔ T	13.92	3
F ↔ YS	7.33	7
F ↔ OS	10.48	5
T ↔ OS	1.61	8
T ↔ YS	0.43	10
OS ↔ YS	1.44	9

total family vocalization duration as well as the rank order of these proportions. Across all families, the greatest dyadic interaction is (M → F) followed by (M → TC), (F → M), (F → TC), (T → M), (OS → M), (M → OS), (M → YS), and so on. Several points pertaining to these data are of interest. First, while (M → F) is ranked first, (F → M) is third, indicating that mothers talk more to fathers than fathers to mothers (sign test $p < .001$). Second, the mean rank for mothers talking to children (TC, OS, YS) is 5.3 while for fathers it was 8.0 indicating that mothers engage their children in conversation more than do fathers; this finding holds true for each comparison individually (i.e., M or F to TC, OS, or YS). Children vocalized to mothers more than to fathers ($\overline{X}$ rank 12.0 vs. 8.0). The least talking was between siblings—in particular, between YS and TC—and indicates that in general the parents (particularly the mother) are the focus of the verbal interaction. Of all the children, the TC was spoken to most ($\overline{X} = 3.0$) followed by the OS ($\overline{X} = 8.0$) and YS ($\overline{X} = 9.0$).

The preceding analysis was concerned with the unidirectional nature of the dyads. Table 2 also presents the duration and rank order data by reciprocal dyad; by reciprocal dyad we simply mean to indicate the total amount of interaction engaged in by two individuals regardless of which individual is the speaker or recipient of the interaction. Here we see that for all families the (M ↔ F) vocalization is the highest, followed by parent–child subsystems (i.e., M ↔ TC and F ↔ TC). The lowest level of interaction was between the two youngest members (TC and YS), that is, between 3-year-olds and their younger siblings. In fact, the data indicate that except for the parent interaction with the target child, all other dyadic vocal interactions are age-ordered. Parent–child vocalization is higher for OS than YS; within the siblings, the order of vocalization follows an age of dyad order: (OS ↔ TC) is highest while (TC ↔ YS) is lowest. That the target child received a mean rank of 3.0 in terms of being spoken to and therefore elevated the verbal exchange level of the parent–target child subsystems may be due to two factors: (1) the only-child status of some first-born target children and (2) focus of interest on the target child as a consequence of our research project.

In this sample of 33 families, there were 5 families who had only children. Because of this artifact, these children, who received a great amount of parental attention, elevated the rank order of all target children. In addition, the effect of continued study of all target children over a 3-year period cannot be overlooked. Our interest in one particular child within the family must certainly affect the focus of the parents' attention and may have increased the level of conversation addressed by parents to the target child. Observing the rank of child to parent-directed dyads—that is (TC → parent), (OS → parent), and (YS → parent)—we find $\overline{X}$ ranks of 8.5,

8.0, and 13.5 respectively. Examining the parent-to-child directed dyads—
that is (parent → TC,), (parent → OS), and (parent → YS)—we note the
ranks of 3.0, 8.0, and 9.0 respectively. The lack of correspondent match for
the rank order of child-to-parent and parent-to-child interaction suggests
that the parents are focusing more attention on the target child than called
for by the child's own vocalization level to the parent. This does not appear
to be the case for the siblings' behavior toward the target child. That is, the
rank order of TC to sibling is similar to the rank order of sibling to TC.
This possible bias in observational research of focusing parental attention
on the child to be studied is one of the many unavoidable problems that
occurs as a function of the study of a phenomenon. Exactly how our 3-year
research project affects the family life is not clear. Perhaps the parents were
more interactive with the target child only when we observed them,
although it may be that having any child in a prolonged study affects the
parent–child interaction even outside the laboratory or observational
period in the field.

Family Size

As we have suggested, the ranking of the set of dyadic interactions that
are generated when considering all two-member possibilities can be used to
characterize family interaction: as such, these may be shown to be affected
by both family size and family configuration. Family configurations vary
within same-size families, since target children can have different ordinal
positions. For example, in a family with four people, there can be a mother,
father, older sibling, and target child or a younger sibling and a target
child. We will consider first family size independent of configuration and
then return to configuration issues as they interact with size.

As was the case with the analysis with all families (as presented in
Table 2), it is possible to generate ranking of each dyad within a family size.
Table 3 presents all possible dyadic interactions, both unidirectional and
reciprocal dyads as well as the rank order for families of different size. We
have averaged all sibling scores to simplify the analysis and will deal with
the issue of different-aged siblings below. Observation of the data reveal
several findings of note. First, we found for all interactions an absolute
decrease in the amount of time per interaction as family size increases.
Given that our duration values are proportions of the time of total family
conversation, these results suggest that although there are more people
around the table, the amount of conversation per total family (the
denominator of our proportion) does not increase. We conclude this from
our observation of the tapes, which indicates that dinnertime itself does not

Table 3. Percentage of Vocalizations and Rank Order by Family Size[a]

| | Family size | | | | | | | |
| | 3 | | 4 | | 5 | | 6 | |
Dyad	Percentage duration	Rank	Percentage duration	Rank	Percentage duration	Rank	Percentage duration	Rank
Unidirectional								
M → T	26.84	1	15.17	1	7.36	3	5.58	2
M → F	20.89	2	14.26	2	10.59	1	12.81	1
F → T	16.09	3	9.34	5	7.26	4	4.70	4
F → M	14.81	4	10.91	3	7.76	2	5.08	3
T → M	14.32	5	9.66	4	6.91	5	2.73	5
T → F	7.05	6	5.66	10	3.53	8	2.67	6
M → S	—	—	8.27	8	2.53	10	1.58	8
F → S	—	—	9.08	6	3.02	9	0.98	10
T → S	—	—	0.88	12	0.34	12	0.18	12
S → M	—	—	9.03	7	4.26	6	2.36	7
S → F	—	—	5.92	9	4.32	7	1.33	9
S → T	—	—	1.83	11	0.52	11	0.28	11
Reciprocal								
M ↔ F	35.70	2	25.17	1	18.35	1	17.89	1
M ↔ T	41.16	1	24.83	2	14.27	2	8.31	2
F ↔ T	23.14	3	15.00	4.5	10.79	3	7.37	3
M ↔ S	—	—	17.30	3	6.79	5	3.94	4
F ↔ S	—	—	15.00	4.5	7.34	4	2.31	5
T ↔ S	—	—	2.71	6	0.86	6	0.46	6

[a]In those cases where there is more than one sibling, we have obtained an average sibling score. Also note that in family size 3 siblings are not present and therefore no interaction can take place between siblings and mother, father, or target child; this fact is indicated by slashes in the column for family size 3.

increase as a function of family size. This is interesting in light of the fact that one might have suspected that more people would talk more and take more time to eat. The duration and amount of conversation at dinner time does not increase with family size; therefore the amount of talking at the table for any dyad decreases. Thus, one result of increased family size is a decrease in conversation time available per dyad. This effect of size has been reported in group-dynamic research (Thomas & Fink, 1963; Willems, 1964) as well as research on the family interaction (Clarke-Stewart, 1978; Lamb, 1977; Pedersen *et al.*, 1979) in the lab and at home. The observed decrease in the quantity of dyad conversation may be related to verbal stimulation level in the parent–child subsystem and may in part be responsible for the finding of an IQ decrease with increasing family size (Feiring & Lewis, 1978; Zajonc & Markus, 1975).

Within the general trend of decreasing amounts of conversation time per dyad, we can observe family structural changes by considering the change in the rank-order structure independent of amount. The parent interaction (M → F) and (F → M) is of some interest. We expected from initial observation of the tapes that mother–father interaction would increase as a function of the other interactions as family size increases. By family size, the average rank for the (M → F) and (F → M) dyads was 3.0, 2.5, 1.5, and 2.0 for family sizes 3, 4, 5, and 6 respectively. In terms of proportional duration values, this finding is also apparent, as the mother–father reciprocal interaction accounts for approximately 33%, 25%, 28%, and 38% of all the reciprocal interactions by family sizes 3, 4, 5, and 6 respectively. As number of children increases, the children's interactions may allow parents more time to interact together (at least for family sizes 4, 5, and 6). This phenomenon may be reflected in the fact that parents often report they find that having more than one child gives them an opportunity to pay more attention to each other, since their children may spend time engaging each other and not require constant parental input. In fact, provision of playmates for their children is often a reason parents give for having more than one child (Feiring & Lewis, 1980).

The data for each family size show that mothers engage fathers more than fathers engage mothers. In fact, in the larger families it is primarily the mother who maintains the contact between parents. Moreover, also there are differences not only in parent level of exchange but also in what they say, a point to be taken up shortly. The biasing effect of attention to the target child is visible for all family sizes. There appears to be some decrease in focus on the target child as family size increases; $\overline{X}$ ranks for (M → TC) and (F → TC) by family sizes of 3, 4, 5, and 6 are 2.0, 3.0, 3.5, and 3.0 respectively. With six people around the table, it is more difficult to focus on any single child, even the one under study.

The target child–father subsystem undergoes some changes as a function of family size. As size increases, both the $(TC \rightarrow F)$ and the $(F \rightarrow TC)$ ranks increase, indicating a decrease in interaction; $\overline{X} = 4.5, 7.5,$ 6.0, and 5.0 for family sizes 3, 4, 5, and 6 respectively. In another analysis (which will not be presented in further detail here), we found that fathers' interaction, unlike the mothers', was much influenced by the sex of the target child, with fathers of boys considerably more interactive than fathers of girls (15% more). This father–sex-of-child interaction has been reported in the infancy data (Lewis, 1980; Lewis & Weinraub, 1979) and can also be observed with older children. Although, fathers appear to decrease their interaction with the target child, they seem to increase their interaction with the children other than the target. Fathers increased their interaction toward older rather than younger children, although this finding is not apparent when the data across siblings are collapsed. In our next analysis, this becomes evident.

Sibling interaction remains the lowest set of interaction and suggests that even though parents interact more with siblings as family size increases (probably due to the obvious fact that more children other than the target are present in larger families), there is not an appreciable increase in parent-to-child input as family size increases. However, sibling interaction is affected by age of siblings and this variable must be considered in order to understand the family interaction more fully.

Age of Sibling

The age of the sibling should have an effect not only on the target child but on the parents as well. There is now considerable research on first- and second-born differences in family interaction, and much of this work is on infants. Within this same sample, Lewis and Kreitzberg (1979) reported that mothers talk to, smile at, and handle first borns more than second borns when the children are 3 months old. Others also have found that first borns in general receive more parental attention than later borns (Terhune, 1974). In order to explore the relationship between family interaction and the nature of child–sibling structure, families with two children were looked at separately. Specifically, family size 4 with a first-born target child and younger sibling and family size 4 with a second-born target child and older sibling were examined. Table 4 presents the data for the two types of sibling structure for family size 4.

Two points are of immediate interest here. Fathers interact more with the target child if it is the older of two than if it is the younger (first born, rank = 6.0; second born, rank = 7.0; Mann-Whitney U-test, $p < .05$). This finding of first borns receiving more parental attention than second borns of family size 4 also applies to mothers. First borns get more attention than

Table 4. Family Size 4 Target Children with Younger and Older Sibling

Dyad	TC, 1st born; Younger sibling $n = 5$		TC, 2nd born; Older sibling $n = 9$	
	Percentage duration	Rank	Percentage duration	Rank
Unidirectional				
M → T	22.82	1	10.92	3
M → F	11.96	3	15.53	1
F → T	11.24	4	8.28	6
F → M	9.27	5	11.83	2
T → M	12.59	2	8.03	8
T → F	5.10	9	5.97	10
M → S	8.74	6	8.00	7
F → S	8.48	7	9.42	5
T → S	0.23	11	1.24	12
S → M	5.85	8	10.79	4
S → F	3.50	10	7.26	9
S → T	0.20	12	2.74	11
Reciprocal				
M ↔ T	35.41	1	18.95	2
M ↔ F	21.23	2	27.36	1
F ↔ T	16.34	3	14.25	5
S ↔ M	14.59	4	18.79	3
S ↔ F	11.99	5	16.68	4
S ↔ T	0.43	6	3.98	6

second borns, a finding consistent with these parents' early behavior (Lewis & Kreitzberg, 1979) and with much of the literature.

When the target child is younger (second born), there is more time spent in interaction between siblings than when the target child is older (first born). Although the rank orders vis-a-vis the other dyads does not reflect this finding, the duration differences are 10 times greater (Mann-Whitney U-test, $p < .05$).

Mothers and fathers (M → F, F → M) both talk more to each other when the target child is second born than when the target child is first born ($\overline{X}$ rank 1.5 versus 4.0 for second borns and first borns respectively). We believe this is due to the fact that when the target child is younger there are two children age 3 and above; however, when the target child is older, there are two children age 3 and under. The older the children, the more likely they are to talk to each other (3.98 [TC ↔ OS] vs. 0.43 [TC ↔ YS]) and therefore the more time the parents have to spend talking together.

These results demonstrate the interrelatedness of family size, birth order, and age of children and suggest that these demographic variables must be considered in order to understand the family interaction patterns. In this regard, it should be noted that SES differences in (M ⟷ F) interaction rank orders have been observed in this sample; higher-SES dyads spend more time interacting than low-SES (M ⟷ F) dyads. Certainly other variables related to the personality of the family members—their cognitive capacity, values, and goals—all affect the dinnertable interaction. The method of ranking the dyads, together with consideration of the duration data, should be sensitive to these kinds of effects. Although an exploration of the goals and values of the families is beyond the scope of this paper, the types of conversations or the functions families engage in at the table are of interest here. Also, functions by family sizes are considered in order to understand the effects of this variable on family interaction.

Family Functions

As we indicated previously, any examination of the family as a social system should include the study of what kinds of functions characterize the family interaction as well as which family members perform these functions. In a preliminary analysis of 15 families, we have begun to explore issues related to person-by-function patterns in the family as they relate to the functions of information seeking (IS), nurturance (N), and caregiving (C). See Table 5. These three functions were chosen to be looked at first, after observation of the videotapes indicated that they occurred with reliable frequency. The functions yet to be looked at are play, control, and teaching; their absence in the present analysis limits any conclusion. The data presented in Table 5 are the mean frequency of social-function interactions over 15 minutes of coded mealtime situation for each family member toward the other. The data indicate that both mothers and fathers direct a similar amount of information seeking, nurturance, and caregiving to the child (no significant differences). Given Parsons' and Bales' (1955) distinction of instrumental and expressive role differences, we were surprised that there were no sex differences in parents' behavior to their children. Information seeking appears to be the most frequently observed function, followed by nurturance and caregiving (IS versus N and C, Sign test, $p < .05$). It is surprising to find that the function of information seeking was performed more than caregiving. Although a great deal of time during the meal situation was spent in silent eating, the function of caregiving, which we defined in terms of ministering to another's physical needs—such as feeding another person or serving their food—was not a frequent occurrence. Given the fact that most family members could feed themselves and that the time necessary to serve and pass food is minimal,

Table 5. Family Interactions by Function for Directed Dyads for Mean
Frequency of Interaction over 15 Minutes of Coded Interaction $(n = 15)$[a]

	Information seeking[b]	Nurturance[c]	Caregiving[d]
M → TC	9.6	4.1	4.3
F → TC	9.5	3.3	3.3
TC → M	3.5	2.0	0.40
TC → F	1.9	2.0	0.33
M → F	3.2	3.9	1.6
F → M	4.7	2.7	0.53

[a] The data and this table also appear in "The Father as a Member of the Child's Social Network" by M. Lewis, C. Feiring, and M. Weinraub. In M. Lamb (Ed.), *The Role of the Father in Child Development* (2nd ed.). New York: Wiley, 1981.
[b] *Information Seeking* is defined as any type of question asking and includes "requests for information" (in which information previously unavailable is solicited) as well as "test questions" (in which the answer is already known) and "directive questions" (in which a behavior is requested).
[c] *Nurturance* is defined as any expression of warmth, whether verbal (such as praise) or nonverbal (such as smiles, kisses, and hugs).
[d] *Caregiving* is defined as taking care of the physical needs of another, such as offering and serving food, feeding food, cleaning, anc assistance with toileting.

caregiving does not take up much family mealtime. Consequently, family interaction during the meal was characterized by finding out about what had happened to the family members during the day, that is, information seeking and then in eating. Fathers and mothers sought more information from the child than from each other, and although fathers sought more information from the mothers than mothers from fathers, this difference is not reliable. Children sought more information from their mothers than from their fathers (Mann-Whitney U-test; $p < .10$). Children spent more time with their mothers in information seeking than in the functions of caregiving or nurturance (Mann-Whitney U-test; $p < 0.5$), although there is no difference between N and IS for fathers. Observation of vocal content as viewed from the tape suggests that fathers tend to ask mothers and children about how they have spent their day. Mothers inquire about the fathers' day away from home but appear to spend more time asking the children questions in order to get the children to tell their fathers about their daily activities. For example, mothers would typically ask rhetorical questions of the child, such as, "Alice, who did you play with today?" or "Steve, where did we go after lunch?" in order to get the children to inform their fathers as well as converse with them. Similarly, fathers asked the children what they did and where they went, often following the mothers' lead. Thus, the data suggest that the mother's role at mealtime is one of maintaining a connection between the father and the children and herself through the exchange of information with each family member concerning activities that take place when they are not together. The father seeks information from the mother and children while the mother is interested in facilitating information exchange between the father and the family. Although the parents' information seeking may have as a primary focus the purpose of maintaining family relationships, the children's question asking to parents and especially to the mothers may be of a different nature. Examination of the content of the children's information seeking behavior suggests that the children ask their mothers for information concerning future activities (i.e., "When can we go to the zoo?") or for information concerning social interaction rules at the table (e.g., "May I leave the table?"). In general, given the limited number of functions thus far studied, information seeking characterizes the family mealtime interaction of these 15 families; as such, it may be a function that operates to maintain the family as a viable social system by informing all members of each member's current status.

Family Functions by Family Size

We have preliminary data on functions by family size for at least family sizes 3, 4, and 5. These data are presented in Table 6 and are related to our discussion of family interactions measured by the duration of conversation rather than function. For most functions, at least those studied, increase in family size leads to a decrease in the occurrence of that function. As we shall see, this is more true for some functions than for others.

For both (M → F) and (F → M) interactions, information seeking

Table 6. Family Interactions by Function for Directed Dyads by Family Size[a]

	Family size								
	3 (n = 5)			4 (n = 5)			5 (n = 5)		
Dyads	IS[b]	N[c]	C[d]	IS	N	C	IS	N	C
M → TC	14.6	7.4	4.4	9.4	2.6	4.8	4.8	2.2	3.8
F → TC	12.8	5.6	2.2	7.0	2.4	2.4	8.6	2.0	5.4
TC → M	6.0	3.2	0.6	4.6	1.4	0.4	1.8	2.0	0.2
TC → F	4.2	1.2	0.0	0.4	1.0	0.0	1.2	3.8	1.0
M → F	3.2	5.0	1.6	3.0	4.4	1.2	3.4	2.4	2.0
F → M	4.0	4.2	0.6	5.6	2.6	0.2	4.4	1.2	0.8

[a]The data represented are mean number of interactions over 15 minutes of dinner time.
[b]IS = Information Seeking.
[c]N = Nurturance.
[d]C = Caregiving.

remains relatively constant over changes in family size. Caregiving, always a low occurrence, also remains constant. In contrast, nurturance, the expression of warmth and affection, is influenced by family size. Nurturance decreases with increasing family size for both parents, so that there is a 50% drop in its expression from family sizes 3 to 5 (Mann-Whitney U-test, $p < .05$). This finding is consistent with a drop in marital satisfaction with increase in family size at this stage of the family life cycle (Rollins & Galligan, 1978).

Parents' interaction with the target child is also affected by family size, with information seeking and nurturant behavior showing marked declines as family increases (Mann-Whitney U-test, $p < .05$ for family sizes 3 through 5 for both functions). With increased family size, both mother and father have less time to ask questions and to be nurturant toward any one child, most probably because they have other children who also want and need their attention. However, the decline in parental involvement is not uniform across all functions, since the parental caregiving function remains consistent across increasing family size. This suggests that as there are more children to care for, caregiving is maintained at the expense of the other functions of nurturance and information-seeking.

The increasing role of the father at the dinner table as related to an increase in family size is indicated by a more than 50% increase in father's caregiving function from family sizes 3 to 5, while no such increase occurs for mothers. In a single-child family, it is the mother rather than the father who engages in the most caregiving (twice as much); however, at least with the target child, the father is engaged in 70% more caregiving in a family with three children (size 5). The maintenance of caregiving and the decline of the information-seeking and nurturant behaviors, at least at the dinner table, suggests that family size has important effects on the way parents interact with their children. Although we have no data to support our belief, it may be the case that increase in family size has similar consequences across any number of situations other than dinner.

The target child's behavior toward its parents also shows the effect of family size. With increasing family size, there is a marked decline in information seeking, with a drop of 50% in IS from target child to both parents. The target child's caregiving activity toward the parents was too low to consider. The target child's nurturant behavior, rather than showing a decline with family size, shows the same patterns as does parental caregiving behavior; the target child's nurturant behavior remains constant over family size toward mothers and actually increases toward fathers (Mann-Whitney U-test $p < .05$, family sizes 3 to 5). The differences between parents as related to family size also supports the suggestion that the father's role in the family increases as family size increases. In family size 3, the target child directs considerably more nurturance to the mother than toward the father; but for family size 5, the father receives more than the mother.

The results concerning function and family size support and would appear to extend the findings from the vocalization duration data; taken together, our data suggest the pervasive impact of family size (number of children) on the characteristic nature of family systems. The increased role of the father, necessitated by the large number of children requiring care and nurturance, points toward the operation of steady states in the family system—states in which interactions and roles may become modified by the tasks of the system as a whole. As opposed to a view of the family as a system with set roles, functions, and rules, the view of a family as a changing and flexible system needs to remain central when we study interactions between family members.

Summary

Although much progress has been made in both the theory and measurement of dyadic relations, little work or theory has been directed to the study of relations containing more than two members (Bronfenbrenner, 1977; Feiring & Lewis, 1978; Lewis, Feiring, & Weinraub, 1981; Parke et al., 1979). The study of families necessitates the consideration not only of comparisons of various dyads but also a concern for a systems approach. Moreover, the study of families need not be restricted to two parents and a single child, since families are made up of multiple members and the defining characteristics of families, although changing, usually comprise important adult persons and children. Research on the influence or even the presence of these others on socialization is lacking, although our network data indicate that 3-year-old children have frequent and prolonged contact with adults other than parents as well as with children other than siblings.

By looking at family size, we have required our study of families at dinner to consider multiple children and have observed how children play a role in the family dynamic by orienting the goals and behavior at the dinner table as well as by affecting the specific level and type of interaction at the dyad level. Traditional role structures were shown to be affected by system-maintenance goals. Specifically, the increased involvement of the father in caregiving was noted as more children to feed required more adult assistance. The degree of flexibility of individuals in social systems must be one of the major considerations in any systems research on the family. Role definitions should become flexible as a function of the demands of the systems, as suggested even by our limited analysis of mealtime interaction. The effects on the parents of multiple children and their relationship also illustrate that interactions are almost never unidirectional and that, especially in multiple member systems, there are always reciprocal effects on each member regardless of the degree of developmental maturity, status, or role of the family member.

Finally, even in light of the present analysis, we still feel that measurement of any system greater than the dyadic one remains elusive. Multiple ways of measuring system effects are needed before we shall be able to sort out which ones are particularly useful for the issues concerning families that we wish to explore. Certainly there are no immediately obvious answers; if the history of interaction research on dyads is of any predictive value, it will be many years before suitable methods evolve. Tolerance is called for in the development of measures, although one must recognize that measurement procedures are almost always tied to theories (whether these theories are explicit or not) and to specific questions being proposed. The system of measurement we have suggested here, either in the measurement of duration of conversation or the measurement of function, at the very least results in similar findings and encourages further exploration as a way of characterizing family systems.

ACKNOWLEDGMENTS

The assistance of M. Berger, E. Hay, J. Jaskir, P. Ritter, and N. Sherman in coding and analyzing the data is gratefully acknowledged, as is the patience of A. Lamendola in typing the manuscript.

References

Ainsworth, M. D. S., & Wittig, B. A. Attachment and exploratory behavior of one-year-olds in a strange situation. In B. M. Foss (Ed.), *Determinants of infant behavior* (Vol. 4). London: Methuen, 1969.

Ban, P., & Lewis, M. Mothers and fathers, girls and boys: Attachment behavior in the one-year-old. *Merrill-Palmer Quarterly*, 1974, *20*(3), 195–204.

Bowen, M. Family therapy and family group therapy. In H. I. Kaplan & B. J. Sadock (Eds.), *Group treatment of mental illness*. New York: Dutton, 1972.

Bronfenbrenner, U. Toward an experimental ecology of human development. *American Psychologist*, 1977, *32*, 513–531.

Cairns, R. B. (Ed.). *The analysis of social interactions: Methods, issues, and illustrations*. Hillsdale, N.J. Lawrence Erlbaum, 1979.

Cicerelli, V. G. Effects of mother and older sibling on the problem solving behavior of the younger child. *Developmental Psychology*, 1975, 11, 749–756.

Clarke-Stewart, A. Interactions between mothers and their young children: Characteristics and consequences. *Monographs of the Society for Research in Child Development*, 1973, *38* (Serial No. 153).

Clarke-Stewart, A. Recasting the lone stranger. In J. Glick & A. Clarke-Stewart (Eds.), *Studies in social and cognitive development: The development of social understanding* (Vol. 1). New York: Gardner Press, 1978.

Dreyer, A. S., & Dreyer, C. A. *Family interaction and cognitive style: Power around the dinner table*. Paper presented at the meeting of the Society for Research in Child Development, Philadelphia, March 1973. (a)

Dreyer, C. A., & Dreyer, A. S. Family dinner time as a unique behavior habitat. *Family Press*, 1973, *12*, 291–301. (b)

Dunn, J., & Kendrick, C. Interaction between young siblings in the context of family relationships. In M. Lewis & L. Rosenblum (Eds.), *The child and its family: The genesis of behavior* (Vol. 2). New York: Plenum Press, 1979.

Dunn, J.,& Kendrick, C. The arrival of a sibling: Changes in interaction between mother and first-born child. *Journal of Child Psychology and Psychiatry*, 1980, *21*, 119–132.

Dunn, J., Wooding, C., & Hermann, J. Mothers' speech to young children: Variation in context. *Developmental Medicine and Child Neurology*, 1977, *19*, 629–638.

Edwards, C. P., & Lewis M. Young children's concepts of social relations: Social functions and social objects. In M. Lewis & L. Rosenblum (Eds.), *The child and its family: The genesis of behavior* (Vol. 2). New York: Plenum Press, 1979.

Feiring, C. *The influence of the child and secondary parent on maternal behavior: Toward a social systems view of early infant–mother attachment*. Unpublished doctoral dissertation, University of Pittsburgh, 1975.

Feiring, C., & Lewis, M. The child as a member of the family system. *Behavioral Science*, 1978, *23*, 225–233.

Feiring, C., & Lewis, M. Middle class differences in the mother–child interaction and the child's cognitive development. In T. Field (Ed.), *Culture and early interactions*. Hillsdale, N.J.: Lawrence Erlbaum, 1982.

Feiring, C., & Lewis, M. *Children, parents and siblings: Possible sources of variance in the behavior of first born and only children*. Paper presented at a Symposium for Cognitive and Social Consequences of Growing Up Without Siblings. Convention of the American Psychological Association, Montreal, Canada, 1980.

Gottman, J. M., & Bakeman, R. The sequential analysis of observational data. In M. E. Lamb, S. J. Suomi, & G. R. Stephenson (Eds.), *Social Interaction analysis*. Madison, Wis.: The University of Wisconsin Press, 1979.

Hill, R. Modern systems theory and the family: A confrontation. *Social Science Information*, 1973, *10*(5), 7–26.

Lamb, M. E. (Ed.). *The role of the father in child development*. New York: Wiley, 1976.

Lamb, M. E. Father–infant and mother–infant interaction in the first year of life. *Child Development*, 1977, *48*, 167–181.

Lamb, M. E., Suomi, S. J., & Stephenson, G. R. (Eds.). *Social interaction analysis: Methodological issues*. Madison Wis.: University of Wisconsin Press, 1979.

Lewis, M. State as an infant-environment interaction: An analysis of mother–infant interaction as a function of sex. *Merrill-Palmer Quarterly*, 1972, *18*, 95–121.

Lewis, M. Situational analysis and the study of behavioral development. In L. Pervin & M. Lewis (Eds.), *Perspectives in interactional psychology*. New York: Plenum Press, 1978.

Lewis, M. *Newton, Einstein, Piaget and the concept of self*. 10th Anniversary invited address before the Jean Piaget Society plenary session, Philadelphia, May–June 1980.

Lewis, M. The social network systems: Toward a theory of social development. In T. Field (Ed.), *Review of Human Development* (Vol. 1). New York: Wiley, 1982.

Lewis M., & Feiring, C. The child's social world. In R. M. Lerner & G. D. Spanier (Eds.), *Child influences on marital and family interaction: a life-span perspective*. New York: Academic Press, 1978.

Lewis, M., & Feiring, C. The child's social network: Social object, social functions and their relationship. In M. Lewis & L. Rosenblum (Eds.), *The child and its family: The genesis of behavior* (Vol. 2). New York: Plenum Press, 1979.

Lewis, M., & Feiring, C. Direct and indirect interactions in social relationships. In L. Lipsitt (Ed.), *Advances in infancy research* (Vol. 1). New York: Ablex, 1981.

Lewis, M., Feiring, C., & Weinraub, M. The father as a member of the child's social network. In M. Lamb (Ed.), *The role of the father in child development* (2nd ed.). New York: Wiley, 1981.

Lewis, M., & Freedle, R. Mother–infant dyad: The cradle of meaning. In P. Pliner, L. Krames, & T. Alloway (Eds.), *Communication and affect: Language and thought*. New York: Academic Press, 1973.

Lewis, M., & Freedle, R. The mother and infant communication system: The effects of poverty. In H. McGurk (Ed.), *Ecological factors in human development*. Amsterdam: North-Holland Publishing, 1977.

Lewis, M., & Goldberg, S. Perceptual–cognitive development in infancy: A generalized expectancy model as a function of the mother–infant interaction. *Merrill-Palmer Quarterly*, 1969, *15*, 81-100.

Lewis, M., & Kreitzberg, V. The effects of birth order and spacing on mother–infant interactions. *Developmental Psychology*, 1979, *15*(6), 617-625.

Lewis, M., & Lee-Painter, S. An interactional approach to the mother–infant dyad. In M. Lewis & K. Rosenblum (Eds.), *The effect of the infant on its caregiver*. New York: Wiley, 1974.

Lewis, M., & Weinraub, M. The father's role in the infant's social network. In M. Lamb (Ed.), *The role of the father in child development* (Vol. 1). New York: Wiley, 1976.

Lewis, M., & Weinraub, M. Origins of early sex-role development. *Sex Roles*, 1979, *5*, 135-153.

Lynn, D. B., & Cross, A. DeP. Parent preference of preschool children. *Journal of Marriage and the Family*, 1974, *36*, 555-559.

Mischel, W. Sex-typing and socialization. In P. Mussen (Ed.), *Carmichael's manual of child psychology* (Vol. 2). New York: Wiley, 1970.

Monane, J. H. *A sociology of human systems*. New York: Appleton Century Crofts, 1967.

Parke, R. D., & O'Leary, S. Father–mother–infant interaction in the newborn period: Some findings, some observations, and some unresolved issues. In K. Riegel & J. Meacham (Eds.), *The developing individual in a changing world: Social and environmental issues* (Vol. 2). The Hague: Mouton, 1975.

Parke, R. D., Power, T. G., & Gottman, J. M. Conceptualizing and quantifying influence patterns in the family triad. In M. E. Lamb, S. J. Suomi, & G. R. Stephenson (Eds.), *Social interaction analysis*. Madison, Wis.: Wisconsin University Press, 1979.

Parsons, T., & Bales, R. F. *Family socialization and interaction process*. Glencoe, Ill.: Free Press, 1955.

Patterson, G. R. A performance theory for coercive family interaction. In R. B. Cairns (Ed.), *The analysis of social interactions*. Hillsdale, N.J.: Lawrence Erlbaum, 1979.

Patterson, G. R., & Moore, D. Interactive patterns as units of behavior. In M. E. Lamb, S. J. Suomi, & G. R. Stephenson (Eds.), *Social interaction analysis*. Madison, Wis.: The University of Wisconsin Press, 1979.

Pedersen, F. A. *Mother, father and infant as an interactive system*. Paper presented at the Convention of the American Psychological Association, Chicago, September 1975.

Pedersen, F. A., Anderson, B. J., & Cain, R. L. *An approach to understanding link-ups between the parent–infant and spouse relationship*. Paper presented at the meeting of the Society for Research in Child Development, New Orleans, 1977.

Pedersen, F. A., Yarrow, L. J., Anderson, B. J., & Cain, R. L. Conceptualization of father influences in the infancy period. In M. Lewis & L. Rosenblum (Eds.), *The child and its family: The genesis of behavior* (Vol. 2). New York: Plenum Press, 1979.

Pervin, L., & Lewis, M. Overview of the internal–external issue. In L. Pervin & M. Lewis (Eds.), *Perspectives in interactional psychology*. New York: Plenum Press, 1978.

Riegel, K. F. The dialectics of human development. *American Psychologist*, 1976, *31*, 689–700.

Riegel, K. F., & Meacham, J. A. Dialectics, transaction, and Piaget's theory. In L. A. Pervin & M. Lewis (Eds.), *Perspectives in interactional psychology*. New York: Plenum Press, 1978.

Rollins, B. C., & Galligan, R. The developing child and marital satisfaction of parents. In R. M. Lerner & G. B. Spanier (Eds.), *Child influences on marital and family interaction*. New York: Academic Press, 1978.

Rosenblatt, P. C. Behavior in public places: Comparisons of couples accompanied and unaccompanied by children. *Journal of Marriage and the Family*, 1974, *36*, 750–755.

Sackett, G. P. The lag sequential analysis of contingency and cyclicity in behavioral interaction research. In J. Osofsky (Ed.), *Handbook of infant development*. New York: Wiley, 1978.

Slater, P. Parental role differentiation. In R. L. Coser (Ed.), *The family: Its structures and functions* (2nd ed.). New York: St. Martin's, 1974.

Terhune, K. W. *A review of the actual and expected consequences of family size*. U.S. Department of Health, Education and Welfare, Public Health Service, National Institute of Health Publication No. (NIH) 75-779, 1974.

Thomas, E. J., & Fink, C. Effects of group size. *Psychological Bulletin*, 1963, *60*, 371–384.

Von Bertalanffy, L. *Robots, men and minds*. New York: Braziller. 1967.

Weinraub, M., & Lewis, M. The determinants of children's responses to separation. *Monographs of the Society for Research in Child Development*, 1977, *42* (4, Serial No. 172).

Weinraub, M., Brooks, J., & Lewis, M. The social network: A reconsideration of the concept of attachment. *Human Development*, 1977, *20*, 31–47.

Willems, E. P. Review of research. In R. Bular & P. V. Gump (Eds.), *Big school small school*. Stanford, Calif.: Stanford University Press, 1964.

Willems, E. P. Planning a rationale for naturalistic research. In E. P. Willems & H. L. Rausch (Eds.), *Naturalistic viewpoints in psychological research*. New York: Holt, Rinehart & Winston, 1969.

Zajonc, R. B., & Markus, G. B. Birth order and intellectual development. *Psychological Review*, 1975, *82*, 74–88.

Zukav, G. *The dancing Wu Li masters*. New York: William Morrow, 1979.

CHAPTER 5

Play as a Context for Early Learning
Lab and Home Analyses

THOMAS G. POWER and ROSS D. PARKE

Father picks up 7-month-old Nathan, tosses him into the air, and then throws his head back so that he and Nathan are face to face. As Nathan giggles and chortles, father lowers him, shakes him, and tosses him up in the air again.

Mother is busy with her daily housework routine of sweeping the kitchen floor. To keep Anna, her 10-month-old, occupied, she opens up the kitchen cabinet which is full of pots, pans, and baking dishes. Mother pulls out a stack of three nested pots and two wooden spoons and sets them all in front of Anna. Anna smiles and busily begins her own musical concert of spoons and pans. Mother continues her housekeeping.

Mother sits 7-month-old Timothy on her lap and pulls out Timothy's favorite toy—a green donkey that brays when you squeeze him. Timothy smiles and for the next few minutes mother moves the donkey in front of her son's eyes, makes it "bray," and talks animatedly to her son. Timothy watches intently, smiles, and occasionally reaches out for the donkey.

Mother says gently, "No, you can't go into that room," shuts the door, and cuts short 10-month-old Lisa's expedition into the guest room.

These examples illustrate the wide range of ways in which parents structure the nature of their infants' experiences in the home environment. Through play, through caretaking, and through the restriction and encouragement of infant exploration, parents undoubtedly play an important role in influencing the course of early learning. Unfortunately, few

THOMAS G. POWER ● Department of Psychology, University of Houston, Houston, Texas 77030.   **ROSS D. PARKE** ● Department of Psychology, University of Illinois, Urbana-Champaign, Illinois 61820. This research was supported by a grant from the NICHD Program project Grant HD 05951 and a grant from the National Foundation March of Dimes 12-55.

empirical attempts have been made to describe and compare the wide range of ways in which parents play this role. The purpose of this chapter is to provide such data through a descriptive analysis of early parent–infant interaction patterns across a number of naturally occurring interactional contexts. Specifically, parent–infant interaction in the play, caretaking, housekeeping, and adult leisure contexts are compared in order to generate some hypotheses concerning the influence of these interactions on infant social and cognitive development.

Data from two recent studies are presented. In the first investigation, the nature of parent–infant play was examined in a laboratory setting. In the second study, parent–infant interactions were examined across a number of play and nonplay contexts in the home. In both studies, the nature of mother– *and* father–infant interaction was examined, since recent research has indicated that fathers as well as mothers are important interactive partners in the early family environment (Lamb, 1976; Parke, 1979b). Together, these studies provide descriptive data concerning the role of contextual factors in determining the nature of early parent–infant interaction, the similar and different roles played by mothers and fathers in early interaction, and the possible impact of these early parent–infant exchanges for infant development.

Study I: Play as an Early-Learning Context

Parent–infant play is increasingly being recognized as a context in which the infant may learn and develop a number of social and cognitive skills (Schaffer, 1977, 1978; Stern, 1977; Ross & Kay, 1980). For example, researchers have suggested that parent–infant play facilitates infant development in such diverse areas as goal-directed behavior (Pawlby, 1977; Schaffer, 1977; Schaffer & Crook, 1978), object permanence (Schaffer, 1978), and the acquisition of turn-taking skills (Pawlby, 1977; Schaffer, 1978; Stern, 1977). Although the findings of these studies provide some preliminary support for the developmental importance of parent–infant play, our understanding of the nature of these interactions is quite limited. This is so because researchers have often chosen to focus on certain forms of parent–infant play interactions at the expense of numerous others. Specifically, studies of parent–infant play have generally focused on the description of either early face-to-face interaction patterns during the first 4 months of life (e.g., Brazelton, Koslowski, & Main, 1974; Blehar, Lieberman, & Ainsworth, 1977; Kaye & Fogel, 1980; Stern, 1977) or on the description of ritualized turn-taking interactions (parent–infant games) during the second half-year (e.g., Crawley, Rogers, Friedman, Iacobbo,

Criticos, Richardson, & Thompson, 1978; Gustafson, Green, & West, 1979; Ross & Kay, 1980).

In contrast, studies of physical and/or object-mediated play that do not restrict their analyses to the description of ritualized turn-taking interactions are relatively uncommon. This is unfortunate, as the results of a recent study showed that conventional parent–infant games accounted for only about 10 percent of all the interactions that mothers engaged in with their 6- to 12-month-old infants in the home (Green, Gustafson, & West, 1980). Approximately another 60% of the interactions could be coded as some form of physical or object-mediated play. Thus, in spite of the fact that a number of investigators have devoted considerable time and effort to the study of parent–infant play during the second half year of life, very sparse descriptive data are currently available concerning the *predominant* kinds of play interactions that occur during this period.

The purpose of the present study was to provide such data by carrying out a descriptive analysis of the various kinds of play interactions that mothers and fathers engaged in with their 8-month-old infants. In addition to providing descriptive data, this analysis aided in the generation of hypothesis concerning the ways through which different types of parent–infant play interactions may facilitate the development of infant social and cognitive skills. That is, by examining the "structure" of the various kinds of parent–infant play interactions, it was possible to speculate about the effects that these interactions may have on the infant's development. Both mothers and fathers were included in this study, since a number of recent findings indicate that the differential role of mother- and father–infant interaction occurs primarily in the play context. First, in most families, the majority of father–infant interactions occur during play (Clarke-Stewart, 1978; Lamb, 1976; Kotelchuck, 1976; Parke, 1979b; Rendina & Dicker-scheid, 1976), and, second, when mother–father differences in parent–infant interaction style are found, they are generally found in play, not in caretaking (Parke & Sawin, 1980).

The observational system utilized in this study was designed in light of a number of recent methodological advances. In recognition of the fact that multiple levels of analysis (molar and molecular) are often necessary to describe interaction patterns adequately (Cairns & Green, 1979; Hinde, 1976a,b; Patterson & Moore, 1979; Sackett, 1978), a primary purpose of this study was to develop an observational system that could codify molar units of parent–infant play interaction while also providing a detailed description of the content and structure of these interactions. This kind of analysis was employed because several methodologists have recently suggested that units of social interaction corresponding to extended sequences of social behaviors might be more meaningful in describing the nature of social interaction than would discrete, molecular units that correspond to the occurrence of individual social behaviors. These methodologists have argued that without the use of molar units, it is often impossible to specify the behavioral context in which a given behavior occurs (Hinde, 1976a,b; Sroufe & Waters, 1977). This is important, since the behavioral context often gives the molecular behavior its meaning. Sroufe and Waters (1977) provide some examples:

> The same behavior may act as a member of class X in one context, class Y in another. For example, most babies turn away when their nose is wiped. Such a response is of limited interest and would not predict turning away when picked up in the course of seeking contact. The latter has a radically different meaning, and tallying the two responses together is certain to obscure results. Contact seeking mixed with squirming to get down, pushing away, or general petulance has a different meaning than relaxed molding to the caregiver (though both would contribute to total scores for time in contact). Looking at the mother, when combined with bounding and smiling upon the caregiver's entrance, has different significance (positive greeting) than mere looking sometime later. (pp. 1188-1189)

These examples clearly illustrate why larger units are often necessary to capture the meaning of various social interchanges (Patterson & Moore, 1979; Sackett, 1978). Therefore, a central problem in coding social interaction is the relationship between levels of analysis; specifically, this requires the articulation of how molecular behaviors relate to specific molar units (Hartup, 1979).

In this study, units at two levels were utilized. Specifically, molar units which we termed play *bouts* were identified; these corresponded to extended sequences of parent and infant behaviors that occurred frequently during the play interactions. In addition, molecular behaviors such as "smile," "touch," and "vocalize" that served as the smaller units within these molar bouts were coded. Thus, through simultaneous use of both molar and molecular units, the structure of the parent–infant play interactions could be described more adequately.

A final methodological consideration is this study concerned the way in which the parent–infant bouts were identified. As the purpose of this study was to describe the nature of various parent–infant play interactions in such a way as to generate hypotheses about how these interactions may influence the course of infant development, the bouts in this study were defined in such a way as to be explicit about the parent's and the infant's role in each of these interactions. Such an analysis has rarely been conducted in previous studies of parent–infant play. For example, in three recent studies of parent–infant play during the second half-year of life, play was coded as being either conventional/nonconventional (Crawley et al., 1978; Lamb, 1977a) or as requiring or not requiring an active role on the part of the infant (Crawley *et al.*, 1978; Gustafson *et al.*, 1979). These distinctions do not adequately reflect the nature of play in terms of the requisite infant skills. Thus, although two of these studies found that the infant took a more "active motor role" as he or she got older (Crawley *et al.*, 1978; Gustafson *et al.*, 1979), what is not clear from these analyses are the specific ways in which the nature of the infant's role changed developmentally. In the present study, an analysis of the infant's role was made possible by coding for each bout the specific parent and infant behaviors that the bout tapped or required. Therefore, whenever the nature of the play interaction changed in terms of the infant's or parent's role, a new bout was coded. In this way, the nature of each participant's role was clearly defined within each play interaction.

Method

Mothers and fathers were videotaped while playing with their firstborn, 8-month-old infants in a laboratory playroom. Twenty-four families participated. Half the infants were boys and half were girls. Families were predominantly white, middle to upper-middle class; eight of the mothers of boys and eight of the mothers of girls worked full or part time. Parents were told that we were "interested in the ways in which mothers and fathers played with their infants," were provided with four small toys, and were instructed to use these toys in play with their infants. A counterbalanced schedule of parent departures and arrivals made possible the assessment of 5 minutes of mother–infant, 5 minutes of father–infant, and 10 minutes of triadic play.

A coding system was developed that identified those parent–infant interaction bouts that occurred frequently during the play session. This system involved (1) scoring all parent–infant interactions along three independent dimensions (toy versus no-toy, degree of physicalness, and play type), (2) identifying those interactions that constituted the most frequently occurring parent–infant interaction bouts (bouts that accounted for more than 3% of the bouts identified), and then (3) coding the sequential patterning of molecular infant and parent behaviors within 10 examples of each bout. The dimensions described aspects of the parent's and infant's role within each bout: degree of physicalness referred to the amount of physical stimulation that the parent used during the particular play interaction (no physical stimulation, tactile stimulation, or kinesthetic stimulation); coding on the play-type scale reflected the most complex infant motor behavior required by the type of play if played successfully. The seven play types that were coded (in order of increasing complexity) were *no motor* behavior required, *watching* an object, *grasping* an object, *retrieving* an object, *imitating* a parent motor behavior, *giving* the parent an object, and engaging in a *turn-taking* interaction. The 10 examples of each bout were chosen through a method designed to identify representative examples of the various bouts based primarily on bout duration, and all examples chosen were analyzed through the use of an extensive second-by-second molecular coding system that included codes of parent and infant affective, vocal, verbal, looking, and motor behavior. Thus, through the use of this three-step procedure, it was possible to (1) identify those parent–infant interaction bouts that made up the vast majority of parent–infant play interactions and (2) specify in some detail the nature of the parent's and infant's role during these interactions by specifying the sequences of parent and infant behaviors that characterized these bouts.[1] Once the various bouts were identified and described, mother–father differences in the frequency and sequencing of these bouts were explored.

Results: Bout Identification

Seven distinctive parent–infant interaction bouts were identified; these accounted for 88% of the play interactions observed. Sequential lag, conditional probability, and frequency analyses were employed to describe and compare the structure of each of these bouts. The results of these analyses are summarized in Table 1. As can be seen in the table, the seven bouts identified were watching, toy-touching, minor physical, grasping, retrieving, face, and lifting bouts. Presented in Table 1 for each of these bouts is (1) a description of the significant sequences of parent and infant behavior that characterized the bout, (2) a description of the parent verbalizations (if any) that generally accompanied the bout, (3) an analysis of the degree to which the bout was characterized by positive affect on the part of the infant (parents were equally likely to smile during any of the bouts), and (4) the percentage of the total play interactions accounted for by that bout. Data on parent verbalizations and infant affect came from the results of a series of one-way analyses of variance that compared the seven bouts for the frequency of occurrence of infant smiling and various parent verbalizations. The parent verbal categories were *commands/invitations*, *directs attention*, *provides/requests information (infant activities)*, *provides/requests information (parental activities)*, and *provides/requests information (objects)*. These were the categories used by Sherrod and

---

[1]A more detailed description of the procedure, coding reliability, and results of the laboratory study can be found in Power (1980).

Table 1. Descriptions of Bout Structure: Laboratory Study

Bout		Parent verbalizations	Infant affect[a]	Percentage
Attention/arousal-regulating bouts				
Watching	Parent presents toy → Make toy salient (make noise, move) → Present toy	—	o	11
Toy touching	Parent presents toy → [Move toy → with toy] Touch[b] → Present toy	—	o	10
Minor physical	Parent touches, tickles, bounces, or shakes infant	Nonverbal	o	16
Exploratory bouts				
Grasping	Parent presents toy → Infant reaches → Infant grasps toy → Parent vocalizes	Attention directing Information: objects	o	25
Retrieving	Parent presents toy out of reach → Infant crawls and reaches → Infant grasps toy	Commands Information: objects	o	12
Communicative bouts				
Face	Parent positions face in front of infant's face → Eye contact → Infant looks away → Parent moves own face away	Information: parent/infant	+	11
Lifting	Parent lifts Infant in air → Parent positions infant in face-to-face orientation → Face bout → parent shakes infant → Parent lowers to lap	Information: parent/infant	+	3

[a] Two symbols are used to indicate the predominant level of infant affective involvement: o for predominantly neutral affect and + for predominantly positive affect.
[b] The sequence in the bracket was often repeated a number of times.

associates (Sherrod, Crawley, Petersen, & Bennett, 1978) in their study of maternal speech to 4- to 8-month-old infants.

Comparison of the structure of the bouts indicated that they fell into three general categories of bouts in which the parent attempted to (1) focus or otherwise manipulate the infant's attention or level of affective arousal (attention/arousal-regulating bouts), (2) influence or direct the infant's motor exploration of a toy (exploratory bouts), or (3) engage the infant in face-to-face social interaction (communicative bouts). Each of these categories will be considered below.

Attention/Arousal-Regulating Bouts

Examination of the structure of watching, toy-touching, and minor physical bouts revealed a basic similarity: when parents engaged in these interactions with their infants, they appeared to be attempting to influence their infants' attentional and/or affective behavior. In the case of watching and toy-touching bouts, parents appeared to be directing their infants' attention toward a toy through presenting the toy, making it salient, and then presenting the toy again; in toy-touching and minor physical bouts, parents appeared to be manipulating the infant's state of affective arousal through physical stimulation (presumably to a level optimal for play). See Table 1.

Parents generally did not vocalize to their infants when engaging in these interactions; even when they did (minor physical bouts), they only engaged in nonverbal vocalizations. Although two of these bouts were characterized by physical stimulation, the probability of infant positive affect was not significantly higher than in any of the other bouts. Together, these bouts accounted for over one-third of all parent–infant play interactions (37%).

Exploratory Bouts

Examination of the structure of grasping and retrieving bouts also revealed a basic similarity: in both cases, parents attempted to structure their infants' exploration of a toy through verbal and nonverbal means. In grasping bouts, the parent would provide the infant with a toy and then verbally direct the infant's attention toward some aspect of that toy; in retrieving bouts, parents would verbally encourage the infant to crawl to and then grasp a toy while presenting the toy out of the infant's reach (see Table 1).

Parents generally talked to their infants when engaging in exploratory bouts, and verbalizations generally served either to direct the infant's attention or to provide or request information about objects. Infant affect was generally neutral during these interactions. As was the case for attention/arousal-regulating bouts, exploratory bouts also accounted for over one-third of all parent–infant interaction bouts (37%).

Communicative Bouts

Finally, the structure of face and lifting bouts had similarities: in both cases, parents appeared to be attempting to elicit infant positive affect and vocal behavior through face-to-face interactions with their infant. In face bouts, parents established eye contact by positioning their *own* faces in front of the infant's face; in lifting bouts, eye contact was established by the parent lifting the infant in the air and positioning the *infant's* face for face-to-face interaction (see Table 1). In addition, both bouts were characterized by high levels of infant positive affect and parent verbalizations. In contrast to the exploratory bouts, verbalizations during communicative bouts generally involved providing or requesting information about infant or parental activities. Together, these bouts accounted for 14% of all parent–infant interaction bouts.

Parent-Infant Bouts: A Discussion of Possible Implications for Infant Development

An analysis of the structural similarities of the parent–infant interactions within each of the three categories presented above aids in the generation of hypotheses concerning their differential implications for infant development. The first set of bouts, the attention/arousal-regulating bouts, all appear to serve in the regulation of the infant's attentional and affective behavior during play. It is likely that such regulation is particularly important for parent–infant play to progress smoothly, as it has been argued that the success of play is often contingent on the parent's ability to keep the infant at an "optimal level" of affective arousal (e.g., Stern, 1977). Therefore, it is hypothesized that watching, toy-touching, and minor physical bouts during the course of parent–infant play operate primarily to serve this short-term regulatory function. Thus, it is argued that these interactions have long-term implications for the infant's development only if the opportunity to engage in extended, successful play interactions with its parents influences the course of the infant's social and cognitive development. To understand how these extended interactions might be influential, we must turn to the parent–infant interaction bouts with apparent long-term effects: the exploratory and communicative bouts.

Exploratory bouts were characterized by the parent actively structuring the infant's exploration of a toy. In both grasping and retrieving bouts the parent did two things: first, the parent provided the infant with what he or she considered to be the appropriate environmental stimulus; second, the parent directed the infant's manipulatory or locomotor behavior toward some aspect of that toy. As the ways in which parents actively structure the nature of their infant's early environmental exploration may have implications for the infant's exploratory and cognitive development (Clarke-Stewart, 1973; Parke, 1978; Schaffer, 1978; Power, 1980), the structural analysis of these two bouts has aided in the identification of two specific contexts in which this influence may occur.

The analysis of the structure of communicative bouts also aids in the generation of hypotheses concerning developmental implications. Since face-to-face interactions and infant positive affect were characteristics of cummunicative bouts, it is possible that such interactions may be important for infant social and communicative development. This is hypothesized because several investigators have emphasized the role of early face-to-face interactions in the development of certain social and communicative skills (e.g., Blehar et al., 1977; Stern, 1977). Furthermore, as face bouts were the only bouts identified in which the infant consistently controlled the length of the interaction (see Table 1), parent–infant interactions in the context of face bouts may be important in facilitating the development of turn-taking skills and in providing early lessons in control of the social environment.

These, then, are some hypotheses concerning possible effects of the various parent–infant interaction bouts on the infant's social and cognitive development. Although it was hypothesized that attention/arousal-regulating bouts serve primarily in the short-term facilitation of parent–infant play interactions, it was hypothesized that exploratory bouts may have long-term implications for infant cognitive development and communicative bouts may have long-term implications for social development. We now turn to an examination of mother–father differences in the duration and sequencing of these various bouts in order to provide some hypotheses concerning differences in the developmental implications of mother– and father–infant play.

Results: Mother–Father Differences[2]

Two sets of analyses were carried out to examine differences in mother– and father–infant play: analyses of bout duration and analyses of the

[2]As mother–father differences were more pronounced in the dyadic (mother–infant and father–infant) than in the triadic sessions (mother–father–infant), only analyses from the dyadic sessions will be presented below.

sequencing of these bouts within the interaction sessions. Results from each of these will be presented below.

Duration Analyses

In the duration analyses, the comparisons of mother- and father-infant play revealed more similarities than differences. Although there were no effects of parent sex or infant sex on the amount of time that parents spent playing during either of the exploratory bouts, differences *did* emerge for two of the attention/regulating and one of the communicative bouts. Fathers spent more time playing toy-touching bouts than did mothers [F $(1,20) = 4.51$, $p < .05$; fathers—25.12 sec; mothers—9.60 sec], mothers spent more time playing watching bouts [F $(1,20) = 4.04$, $p < .06$; fathers—12.26 sec; mothers—34.95 sec]. Fathers, especially fathers of boys, spent the most time engaged in lifting bouts [F $(1,20) = 8.06, p < .2$; fathers of boys—35.25 sec; fathers of girls—6.00 sec; mothers of boys—1.80 sec; mothers of girls—6.51 sec].

Sequential Analyses

Analyses of mother–father differences in the sequencing of the various bouts revealed a number of other differences. For these analyses, the bouts were combined across functional categories and a distinction was made between successful and unsuccessful bouts.[3] In a successful bout, the infant successfully engaged in the infant behavior that defined the bout; in an unsuccessful bout, he or she did not. Specifically, grasping a toy defined success in grasping bouts, crawling to and grasping a toy defined success in retrieving bouts, and looking at the toy defined success in attention-regulating bouts.

Figure 1 presents the results of a lag sequential analysis (Gottman & Bakeman, 1979; Sackett, 1979) run on the sequential data after the data were recoded by functional category. Since the effects of infant sex were minimal,[4] data from boy and girl infants were combined. Lag-1 and lag-2 sequences are illustrated. The straight arrows represent significant lag-1 sequences (that is, the probability of the second bout following the first is significantly greater—$z > 1.96$—than the baseline probability of the second bout), while the curved arrows represent significant lag-2 sequences. In

---

[3]Only one significant finding concerning the *duration* of unsuccessful bouts was found—fathers of boys were more likely than any other parents to engage in unsuccessful watching bouts.

[4]Only one sequence was consistently qualified by infant sex: fathers of boys were more likely to respond to unsuccessful attention-regulating play with arousal-regulating play than were fathers of girls.

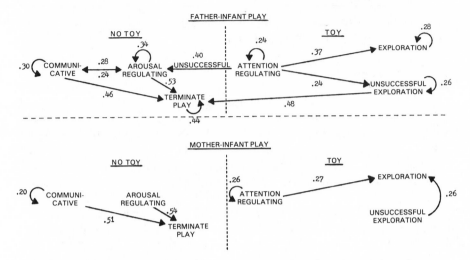

Figure 1. Flow diagram illustrating the structure of mother- and father-infant play.

a lag-2 sequence, the probability calculated is the probability of one bout following another after the occurrence of an unspecified intermediate bout (in this case, the baseline probability for comparison is the baseline probability of the third bout in the chain). In addition, the conditional probabilities associated with the sequences are printed above the arrows.[5]

Two mother–father differences in interaction style are highlighted in this analysis. First, three sequences indicated that fathers were more likely than mothers to engage in extended physical no-toy play interactions with their infants. This is indicated by the bidirectional lag-1 relationship between arousal-regulating and communicative bouts for fathers, the lag-2 relationship between arousal-regulating and arousal-regulating bouts for fathers, and the lag-1 relationship between arousal regulating bouts and terminate play for mothers. Thus, while fathers often alternated between physical and communicative, no-toy play, mothers generally terminated play after becoming physical.

Second, several findings indicate that although fathers showed a preference (and possibly greater skill) for interaction in the social, no-toy realm, mothers appeared to be more skillful at engaging in extended, successful sequences of exploratory play. This is indicated primarily by the sequences involving unsuccessful exploratory play. Although mothers often followed unsuccessful exploratory play with successful exploratory

[5]For the one double arrow, .28 is the probability from communicative to arousal-regulating while .24 represents the probability from arousal-regulating to communicative.

play (after the occurrence of an unspecified bout), fathers who engaged in unsuccessful exploratory play often terminated play or engaged in more unsuccessful exploration. Furthermore, though engaging in successful attention regulating play often led to successful exploratory play for mothers, it also often led to *unsuccessful* exploration for fathers. Finally, if fathers failed to focus their infant's attention on a toy, this often led to physical, no-toy play.

Mother–Father Differences: Implications

These results replicate and extend the findings of previous studies of mother- and father-infant play patterns. The finding that fathers had a tendency to engage in physical bouts (i.e., toy-touching and lifting) while mothers were more likely to engage in nonphysical bouts (i.e., watching) is consistent with the pattern of results reported in most studies of mother- and father-infant play. For example, in a study of the face-to-face interactions between parents and their 2-week- to 6-month-old infants, Yogman and associates (Yogman, Dixon, Tronick, Als, & Brazelton, 1977) found that fathers touched their infants with rhythmic tapping patterns more often than did mothers, while mothers vocalized more often to their infants. Lamb (1977a,b), in a home-based study, found a similar pattern: fathers played more physical games and engaged in more parallel play with their infants while mothers, in contrast, engaged in more conventional play activities (peek-a-boo), stimulus toy play, and reading. This pattern of results is also found in studies of older infants. In a study of 15 to 30-month-old infants and their parents, Clarke-Stewart (1978) found that father-infant play was more likely than mother–infant play to be physical and arousing and less likely to be didactic, intellectual, or mediated by objects.

Results of the sequential analyses extend the results of the duration analyses in showing that fathers were more likely than mothers to engage in *extended* physical interactions with their infants and that fathers often engaged in these interactions in response to unsuccessful toy play. Mothers, in contrast, appeared to be more skillful at engaging in extended, *successful* sequences in nonphysical play with objects. This pattern may reflect, in part, a general tendency for parents to rely on familiar and predominant modes of play when infant interest lessens; for mothers, this involved prolonging toy play while for fathers it involved shifting to physical play. Perhaps fathers would be more successful than mothers in maintaing bouts of physical play, and a lack of interest in physical play on the part of the infant would lead mothers to shift back to their preferred mode—object-mediated play. Clearly, a detailed study of mother–father differences in physical play is necessary to adequately test the relationship between infant disinterest and the reliance on preferred parental play modes.

What are the implications of these differences in mother–father play style for the infant's development? The fact that father–infant play was more physical than mother–infant play (especially for fathers of boys) indicates that fathers may play an important role in their infants' *social* development. This is suggested because the descriptive analysis of the physical bouts (especially the lifting bouts) showed that these bouts often serve as contexts for a wide range of communicative and affectively charged social interactions between parents and their infants. Therefore, through such interactions fathers may play an important role in facilitating the development of communicative skills and the formation of social relationships.

Another implication of the physical play between fathers and their male infants is suggested by the earlier work of Harlow and his colleagues (Suomi & Harlow, 1971). In this research, infant monkeys who were deprived of opportunities for physical interaction with either peer or adult monkeys showed serious deficits in their ability to regulate physical social exchanges, particularly aggression. Therefore, we might expect that early physical play may be important both as an antecedent of later peer-peer play and in the regulation of agonistic and aggressive interactions. Since boys are more likely to engage in physical aggression, this type of early father–infant physical play may be more important for boys than for girls.

Finally, since the results of the sequential analyses indicated that mothers were more successful than fathers in engaging their infants in extended sequences of toy play (and thereby played a greater role in structuring their infants' early environmental exploration), it is hypothesized that mother–infant play may have its greatest influence in the realm of early exploratory and cognitive development.

Study II: Beyond Play—A Study of Parent–Infant Play and Nonplay Interactions in the Home Setting

The next step in our research program served to answer two questions raised by the laboratory investigation. First, as many researchers have noted in recent years (Bronfenbrenner, 1979; McCall, 1977; Parke, 1976, 1979a), it is important to address the extent to which patterns of family interaction identified in the laboratory are generalizable to more naturalistic settings. Otherwise, there is the possibility of generating a "mythology of childhood" (Baldwin, 1967) in which the effects that were identified in the laboratory are, in fact, assumed to take place in naturalistic socialization contexts. Without directly testing this issue by examining the types of parent-infant play generated by our lab analysis, we may develop a theory of early learning that is neither a necessary nor sufficient account of how this early learning proceeds. Second, as a large number of naturally occurring parent-infant interactions occur outside the play context, it is important to expand our descriptive analysis to include these nonplay contexts. To address these issues, the coding system used in the laboratory was refined and employed in an observational study of parent-infant interaction across a wide variety of contexts in the home setting. Before turning to a description of this study, we will consider the issue of context in more detail.

The Home Environment: A Setting of Multiple Contexts

In spite of the growing recognition of the influence of the immediate context or setting on parent-infant interaction patterns, there has been little effort to develop a descriptive taxonomy of contexts or settings within the home. Distinctions between home versus laboratory are inadequate to capture the differences across settings. Just as the laboratory can be described along a continuum of naturalness (Parke, 1979a), a series of setting distinctions in the home environment must be made not only for the purposes of cross-study comparison but also to describe more adequately the degree of restraint that different contexts in the home place on parent-infant interaction.

The necessity of developing a better taxonomy of contexts within home environments comes from two sources. First, our own observations of parent-infant play in the home showed that a large number of parent-infant "play" interactions (bouts) that were identified in the laboratory study often occurred in the home in contexts other than play. Often, these "play" interactions occurred during such activities as routine housework, care-taking, or TV viewing. Second, a group of investigators (Green, Gustafson, & West, 1980) recently found that a significant proportion of all naturally occurring mother-infant interactions in the home occurred outside of the play context. Thus, it seemed necessary to develop a descriptive taxonomy of contexts in the home and to determine how play and nonplay contexts differ in terms of the kinds of parent-infant bouts that characterize them. Once we began this undertaking, however, it immediately became clear that another issue needed to be addressed: that of direct and indirect learning in the home.

Direct and Indirect Learning in the Home: Parent as Stimulator and Manager

In investigating the nature of parent–infant interactions outside the play context, it is evident that learning in the home takes place in at least two ways. First, parents *directly* influence their infant's development through parent–infant interactions such as those that were examined in the laboratory study. Second, parents *indirectly* influence their infant's social and cognitive development through the ways in which they organize and arrange the infant's home environment and set limits on the range of the home setting to which the infant has access (Parke, 1978). Only recently have theorists and researchers begun to recognize this "managerial"function of parents and to appreciate the impact of variations in how this function influences the infant's development. In fact, the managerial role may be just as important as the parent's role as stimulator, since the amount of time that infants spend interacting with the inanimate environment far exceeds their social interaction time. Here are some recent estimates based on extensive home observations by White and his colleagues (White, Kaban, Shapiro, & Attonucci, 1976):

> For 12-month-old to 15-month-old children, the figures were 89.7% for nonsocial tasks versus 10.3% for social tasks. By 18–21 months the figures are 83.8% nonsocial and 16.2% social: at 24–27 months 80.0% nonsocial and 20.0% social and at 30–33 months they were 79.1% nonsocial and 20.0% social. (p. 125)

Others report similar findings (Clarke-Stewart, 1973; Wenar, 1972). Secondly, White *et al.* (1976) noted that, over 85% of the time, 12 to 33 month-old infants initiated their own activities. In short, the way that the mother or other caretaker organizes the child's physical environment may be just as important as the direct social interactions between the child and caretaker.

A number of aspects of this managerial role appear to be important for the infant's development. Studies by several investigators (Bradley & Caldwell, 1976; Klaus & Gray, 1968; Wachs, 1976) show that the level of predictability or regularity in the child's home environment is positively correlated with early cognitive development. Furthermore, the boundaries of the home environment to which the child has access for exploration and play influence the child's cognitive development. White *et al.* (1976) argue that:

> the effective child-rearer makes the living area as safe as possible for the naive newly crawling or walking child and then provides maximum access to the living area for the child. This immediately sets the process of development off in a manner that will lead naturally to the satisfaction of and the further development of the child's curiosity; the opportunity to learn about the world at large; and the opportunity to enter into natural useful relationships with

people. The child-rearer not only provides maximum access to the living area, but in addition he or she makes kitchen cabinets attractive and available and then keeps a few materials in reserve for those times when the child may become a bit bored. (pp. 150-151)

This hypothesis has been supported in a number of empirical investigations: positive correlations are often reported between infant cognitive development and floor freedom—the degree to which mothers allow their infants to explore the physical environment freely (Beckwith, Cohen, Kopp, Parmelee, & Marcy, 1976; Wachs, 1979; Wachs, Uzgiris, & Hunt, 1971)—while negative correlations are generally reported between infant cognitive development and various measures of verbal and physical maternal restrictiveness (Clarke-Stewart, 1973; Elardo, Bradley, & Caldwell, 1975; Wenar, 1976; White & Watts, 1973).

Given the importance and prevalence of these boundary-setting behaviors in the home (boundary setting was rarely necessary in the laboratory setting), it was therefore necessary to expand the home coding system to include these interactions. The boundary-setting techniques (or managerial interactions) that were identified in the home study will be presented below.

Method

In this second study, 20 families of first-born infants (10 boys and 10 girls) were observed in their homes: half the infants were 7½-month-olds; half were 10½-month-olds. The families were white and predominantly middle- and upper-middle class. All the fathers and nine of the mothers worked full time.

All families were observed in the early evening, when both parents were at home. For those mothers who were home alone during the day with their infants, an afternoon observation was also scheduled. This procedure ensured a larger sample of interactional contexts for analysis. All observations were 45 minutes long. Parents were instructed to ignore the observers and to go about doing what they ordinarily did during that particular time of day.

During each visit, a male and a female observer, using a paper-and-pencil coding system, coded the frequency and sequencing of all the parent–infant interaction bouts that were identified in the laboratory study, along with the frequency and sequencing of a number of "managerial interactions" and any parent–infant interaction bouts that were unique to the home context.[6] In addition, observers coded the context in which each interaction

---

[6]A more detailed description of the coding system used can be obtained by writing to the authors.

bout or managerial interaction occurred. *Context* was defined as the ongoing parental activity in which the particular activity was embedded, and five contexts were identified that occurred with sufficient frequency for analysis: housework, caretaking, individual parent leisure (e.g., watching TV, reading), husband–wife leisure (primarily conversation between the spouses), and parent–infant play. Play was defined as any noncaretaking parent–infant interaction in which the parent's total attention was directed toward the infant (i.e., the parent was not already engaged in an activity that did not involve the infant).[7] Furthermore, whenever the parent interrupted a noninfant activity for three or more consecutive noncaretaking parent–infant interaction bouts, the entire interaction was coded as play. We now turn to a description of the bouts and managerial interactions that were identified in the home observations.

Results: Bout Identification

At the end of the study, 10 parent–infant interaction bouts and 3 managerial interactions that accounted for 85% of all interactions in the home setting were identified. The 10 bouts included 6 of 7 bouts identified in the laboratory study (toy touching occurred with very low frequency in the home) and 4 new bouts. Reliabilities for the frequency of bouts and managerial interactions ranged from .80 to .97 with a mean reliability of .88. Each of the new bouts is presented in Table 2 and will be described below. In addition, the categories developed in the laboratory study were adapted to include the new bouts and managerial interactions; these categories are presented in Table 3. Also presented are the relative frequency of occurrence of the bouts and managerial interactions within each of these categories.

Social/Affective Bouts

As can be seen in Table 3, two of the categories of parent–infant bouts that were identified in the laboratory study—arousal regulating bouts and communicative bouts—were classified as social/affective bouts in the home study. Social/affective bouts included all parent–infant interactions that were *not* centered around objects and were characterized by physical stimulation, infant positive affect, and face-to-face communicative inter-

[7]This definition of play differs considerably from other, narrower definitions available in the literature (cf. Green *et al.*, 1980; Goldman & Ross, 1978). This definition was chosen because it encompassed all noncaretaking interactions that were observed when parents were instructed to "play" with their infants in the laboratory study.

Table 2. Descriptions of Bouts Unique to Home Setting

Bout	Sequential description
Large motor assisting	Parent assists infant in crawling, walking, climbing, etc.
Imitating	Parent demonstrates motor behavior with or without Object → Parent gives object to infant → Infant imitates motor behavior
Searching	Parent hides object → Infant searches → Infant finds object OR Verbal instructions to find object (e.g., "Where's your Doggie?") → Infant searches → Infant finds object
Vocal	Parent asks question answerable by one word → Infant utters word OR Parent labels object → Infant labels object

Table 3. Parent–Infant Interaction Bouts and
Managerial Interactions: Home Study

Bouts	Percentage of total interactions	Percentage of total play interactions
Social/affective bouts		
Arousal-regulating bouts		
Minor physical	12	10
Communicative bouts		
Face	4	4
Vocal	9	8
Lifting	6	4
Exploratory bouts		
Attention-regulating bouts		
Watching	11	12
Large-motor bouts		
Retrieving	3	3
Large-motor assisting	5	5
Fine-motor bouts		
Grasping	14	12
Searching	3	3
Imitating	6	7
Managerial interactions		
Restrictions		
Verbal	4	2
Physical	2	4
Directions		
Verbal	6	6

action between parent and infant. As was also the case in the laboratory study, arousal-regulating bouts included those interactions where the parent attempted to manipulate the infant's state of affective arousal through the means of physical stimulation; and communicative bouts included those interactions where the parent attempted to elicit infant positive affect or vocal behavior through affectively charged face-to-face interaction.

As can also be seen in the table, one of the arousal-regulating bouts (minor physical bouts) and both of the communicative bouts (face and lifting bouts) that were identified in the laboratory study were also found in the home. The other arousal-regulating bout identified in the laboratory study (toy-touching bouts) was not included in the table, since it occurred with very low frequency in the home. However, a new communicative bout was added: the vocal bout. As illustrated in Table 2, vocal bouts consisted of extended parent–infant interactions where the parent attempted to elicit vocal behavior from the infant. Vocal bouts had not been coded in the laboratory study, since the coding system used in that study had not included a description of parent–infant play interactions that involved only verbal behavior on the part of the parent. Since these interactions did appear to make up a small but significant proportion of all parent–infant interactions in the home, they were included in the present study. Together, social/affective bouts accounted for 31% of the total parent–infant interactions in the home.

Exploratory Bouts

Three categories of exploratory bouts were identified in the home: attention-regulating bouts, large-motor bouts, and fine-motor bouts (see Table 3). Bouts in these categories were parent–infant interactions that were generally centered around an object, and each consisted of a parental attempt to structure the infant's exploration of the physical environment. Attention-regulating bouts included attempts on the part of the parent to actively direct the infant's attention, while large-motor and fine-motor bouts included parental attempts to influence, facilitate, or otherwise control infant large-motor and fine-motor behavior respectively. Three bouts identified in the laboratory study (watching, retrieving, and grasping bouts) and three new bouts (large-motor assisting, searching, and imitating bouts) are listed in Table 3. In each of the new bouts, parents actively attempted to get their infants to engage in some form of large- or fine-motor exploration. Parents engaging in large-motor assisting bouts assisted the infant in engaging in some large-motor or locomotor behavior; parents engaging in searching bouts attempted to get the infant to search for an object not in view; and parents engaging in imitating bouts attempted to get the infant to imitate a parent motor behavior. Together, exploratory bouts accounted for 42% of the total parent–infant interactions coded.

Managerial Interactions

Three managerial interactions were identified in the home study: verbal restrictions, physical restrictions, and verbal directions (see Table 3). As described above, these interactions occurred when the parent attempted to set the boundaries on the infant's exploration of the home environment. Physical restrictions differed from the other two managerial interactions, since these interactions involved physical contact between parent and infant (parent moves infant out of the way, parent slaps infant's hand, etc.). Verbal directions differed from verbal and physical restrictions, since these interactions were characterized by the parent trying to direct infant's fine motor or locomotor exploration verbally without resorting to a verbal prohibition. For example, in a verbal direction the parent might distract the infant from a prohibited object by saying, "Come play with your toys." Together, managerial interactions accounted for 12% of the total parent–infant interactions coded.

Bouts Unique to the Home Setting: A Discussion of Possible Implications for Infant Development

As mentioned above, four bouts that were not identified in the laboratory study were identified in the home: large-motor assisting, searching, imitating, and vocal bouts. The analysis of the structure of each of these bouts presented in Table 2 aids in the generation of hypotheses concerning their differential implications for infant development. Implications for both cognitive and social development are evident. For example, it is hypothesized that large-motor assisting, searching, and imitating bouts may have long-term implications for infant exploratory and cognitive development, since in each of these interactions the parent actively encouraged the infant to engage in some kind of exploratory behavior. This was particularly true for searching and imitating bouts, for in each case the parent made some aspect of the object salient to the infant. In searching bouts the parent demonstrated for the infant the permanence of the object, while in imitating play the parent had the opportunity to demonstrate and highlight the object's unique properties.

Hypotheses concerning social development involve vocal and imitating bouts: although the encouragement of vocal behavior (vocal bouts) may facilitate the development of language and communicative skills, the encouragement of imitative behavior (imitating bouts) may facilitate the development of a variety of social skills, since imitation plays such an important role in childhood socialization.

Results: Contextual Effects

We now turn to a presentation of some preliminary data on the effects of context, parent sex, and infant sex on the nature of parent–infant interaction patterns. Infant age effects were minimal across this small range (7 ½ to 10 ½ months), so for most analyses the data were collapsed across age. As the number of interactions per family member and per context varied across families, it was necessary to transform the data into percentages. In these preliminary analyses, the frequency of successful and unsuccessful interactions were combined. We will first consider the effects of context.

**Table 4. Contextual Effects: Percentage of Total Interactions in Each
of the Three Functional Categories across Five Contexts[a]**

	Housework	Caretaking	Individual leisure	H–W leisure	Play
Exploratory[b]	54%	19%	43%	39%	40%
Social/Affective	16%	11%	22%	27%	28%
Managerial	18%	15%	25%	23%	18%

[a] It should be noted that the percentages do not total to 100% for each context. The remaining interactions were either idiosyncratic interactions (interactions that constituted a total of 15% of the total interactions) or caretaking interactions (feeding or pacifying).
[b] $p < .05$.

Interactional context had a limited effect on the kinds of interactions that parents engaged in with their infants. For this analysis, the percentage of interactions that fell into each of the three major categories (exploratory bouts, social/affective bouts, and managerial interactions) was calculated for each of the five contexts. Only the 12 families (7 boys and 5 girls) that engaged in interactions in each of the five contexts were included. Analyses of variance showed that the parent and infant sex effects were minimal across the five contexts and that the context main effect was only significant for exploratory bouts [$F (4,40) = 2.73$; $p < .05$]. The means for the five contexts are listed in Table 4: exploratory bouts were highest in housework, lowest in caretaking, and at an intermediate level in individual leisure, husband–wife leisure, and play.

Results: Mother–Father Differences

For both exploratory and social/affective bouts, significant effects of parent sex and infant sex were found, but only in the play context. These effects took the form of a number of significant parent-sex × infant-sex interactions. These interactions and the corresponding means are listed in Table 5. Examination of the table shows that this interaction approached significance for half the bouts: watching, large-motor assisting, retrieving, imitating, and vocal bouts. In addition, there was a parent-sex main effect for both the physical bouts (see Table 5, note *b*).

Examination of the means shows that together, these interactions present a fairly consistent picture. Fathers showed greater differential treatment of the sexes than did mothers: fathers were more likely to encourage visual, large-motor, and fine-motor exploration in their sons (watching, large-motor assisting, retrieving, and imitating) while they encourage the vocal behavior of their daughters. Furthermore, fathers

Table 5. Play Interactions—Significant Parent Sex × Infant Sex Interactions

Bout	F (1,15)	p	Father-boys	Father-girls	Mother-boys	Mother-girls
Watching	4.07	.07	14.12[a]	4.98	10.29	13.76
Large Motor Assisting	4.71	.05	5.31	1.43	4.78	6.71
Retrieving	5.33	.04	5.77	0	1.55	2.44
Grasping	.73	—	8.51	13.35	18.19	15.97
Searching	.03	—	1.94	1.87	4.06	4.45
Imitating	3.03	.10	6.42	.71	6.42	6.81
Minor Physical[b]	.01	—	16.06	13.83	9.24	7.87
Lifting[b]	.55	—	11.81	5.99	2.04	1.22
Face	.32	—	2.23	3.90	6.46	5.23
Vocal	3.90	.07	5.44	22.90	5.48	6.69

[a] Percentage of total play interactions.
[b] Parent sex main effect was significant for these variables: minor physical—$F(1,15) = 3.47$, $p < .09$; lifting—$F(1,15) = 5.40, p < .04$.

engaged in more physical play than did mothers, although it is not clear whether or not fathers favor their boys in such interactions, as was found in the laboratory study (although the parent sex × infant sex interaction was not significant for lifting bouts in this study, the means in Table 5 are in the predicted direction).

The only mother–father difference identified outside the play context concerned managerial interactions. The analyses for these interactions differed slightly from those presented thus far: for managerial interactions, the dependent variables were the frequencies of the various managerial interactions that parents engaged in when they both were involved in non-infant-centered activities (husband–wife and individual leisure). Only those interactions that occurred when both parents were in the same room were included, since this situation served as an excellent test of differences between the maternal and paternal roles: when the infant got into something, one parent or the other had to restrict its behavior. In most cases, it was the mother: during both individual and husband–wife leisure, mothers were three times as likely as fathers to restrict their infant's behavior, verbally or physically. This finding was only significant for 10-month-old infants [F (1,8) $= 7.69$; $p < .03$]. Thus, once the infant had developed the significant locomotor skills that necessitated frequent restriction, mothers engaged in more restrictive behavior than fathers. Other data showed that fathers *did* engage in such behavior, but they generally did so only when the mother was not present.

Some supplementary data highlight the mother's greater managerial role: whenever the infant's locomotor behavior was restricted through the use of a restraining device (such as a playpen or high chair), mothers were more likely to be responsible for restraining the infant's locomotion in this way than were fathers. For those 10 families in which such restriction was observed, 9 mothers and only 2 fathers engaged in this behavior ($p < .02$— sign test). No significant parent-sex $\times$ infant-sex interactions were found for any of the managerial interactions.

Contextual, Parent Sex, and Infant Sex Effects: Implications

Data from this study have implications for understanding the effects of setting (lab vs. home), interactional context, parent sex, and infant sex on the nature of parent–infant interaction. Each of these will be considered in turn.

Home versus Laboratory: The Effects of Setting

Comparison of the findings of the home study with findings of the laboratory study revealed a number of differences. Even when interactional context was held constant by focusing on play interactions, differences between the home and lab settings were evident in both the parent–infant interaction bouts that were identified and in their frequency of occurrence. For example, although six of the seven bouts identified in the laboratory study were also identified in the home, one of the laboratory bouts (toy touching) rarely occurred in the home setting and four bouts that occurred very infrequently in the lab were quite common in the home (vocal, imitating, searching, and large motor bouts). In addition, managerial interactions, which were very common in the home setting, rarely occurred in the lab.

Several differences between the home and laboratory settings appeared to indicate why certain interactions were common only in a particular setting. First, the physical setup of the lab resulted in a low frequency of large-motor assisting and managerial interactions in this setting. This was the case because videotaping was done in a small room in which the opportunities for locomotor exploration were limited. Second, searching bouts were uncommon in the laboratory, since few places in which to hide objects were available. Third, imitating bouts were relatively uncommon in the lab, probably as a function of the simple toys used in the play sessions (the toys had few manipulable parts). Finally, differences in the instructions between the two settings indicated why toy-touching bouts were only common in the laboratory: as parents in the lab were instructed to play with the *toys*, the probability of physical toy play (toy-touching) was probably increased over baseline levels, especially for those parents who were generally physical without toys. Thus, no single difference between the laboratory and the home settings accounted for these findings: a number of factors appeared to be important.

Together, these findings indicate that caution must be used when generalizing the results of laboratory studies to more naturalistic settings. However, this statement should not be interpreted to mean that laboratory investigations are of limited value. In fact, the laboratory study discussed above was useful in identifying a number of parent–infant interaction bouts that *did* occur in the home setting (recall that six out of the seven laboratory bouts were identified in each study). In addition, the laboratory analysis also allowed us to investigate a number of subtle mother–father differences in interaction style that could not be easily studied in the home. Specifically, the use of the laboratory setting made it possible to study the sequencing of parent–infant interaction bouts within the interaction sessions and to investigate the sequential patterning of parent and infant behavior within these bouts. Therefore, it is suggested that the laboratory and home setting can best be used in a complementary fashion in trying to unravel the complexities of early parent–infant interaction. However, as discussed above, researchers should still be aware of the limitations of carrying out observations in either of these settings and should develop innovative approaches in designing multi-method investigations that employ observations from both settings (Parke, 1979a).

Finally, whenever one *does* need to generalize the results of a study from one setting to another, it is suggested that a detailed analysis of the differences between the two settings be undertaken and that the implications of each of these differences for the behavior of interest be examined. Only after such an analysis has been carried out should any attempt at generalization be made.

Contexts within a Setting: The Effects of Interactional Context

Results of the contextual analyses showed that exploratory inter-actions varied the most across interactional context. This makes it possible to describe the restraints of the various home contexts on parent–infant interaction: while social interaction and management were equally pos-sible (and often necessary) in all five contexts (housework, individual leisure, spouse–spouse leisure, caretaking, and play), exploratory inter-actions occurred infrequently during caretaking (these interactions—diapering, soothing, bathing—were rarely centered around objects) and quite frequently during housework.

The high percentage of exploratory bouts in the housework context appeared to be the result of a particular pattern of maternal behavior: when mothers started to engage in a housework task, they generally would provide their infant with something to manipulate. For example, when mothers would start fixing dinner, they would open the cupboard and let the infant play with the pots and pans; before mothers started to clean the house, they would give the infant some toys to play with. Subsequently, when mother–infant interactions occurred during housework, they were generally centered around these objects.

Thus, the results of this contextual analysis indicate that parent–infant interactions during housework and caretaking differ considerably from interactions during the three leisure contexts (individual leisure, husband–wife leisure, and parent–infant play), particularly concerning the percentage of exploratory interactions. Conversely, with the exception of differences in duration (play interactions were generally made up of longer sequences of parent–infant bouts than interactions in the other contexts), interactions that occurred during the three leisure contexts differed little in their content. Together, these data provide a preliminary description of the nature of parent–infant interactions across a number of naturally occurring interactional contexts in the home and highlight the importance of including interactional context as a variable in the study of early parent–infant interaction. It is hoped that future studies including cross-contextual analyses will provide additional evidence for the importance of this variable.

Mother–Father Differences

The findings of this study concerning mother–father differences in parent–infant interaction style are consistent with both the laboratory study and a number of previous investigations. First, the mother–father difference in physical play replicates the laboratory study and parallels the findings of previous studies that have documented the physical nature of father–infant play (Field, 1978; Lamb, 1977a; Trevarthen, 1974; Yogman *et al.*, 1977; Weinraub & Frankel, 1977). Second, the finding that fathers (but not mothers) encourage visual, locomotor, and fine-motor exploration in their boys and vocal behavior in their girls is consistent with data on later differences in the behavior paterns of male and female children (verbal ability in girls and visual–spatial abilities in boys—Maccoby & Jacklin, 1974) and with data on the father's paramount role in sex-role socialization during the preschool years (Goodenough, 1957; Johnson, 1963; Sears, Maccoby, & Levin, 1957).

Finally, the finding that mothers played a more active managerial role than fathers in infancy is consistent with previous research which indicates that caretaking is more often a maternal responsibility (see Parke, 1979b, for a review). This finding that mother, in contrast to father, plays the instrumental and disciplinary role in this early period of infancy is in contrast to traditional theorizing that has allocated this role to the father (cf. Parsons, 1954). However, these differential responsibilites associated with mother and father roles must be carefully monitored over time to assess the impact of secular trends on these role definitions. Possibly fathers will assume a larger managerial role as a higher percentage of mothers of infants enter the work force.

In any case, the finding that mothers were more likely than fathers to play the managerial role indicates that mothers may influence their infants' learning in a wider variety of ways than do fathers: while the father's influence appears to be mediated through direct interaction with the infant, the mother's influence appears to be mediated directly as well as indirectly through her role as manager of the infant's interactions with the physical environment. Since many studies have shown that the opportunity for exploration of the physical environment has implications for infant exploratory and cognitive development, the data from the home study once again confirm the findings of the laboratory study: in both cases the data indicate that fathers may have their greatest influence in the area of sex role and social development while mothers may have their greatest impact through the ways in which they influence the development of exploratory and cognitive skills.

Conclusions

In conclusion, the present set of studies indicate that opportunities for infant social and cognitive development are found to occur in a wide variety of contexts in the home environment. Parent–infant interactions that were first identified in the play context were also found to occur in other naturally occurring contexts in the home, and many of these interactions appear to be the contexts in which much of early learning may occur. The task that remains is to specify how the interactional experiences that mothers and fathers offer their infants within these varied contexts facilitate the development of specific infant social and cognitive skills. It is unlikely that this analysis can be satisfactorily achieved through reliance on observational strategies alone. Instead, a wide range of strategies, including experimental approaches, must be more heavily utilized. Such strategies as the specific training of parental play skills (Zelazo, Kotelchuck, Barber, & David, 1977) or the manipulation of parental play through instructions combined with short- as well as long-term evaluation of the impact of these shifts in parental interactive style on infant development would be helpful. The use of surrogate caregivers who are trained to provide infants with particular types of social experience is another underutilized strategy (Parke, 1979a). Finally, the application of path-analytic and other "causal" modeling techniques will make better use of nonexperimental data. By a careful combination of strategies, we may be able to answer the questions that are raised in this chapter and indicate more precisely the ways in which the family contributes to the infant's early learning and development.

ACKNOWLEDGMENTS

Thanks are extended to Debbie Albright and Toby Nathan for their invaluable contribution as observers and research assistants.

References

Baldwin, A. *Theories of child development.* New York: Wiley, 1967.

Beckwith, L., Cohen, S. E., Kopp, C. B., Parmelee, A. J., & Marcy, T. Caregiver–infant interaction and early cognitive development in preterm infants. *Child Development,* 1976, *47,* 579-587.

Blehar, M. C., Lieberman, A. F., & Ainsworth, M. D. Early face-to-face interaction and its relations to later infant–mother attachment. *Child Development,* 1977, *48,* 182-194.

Bradley, R. H., & Caldwell, B. M. The relation of infants' home environments to mental test performance at fifty-four months. *Child Development,* 1976, *47,* 1172-1174.

Brazelton, T. B., Koslowski, B., & Main, M. The origins of reciprocity: The early mother–infant interaction. In M. Lewis & L. A. Rosenblum (Eds.), *The effect of the infant on its caregiver.* New York: Wiley–Interscience, 1974.

Bronfenbrenner, U. *The ecology of human development.* Cambridge, Mass.: Harvard University Press, 1979.

Cairns, R. B., & Green, J. A. How to assess personality and social patterns: Observations or ratings? In R. B. Cairns (Ed.), *The analysis of social interactions.* Hillsdale, N.J.: Lawrence Erlbaum, 1979.

Clarke-Stewart, K. A. Interactions between mothers and their young children: characteristics and consequences. *Monographs of the Society for Research in Child Development,* 1973, *38*(6-7, Ser. 153).

Clarke-Stewart, K. A. And daddy makes three: The father's impact on the mother and young child. *Child Development,* 1978, *49,* 466-478.

Crawley, S. B., Rogers, P. P., Friedman, S., Iacobbo, M., Criticos, A., Richardson, L., & Thompson, M. A. Developmental changes in the structure of mother–infant play. *Developmental Psychology,* 1978, *14,* 30-36.

Elardo, R., Bradley, R., & Caldwell, B. The relation of infants' home environments to mental test performance from six to thirty-six months: A longitudinal analysis. *Child Development,* 1975, *46,* 71-76.

Field, T. Interaction patterns of primary versus secondary caretaker fathers. *Developmental Psychology,* 1978, *14,* 183-185.

Goldman, B. D., & Ross, H. S. Social skills in action: An analysis of early peer games. In J. Glick & K. A. Clarke-Stewart (Eds.), *Studies in social and cognitive development* (Vol. 1): *The development of social understanding.* New York: Gardner Press, 1978.

Goodenough, E. W. Interest in persons as an aspect of sex difference in early years. *Genetic Psychology Monographs*, 1957, *55*, 287-323.

Gottman, J. M., & Bakeman, R. The sequential analysis of observational data. In M. E. Lamb, S. J. Suomi, & G. R. Stephenson (Eds.), *Social interaction analysis.* Madison, Wis.: The University of Wisconsin Press, 1979.

Green, J. A., Gustafson, G. E., & West, M. J. Effects of infant development on mother–infant interaction. *Child Development*, 1980, *51*, 199-207.

Gustafson, G. E., Green, J. A., & West, M. J. The infant's changing role in mother–infant games: The growth of social skills. *Infant Behavior and Development*, 1979, *2*, 301-308.

Hartup, W. W. Levels of analysis in the study of social interaction: An historical perspective. In M. E. Lamb, S. J. Suomi, & G. R. Stephenson (Eds.), *Social interaction analysis: Methodological issues.* Madison, Wis.: The University of Wisconsin Press, 1979.

Hinde, R. A. On describing relationships. *Journal of Child Psychology and Psychiatry*, 1976, *17*, 1-19. (a)

Hinde, R. A. Interactions, relationships, and social structure. *Man*, 1976, *11*, 1-17. (b)

Johnson, M. M. Sex role learning in the nuclear family. *Child Development*, 1963, *34*, 315-333.

Kaye, K., & Fogel, A. The temporal structure of face-to-face communication between mothers and infants. *Developmental Psychology*, 1980, *16*, 454-464.

Klaus, R. A., & Gray, S. W. The early training project for disadvantaged children: A report after five years. *Monographs of the Society for Research in Child Development*, 1968, *33*(4, Ser. 120).

Kotelchuck, M. The infant's relationship to the father: Experimental evidence. In M. E. Lamb (Ed.), *The role of the father in child development.* New York: Wiley, 1976.

Lamb, M. E. The role of the father: An overview. In M. E. Lamb (Ed.), *The role of the father in child development.* New York: Wiley, 1976.

Lamb, M. E. Father–infant and mother–infant interaction in the first year of life. *Child Development*, 1977, *48*, 167-181. (a)

Lamb, M. E. The development of mother–infant and father–infant attachments in the second year of life. *Developmental Psychology*, 1977, *13*, 639-649. (b)

Maccoby, E. E., & Jacklin, C. N. *The psychology of sex differences*, Stanford, Calif.: Stanford University, 1974.

McCall, R. B. Challenges to a science of developmental psychology. *Child Development*, 1977, *48*, 333-334.

Parke, R. D. Social cues, social control, and ecological validity. *Merrill-Palmer Quarterly*, 1976, *22*, 111-123.

Parke, R. D. Children's home environments: social and cognitive effects. In I. Altman & J. F. Wohlwill (Eds.), *Children and the environment* (Vol. 3): *Human behavior and environment.* New York: Plenum Press, 1978.

Parke, R. D. Interactional designs. In R. B. Cairns (Ed.), *The analysis of social interactions: Methods, issues, and illustrations.* Hillsdale, N.J.: Lawrence Erlbaum, 1979. (a)

Parke, R. D. Perspectives on father–infant interaction. In J. Osofsky (Ed.), *The handbook of infant development.* New York: Wiley, 1979. (b)

Parke, R. D., & Sawin, D. B. The family in early infancy: Social interactional and attitudinal analyses. In F. A. Pedersen (Ed.), *The father–infant relationship: observational studies in the family setting.* New York: Praeger, 1980.

Parsons, T. The father symbol: An appraisal in the light of psychoanalytic and sociological theory. In L. Bryson, L. Kinkelstein, R. M. MacIver, & R. McKeon (Eds.), *Symbols and values*. New York: Harper & Row, 1954.

Patterson, G. R., & Moore, D. Interactive patterns as units of behavior. In M. E. Lamb, S. J. Suomi, & G. R. Stephenson (Eds.), *Social interaction analysis: Methodological issues*. Madison, Wis.: University of Wisconsin Press, 1979.

Pawlby, S. J. Imitative interaction. In H. R. Schaffer (Ed.), *Studies in mother-infant interaction*. New York: Academic Press, 1977.

Power, T. G. *Mother- and father-infant play: an exploratory analysis of structure and function*. Unpublished master's thesis, University of Illinois, 1980.

Rendina, I., & Dickerscheid, J. D. Father involvement with first-born infants. *Family Co-ordinator*, 1976, *25*, 373-379.

Ross, H. S., & Kay, D. A. The origins of social games. In K. Rubin (Ed.), *Children's play*. San Francisco: Jossey-Bass, 1980.

Sackett, G. P. Measurement in observational research. In G. P. Sackett (Ed.), *Observing behavior* (Vol. 2). Baltimore: University Park Press, 1978.

Sackett, G. P. The lag sequential analysis of contingency and cyclicity in behavioral interaction research. In J. D. Osofsky (Ed.), *The handbook of infant development*. New York: Wiley, 1979.

Schaffer, H. R. *Mothering*. Cambridge, Mass.: Harvard University Press, 1977.

Schaffer, H. R. Acquiring the concept of the dialogue. In M. H. Bornstein & W. Kesson (Eds.), *Psychological development from infancy*. Hillsdale, N.J.: Lawrence Erlbaum, 1978.

Schaffer, H. R., & Crook, C. K. The role of the mother in early social development. In H. McGurk (Ed.), *Childhood social development*. London: Methuen, 1978.

Sears, R. R., Maccoby, E. E., & Levin, H. *Patterns of child rearing*. Evanston, Ill.: Row, Peterson, 1957.

Sherrod, K. B., Crawley, S., Petersen, G., & Bennett, P. Maternal language to prelinguistic infants: Semantic aspects. *Infant Behavior and Development*, 1978, *1*, 335-345.

Sroufe, L. A., & Waters, E. Attachment as an organizational construct. *Child Development*, 1977, *48*, 1184-1199.

Stern, D. *The first relationship: infant and mother*. Cambridge, Mass.: Harvard University Press, 1977.

Suomi, S., & Harlow, H. Abnormal social behavior in young monkeys. In J. Helmuth (Ed.), *Exceptional infant: studies in abnormalities* (Vol. 2). New York: Brunner Mazel, 1971.

Trevarthen, C. Conversations with a two-month-old. *New Scientist*, 1974, May 2, 230-235.

Wachs, T. D. Utilization of a Piagetian approach in the investigation of early experience effects: A research strategy and some illustrative data. *Merrill-Palmer Quarterly*, 1976, *22*, 11-30.

Wachs, T. D. Proximal experience and early cognitive-intellectual development: The physical environment. *Merrill-Palmer Quarterly*, 1979, *25*, 3-42.

Wachs, T. D., Uzgiris, I. C., & Hunt, J. McV. Cognitive development in infants of different age levels and from different environmental backgrounds: An exploratory investigation. *Merrill-Palmer Quarterly*, 1971, *17*, 283-317.

Weinraub, M., & Frankel, J. Sex differences in parent-infant interaction during free play, departure, and separation. *Child Development*, 1977, *48*, 1240-1249.

Wenar, C. Executive competence and spontaneous social behavior in one-year-olds. *Child Development*, 1972, *43*, 256-260.

Wenar, C. Executive competence in toddlers: A prospective, observational study. *Genetic Psychology Monographs*, 1976, *93*, 189-285.

White, B. L., & Watts, J. C. *Experience and environment*. Englewood Cliffs, N.J.: Prentice-Hall, 1973.

White, B. L., Kaban, B., Shapiro, B., & Attonucci, J. Competence and experience. In

I. C. Uzgiris & F. Weizmann (Eds.), *The structuring of experience*. New York: Plenum Press, 1976.

Yogman, M. J., Dixon, S., Tronick, E., Als, H., & Brazelton, T. B. *The goals and structure of face-to-face interaction between infants and fathers.* Paper presented at the biennial meeting of the Society for Research in Child Development, New Orleans, March 1977.

Zelazo, P. R., Kotelchuck, M., Barber, L., & David, J. *Fathers and sons: An experimental facilitation of attachment behaviors.* Paper presented at the biennial meeting of the Society for Research in Child Development, New Orleans, March 1977.

CHAPTER 6

On the Familial Origins of Personality and Social Style

MICHAEL E. LAMB

Since Freud made his seminal contributions to the study of affective and personality development, no one has seriously challenged the notion that intrafamilial relationships have an enormous impact on psychosocial development. There remains a good deal of disagreement, however, about the nature of their influence, the mechanisms whereby these influences are mediated, and the ways in which these processes can profitably be studied. In this chapter, I plan to review the issues I believe to be most pressing and the strategies that seem most promising. My goal is to show how several rather different studies and approaches should be viewed in relation to one another, for they represent attempts on my part to examine different aspects of a common puzzle. My goal is not to present extensive and comprehensive amounts of data. Rather, I wish to sketch a perspective for the examination of family influences on infant development while also underscoring the diverse issues that should occupy our collective attention as we seek a clearer and more complete understanding of the nature and process of early personality development.

Several questions have dominated my work on parent–infant relationships ever since I began research in this area. A concern with the origins and implications of individual differences is of superordinate importance, subsuming interests in the following questions: What accounts for individual differences in parental behavior? What dimensions of parental behavior have greatest impact on children, and how are these effects

MICHAEL E. LAMB ● Department of Psychology, Psychiatry, and Pediatrics, University of Utah, Salt Lake City, Utah 84112. The author is grateful for financial support from the Foundation for Child Development, the Spencer Foundation, and the Riksbankens Jubileumsfond of Sweden.

mediated? How do parent-infant, sibling-infant, and peer relationships influence one another? Finally: How do infant experiences affect later development? Obviously, I would not be able to answer all these questions in one chapter even if all the necessary information were available. Nevertheless, awareness of these concerns may help us understand the common goal and motivation underlying the diverse specific studies I discuss.

My interpretive framework is based on the ethological attachment theory presented and elaborated by Ainsworth (1973; Ainsworth, Bell, & Stayton, 1974; Ainsworth, Blehar, Waters, & Wall, 1978) and Bowlby (1958, 1969). According to the proponents of this theory, human infants and adults are biologically predisposed to behave toward one another in ways that maximize the probability of infant survival. Over the course of evolution, the ethologists suggest, human infants have acquired a tendency to emit behaviors that promote proximity to protective and caring adults. Initially, infants are motorically incompetent; therefore adult-infant proximity can be promoted and maintained by infants only by emitting signals (crying is the best example) that attract adults to approach and minister to them. The ability of infants to promote proximity is thus wholly dependent on the propensity of adults to respond to the infants' signals. For this reason, the intermeshing of adult and infant propensities and behaviors becomes extremely important. Of the many dimensions of parental behavior that one might choose to emphasize, therefore, proponents of the ethological attachment theory often focus on parental sensitivity—the parent's tendency to respond promptly and appropriately to the infant's signals and physiological needs.

The concept of parental sensitivity will be of major importance to the arguments presented in the first two-thirds of this chapter. Following Ainsworth and her colleagues (1974, 1978), I assume that variations in the sensitivity of parents largely determine the quality of parent-infant attachment. This assumption is, of course, a testable one, and some relevant data have already been presented by Ainsworth and her colleagues. Agreement regarding the formative significance of parental sensitivity, however, demands that we consider two related issues: (1) What factors influence individual differences in parental sensitivity? and (2) What implications do variations in the security of parent-infant attachment have for later development? Discussion of these issues dominates the first substantive section.

The nature of parent-infant attachment appears to be determined by variations in the quality of parental responsiveness to infant signals and needs. As I have suggested elsewhere, differences in security/insecurity seem to reflect the infants' expectations concerning the likelihood of receiving predictable responses of a certain kind (Lamb, 1981). Secure relationships are likely to develop when parent and infant are "well meshed," able to read each other's behavior easily and respond promptly and appropriately to one another. By contrast, insecure relationships develop when the parental responses are either inconsistent or reliably aversive and rejecting (Ainsworth, Bell, & Stayton, 1974). It is clearly possible, therefore, for two parents to promote secure attachments by being equivalently sensitive while still engaging in very different types of interaction. These differences too are probably important, just as the different behavioral styles of parents and siblings undoubtedly make for different types of influence on infant development. In the last third of this chapter I discuss the different behavioral repertoires of mothers, fathers, and siblings.

Quite clearly, the scope of this chapter is broad, and I am able only to illustrate, rather than explore thoroughly, each of the issues identified above. In the next section, I discuss the antecedents and determinants of individual differences in parental behavior. Then I consider the assessment of parental behavior and its relationship to the quality or security of infant–parent attachment. This sets the stage for a discussion of the ways in which the quality of parent–infant attachment affects the developing child's integration into the social world beyond the family. In the final section, I discuss the possibility that mothers, fathers, and siblings have distinctive influences on infant development by virtue of the fact that they represent characteristically different types of experiences for young infants.

Origins of Individual Differences in Parental Sensitivity

I have reviewed and speculated about likely influences on parental behavior in a number of recent chapters (Lamb, Chase-Lansdale, & Owen, 1979; Lamb & Easterbrooks, 1981; Lamb, Owen, & Chase-Lansdale, 1980). so I will not attempt a comprehensive discussion here. Rather, I will mention only those attributes or factors that are the focus of research in which several collaborators and I are currently engaged. Two projects are pertinent: the "maternal employment" study, which involves collaboration with Margaret Owen and Lindsay Chase-Lansdale, and the "Swedish" study, involving Ann Frodi, Majt Frodi, and Philip Hwang.

In a recent review, Lamb and Easterbrooks (1981) identified three types of influence on parental sensitivity. First of all, there are the enduring dispositions, values, and traits of the individual. Second, there are the characteristics of the child and the way these are perceived by the parent.

Finally, there is the social context in which the parents, and more broadly the families, are embedded. Needless to say, these are interrelated sources of influence, and this interrelatedness complicates attempts to investigate explanatory models.

In most discussions, parental sensitivity is portrayed as an enduring attribute or trait of the individual (Lamb & Easterbrooks, 1981). This assumption is particularly notable in the writing of psychoanalysts like Brody (e.g., Brody, 1956; Brody & Axelrad, 1978) as well as ethological attachment theorists like Ainsworth (e.g., Ainsworth *et al.*, 1974). Adjectives such as *self-centered*, *obsessive*, and *ignoring* consistently recur in their descriptions of insensitive mothers, whereas sensitive mothers are described with the words *warm*, *empathic*, and *accessible*. Unfortunately, it is seldom possible to determine whether these clinical impressions are either reliable or valid, and it is not clear that they help us to understand the origins of parental sensitivity or insensitivity even though they may clarify what we mean when we describe a parent as sensitive or insensitive. Furthermore, measurement difficulties are such that neither a sensitivity "trait" nor the correlated dimensions can be investigated very profitably at this stage.

It might be more useful, in fact, to focus on the interaction between certain directly relevant aspects of parental personality and the social context in which the family is embedded. As suggested in an earlier chapter (Lamb *et al.*, 1979), parental sensitivity may be affected substantially by conflicts over the competing motivations for fulfillment through parenthood and through employment. Consequently, we have focused on two parental characteristics or values—value of parenthood and value of work—in our research. *Value of parenthood* refers to the individual's motivation for seeking to become a parent; our scale focuses on *why* the person wants a child rather than whether or not he or she does. To the person assigned a high score on our scale, becoming a parent is a deeply internalized desire, one that contributes to the individual's sense of fulfillment or self-worth. By contrast, an individual who wants to become a parent simply because it is socially expected or for some vague and uncompelling reason would be deemed to have a low value of parenthood.

Analogously, *value of work* concerns the extent to which each individual's sense of fulfillment is derived from his or her employment. A low value is assigned when the person claims to work simply because it is economically necessary; a higher value is assessed when the job or its financial rewards bring a sense of fulfillment or personal worth. Both value of parenthood and value of work can be assessed pre- and postnatally, and they can be assessed in mothers as well as fathers.

We chose to focus on these two constructs out of a belief that for an increasing number of western adults—particularly women—parenthood involves complex evaluations of the relative importance of parenthood and work involvement. Especially in the United States, work roles are an important form of self-definition. As far as women are concerned, this is a relatively new development, since traditionally they were supposed to obtain fulfillment directly through motherhood and vicariously through their husbands' work or careers. In our current research, we wish to determine whether conflicts arise in the pursuit of these two sources of fulfillment and self-definition, and if so, whether the conflicts affect parental behavior.

We expect to find that value of parenthood directly predicts both parental sensitivity and the security of parent–infant attachment. Our predictions regarding the relationship between value of work and sensitivity/security are a little more complicated. Essentially, we expect that value of work will be negatively correlated with sensitivity when work involvement is interrupted by parenthood, although we expect the relationship to hold only for those whose value of parenthood is low.

As I indicated earlier, these parental characteristics cannot be viewed in isolation from two other sources of influence: (1) perceptions of the infant and (2) the supportiveness of the social context in which the parents are embedded. Let me first consider the parents' perceptions of their infant. After several years of neglect, the concept of *temperament* is becoming respectable among psychologists once again. Temperament is an inclusive construct that attempts to measure intrinsic characteristics of the infant that are most likely to influence the parents' behavior. Several researchers have suggested that parental behavior may be affected by perceived infant temperament, and we would like to verify the prediction. In addition, we wish to determine how perceived temperament interacts with parental characteristics in affecting parental behavior and how differences in temperament may affect the way in which infants are affected by their parents' behavior.

Another construct of interest to us is societal and familial *support*. Feiring and Taylor (1978) have noted the importance of emotional support in promoting the success of parenting; its absence is repeatedly identified in the constellation of circumstances escalating the probability of parental failure and child abuse (Belsky, 1978; Garbarino, 1976; Parke, 1977; Parke & Collmer, 1975). In many studies, however, support has been inferred from the existence of potentially supportive relationships and is thus viewed as the opposite of social isolation. Within the relatively affluent populations we study, it seems important to consider both the closeness or intimacy of extrafamilial relationships as well as the attitudinal supportiveness of significant others. We rate support highest when the relationships seem to be close and the others' attitudes are congruent with those of the interviewee. By contrast, we consider support to be lowest when the relationships are close but strong attitudinal discrepancies are reported. We reasoned that the closeness of the relationships determines the salience of the attitudinal dissonance or congruence.

The attitudes of relatives and friends concerning the child care arrangements chosen by new or expectant parents are of great relevance today and are of central concern to our researchers. Both paternal involvement (in caretaking) and maternal employment are currently issues that are salient to young parents and are controversial enough that significant others usually have clear opinions. The supportiveness of the noncaretaking parent is also important in modulating the adjustment to parenthood, particularly when the child care option chosen is one that is controversial and/or novel or one about which the parent experiences some conflict. Most women today are employed prior to and during their pregnancies, and it is usually *their* work involvement rather than their husbands' that is affected by parenthood. In these circumstances, the fathers' concrete assistance constitutes another important form of support.

Value of parenthood, value of work, and support (both emotional and practical) from spouse, relatives, and friends are all constructs that can be assessed both pre- and postnatally. In our efforts to understand individual differences in parental behavior, however, we also focus on a number of parental conceptions and attitudes that can only be assessed postnatally. It is, of course, much more difficult to demonstrate the direction of effects between attitudes and behaviors when both are assessed postnatally; in most cases, it is likely that variations in parental behavior are both consequences and determinants of reported attitudes and values.

Consider, for example, the parents' *satisfaction with parenthood*. It seems reasonable to assume that the more content parents are with the way things have worked out, the more responsive and sensitive they will be with their infants. It is also likely, however, that the temperamentally "easy" baby will be more enjoyable to interact with, and this should enhance the parents' satisfaction with the experience. If this were true, it would indicate that satisfaction might be determined jointly by the parents' expectations, their mesh with the infants' characteristics, and the smoothness of the interaction between parents and infants. The more seriously one investigates early parent–infant relationships, the more difficult it becomes to identify causes and effects. At best, it may be possible (using cross-lagged panel correlations) simply to determine whether one construct seems more cause than consequence of changes in another.

Let me consider one final factor that seems likely to influence parental behavior—the parents' view of their own adequacy and competence, which we refer to as *perceived effectance* (see Goldberg, 1977). Perceived effectance involves an implicit comparsion between the parent being interviewed and other potential caretakers, a comparison between her or his expectations and the postnatal realities, and the tendency not to attribute parenting problems to personal deficiencies. Parents who perceive themselves as competent and effective are likely to be more sensitive and persistent than parents who doubt their own efficacy.

Summary

Value of parenthood, value of work, support, perceived effectance, and satisfaction with parenthood are all likely to influence the quality of parental behavior. In two longitudinal studies, we are attempting to assess the relationships among these and other variables. Regardless of the fruitfulness of these studies, the approach they represent exemplifies several important issues.

First, the behavior of any parent has to be viewed in the context of her or his attitudes; the attitudes and behavior of his or her spouse, relatives, and peer group; and the characteristics of the infant involved. The necessary data can be gathered in a variety of ways, but the parents' own reports and perceptions may be especially important. It has become common to criticize the unreliability of parental reports, but as Parke (1978) remarked, parental reports may be valuable and informative provided we recognize their subjectivity and choose carefully which constructs to assess by way of parental interviews and reports.

Second, as a Briton investigating attitudes toward parenting in the United States, Israel, and Sweden, I am continually reminded of the cultural relativity of many of the issues we study. There are inter- as well as intracultural differences in value of parenthood and value of work, for example, just as the arrangements for which support is important vary from culture to culture. (In the United States, it is the woman's attempt to combine working and mothering that is at issue, whereas in Sweden, it is the man's willingness to take leave in order to care for the new baby.) In the United States married couples are still expected to become parents, whereas in Sweden the decision to have a baby must be justified and defended. It is crucial that we study diverse cultures in our attempts to understand parenting and its influence on infant development.

Parental Sensitivity and Behavior

As I have repeatedly suggested, the attitudes and values mentioned above can affect infant development only if they are translated into differences in the way parents behave. Testing this assumption involves difficult decisions about the manner in which parental behavior will be assessed. Roughly halfway through many studies I undertake, I become dissatisfied with the behavioral measures I have chosen, and I certainly have doubts about some of the measures being used in the projects described above. Consequently, the next few paragraphs will be focused on general issues regarding observational measurement rather than on the specific measures being used in my current research.

In Ainsworth's longitudinal study, prompt responsiveness to the infants' signals was the key dimension of parental behavior. Contingent responsiveness also proved important in Clarke-Stewart's research (1973, 1978); therefore, like Bakeman and Brown (1978) and Parke and Sawin (1980), we tried to quantify parental responsiveness by computing the probability of adult responses to infant signals. One such ratio, for example, quantifies the probability that the adult will respond to a distress vocalization within 5 seconds; another quantifies the probability of responses to behaviors other than distress vocalizations.

There are, unfortunately, problems with such strategies, and I would like to dwell on these as they are currently of central importance not only to me but to all researchers who rely upon observations when gathering information about parental and filial behavior.

The availability of sophisticated data-recording devices and an emphasis on the importance of observational objectivity appear to be responsible for a tendency to discount the integrative and judgmental power of human observers. In retrospect, I wish we had tried to record observers' impressions more systematically than we did. Automated devices, alas, do not think and so cannot handle the exceptions and special circumstances that need to be considered if we are to assess parental sensitivity with great accuracy. As I noted in another recent chapter (Lamb, 1979b), the ready availability of automatic data-recording devices appears to have inhibited capitalization on the enormous capacities of human observers. Thus, we ask observers to record when specific behaviors occur but fail to take advantage of their ability to define behavioral units or constellations and to determine the onset, offset, and quality of inter-actional "bouts." More generally, our units of observation and analysis have become too small—smaller than the unit of meaning, whether that be defined from the point of view of the baby/child or the perspective of the adult.

Ironically, the major problem may be our imbalanced concern with reliability. Certainly, reliability is important, but so too is validity. In the past several years, we have gone from counting behaviors to computing the probability of certain stimulus–response sequences out of the realization that behaviors need to be considered in their context. It is clear, however, that the meaning of behavior is not defined simply by immediate antecedents and consequences. Instead, we must think in terms of larger units of analysis—units that represent the integration, organization, and meaning of behavior, not simply the sequence. Such coding schemes will require greater reliance on the capacities of well-trained observers than we have hitherto deemed desirable.

More specifically, it might be valuable to reconsider the types of decisions we ask observers to make and record. It may be less important to specify that a smile or a vocalization occured than it is to specify the occurrence and intensity of a "social bid" or "social response." Likewise, instead of noting only when a mother touches her baby, we must consider how she does it, or we will be ignoring the most important information. We know that this can be done reliably, for some researchers have developed and employed such measures before. Under the influence of the observational zeitgeist, however, such descriptive categories have been eschewed, and it is high time to reverse the trend. I disagree with Blurton Jones and Woodson's (1979) contention that meaningfulness will just emerge from detailed observations.

In addition to recording larger behavioral units and demanding more sophisticated decisions of our observers, there are other approaches with which we could experiment. I have already noted Parke's (1978) suggestion that we use parents' perceptions systematically to help clarify the meaning of behavior. Another useful strategy has been proposed by Graeme and Alan Russell (personal communication), who plan to observe interactions and then ask parents to recall the incident and explain what happened from their perspective.

Finally, I would counsel against attempts to rely upon any single measure to capture so complex a concept as parental sensitivity. In any particular study, the actual measures chosen should vary depending on the goals of the study, but there should always be a coherent *set* of measures employed. (Clarke-Stewart [1973] has illustrated strategies for combining multiple measures into multivariate measures.)

The Predictive Value of Parental Sensitivity

Ainsworth's longitudinal study indicated that variations in parental sensitivity were the principal determinants of the security of infant–parent attachment (Ainsworth, Bell, & Stayton, 1974). Both the maternal employment study and the Swedish project will ultimately permit us to determine whether variations in parental attitudes, infant temperament, and parental sensitivity indeed predict security of later infant–parent attachment as assessed in the Ainsworth "strange situation" (Ainsworth & Wittig, 1969). These data are not yet available, however, and I wish to shift focus at this point away from these two longitudinal projects.

Those of us who conduct assessments in the strange situation do so because we believe that it reveals social dispositions that influence later behavior in other contexts. I have been particularly interested in determining whether and how the security of infant–parent attachment shapes the infant's integration into the peer group, and I would now like to describe two studies aimed at exploring the relationship between the quality of mother–infant attachment and the child's behavior in interaction with peers. This topic is especially important, because, if such a relationship can be demonstrated, it would indicate that family experiences affect the child's behavior not only within the family but in extrafamilial contexts as well.

Interest in this topic was first stimulated by Ainsworth, who showed in her longitudinal study that infants who behaved differently toward their mothers in the strange situation also behaved differently at home (Ainsworth, Bell, & Stayton, 1972). This finding indicated that there was cross-situational validity to the patterns of attachment observed in the strange situation, and it was not long before researchers attempted to determine whether the patterns of attachment predicted styles of interaction with persons other than the infants' mothers.

In an early study, Main (1973) demonstrated that the patterns of attachment behavior observed in the strange situation at 12 months of age were predictive of the way infants behaved toward a Bayley examiner and an adult playmate 8 to 9 months later. Matas, Arend, and Sroufe (1978) subsequently showed that infants who were securely attached to their mothers at 18 months exhibited more positive affect and enthusiasm in problem-solving situations at 24 months.

In addition to the emergence of autonomous behavior as evidenced in problem-solving situations, toddlerhood is marked by the extension of social networks to include individuals outside the nuclear family. The establishment of peer relationships is probably of special importance. Unfortunately, as Hartup (1979) recently noted, researchers have failed to ask whether there is any developmental continuity between the social styles shown by children in interaction with their parents and that observed later in interaction with peers. Researchers have apparently concluded that because the parent–child and peer "systems" are distinct (e.g., Lamb, 1979a), involving as they do different forms of interaction with different effects on social development, they must be considered totally insulated from mutual influence. It seems unlikely that the child's social world would be compartmentalized thus. Instead, the basic social expectations and styles developed in interaction with parents probably do influence the child's behavior in interaction with peers. Ann Easterbrooks and I have made two attempts to investigate this, one with 18-month-olds and one with 3-year-olds.

In the first study (Easterbrooks & Lamb, 1979), 18-month-olds were observed in the strange situation in order to assess the quality or security of mother–infant attachment by Ainsworth's criteria (Ainsworth *et al.*, 1978). Unlike most other researchers, we chose to focus not on the differences between secure (B), avoidant (A), and ambivalent (C) infants but on the subgroups within the secure (B) category. Ainsworth and her colleagues (e.g., 1978) have identified four subgroups within the secure (B) group. Briefly, the differences are as follows. B_1 infants are active in distance interaction with the parent; even after separation, they greet the parent with distal bids rather than by seeking proximity and contact. By comparison, the B_2 infants are not quite as interested in distance interaction and are somewhat more eager to seek proximity following reunion, although they do not actively seek contact. The B_3 infants actively seek contact in the reunion episodes; once comforted, however, they are able to use the parent as a secure base from which to explore the novel environment. This distinguishes them from the B_4 infants, who are unable to use the parent as a secure base, remaining preoccupied with contact to him or her throughout. In Ainsworth's longitudinal study, the mothers of infants displaying the B_3 pattern had been most sensitively responsive in the preceding months, whereas the mothers of the insecure A and C infants had been most *in*sensitive (Ainsworth, Bell, & Stayton, 1971, 1974; Blehar, Lieberman, & Ainsworth, 1977). The mothers of the B_1 and B_2 infants had attained intermediate ratings on measures of sensitivity. There were no B_4 infants in Ainsworth's original study; therefore there are no data concerning the prior behavior of their mothers. The clingyness of these infants, their inability to use the attachment figure as a secure base, and their inability to soothe themselves or modulate their own states are all indicative of insecurity, although these infants lack the avoidant and angry behavior characteristic of the A and C infants. It seems, in fact, that the insecurity and anxiety of the B_4 infants can be attributued to recent traumatic experiences (e.g., fairly lengthy periods during which the primary attachment figures were emotionally or physically inaccessible) that have destabilized basically secure relationships (Ainsworth, personal communication).

Within 2 weeks of the assessment in the strange situation, two infants and their mothers were brought together in a different playroom and the infants' competence in interaction with peers was determined from observations of their behavior in a 30-minute period of unstructured play. Since there is an obvious dependence between measures of the two infants who were observed interacting with one another, we chose to focus primarily on one member of the dyad—the infant who was designated a "target" or "focal" infant (the other was termed a *foil*). Measures of focal and foil infants were never included in the same analyses. Further, since different foils might elicit different behaviors from the target infants, we tried to ensure that the foils were drawn from a homogeneous group by choosing as foils only those infants who had B_1 or B_2 relationships with their mothers as assessed in the strange situation. As indicated earlier, the focal infants were drawn from the four B subgroups, all of which are supposed to exemplify different patterns of secure attachment.

Our analyses of the peer interaction revealed clear subgroup differences between B_1 / B_2, B_3, and B_4 infants. In general, the B_1 and B_2 infants were most sociable. Compared with the B_3 and B_4 infants, they spent more time near the foil infants and directed more positive social behaviors towards the peers. The $B_{1/2}$ focal infants also engaged in more negative interactions with the B_4 infants. The differences are evident in Figure 1 and 2, for which the data presented in the original report have been adapted. In part, these differences probably occurred because the B_1 and B_2 infants (as in the strange situation) spent least time engaged in seeking proximity to and contact with their mothers. The B_3 and B_4 infants, by contrast, engaged in the least interaction with their peers because they spent much of their time

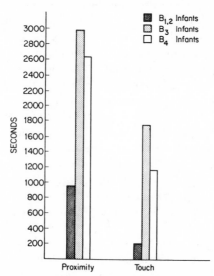

Figure 1. Graphic depiction of data concerning the amount of time $B_{1,2}$, B_3, and B_4 infants spent touching or in proximity to their mothers during the peer session. (Data from Easterbrooks & Lamb, 1979.)

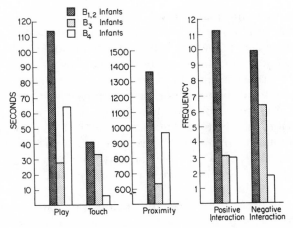

Figure 2. Graphic comparison of the peer interactions of $B_{1,2}$, B_3, and B_4 infants. (Data from Easterbrooks & Lamb, 1979.)

in proximity to or touching their mothers. The differences between B_1/B_2 and B_3/B_4 infants were not accounted for by different amounts of prior experience with peers.

It is clear from this study, therefore, that individual differences in the patterning of infant–mother interaction had implications for the way infants behaved in their initial encounters with unfamiliar peers. From this study, however, we do not know whether the same differences would be evident in established groups or dyads such as those one would find at nursery schools or day care centers. Although neither study examined subgroup differences as closely as we did, two studies have successfully demonstrated a relationship between quality of mother–child attachment and social competence with peers. The most impressive findings were reported by Waters, Wippman, and Sroufe (1979), who showed that toddlers who had secure relationships with their mothers at 15 months of age were more socially competent and assertive among peers in a preschool setting 2 years later. Lieberman (1977) too reported that preschoolders who had insecure relationships with their mothers were less socially competent in interaction with peers. Unfourtunately, however, Lieberman's assessment of security confused actual indices of insecurity with circumstances deemed likely to yield insecurity.

Easterbrooks and I have also attempted to investigate the relationship between patterns of mother–child interaction and social competence in interaction with familiar peers. In our research, we tried to relate characteristics of mother–child interaction in 3-year-olds in both (1) social competence with peers and (2) susceptibility to peer influence. To do this, we had to develop techniques for assessing peer competence as well as ways of assessing the quality of mother–child interaction in 3-year-olds. In retrospect, it is evident that we were unsuccessful on both counts, though a brief description of our failures may be instructive.

We used three techniques to assess the quality of the mother–infant relationship: a separation–reunion sequence, a delay of gratification procedure, and several problem-solving tasks chosen because problem-solving behavior had been related by Matas *et al.* (1978) to prior behavior in the strange situation. Unfortunately, we were unable to extract classifications or measures that were systematically interrelated or related to measures of the child's contemporaneous behavior. Evidently, we had not been successful in our efforts.

Meanwhile, measures of peer interaction were based on twelve 10-minute observations in the preschool. Six of these focused on social competence—indices of the skill manifest in the initiation, reciprocation, and maintenance of bouts of social interaction. Sadly, however, our measures of social competence were deficient: although interobserver reliability was easily obtained, there was poor individual consistency over time, and none of the relevant correlations among conceptually related measures was significant (Lamb, Easterbrooks, & Holden, 1980). Evidently, we had not been able to measure social competence.

The other six observations focused on the effects of peer-administered rewards and punishments on our target children. In an earlier study, we (Lamb *et al.*, 1980) found that susceptibility to peer reinforcement/punishment was a stable individual characteristic, since there was a significant negative correlation between the latency to terminate activities following punishment and the latency to terminate activities following reinforcement. Easterbrooks and I wanted to determine whether this characteristic was related to measures of the parent–child relationship. Our prediction was drawn from several studies showing that adolescents who were alienated from their parents were more susceptible to peer pressure (e.g., Condry & Siman, 1974). In our study, susceptibility to peer influence was unrelated to the measures of the mother–child relationship, however, and we do not know whether this should be attributed to inadequacies of the measures or of the hypotheses.

Considering our unsuccessful attempts to measure both the quality of mother–child interaction and social competence with peers, my earlier comments about observational strategies are germane once again. Happily, there are several innovative leads to report. In their study, Waters *et al.* (1979) emphasized the Q-sort technique, which has been widely used by researchers at Berkeley (e.g., Baumrind, 1971; Block & Block, 1979) but little explored elsewhere. Q-sorts and rating scales may merit wider use as means of formalizing and quantifying observers' impressions about social behavior. Another approach has been developed by Tower (1980), who had observers take notes which they later used to rate the children's behavior along a number of superordinate dimensions. Both these approaches, you will note, demand judgments and the integration of information on the part of observers, and both have proved reliable and empirically valuable. Meanwhile, longitudinal studies such as that being conducted by Egeland and Sroufe permit investigators to test the predictive validity of techniques designed to assess parent–child relationships in preschoolers and school-aged children.

Longitudinal studies, obviously enough, are also necessary if we are to determine how early experiences affect later socioemotional development. It seems unlikely that there is direct or linear continuity over time. Rather it is most likely that the avoidant child (for example) behaves avoidantly when first introduced to peers; this affects their impression of him or her and so affects their later behavior toward him or her. Thus, the effects of insecure attachment would be indirectly mediated via differences in the child's later socializing experiences. In addition, of course, there may be continuity in the parent–child relationship, so that the early "insecure" relationship remains insecure as the child grows older. Continuity makes it difficult to determine whether early family experiences are especially important or whether each of our social experiences simply affects the others in continuing synergistic fashion. In the long run, however, security of parent–infant attachment will be deemed an important construct only if it is shown to have predictive validity. That is why my research maintains its dual focus on the determinants and consequences of individual differences in the security of parent–infant attachment.

The Content of Interactions within the Family

The security of infant–parent attachment reflects the infant's expectations about the probability of receiving prompt and appropriate responses to its signals. Consequently, security is a dimension of the attachment relationship primarily related to the structure (sequencing or meshing) of the prior interaction between parent and infant (Lamb, 1981), although the "content" of the parent's behavior (i.e., its appropriateness) is also important. Following Ainsworth, I believe that the infant's expectations about the probability of eliciting responses from others underlie two important aspects of social and personality development: trust or faith in the parent's propensities (cf. Erikson, 1950) and confidence in one's own efficacy (Lamb, 1981). Studies like those described earlier are designed to determine how interpersonal trust and efficacy affect later behavior. However, parents can be equivalently sensitive—choosing to interact both responsively and appropriately—while engaging in very different types of interaction. In this section, I want to focus exclusively on the types of experiences mothers, fathers, and siblings represent for young infants.

Maternal and Paternal Styles

In my first attempt to elucidate early influences on socioemotional development, I focused on the differences between the types of interactions mothers and fathers represented for their infants. Observational data gathered in this and other studies show that, from very early in their infants' lives, fathers are more likely to engage in physically stimulating and robust types of play than are mothers (Lamb, 1976, 1977c; Yogman, Dixon, Tronick, Adamson, Als, & Brazelton, 1976; Parke, chapter 5). Although at first fathers are distinguished by the type rather than the amount of play they engage in, this changes with time (Clarke-Stewart, 1978), so that by the middle of the second year, fathers are engaging in more play than mothers are. Throughout, fathers appear to engage in more enjoyable play than mothers do (Clarke-Stewart, 1978; Lamb, 1976, 1977c); as a result, male and female toddlers prefer to play with their fathers rather than with their mothers when they have the choice (Clarke-Stewart, 1978; Lynn & Cross, 1974). Mothers, by contrast, generally assume primary responsibility for caretaking, and many of their interactions take place in the course of caretaking. Interestingly, we know that most fathers can be just as responsive and competent as their wives where caretaking is concerned, although they tend to yield responsibility to their wives when both are present (Parke & Sawin, 1980).

The identification of mothers with caretaking and fathers with play is pervasive: it is evident whether one examines time-use data (Kotelchuck, 1976), the purposes for which mothers and fathers pick up and hold their infants (Lamb, 1976, 1977c), or other observational indices of maternal and paternal behavior (Belsky, 1979; Clarke-Stewart, 1978). In all, it is clear that the gender-linked roles assumed by the parents result in differentiated, sex-stereotyped interactions with their infants. Maternal and paternal styles are sufficiently distinctive that even very young babies should be aware of the differences.

Maternal and paternal styles are evident in interactions with both sons and daughters. Indeed, in my first longitudinal study, mothers and fathers treated sons and daughters rather similarly from 7 to 13 months of age (Lamb, 1977c), although several other researchers have found that parents interact preferentially with infants of the same sex from early in the first semester (e.g., Parke & Sawin, 1980). During the second year, however, there is no doubt that fathers initiate much more interaction with their sons (the primary measure in my longitudinal study was of the frequency of parental vocalization) while appearing to withdraw at least temporarily from their daughters (Lamb, 1977a,b, 1978b). The mothers in my study continued to accord equivalent amounts of attention to boys and girls. The net effect of the fathers' behavior was to increase their own salience in the eyes of their sons while (if anything) reducing their salience in the lives of their daughters. As one might expect, the changes in paternal behavior were effective in producing a change in the children's behavior, since, over the course of the second year, the boys developed strong and consistent preferences for their fathers (Lamb, 1977a,b). The girls were much less consistent: some preferred their mothers, some their fathers, and some showed no preference for either parent over the other. What might be happening here, I suggested, was that boys were forming especially close (identificatory?) relationships with a same-sex model. (As noted earlier, there was substantial evidence that the fathers' behavior was indeed sex-typed.)

This study raised many questions for future investigation. Some of these questions are being explored in the Swedish project mentioned earlier. Largely thanks to the social engineering of the old Social Democratic government, Sweden attempts to ensure that fathers can take an active role in the care of their infants without making personal, economic, or professional sacrifices. Our present research there will reveal whether the gender-related differences in maternal and paternal interaction styles (described above) are evident when fathers are more (and mothers less) involved in infant care. In other words, we wish to know whether there are some *gender*-related differences that transcend parental *role* differences. Our second concern is with the gender-differentiated treatment and behavior of infant boys and girls. Do Swedish fathers show the same tendency to favor their sons as American fathers do, we wonder, and is there an analogous tendency on the part of Swedish mothers to prefer their daughters? During the second year, will boys develop preferences for their fathers as they do in the United States, and will daughters too develop preferences for the same-sex parent? Finally, as paternal involvement in caretaking increases, does the security of the father–infant attachment become an increasingly important predictor of the infant's behavior in other situations?

Unfortunately, the answers to these questions and the others of central relevance to the Swedish project are not currently available. Nevertheless, I hope that this brief description of the study and its multiple foci illustrates why we must explore how both the content and the structure of early parent–infant interaction affects children's behavior as they move from the family into the wider world.

Sibling Interaction in Infancy

Interactional "content" was also of primary interest in my studies of sibling interaction in infancy. I chose not to study the security of sibling–infant attachment because in western cultures, infants should not form attachments (strictly defined) to young siblings. Siblings are not assigned responsibility for child care in this culture, are not called on to monitor and respond appropriately to infant signals, and so do not engage in the types of interactions from which attachments emerge. This is not to deny individual differences in the quality of sibling relationships; it is simply to underscore that parent–child and sibling relationships must be viewed in the context of different conceptual frameworks (cf. Weinraub, Brooks, & Lewis, 1977).

In my first study of sibling interaction (Lamb, 1978c), twenty-four 18-month-olds came to my laboratory playroom accompanied by their pre-school-aged siblings (average age, 53 months; range, 38 to 70 months) and both their parents. The families were led into a playroom in which there were a variety of attractive toys. The interaction between the two children as well as that between them and their parents was recorded by observers concealed behind one-way mirrors. The parents were encouraged not to initiate interaction with the children but were free to chat with one another.

Faced with an array of novel toys, the children explored eagerly. There was relatively little social interaction and relatively little parallel or cooperative play—largely, I suspect, because there were so many novel toys that there was little motivation for joint exploration and play. In fact, most of the social interaction that occurred was with the parents rather than with the siblings. Still, the measures of sibling interaction clearly indicated that the older and younger children assumed rather different roles in relation to one another. The younger children were much more interested in the behavior of their siblings than the older children were. Thus, the toddlers frequently watched their siblings and what they were doing, took the initiative in moving toward them (to remain close enough to observe?), and occasionally imitated the older children or took over toys they had recently abandoned. For their part, the preschoolers were more likely to be assertive or dominant. The relevant data are presented in Table 1.

Exactly the same asymmetry of roles was evident in the second investigation (Lamb, 1978a). In this longitudinal study, the infant subjects were observed interacting with their siblings at 12 and again at 18 months of age, and the asymmetric roles were already apparent by the time of the first observation. Furthermore, Abramovitch, Corter, and Lando (1979) have recently completed a home observational study in which the same pattern was evident. All three studies, then, suggest that infants treat their older siblings as people from whom they may learn by observation.

Table 1. Mean Frequency of Interactive Behaviors per Episode:
Sibling–Sibling Interaction

Behavior	Baby to older	Older to baby	Significance of difference
Smile	0.68	1.02	ns
Vocalize	1.64	5.64	$p < .0001$
Look	4.90	2.49	$p < .0001$
Look at other's activities	6.57	1.64	$p < .0001$
Laugh	0.51	0.60	ns
Proffer	0.22	0.58	$p < .015$
Approach	3.97	2.19	$p < .0002$
Fuss	0.46	0.0	ns
Strike	0.19	0.24	ns
Imitate	0.76	0.04	$p < .0002$
Accept toy	0.15	0.04	$p < .066$
Take over toy	1.03	0.25	$p < .0001$
Take toy	0.26	0.39	ns
All measures[a]			$p < .0001$

Note: These data were first published in Michael E. Lamb, "Interactions between 18-month-olds and their preschool-aged siblings." *Child Development*, 1978, *49*, 51–59, Reprinted with permission of the author and the Society for Research in Child Development.
[a]MANOVA comparison.

Siblings, indeed, model types of activities that may be interesting to infants and toddlers, and it is clear that infants are aware of this by 12 months of age. Unfortunately, we do not yet know how much infants actually learn from older siblings.

In my longitudinal study (Lamb, 1978a), in fact, it seemed that the older children were learning from the younger ones, rather than the reverse! This conclusion emerges from analyses in which I correlated the measures of each child's behavior with: (1) measures of its own behavior 6 months later; (2) measures of the sibling's contemporaneous behavior; and (3) measures of the sibling's behavior 6 months later. As the data in Table 2 indicate, the measures of each individual's behavior showed remarkable stability over time, but the most impressive correlations were between the behavior of the young child at Time I and the behavior of the older child 6 months later (Time II). The pattern of correlations suggests that the more sociable an infant was, the more likely it was to elicit attention from its preschool-aged sibling. The prior sociability of the infant was a far better predictor of the older child's later behavior than the reverse.

Although this pattern of correlations is interpretable and impressive, I would very much like to see it replicated. Frankly, I did not expect such high correlations; even though I have attempted to rule out all artifactual sources of spurious correlations, the magnitude of these correlations

Table 2. Significant Correlations among Sibling–Directed Behaviors[a]

Behavior	Inf 1 Inf 2	Pres 1 Pres 2	Inf 1 Pres 2	Pres 1 Inf 2	Inf 1 Pres 1	Inf 2 Pres 2
Smile	.79	.80	.92		.60	.52
Vocalize	.61	.48	.90			.57
Look—person	.63	.91	.63		.55	
Look—activities	.92	.92	.84	.47	.71	
Laugh	.97		.98			.96
Proffer		.50	.87		.41	
Proximity	.65	.65	.65	.65	*	*
Approach	.90	.90	.85	.44	.66	.69
Touch	.98	.98	.90	.98	*	*
Hit	1.00	.50	.55			.55
Imitate	.89		.87			.63
Same play materials	.89	.89	.89	.89	*	*
Accept	.88	.81				
Take over	.94	.81	.91	.50	.65	.84
Take	.90		.86			.77
Struggle	.88	.88	.88	.88	*	*
Coordinate play	.93	.93	.93	.93	*	*

[a] From "The Development of Sibling Relationships in Infancy: A Short-Term Longitudinal Study" by Michael E. Lamb, *Child Development*, 1978, *49*, 1189–1196. Reprinted with the permission of the Society for Research in Child Development.

Note: Inf. = infant's behaviors directed to sibling; Pres = preschooler's behavior directed to infant; 1 = behaviors in first observation; 2 = behavior in second observation. $r > .40, p < .05; r > .52, p < .01; r > .61, p < .001$.

*Correlations of these dyadic measures cannot be computed.

remains incredible. Nevertheless, the apparent direction of effects is instructive. These data add to the growing evidence that the outcome of any social interaction depends on the characteristics of both the participants. The complexity is multiplied when one is considering relationships over time within a social network—the family—involving two adults as well as one or two children.

Although a great deal has been written about "the infant's social network" (e.g., Weinraub *et al.*, 1977), few researchers have explored the network empirically. It would be extremely valuable to determine whether the quality of parent–child relationships is systematically associated with certain kinds of sibling relationships. To what extent are parental influences on child development supplemented (or weakened) by indirect influences mediated through parental influences on siblings? Although we know that parents treat first and second borns differently, we don't know how important these differences are nor how they vary depending on the sex and temperament of the two children and the parents' attitudes and expectations.

Conclusion

In this chapter I have repeatedly noted the need to gather multiple types of data representing several levels of analysis and drawn from several sources. I plan to close by reiterating this point. Over the last decade, we have significantly improved the reliability and "objectivity" of observational data-gathering procedures, but in the process I fear we have chosen to ignore the integrative capacities of human observers. We often allow technology to dictate the size of behavioral units; consequently, we fail to consider the organization and affective quality of the behaviors we observe. Observers *can* make reliable judgments about the behavior they view, and we should use these judgments more systematically. Subjective and biased as they are, furthermore, the parents' perspectives are also important, not as direct predictors of their behavior but as interpretive filters through which we may understand their behavior (Parke, 1978).

Assuming that we adopt more complex and inclusive means of data gathering, there are three substantive issues of paramount importance to progress in this area. First, we need to take the diversity among families seriously and attempt to determine *how* individual differences in parental attitudes, values, and behavior affect dimensions of infant development. Second, the social network within the family still awaits systematic empirical examination. The tangled web of direct and indirect effects ensures that investigation will remain complex and frustrating and that progress will consequently be slow. Finally, we need to ask how and how much relationships within the family affect integration into the wider social world. We often operate as if all experiences within the family (both normative and individually differentiating) had significant developmental implications, and it is now past time to investigate this assumption empirically.

Acknowledgments

Ann Easterbrooks, Margaret Owen, Lindsay Chase-Lansdale, and especially Dr. Ann Frodi made helpful comments on an earlier draft of this chapter.

References

Abramovitch, R., Corter, C., & Lando, B. Sibling interaction in the home. *Child Development*, 1979, *50*, 997–1003.

Ainsworth, M. D. S. The development of infant–mother attachment. In B. M. Caldwell & H. N. Ricciuti (Eds.), *Review of child development research* (Vol. 3). Chicago: University of Chicago Press, 1973.

Ainsworth, M. D. S., Bell, S. M., & Stayton, D. J. Individual differences in strange situation behavior of one-year-olds. In H. R. Schaffer (Ed.), *The origins of human social relations*. London: Academic Press, 1971.

Ainsworth, M. D. S., Bell, S. M., & Stayton, D. J. Individual differences in the development of some attachment behaviors. *Merrill-Palmer Quarterly*, 1972, *18*, 123–143.

Ainsworth, M. D. S., Bell, S. M., & Stayton, D. J. Infant–mother attachment and social development: Socialization as a product of reciprocal responsiveness to signals. In M. P. M. Richards (Ed.), *The integration of a child into a social world*. Cambridge: Cambridge University Press, 1974.

Ainsworth, M. D. S., Blehar, M. C., Waters, E., & Wall, S. N. *Patterns of attachment*. Hillsdale N.J.: Lawrence Erlbaum, 1978.

Ainsworth, M. D. S., & Wittig, B. A. Attachment and exploratory behavior of one-year-olds in a strange situation. In B. M. Foss (Ed.), *Determinants of infant behaviour*. London: Methuen, 1969.

Bakeman, R., & Brown, J. V. Behavioral dialogues: An approach to the assessment of mother–infant interaction. *Child Development*, 1977, *48*, 195–203.

Baumrind, D. Current patterns of parental authority. *Developmental Psychology Monographs*, 1971 (*4*, Whole No. 1).

Belsky, J. Three theoretical models of child abuse: A critical review. *Child Abuse and Neglect*, 1978, *2*, 37–49.

Belsky, J. Mother–father–infant interaction: A naturalistic observational study. *Developmental Psychology*, 1979, *13*, 601–607.

Blehar, M., Lieberman, A. F., & Ainsworth, M. D. S. Early face-to-face interaction and its relation to later infant–mother attachment. *Child Development*, 1977, *48*, 182–194.

Block, J. H., & Block, J. The role of ego-control and ego-resiliency in the organization of behavior. In W. A. Collins (Ed.), *Minnesota symposia on child psychology* (Vol. 13). Hillsdale, N.J.: Lawrence Erlbaum, 1979.

Blurton Jones, N. G., & Woodson, R. H. Describing behavior: The ethologists' perspective. In M. E. Lamb, S. J. Suomi, & G. R. Stephenson (Eds.), *Social interaction analysis: Methodological issues*. Madison, Wis.: University of Wisconsin Press, 1979.

Bowlby, J. The nature of the child's tie to his mother. *International Journal of Psychoanalysis*, 1958, *39*, 350–375.

Bowlby, J. *Attachment and loss* (Vol. 1): *Attachment*. New York: Basic Books, 1969.

Brody, S. *Patterns of mothering*. New York: International Universities Press, 1956.

Brody, S., & Axelrad, S. *Mothers, fathers, and children*. New York: International Universities Press, 1978.

Clarke-Stewart, K. A. Interactions between mothers and their young children: Characteristics and consequences. *Monographs of the Society for Research in Child Development*, 1973, *38* (Serial No. 153).

Clarke-Stewart, K. A. And daddy makes three: The father's impact on mother and young child. *Child Development*, 1978, *49*, 466–478.

Condry, J., & Siman, M. L. Characteristics of peer- and adult-oriented children. *Journal of Marriage and the Family*, 1974, *36*, 543–554.

Easterbrooks, M. A., & Lamb, M. E. The relationship between quality of infant–mother attachment and infant competence in initial encounters with peers. *Child Development*, 1979, *50*, 380–387.

Erikson, E. H. *Childhood and society*. New York: Norton, 1950.

Feiring, C., & Taylor, J. *The influence of the infant and secondary parent on maternal behavior: Toward a social systems view of infant attachment*. Unpublished manuscript, Educational Testing Service, 1978.

Garbarino, J. A preliminary study of some ecological correlates of child abuse: The impact of socioeconomic stress on mothers. *Child Development*, 1976, *47*, 178–185.

Goldberg, S. Social competence in infancy: A model of parent–infant interaction. *Merrill-Palmer Quarterly*, 1977, *23*, 163–177.

Hartup, W. W. Two social worlds: Family relations and peer relations. In M. Rutter (Ed.), *Scientific foundations of developmental psychiatry*. London: Heinemann, 1979.

Kotelchuck, M. The infant's relationship to the father: Experimental evidence. In M. E. Lamb (Ed.), *The role of the father in child development*. New York: Wiley, 1976.

Lamb, M. E. Interactions between eight-month-old children and their fathers and mothers. In M. E. Lamb, (Ed.), *The role of the father in child development*. New York: Wiley, 1976.

Lamb, M. E. The development of mother–infant and father–infant attachments in the second year of life. *Developmental Psychology*, 1977, *13*, 637–648. (a)

Lamb, M. E. The development of parental preferences in the first two years of life. *Sex Roles*, 1977, *3*, 495–497. (b)

Lamb, M. E. Father–infant and mother–infant interaction in the first year of life. *Child Development*, 1977, *48*, 167–181. (c)

Lamb, M. E. The development of sibling relationships in infancy: A short-term longitudinal study. *Child Development*, 1978, *49*, 1189–1196. (a)

Lamb, M. E. The father's role in the infant's social world. In J. H. Stevens & M. Mathews (Eds.), *Mother/child, father/child relationships*. Washington, D.C.: National Association for the Education of Young Children, 1978. (b)

Lamb, M. E. Interactions between 18-month-olds and their preschool-aged siblings. *Child Development*, 1978, *49*, 51–59. (c)

Lamb, M. E. The effects of the social context on dyadic social interaction. In M. E. Lamb, S. J. Suomi, & G. R. Stephenson (Eds.), *Social interaction analysis: Methodological issues* Madison, Wis.: University of Wisconsin Press, 1979. (a)

Lamb, M. E. Issues in the study of social interaction: An introduction. In M. E. Lamb, S. J. Suomi, & G. R. Stephenson (Eds.), *Social interaction analysis: Methoodological issues*. Madison, Wis.: University of Wisconsin Press, 1979. (b)

Lamb, M. E. The development of social expectations in the first year of life. In M. E. Lamb & L. R. Sherrod (Eds.). *Infant social cognition: Empirical and theoretical considerations*. Hillsdale N.J.: Lawrence Erlbaum, 1981.

Lamb, M. E., Chase-Landsale, L., & Owen, M. T. The changing American family and its implications for infant social development: The sample case of maternal employment. In M. Lewis & L. A. Rosenblum (Eds.). *The child and its family*. New York: Plenum Press, 1979.

Lamb, M. E., & Easterbrooks, M. A. Individual differences in parental sensitivity: Origins, components, and consequences. In M. E. Lamb & L. R. Sherrod (Eds.), *Infant social cognition: Empirical and theoretical considerations*. Hillsdale, N.J.: Lawrence Erlbaum, 1981.

Lamb, M. E., Easterbrooks, M. A., & Holden, G. W. Reinforcement and punishment among preschoolers: Characteristics, effects and correlates. *Child Development*, 1980, *51*, 1230–1236.

Lamb, M. E., Owen, M. T., & Chase-Lansdale, L. The working mother in the intact family: A process model. In R. R. Abidin (Ed.), *Handbook of parent education*. Springfield Ill.: Charles C Thomas, 1980.

Lieberman, A. F. Preschoolers' competence with a peer: Relations with attachment and peer experience. *Child Development*, 1977, *48*, 1277–1287.

Lynn, D. B., & Cross, A. R. Parent preference of preschool children. *Journal of Marriage and the Family*, 1974, *36*, 555–559.

Main, M. B. *Exploration, play, and cognitive functioning as related to child–mother attachment*. Unpublished doctoral dissertation, Johns Hopkins University, 1973.

Matas, L., Arend, R., & Sroufe, L. A. Continuity in adaptation: Quality of attachment and later competence. *Child Development*, 1978, *49*, 547–556.

Parke, R. D. Socialization into child abuse: A social interactional perspective. In J. L. Tapp & F. J. Levin (Eds.), *Law, justice, and the individual in society: Psychological and legal issues.* New York: Holt, Rinehart & Winston, 1977.

Parke, R. D. Parent-infant interaction: Progress, paradigms and problems. In G. P. Sackett (Ed.), *Observing behavior* (Vol. 1): *Theory and applications in mental retardation.* Baltimore: University Park Press, 1978.

Parke, R. D., & Collmer, C. W. Child abuse: An interdisciplinary analysis. In E. M. Hetherington (Ed.), *Review of child development research* (Vol. 5). Chicago: University of Chicago Press, 1975.

Parke, R. D., & Sawin, D. B. The family in early infancy: Social interactional and attitudinal analyses. In F. A. Pedersen (Ed.), *The father-infant relationship: Observational studies in a family context.* New York: Praeger Special Publications, 1980.

Tower, R. Parents' self-concepts and preschool children's behaviors. *Journal of Personality and Social Psychology*, 1980, *39*, 710-718.

Weinraub, M., Brooks, J., & Lewis, M. The social network: A reconsideration of the concept of attachment. *Human Development*, 1977, *20*, 31-47.

Yogman, M. W., Dixon, S., Tronick, E., Adamson, l., Als, H., & Brazelton, T. B. *Development of infant social interaction with fathers.* Paper presented to the Eastern Psychological Association, New York, April 1976.

Waters, E., Wippman, J., & Sroufe, L. A. Attachment, positive affect, and competence in the peer group: Two studies in construct validation. *Child Development*, 1979, *50*, 821-829.

CHAPTER 7

Variation in Infant Experience Associated with Alternative Family Roles

FRANK A. PEDERSEN, RICHARD L. CAIN, JR., MARTHA J. ZASLOW, and BARBARA J. ANDERSON

Observational data on the young child interacting with either mother or father derive primarily from studies of families with traditional roles: the mother characteristically is the infant's primary caregiver and the father fulfills the wage-earner role. Conceptualizations of maternal and paternal relationships, particularly theories stemming from the psychoanalytic tradition, similarly assume this family-role organization. Contrary to the dominant empirical and conceptual notions of early experience, however, there is a clear secular trend among all industrialized nations toward families more typically having two wage earners even when there are very young children (Cook, 1978). Indeed, the rate of increase in employment rates for U.S. mothers is greatest for those with young children. In the period in which employment rates doubled for mothers with school-age children, there was a threefold increase for mothers with pre-school-age children. In 1979 over 40% of U.S. mothers with children under age 3 were employed outside the home (U.S. Department of Labor, 1979). Despite the increasing prevalence of dual-wage-earner families, little is known about whether families with two wage earners have different styles of interacting

FRANK A. PEDERSEN ● National Institute of Child Health and Human Development, Bethesda, Maryland 20205. **RICHARD L. CAIN, JR.** ● National Institute of Child Health and Human Development, Bethesda, Maryland 20205. **MARTHA J. ZASLOW** ● National Institute of Child Health and Human Development, Bethesda, Maryland 20205. **BARBARA J. ANDERSON** ● University of Michigan, Ann Arbor, Michigan 48103.

with and caring for the young infant than is characteristically found in the traditional single-wage-earner family.

There are several reasons why this is an important question. First, it provides a different emphasis than the current research that focuses on the nature and effects of substitute care for the child. For example, the mother–infant attachment relationship has been examined to determine whether repeated separation from the mother associated with day care has an adverse effect (Blehar, 1974; Caldwell, Wright, Honig, & Tannenbaum, 1970; Ricciuti, 1974). Measures of cognitive development on children in group care arrangements have been obtained to see whether these environents have either beneficial or harmful influences (Golden & Birns, 1976; Kagan, Kearsley, & Zelazo, 1978; Ramey & Smith, 1976). There has also been some investigation of the substitute care environment (Cochran, 1977; Rubenstein, Pedersen, & Yarrow, 1977; Rubenstein & Howes, 1979), identifying the ways in which varied forms of substitute care differ from maternal care in the home setting. In addition to this focus on the substitute care environment, there is need for investigations to identify variation in the child's experiences in the *family* setting as a consequence of alternative role organizations. Except for the acknowledgment that separations from the mother occur concomitantly with substitute care, there has been an unexamined assumption that parental behavior is relatively unaffected by maternal employment.

A second reason for investigating families with alternative role organizations is that results may qualify generalizations emerging in the literature regarding differences between the maternal and paternal relationship with the infant. Although there has been a burgeoning of observational studies on early father–child interaction (Lamb, 1976, 1977; Clarke-Stewart, 1978; Belsky, 1979; Parke & Sawin, 1980; Pedersen, Anderson, & Cain, 1980), virtually all families in these investigations maintained traditional roles. As data are becoming available regarding paternal behavior, there is a danger that oft-repeated findings are accorded very great generality when, in fact, they should be seen as specific to the samples that were investigated.

Several investigators (Clarke-Stewart, 1978; Kotelchuck, 1976; Lamb, 1976; Lewis & Weinraub, 1976; Parke, 1979) have highlighted the distinction between caregiving behavior and social play, emphasizing the former as a specialty of mothers and the latter as a specialty of fathers. The caregiving role of the mother is underscored because she typically is responsible for all of the child's needs during the period when the father is not in the home. Even periods when both parents are available or in research situations that carefully control each parent's time with the child, mothers characteristically assume greater responsibility for caregiving.

Studies of two-wage-earner families, however, suggest that caregiving activities are sometimes more equally shared by the mother and father. In Young's research based on parental report (Young, 1975), fathers whose wives were employed spent more time in close proximity to their 1-year-old children and engaged in more caregiving activities than fathers in families with mothers who were full-time caregivers. A similar adaptation pattern was described by Fein (1976), also based on self-report, in which a father's more active participation in child care was often associated with well-defined career commitments on the part of the mother.

Physically robust play has been described as the hallmark of father–infant interaction, and studies show that fathers who are infrequently involved as caregivers may nontheless be highly involved with the young child as a partner in play. The fact that nonhuman male primates engage in bouts of physical play with the young provides a basis for interpreting this behavior as a biologically prepotent mode of interacting for fathers (Suomi, 1977). It is also possible, however, that the father's proclivity to engage the young child in play is in some way a product of social roles that separate father and infant for relatively long periods of the day and then bring them together in a manner that facilitates more intense interactions. Although recent replication of gender differences in parental behavior is impressive, it is important to recognize that findings differentiating maternal and paternal behavior are primarily from studies of traditional families. Before statistical differences between maternal and paternal behavior become reified, it is important also to examine behavior in families with somewhat less traditional role organization.

Finally, a focus on the child's experiences in the family may shed light on the frequently debated issue of quality versus quantity of maternal care. Mothers sometimes have argued that *quality* of time spent with the child may be improved by the opportunity to engage in a self-esteem-enhancing work role, especially when the work setting also provides relief from a sense of isolation and the engulfment with child care and household responsibilities often characteristic of the full-time caregiver in this society. Because much research on maternal employment has been restricted to examining effects on the child, this question has received surprisingly little attention. One investigation (Cohen, 1978), based on a sample of premature infants and including a high proportion of single-parent mothers, did not provide support for the view that employed mothers show an enhanced quality of interacting with their children. Studies of children born at term in two-parent families are obviously needed.

In the investigation reported in this chapter, we observed mother– and father–infant interaction at age 5 months in single-wage-earner families and in families where both the mother and father were employed.

Observations were conducted in the natural home environment during time periods that characteristically included all three family members on a day-to-day basis. In addition, we observed mother–infant interaction during a period when the father was not in the home. Finally, we examined the infant's developmental status. Although no investigation has reported effects of maternal employment on overall development measurable in the first year of life, Cohen's (1978) study did find even with statistical controls for single-parent status, that 21-month-old children were adversely affected when mothers worked outside the home. We will present appraisals of the infants based on the Bayley Scales of Infant Development.

Methodology

Sample

The participants in this investigation were 41 families with a first-born 5-month-old infant. In 13 families the mother was employed outside the home on a full- or part-time basis; in 28 families the mother was a full-time caregiver. In all families but one, the father was employed full time; the one exception was a father who was employed on a part-time basis while making a career change. Participants were recruited through childbirth preparation groups in 1976, which encourage low-medication deliveries and active participation on the part of both parents in the birth process. Most parents had college-level educations, with a mean of 16.1 years of education for mothers and 17.3 years for fathers. The mean age of mothers was 29 years and 31 years for the fathers, reflecting the deferral of childbirth that has recently occurred among more highly educated parents. The couples had been married a mean of 4.6 years. The two groups of families, those with one and those with two wage earners, were comparable on all demographic and background variables such as parental age, education, years of marriage, and the sex composition of the groups.

Observational Methodology

The observational methodology was designed to provide simultaneous time-sampled descriptions of interaction among the three possible dyadic units in a three–person family: mother and infant, father and infant, and husband and wife. The parent–infant units are the primary focus of this report. The time-sampling cycle was a 10-second observing period followed by a 20-second recording period; these were repeated throughout the observation sessions conducted in the home.

Parental behavior categories were selected on the basis of theoretical considerations or previous empirical findings relevant to differential developmental outcomes in the child and/or parental role specialization. Of an original pool of 18 measures, 13 categories of parental behavior met the conditions of adequate interobserver agreement and a mean rate of occurrence of at least 1% of the observation intervals. There were four categories of distance receptor interaction: (1) mutual visual regard, (2) verbalizations, (3) vocalizations (i.e., "baby talk," playful sounds, or other distortions of normal speech); and (4) smiles. There were also four categories of near receptor interaction: (1) holding, moving, or supporting the child; (2) rocking or cuddling; (3) vigorous tactile or kinesthetic stimulation; and (4) active touching, such as a pat or caress. Two types of play were distinguished: (1) focused social play and (2) play that involved directing the child's attention to toys or other inanimate objects. Finally, there were three categories of caregiving: (1) feeding liquids, (2) feeding solids, and (3) other caregiving, which included cleaning, changing diapers, or dressing the infant.

The infant behaviors sampled were similar to those of other investigations at this developmental stage (Yarrow, Rubenstein, & Pedersen, 1975) and included the baby's visual focus on the mother's or father's face, positive vocalizations, smiling, fussing or crying, and exploratory behavior with inanimate objects.

Three observers, each visiting comparable numbers of families, collected all the data, and each observer was "blind" as to the hypotheses of this investigation. Interobserver agreement was achieved through intensive participation in the code development phase and in the observation of 10 families by pairs of observers before and during the data-collection period. Periodic reviews of videotaped family interaction were done during the data-collection period to ensure adherence to category definitions. Reliability of all behavior categories range from .70 to .99 on the basis of product–moment correlations between pairs of observers utilizing frequency scores derived in identical fashion to those used in the data analyses.

The data derive from four visits made to each home around the time the infant was 5 months old. The purpose of the first visit was to explain the investigation in detail, secure informed consent, obtain background information, and encourage the parents to feel at ease with the observer. Subsequently, three home observations were made within a 7- to 10-day interval. The second and fourth visits included the father and were conducted during a period when both parents were typically home and the infant was expected to be awake, most often during the early part of the evening. These observations were 1 hour in length. The third visit was a 90-minute observation of mother–infant interaction at a time when mother and infant were alone. This was normally conducted during the day. We emphasized to the parents that our interest was in the baby's "typical" experiences during these periods. Although most observations included a feeding, no constraints were placed upon the parents to stay in the same room, to engage the infant in prescribed ways, or to avoid certain behavior or activities.

Results and Discussion

The sample was dichotomized into single-wage-earner and dual-wage-earner families and the data were analyzed in two different ways. For the evening observations of mother–infant and father–infant interaction, frequency counts of behavior were pooled for the two visits and two-factor analyses of variance were performed: a repeated-measure factor (gender of parent) and a between-subject factor (role organization). In this way we examined differences related to gender of parent that were consistent for the entire sample (independent of family role organization), differences related to role organization that obtain for both parents (independent of parental gender), and for possible interactions between role organization and gender of parent. The latter possibility in regard to parental behavior appeared especially interesting because it would be an important qualification of existing knowledge regarding maternal and paternal behavior. Similarly, analyses of variance were applied to infant behaviors involving either parent in the two types of families. Infant behaviors that were undirected (e.g., fussing or crying, or directed to inanimate objects), of course, were compared only for effects of role organization. In the case of the daytime observations of mother–infant interaction, comparisons of maternal and infant behavior rates were made with t tests for the two groups of families.

For all of the analyses, separate comparisons were first made for male and female infants. Considering the total number of comparisons made, gender of infant showed fewer main effects or interactions than would be expected by chance. Therefore, male and female infants were combined in all analyses. The absence of differences associated with gender of the child may appear discordant with the emphasis on such findings in other investigations (Parke, 1979). We speculate that there are two explanations for this difference. First, it is possible that the degree of influence of infant gender is less prominent in the first year of life than it is at either the newborn period (when parental gender stereotyping may be strong) or at later ages (when behavioral differences between male and female children may be emerge more clearly). Second, the parents in this investigation may have been more committed, consciously or implicitly, to "androgynous parenting" than the parents in other samples. This possibility is suggested by our recruitment of research participants through groups involved in preparation for childbirth, an experience that may have been selectively attractive to parents with less traditional sex-typing behaviors.

Gender of Parent

Table 1 reports the group means for frequency counts of parental behavior observed in the two visits that included mother, father, and infant. Considering first parental gender differentiations that are consistent for the sample as a whole, it is clear that mothers rather consistently provided more distance receptor stimulation than the fathers did. Compared to fathers, mothers more frequently talked to the infants, smiled, and maintained eye contact. On the whole, these results are generally consistent with findings in the literature that are based on single-wage-earner families in which the mother is the primary caregiver. Studies of small samples of toddlers in the home setting by Fagot (1974) and Clarke-Stewart (1978) show that mothers interact verbally with children more frequently than do fathers. Other studies, primarily with younger infants, report that mothers tend to smile more frequently than fathers (Parke, O'Leary, & West, 1972; Parke & O'Leary, 1976). Field (1978) also found this to be true when she compared mothers and primary-caregiver fathers in a brief, structured interactional situation. Our findings in regard to eye contact are consistent with this pattern, although other investigations rarely included this variable.

We also found that mothers, as compared with fathers, consistently performed more of *one* type of caregiving behavior: feeding liquids. A very high proportion of the mothers in the total sample breast-fed their infants at least initially. Even though the mothers who were employed more often fed by bottle ($p < .05$), the overall pattern of maternal responsibility for feeding liquids held for the sample as a whole.

Our data also highlight some important "nonfindings," absences of main effects related to gender of parent in areas where differences might be expected on the basis of past research. Two out of three caregiving measures did not differentiate mothers and fathers, which suggest somewhat more shared responsibility for caregiving in our sample than in those studied by others. Mothers and fathers also did not differ significantly in rates of vocalization (i.e., high pitched, often imitative sounds and ways of speaking very uncharacteristic of adult-to-adult conversation). This style, sometimes called "motherese," has been identified by Ferguson (1964) as characteristic of mothers in six cultures; in our sample, speaking this way to the infant was equally characteristic of mothers and fathers, just as Field (1978) found for mothers and primary-caregiver fathers. Finally, social play

Table 1. Comparisons of Maternal and Paternal Behaviors in Families with Alternative Role Organization[a]

Variable	Single-wage-earner families		Dual-wage-earner families		F ratios		
	Mothers	Fathers	Mothers	Fathers	Sex of parent	Role organization	Interaction
Distance receptor interaction							
Mutual visual regard	17.4	15.3	24.7	14.0	4.18[c]	—[b]	—
Verbalization	55.5	47.4	70.3	39.2	14.45[d]	—	5.05[c]
Vocalization	14.2	16.1	22.1	12.6	—	—	—
Smile	16.8	10.4	17.8	11.0	10.24[d]	—	—
Near receptor interaction							
Hold, move, support	44.3	44.2	47.6	41.8	—	—	—
Rock–cuddle	5.4	4.5	4.8	1.9	—	—	—
Vigorous tactile/kinesthetic	1.6	3.0	2.1	2.9	—	—	—
Touch	15.5	16.1	11.5	7.2	—	3.94[c]	—
Play							
Focused social play	6.0	9.5	7.5	3.9	—	—	4.31[c]
Play with objects	7.0	7.2	9.1	5.3	—	—	—
Caregiving							
Feed liquids	13.2	5.5	18.5	9.1	4.88[c]	—	—
Feed solids	12.4	10.4	11.5	7.3	—	—	—
Other caregiving	5.5	7.2	6.0	7.2	—	—	—

[a]Entries are frequency counts based on 240 observation units.
[b]— indicates F value is not significant.
[c]$p < .05$.
[d]$p < .01$; $df = 1/40$ for all comparisons.

and physically robust handling of the infant, behaviors that have been called the hallmark of paternal interactional styles, were engaged in equally by mothers and fathers across the total sample.

Role Organization

Table 1 also presents results regarding main effects of role organization, or variation in parental behavior related to having one or two wage earners that is consistent for both parents. There is one such finding: both parents in the single-wage-earner families provided significantly more tactile stimulation in the form of touching, stroking, patting, or caressing the infant. A fair amount of this, we believe, is gentle patting to relieve ingested air, or "burping." One of the interesting properties of this behavior is that it is often continued for long intervals after an infant "burps," even when the infant may have no particular "need" for it. Extra tactile stimulation of this nature, provided by both mother and father in single-wage-earner families, may occur because of a generally more leisurely tempo in managing caregiving and other routines in these families. In studies of two-wage-earner families, such as that of Rapoport and Rapoport (1976), parents often described a sense of "overload" and said that *time* is a scarce commodity. The dual-wage-earner families in our sample may have given expression to these feelings by not providing as much time for simple tactile stimulation of the infant. Theorists such as Frank (1957) have emphasized the importance of tactile stimulation for maintaining the young infant's equilibrium, and inference to human experience has often been made from Harlow's (1958) research on contact-deprived rhesus monkeys. Our research suggests that this is an area worthy of increased attention.

Gender of Parent by Role Organization Interactions

There were also two significant interactions of gender of parent and role organization on parental behavior. Although mothers as a group talked to infants more frequently than fathers did, the employed mothers directed an extraordinarily great amount of verbal stimulation to their babies. Paired comparison t tests show a highly significant difference between mothers and fathers in dual-wage-earner families ($t = 3.30$; $p < .01$) and a significant difference between mothers in the two types of families ($t = 2.10$; $p < .05$); mothers and fathers in single-wage-earner families, however, were not significantly different from each other. This result, an intensification of verbalization rates among employed mothers, is a much stronger finding than the similar trend reported by Schubert, Bradley-Johnson, and Nuttel (1980), based on laboratory observations of mothers and toddlers. The latter study did not include observations of fathers and therefore could not address an important point evident in our data: influences of work roles on parental behavior may take on special meaning by virtue of *differential* effects on mothers and fathers, which provide different contrasts in the infant's experiences. Looking only at maternal behavior would not uncover these effects.

The second statistical interaction occurred in regard to focused social play. Here the pattern of degree of maternal and paternal involvement was *reversed*, depending upon the family's role organization. In single-wage-earner families, fathers played with the infant significantly more than mothers did ($t = 2.09$; $p < .05$), which is in line with what other research in traditional families reports as especially characteristic of the male parent. In the two-wage-earner family, however, the mother's rate of social play was relatively high while the father's was very low. Fathers' rates of play in the two types of families were significantly different from each other ($t = 2.51$; $p < .05$), a mirror image of the set of findings in regard to maternal verbalizations. This finding means that generalizations about fathers and mothers in regard to social play must be qualified by consideration of the family's role organization. What has been described in other studies as the father's special mode of involvement with the young child seems rather to be a technique for reestablishing contact and affectively intense interaction with the baby, which, for the employed mother, may exert a stronger "pull" than it does for the father.

Finally, there is an overall *pattern* in the measures in Table 1 that warrants attention. Looking across all categories of parental behavior, the four classifications of gender of parent by role organization are not randomly distributed. Mothers in two-wage-earner families tended to score highest and fathers in the same families tended to score lowest; either parent in the single-wage-earner family was often intermediate.[1] Instead of the two-wage-earner family appearing more egalitarian in child care, as suggested in studies based on parental report (Fein, 1976; Young, 1975), observational data indicate the reverse.

---

[1] This patterning in the total number of measures did not emerge as significant in a MANOVA; however, the power of multivariate tests with our sample size, number of measures, and relatively low-order intercorrelations among measures is poor (Stevens, 1980). Treating the four group means on each variable as an independent observation (partially justified because of the low-order correlations among measures) and evaluating the groups by ranks with the Kruskal-Wallis analysis of variance (Siegel, 1956) yields a significant result ($p < .05$).

Infant Behavior

Table 2 compares (1) the infant's affiliative behavior to either parent and (2) behavior directed toward the inanimate environment for the two types of role organization. Although the measures of socially directed behaviors fell short of statistically significant differences, there is a clear tendency for higher rates of behavior to occur toward mothers in the two-wage-earner families. This pattern parallels the higher rates of maternal verbal stimulation these infants received.

There were two significant differences in the infants' behavior directed toward the inanimate environment. Infants from dual-wage-earner families engaged in more manipulation of inanimate objects and vocalized more while exploring toys or play materials. It is possible that the higher rates of maternal verbal stimulation that these infants received promoted greater manipulative exploration of the inanimate environment. Vocalizations during exploration, moreover, are thought to reflect possible information processing during these periods. Our findings are consistent with Rubenstein's (1967) report of significant associations between maternal social stimulation observed in the home environment and an independent appraisal of the infant's exploratory behavior.

Mother–Infant Observation

Table 3 reports the analyses with t tests of mother–infant interaction observed during periods when the father was not a part of the situation. On the whole, the *pattern* of findings is similar to the mother–infant data derived from observations that included the father. That is, on 10 out of 13 measures, the employed mothers showed *higher* rates of social stimulation toward their infants than did mothers in single-wage-earner families. Only one measure, vocalizations to the baby, showed a statistically significant difference, however, and that variable did not replicate precisely the findings from the three-person observations which were in regard to verbalizations. Vocalizations are "baby talk," departures from more conventional conversational forms. Although findings from both settings show higher rates of verbal stimulation for employed mothers, one can only speculate as to why different types of verbal stimulation might be affected. Parenthetically, two variables that were not elevated in the employed-mother group involved tactile contact, active touching, and rocking or cuddling the infant, which is also consistent in direction with the findings from the evening observations.

Findings in regard to the infants' behavior are generally consistent with those obtained in the evening observation, but none of the differences

Table 2. Comparisons of Infant Behavior in Families with Alternative Role Organizations[a]

Variable	Single-wage-earner families		Dual-wage-earner families		F ratios		
	To mother	To father	To mother	To father	Sex of parent	Role organization	Interaction
Socially directed behavior							
Looks at face	25.07	23.39	31.23	23.00	—[b]	—	—
Smiles	3.75	3.50	4.92	3.08	—	—	—
Vocalizes	6.54	5.54	9.08	4.62	—	—	—
Behavior directed to inanimate environment					Role-Organization Analysis Only		
Looks at object	43.54		47.62			—	
Manipulates object	39.11		53.23			5.97[c]	
Vocalizes during exploration	10.07		14.46			4.39[c]	
Fret/Cry	17.61		18.15			—	

[a]Entries are frequency counts based on 240 observation units.
[b]— Indicates F value is not significant.
[c]$p = <.05$; $df = 1/40$ for all comparisons.

Table 3. Comparisons of Means for Maternal and Infant Behaviors in Families with Alternative Role Organization[a]

Variable	Single-wage-earner families	Dual-wage-earner families	t
Maternal behaviors			
Distance receptor interaction			
Mutual visual regard	20.2	26.8	—[b]
Verbalization	77.9	87.2	—
Vocalization	14.2	25.6	2.32[c]
Smile	14.5	16.8	—
Near receptor interaction			
Hold, move, support	49.3	53.1	—
Rock–cuddle	10.1	7.2	—
Vigorous tactile/kinesthetic	1.9	2.8	—
Touch	15.5	15.1	—
Play			
Focused social play	7.7	10.5	—
Play with objects	11.4	12.2	—
Caregiving			
Feed liquids	12.9	19.9	—
Feed solids	11.6	13.5	—
Other caregiving	21.4	15.8	—
Infant behaviors			
Socially directed behavior			
Looks at face	26.3	34.2	—
Smiles	5.1	5.2	—
Vocalizes	8.5	8.1	—
Behavior directed to inanimate environment			
Looks at object	43.5	44.3	—
Manipulates object	37.7	48.9	—
Vocalizes during exploration	10.2	7.8	—
Fret/Cry	14.6	9.8	—

[a]Entries on frequency counts based on 180 observation units.
[b]— Indicates t value is not significant.
[c]$P < .05$; $df = 39$.

are of sufficient magnitude to be statistically significant. It is possible, then, that the impact of maternal employment on parent–infant interaction is heightened in the evening periods, a time that includes the father and is often described by parents (of either role organization) as relatively more stressful because of competing adult and child needs. The influence of an outside role activity, maternal employment, appears a bit more attenuated in daytime mother–infant interaction periods.

Infant Development

In spite of differences in infant behavior observed in the three-person home setting, there were no differences on either the Mental or Psychomotor Quotients of the Bayley Scales of Infant Development that related to role organization. This suggests that either pattern of parental behavior was within the adaptational limits of the infant.

Implications for Understanding the Family as a Learning Environment

The findings of this observational investigation of first-born 5-month-old infants indicate that in several respects experiences vary with *both* mother and father, depending upon the family's role organization. Infants reared in single-wage-earner families, as contrasted to those reared in dual-wage-earner families, received more tactile stimulation from both their mothers and fathers. Mothers in dual-wage-earner families provided a much higher amount of verbal stimulation, more than the fathers in the same families and more than mothers in single-wage-earner families. Fathers in single-wage-earner families provided more focused social play than did mothers in the same families, but in dual-wage-earner families this pattern was reversed: mothers, as contrasted to fathers, provided more social play. Looking across all categories of interaction with the child, employed mothers tended to show elevated rates of interaction in most areas except for simple tactile stimulation. This pattern was consistent in both evening and daytime observations, although the effects of employment on interaction with the child may be slightly attenuated in time periods that do not include the father. Across most categories of parental behavior, fathers whose wives were employed showed a general pattern of low rate of interaction. Infants reared in dual-wage-earner families showed higher rates of exploratory behavior in the home setting, but no differences emerged on the Bayley Scales of Infant Development.

In evaluating our results in relation to previous research, there is some discrepancy between findings based on parental report, which stress egalitarian sharing of caregiving between mothers and fathers in dual-wage-earner-families (Fein, 1976; Young, 1975), and our observational findings which suggest *less* egalitarian social interaction rates in dual-wage-earner families. Caregiving *per se* appeared unaffected by role organization.

A difference in results obtained by different methods, for example, observation and parental report, may not necessarily mean that one method is valid and the other invalid. It is perhaps more likely that a research participant's social desirability motive may show itself differently. When *talking* about behavior, the two-wage-earner family may stress a "fair" division of labor and emphasize egalitarian practices: when babies in these families are *observed*, however, the mother may feel under special scrutiny and be drawn in to provide higher amounts of focused stimulation such as verbalization and social play. In addition to the influence of being observed and/or interviewed, time periods that are seldom observed (e.g., mornings and weekends) may be weighted differentially in parental report just as observations can have their own differential bias. For example, the evening observations of mother, father, and infant may have a strong pull toward highlighting egalitarian behavior in single-wage-earner families because this is often "prime time" for father and infant and the only opportunity for the mother to find some respite from the child care role. The demand character of this time period might then show itself in rather similar rates of maternal and paternal behavior overall.

In spite of the likelihood that no research method is entirely free of bias, there are several reasons to believe that our findings are representative of the infant's natural environment. Precautions were taken to maximize the ecological validity of the observations and to ensure the greatest possible generalization to enduring experiences. Families were observed in their home settings during time intervals that characteristically occurred on a day-to-day basis. A familiarization visit by the home observer preceded all visits for data collection, and the total amount of time spent with the families was long enough to overcome highly guarded modes of behaving. Thus, we have reasonable confidence that our results do generalize to the infant's early experiences.

One of the most interesting issues is why parental behaviors differed in the particular way that was observed. Why should mothers in the work force show an intensification of verbal interaction with their babies, and why should fathers in these families show an attenuation in their interactions, especially those involving play? Our explanation is in terms of the behavioral hierarchies with which parents engage children, developmental considerations, and the present cultural context in regard to family roles.

That mothers in dual-wage-earner families should be drawn toward their infants with increased verbal interaction, especially, as opposed to other ways of relating to the child, is in line with findings that females generally are verbally inclined. Indeed, our own data show a main effect of parental gender on rates of verbal stimulation in addition to the statistical interaction of gender and role organization. Verbal and vocal stimulation, then, are behaviors high on the mother's hierarchy of responses with which to engage an infant.

A style of interacting that has been identified as especially prominent in the behavioral hierarchy of fathers, social play, was precisely the area that showed a diminution for fathers in dual-wage-earner families. It is possible that the working mother's special need to interact with the infant inhibited or "crowded out" the father in his specialty. This effect on the father also appears in the overall pattern of the other behavioral categories, even though only social play was statistically significant. One of the participants in our investigation verbalized the possibility that his relationship with his child might be indirectly affected by his wife's needs to interact with the infant. He said he was glad that his wife did not accept a job outside the home because he sensed that if she did, he would lose some of "his time" with the baby. This suggests a different hypothesis from the way maternal employment has been conceived of in the past: infants whose mothers are in the work force may not be deprived of interaction in ways in which their mothers specialize. Instead, it is the father–infant relationship that shows some inhibition—at least during this stage of the child's development and in this cultural context.

Other factors that may affect the mother's behavior relate to the developmental level of the child and the psychological meaning of the time spent in substitute care. The 5-month-old infant is in the process of rapidly expanding its capacity to interact with the parent. It seems reasonable, then, that the infant would be particularly responsive to increased amounts of verbal stimulation. The mothers in dual-wage-earner families in our sample, moreover, made the transition from being full-time caregivers to being employed people as well as part-time caregivers within a relatively short period—a month or two for the most part—prior to the time of the observations. Therefore our findings may in some measure reflect a *transition period* for the mothers rather than an adaptational pattern that has stabilized and is expected to persist over a long time span.

Finally, it is likely that the mother's behavior may reflect some conflict and uncertainty over the choice to be in the work force during the infant's first year of life. Developmental psychologists, such as Kagan and Fraiberg, disagree about what is best for infants, and the parents in our study were noticeably ambivalent about nonmaternal care. It is possible, then, that mothers in the work force were in part motivated to "make up" or compensate for what might be missed during the periods the mother was not available. A cultural context that could assure mothers that their children were not being harmed by separations and substitute care might produce a different pattern of behavior. The motivational process behind the heightened mother–infant interaction, however, might be bidirectional in character in the age period when focused relationships are being established: the infant may show a need to reestablish interaction with the mother just as the mother may with the infant.

As to why the father in a dual-wage-earner family shows attenuated rates of interaction, we have already suggested that he is being "crowded out" by the mother's needs to interact with the baby. Two other factors are also relevant. In spite of increased research on fathers generally and a rather large interest in this topic appearing in the media, we suspect that many fathers are not totally convinced that what they have to offer the child is vitally important. Certainly there is very little institutional support for fathering, and it is rare for a father to experience the role of full-time caregiver. Thus, fathers are likely to yield readily to their wives' interests in engaging the child. Again, a different cultural context, one that greatly valued the father–infant relationship, might produce a different picture. A second reason accounting for our findings in regard to fathers is that, at this development period, the child may still be rather limited in its capacity to *seek out* the father. At older ages, it is possible for the child to express preferences more strongly and to engage in activities that are especially available in the father's repertoire. Therefore, a very important question is whether the picture that we saw at 5 months is predictive of the longer-term family adaptation.

Acknowledgments

The authors gratefully acknowledge the assistance of Nancy Gist, who assisted in enrolling the participants in the study, and Barbara Wright, who prepared the manuscript.

References

Belsky, J. Mother–father–infant interaction: A naturalistic observational study. *Developmental Psychology*, 1979, *15*, 601–607.

Blehar, M. Anxious attachment and defensive reaction associated with day care. *Child Development*, 1974, *45*, 683–692.

Caldwell, B. M., Wright, C. M., Honig, A. S., & Tannenbaum, J. Infant care and attachment. *American Journal of Orthopsychiatry*, 1970, *40*, 397–412.

Clarke-Stewart, K. A. And daddy makes three: The father's impact on mother and young child. *Child Development*, 1978, *49*, 466–478.

Cochran, M.M. Comparison of group day and family child-rearing patterns in Sweden. *Child Development*, 1977, *48*, 702–707.

Cohen, S. E. Maternal employment and mother–child interaction. *Merrill–Palmer Quarterly*, 1978, *24*, 189–197.

Cook, A. H. *The working mother: A survey of problems and programs in nine countries.* Ithaca, N.Y.: Cornell University, 1978.

Fagot, B. J. Sex differences in toddlers' behavior and parental reaciton. *Developmental Psychology*, 1974, *10*, 554–558.

Fein, R. A. Men's entrance to parenthood. *Family Coordination*, 1976, *25*, 341–348.

Ferguson, C. A. Baby talk in six languages, *American Anthropologist*, 1964, *66*, 103–114.

Field, T. Interaction behaviors of primary versus secondary caretaker fathers. *Developmental Psychology*, 1978, *14*, 183–184.

Frank, L. K. Tactile communication. *Genetic Psychology Monographs*, 1957, *56*, 209–225.

Golden, M., & Birns, B. Social class and infant intelligence. In M. Lewis (Ed.), *Origins of Intelligence*. New York: Plenum Press, 1976.

Harlow, H. F. The nature of love. *American Psychologist*, 1958, *13*, 673–685.

Kagan, J., Kearsley, R. B., & Zelazo, P. R. *Infancy: Its place in human development*. Cambridge, Mass.: Harvard University Press, 1978.

Kotelchuck, M. The infant's relationship to the father: Experimental evidence. In M. E. Lamb (Ed.), *The role of the father in child development*. New York: Wiley, 1976.

Lamb, M. E. Effects of stress and cohort on mother- and father-infant interaction. *Developmental Psychology*, 1976, *12*, 435–443.

Lamb, M. E. The development of mother–infant and father–infant attachments in the second year of life. *Developmental Psychology*, 1977, *13*, 637–648.

Lewis, M., & Weinraub, M. The father's role in the infant's social network. In M.E. Lamb (Ed.), *The role of the father in child development*. New York: Wiley, 1976.

Parke, R. D. Perspectives on father-infant interactions. In J. Osofsky (Ed.), *Handbook of infant development*. New York: Wiley, 1979.

Parke, R. D., & O'Leary, S. Father-mother-infant interaction in the newborn period: Some findings, some observations, and some unresolved issues. In M. K. Riegel & J. Meacham (Eds.), *The developing individual in a changing world* (Vol. II). The Hague: Mouton, 1976.

Parke, R. D., O'Leary, S. E., & West, S. Mother-father-newborn interaction: Effects of maternal medication, labor, and sex of infant. *Proceedings of the American Psychological Association*, 1972, 85–86.

Parke, R. D., & Sawin, D. B. The family in early infancy: Social interactional and attitudinal analysis. In F. Pedersen (Ed.), *The father-infant relationship: Observational studies in the family setting*. New York: Praeger, 1980.

Pedersen, F. A., Anderson, B. J., & Cain, R. L. Parent-infant and husband-wife interactions observed at age five months. In F. Pedersen (Ed.), *The father-infant relationship: Observational studies in the family setting*. New York: Praeger, 1980.

Ramey, C., & Smith, B. Assessing the intellectual consequences of early intervention with high risk infants. *American Journal of Mental Deficiency*, 1976, *81*, 318–324.

Rapoport, R., & Rapoport, R. N. *Dual career families re-examined*. London: Martin Robertson, 1976.

Ricciuti, H. Fear and development of social attachments in the first year of life. In M. Lewis & L. A. Rosenblum (Eds.), *The origins of human behavior: Fear*. New York: Wiley, 1974.

Rubenstein, J. R. Maternal attentiveness and subsequent exploratory behavior in the infant. *Child Development*, 1967, *38*, 1089–1100.

Rubenstein, J. R., & Howes, C. Caregiving and infant behavior in day care and in homes. *Developmental Psychology*, 1979, *15*, 1–24.

Rubenstein, J. R., Pedersen, F., & Yarrow, L. What happens when mother is away: A comparison of mothers and substitute caregivers. *Developmental Psychology*, 1977, *13*, 529–530.

Schubert, J. B., Bradley-Johnson, S., & Nuttel, J. Mother-infant communication and maternal employment. *Child Development*, 1980, *51*, 246–249.

Siegel, S. *Nonparametric statistics for the behavioral sciences*. New York: McGraw-Hill, 1956.

Stevens, J. P. Power of the multivariate analysis of variance tests. *Psychological Bulletin*, 1980, *88*, 728–737.

Suomi, S. J. Adult male-infant interactions among monkeys living in nuclear families. *Child Development*, 1977, *48*, 1255–1270.

U.S. Department of Labor, Bureau of Labor Statistics. *Marital and family characteristics of the labor force.* March 1979. Special Labor Force Reprint #237.

Yarrow, L. J., Rubenstein, J. L., & Pedersen, F. A. *Infant and environment: Early cognitive and motivational development.* New York: Halsted Press, 1975.

Young, S. F. *Paternal involvement as related to maternal employment and attachment behavior directed to the father by the one-year-old infant.* Unpublished doctoral dissertation, Ohio State University, 1975.

CHAPTER 8

Family Day Care
The Role of the Surrogate Mother

STEVEN FOSBURG

This chapter is based on data from the National Day Care Home Study (NDCHS), which the author designed and directed.[1]

The chapter begins with an overview of the changing patterns of day care, showing that the steadily increasing labor force participation of women with young children is leading to a rising demand for care, especially for children under 3 years of age. In large measure this increased demand is being met by family day care.

It is important to recognize, however, that the general rubric family day care includes a variety of different settings. The study research design, described below, was intended to incorporate the majority of these settings while including a sufficient number of homes of each type to draw inferences about their similarities and differences. These comparisons are reflected in the paper's description of family day care providers. This description points to the significant differences between the women who provide care in different communities.

The chapter's concluding sections focus on caregiver and child behaviors in family day care homes based on an observation system developed specifically for this study. A synopsis of this system is presented, followed by profiles of caregivers and child behaviors.

---

[1]The study was conducted for the Department of Health, Education, and Welfare, Administration for Children, Youth, and Families, over the 4-year period from 1976 to 1980. A study of the magnitude of the NDCHS is necessarily a collaborative effort of many researchers from a variety of disciplines. This paper draws on the work of Judy Singer and Barbara Goodson, both of Abt Associates, Inc. A much more extensive description of the results of this study are contained in Fosburg (1981).

STEVEN FOSBURG ● Abt Associates, Inc., Cambridge, Massachusetts 02138.

Background

Mothers are entering the work force in ever increasing numbers while the average age of children when their mothers enter the work force is declining. This changing social pattern has made day care—the care of a child by someone other than a member of the nuclear family—a growing and important social and economic support for families. Furthermore, the relative youth of the children entering care has recently brought greater attention to family day care, which provides by far the largest amount of out-of-home care for children under age 3.

A family day care home is generally defined to be a private home in which regular care is given to six or fewer children, including the caregiver's own, for any part of a 24-hour day. Larger homes are sometimes referred to as group homes. However, for purposes of this study, care provided in private homes is considered as family day care regardless of the enrollment in the home as long as the home is not licensed as a day care center.

The importance of and demand for day care is clearly reflected in data on labor force participation rates of mothers, which show a dramatic rise over the past several decades. In 1950, for example, only 20% of all mothers with children under 18 were employed; by 1979, their labor force participation exceeded 50%. The largest increase during this period occurred among mothers of children less than 6 years of age, whose employment rates more than tripled (from 14% to 45.4%). These trends are most striking within the current decade. In the 8 years from 1971 to 1979, the employment of women with children under age 3 rose from 27% to 40.9%. For women with children between 3 and 5; employment increased from 38% to 52% (Bureau of Labor Statistics, 1979).

The substantial number of working mothers translates into large-scale demand for child care. In 1978, almost 30% of the country's 56 million families were using some form of day care. Approximately 7.5 million families regularly use care for 10 hours a week or more. Of this number, fully 45% use family day care. An additional 36% choose substitute care in their own homes, and 17% place their children in day care centers, nurseries, Head Start, and other preschool programs (Rhodes & Moore, 1975).

Family day care constitutes the single largest system of out-of-home care in the United States, both in terms of the number of families using care and in the number of children served. An estimated 1.3 million family day care homes serve an estimated 2.4 million full-time children (over 30 hours per week), 2.8 million part-time children (10 to 29 hours per week), and 16.7 million children in occasional care (less than 10 hours per week) (Rhodes &

Moore, 1975). More than half of the full-time children in family day care homes are under 6 years of age; the greatest proportion of these children are under 3, and approximately 30% are aged 3 to 5. Family day care also represents the most prevalent mode of care for the 5 million schoolchildren between 6 and 13 whose parents work (Rhodes & Moore, 1975).

For the most part, family day care in this country consists of *unregulated* providers who operate informally and independently of any regulatory system or administrative structure. According to estimates from a 1971 Westinghouse–Westat survey, unregulated day care homes may constitute up to 90% of all family day care arrangements (Westinghouse, 1971).

Family day care as an informal, unregulated arrangement is one of the oldest forms of child care provided as a supplement to parental care. Historically, such care was provided without charge by relatives or given by neighbors and friends in exchange for other services. The gradual disappearance of the extended family and the increasing number of women entering the work force, however, have caused the supply of "non-monetized" services to drop off sharply. The full-time working mother's use of nonrelatives for supplemental care of children under 6 is now almost as prevalent as the use of relatives. Most arrangements, however, still involve friends, neighbors, or acquaintances; even when the caregiver is a stranger, the family day care home is usually located in the neighborhood where its clients live (Fosburg, 1981).

A second category of homes consists of *regulated* providers who meet state and/or federal standards and may receive day care subsidies for income-eligible consumer families. Regulated caregivers, like their unregulated counterparts, operate independently but within a regulatory system. Data from the National Day Care Supply Study, conducted in 1976–1971, indicate that there are approximately 100,000 regulated family day care homes (Coelen, Glantz, & Calore, 1979).

Regulated family day care has evolved somewhat differently from unregulated care and has a shorter history. Beginning in the early 1960s, state social welfare agencies began to use family day care as an alternative to foster care in order to prevent the disruption of families. Thus, family day care, supervised by agencies, was seen as a placement service patterned after foster care, with homes to be screened, licensed, and monitored.

The third major category of family day care is made up of the approximately 25,000 regulated providers who operate as part of day care systems or networks of homes under the sponsorship of an administrative agency. *Sponsored* homes are likely to serve subsidized children and may have access to a range of services such as caregiver training and client referral. The trend toward organization of family day care homes into systems is a fairly recent development but one with important implications for future day care programs and policies.

Given the central place of family day care in the care of young children throughout the United States, there is a critical need for increased understanding of family day care and for the development of sound and effective strategies to support parents and caregivers in providing children with high-quality family-based care. Despite the widespread use of family day care and its increasing role in federally supported care, little has been known about the nature of home environments—the populations, programs and processes that characterize family day care—or the costs of providing care in home settings. Until recently, research has focused almost exclusively on day care centers, both because they are visible community facilities with relatively easy access for researchers and because they receive the bulk of day care subsidies. By contrast, family day care homes are scattered thoughout residential communities and may not be known to anyone outside the immediate neighborhood unless they are affiliated with a licensing agency or other local organization.

Thus the narrow focus of previous day care research combined with a growing awareness of both the magnitude of family day care and its importance for the development of a comprehensive child care policy led to the National Day Care Home Study (NDCHS).[2]

The NDCHS represents the first national study of family day care and the first attempt to describe the ecology of family day care as a complex social system. It is the first major study to examine all the principal family day care participants—the caregiver, the children in care, their parents, day care program administrators, and the community institutions that complete the day care milieu. All major forms of family day care are represented in the NDCHS, including regulated homes, sponsored homes, and the first large sample of informal, unregulated family day care homes ever studied.

In addition, the NDCHS represents the only study of national scope to systemically observe the care of children in the home environments using sophisticated and carefully tested instruments. Finally, the study focuses on understanding cultural diversity in family day care among the three groups

[2]The primary responsibility for the design, implementation, and analysis of this study was undertaken for the Administration for Children, Youth, and Families by Abt Associates. Abt was assisted by SRI International in the design, collection, and analysis of observation data in family day care homes and by the Center for Systems and Program Development in the design, collection, and analysis of parent interview data. The observation system used in this study was developed for the study through the cooperative efforts of Jean Carew and SRI International.

who together constitute the largest users of family day care: whites, blacks, and Hispanics.

Major objectives of the NDCHS were to:

1. Describe cultural and demographic patterns of family day care
2. Describe the range of program elements, services and administrative structures in family day care homes
3. Describe the nature of care provided and document the day-to-day experiences of caregivers and children
4. Identify similarities and differences among unregulated, regulated, and sponsored homes
5. Explore parents' needs, preferences, and satisfaction with their day care arrangements
6. Describe the community context for family cay care and identify major factors affecting availability and utilization
7. Identify major economic factors and document the costs of family day care—to the parent, to the government, and to the provider

These objectives reflect the principal goals of the NDCHS: to develop a comprehensive and detailed description of family day care and to provide useful information that will help to improve day care quality, formulate sound day care policies, and assist the day care community.

In this paper, a portion of the data relating to the caregiver and the children being cared for will be explored in an effort to give the reader an understanding of those who care for other people's children in their own homes.

Study Design

In Phase I of the study, a 25-city survey of family day care was conducted in order to provide preliminary data on the distribution of family day care homes. The design of subsequent study phases was largely based on information gathered at this time. The survey showed that 99% of all family day care in this country is provided by caregivers of white non-Hispanic (72%), black non-Hispanic (20%), or Hispanic ethnicity (7%). The study sample therefore was designed to represent these groups. Furthermore, the survey verified that the three most common classifications of family day care homes are—in order of frequency—*unregulated* homes, *regulated independent* homes, and *regulated sponsored* homes.

The three-way classification of family day care homes and the three major ethnic groups of caregivers to be studied together formed the basis for the design of the study, illustrated in Table 1.

Table 1. National Day Care Home Study Design

Caregiver ethnicity	Type of home		
	Sponsored	Regulated	Unregulated
White	Sponsored home/ White caregiver	Regulated home/ White caregiver	Unregulated home/ White caregiver
Black	Sponsored home/ Black caregiver	Regulated home/ Black caregiver	Unregulated home/ Black caregiver
Hispanic	Sponsored home/ Hispanic caregiver	Regulated home/ Hispanic caregiver	Unregulated home/ Hispanic caregiver

The study was conducted in three sites—Los Angeles, Philadelphia, and San Antonio. Since the number of Hispanic caregivers nationally is relatively small, it was decided that a representative sample of these could be obtained by using only two study sites, whereas an adequate representation of white and black care would require three sites. Hispanic caregivers were thus sampled only in Los Angeles and San Antonio; white and black caregivers were sampled in Philadelphia as well.

Statistical power analyses were conducted as part of the design phase in order to determine how many homes would be needed to conduct the range of analyses proposed for the study. It was estimated that 16 homes would be needed in each design cell in each site in order to permit disaggregated analyses.

To form a pool of candidate homes in each site from which participants could be identified, several target communities were selected using both licensing lists and sponsor participant lists; home enlistment activities were concentrated in these communities. Since unregulated homes are considerably more difficult to find (because no list of such homes exists), the bulk of the field effort was devoted to finding an adequate number of these homes. A concentrated search for unregulated care, including door-to-door canvassing, was first conducted in the same communities where regulated homes were found. In addition, other areas were canvassed for unregulated care to ensure sufficient numbers and adequate representatives of these difficult-to-find homes.

In general, interviews were conducted with more unregulated than regulated providers and with more regulated than sponsored caregivers. This was due both to the limited number of sponsored caregivers in some sites and to the anticipation of higher refusal and attrition rates among those providers not sponsored by an umbrella agency, especially among those who were unregulated.

Table 2. National Day Care Home Study Design

	Sponsored homes		Regulated homes		Unregulated homes			
	Overall sample	Observation sample	Overall sample	Observation sample	Overall sample	Observation sample	Overall sample	Overall sample totals
Los Angeles—Phase II Site:								
White	18	14	71	15	49	13	138	42
Black	20	11	40	13	20	12	80	26
Hispanic	24	16	22	7	36	8	32	31
	62	41	133	35	105	33	300	99
San Antonio—Phase III Site:								
White[a]	—	—	61	24	57	19	118	43
Black	9	5	13	7	48	14	70	26
Hispanic	12	11	31	18	80	17	123	46
	21	16	105	49	185	50	311	115
Philadelphia—Phase III Site:								
White	23	15	21	12	29	14	73	41
Black	37	18	39	17	33	13	109	48
	60	33	60	29	62	27	182	89

[a]There were no-white sponsored homes in San Antonio.

Two nested samples of caregivers are relevant to this chapter: (1) the total family day care home sample in which caregiver interviews were conducted and (2) a smaller nested subsample of homes in which observations were also made. A somewhat more stringent set of selection criteria were used for the observation sample in order to guarantee enough children in the home during the morning hours in which the observations were made. A third sample of parents is also referenced. One parent of a child in care was interviewed for each family day care home in which we conducted caregiver observations.

Table 2 presents the sample design for all study sites. For the *overall* sample, the minimum of 16 homes was obtained for essentially all the homes except the sponsored homes in San Antonio. There were very few of these homes (none had white caregivers) and all were therefore included in the sample.

Family Day Care Providers

The complex social and economic forces acting within each community establish an equilibrium between demand and supply in family day care. Because of the complexity of the forces involved, the shape of this equilibrium differs from community to community. In some, young mothers choose to stay at home to care for their own as well as other preschool children, thus becoming family day care providers. In other communities, social and economic pressures force this same group of women to find employment outside of their own homes. In these communities, older relatives, friends, and neighbors generally provide the needed day care.

Subsequent analyses of the characteristics of the caregivers interviewed for this study have shown that many of the most significant similarities and differences among caregivers reflect differences in caregiver ethnicity or differences in the regulatory status of the family day care home. Because of the significant nature of these variations, we have presented many of our findings in terms of tables defined by caregiver ethnicity and regulatory status of the home. That is, many of the results of the study are best presented in the format of Table 1 above. For many of our findings, presentation of a single "average" picture value would have distorted the meaning of the results.

Profile of Family Day Care Providers

The central figure in family day care is the provider. Her background, her motivation for providing care, her child-rearing attitudes and practices and other personal qualities shape the experiences of the children for whom she cares.

Family day care providers are a socioeconomically and culturally diverse group. These women are young and old, married and single, rich and poor; yet they have one thing in common—they care for other people's children in their own homes. In this section, we present a profile of these providers, addressing the question: Who is taking care of the children?

Women expressed a variety of motives for becoming child care providers. Some said that they had always loved children, had always worked with them, and that caring for them in their own homes was the most natural of professions (26.6%). Another 22.4% said they began taking in children because of the extra money they could earn. Still others responded that they had nothing else to do or that they wanted to work but preferred to remain at home.

Despite the varied reasons for starting to provide care, most family day care providers like their job and feel that it is permanent rather than temporary. Across sites, three-quarters of the providers interviewed did not intend to change jobs or stop working. Not surprisingly, sponsored and regulated providers, who have gone through a certification process, most often think of their job as permanent; also, older, more experienced caregivers are more likely to think of their job in these terms. Almost 50 % of the unregulated caregivers, on the other hand, are providing care on a short-term basis and foresee a time or circumstance when they will stop.

Caregivers interviewed in the NDCHS ranged in age from 16 to 76; the vast majority, however, fell between 25 and 55. Across sites, the median age was 41.6, indicating that although a large proportion of the caregiver population is composed of young women, often with young children at home, an equally large fraction of the population consists of middle-aged and older women who have already raised their families.

Table 3 presents the median caregiver age by ethnicity and regulatory status. A most striking finding in this table is that white unregulated caregivers—white women providing informal care outside the regulatory system—are substantially younger than any other group of providers. They are only slightly over 30 years of age, whereas every other group of caregivers averages at least 8 years older. The table is illustrated in Figure 1.

On closer examination, we find that these white caregivers are by and large mothers who have chosen to become family day care providers while their own young children are at home. They tend to come from households with relatively high household incomes, and the income from caregiving represents for them only a small portion of total household earnings.

Black and Hispanic caregivers, on the other hand, tended to be substantially older than the white caregivers, although the difference is

Table 3. Median Caregiver Age

Ethnicity	Sponsored	Regulated	Unregulated	Means
White	40.3	38.4	30.4	34.7
Black	44.5	49.4	46.9	46.6
Hispanic	47.5	39.9	44.8	44.8
Totals	44.5	42.3	38.4	41.6

most striking for unregulated providers, where there is approximately a 15-year difference—a real generational gap. Many of these black and Hispanic women were caring for at least one relative along with a group of unrelated children. However, whereas among whites this was often the caregiver's own child, among blacks and Hispanics it was frequently a grandchild. Household incomes are lower for these women than for their white counterparts; consequently family day care income is often a more significant contribution to the household.

Many women begin family day care by caring for the child of a relative. Fully 56% of all caregivers provide care during the day to at least one related child—their own child, a grandchild, a niece, or a nephew (see Table 4). Relative care is especially common among unregulated caregivers. Over three-quarters of unregulated caregivers were found to care for a related child as compared with only 35% of sponsored caregivers.

The large marjority of family day care providers in this study were

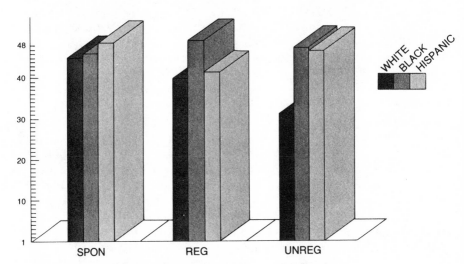

Figure 1. Histogram of Table 3—median caregiver age.

Table 4. Percentage of Homes with Any Related Child[a]

Ethnicity	Sponsored	Regulated	Unregulated	Means
White	34	45	79	57
Black	38	32	68	47
Hispanic	31	49	79	63
Totals	35	42	76	56

[a]Resident and nonresident; caregiver's own and other related children.

married; across sites, three-quarters of those interviewed were currently living with a spouse (see Table 5). Although over 80% of the white and Hispanic caregivers were married, only 50% of black providers were (see also Figure 2). This difference is not surprising, however, given the large proporation of single-parent families within the black population nationally.

Among providers who were married, the large majority (87%) had husbands who were employed. Thus, a sizable proportion of caregivers come from households in which there are two wage earners and caregiving is not the only source of income. Family day care providers spanned a broad range in household income. Many caregivers in our sample had household incomes under $6,000; indeed, this is the modal income category. Nevertheless, a small but important fraction had incomes in excess of $21,000 per year. Median household income across all study providers was found to be just over $10,000 per year. It is noteworthy that white caregivers in all sites were substantially better off economically than either their black or Hispanic counterparts.

Caregiver Qualifications

Three caregiver characteristics are often used as indicators of caregiver professionalism—education, experience, and training. Of the three dimen-

Table 5. Percentage of Married Caregivers

Ethnicity	Sponsored	Regulated	Unregulated	Means
White	88	82	87	84
Black	55	53	49	52
Hispanic	86	92	72	80
Totals	73	75	71	73

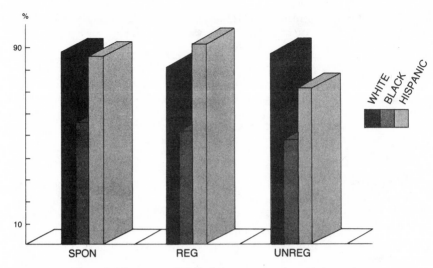

Figure 2. Histogram of Table 5—percentage of married caregivers.

sions of caregiver qualifications described here, educational attainment has traditionally been considered the least relevant index of competence for family day care providers. Nevertheless, it is still held by some to be an index of professionalism and thus is included in this profile of caregiver qualifications (see Table 6).

Although very few of the caregivers under study had a college degree, the majority had completed high school (57%), and some had gone on to take at least some college courses. On the other hand, a full 19% of the caregivers had only an eighth-grade education or less. In keeping with the results of many other studies, the education of caregivers was found to vary significantly across ethnic groups. Hispanic providers had approximately 2 years less education, on average, than black providers, and almost 3 years less than white providers. This reflects the fact that only 5% of white caregivers and 10% of black caregivers had less than a ninth-grade

Table 6. Median Years of Education

Ethnicity	Sponsored	Regulated	Unregulated	Means
White	12.6	12.0	12.2	12.2
Black	11.6	11.5	11.3	11.4
Hispanic	9.4	10.2	9.3	9.6
Totals	11.3	11.5	11.0	11.3

education but over 50% of the Hispanic caregivers never went past grade school. Moreover, in San Antonio, we interviewed several Hispanic providers whose families had forbidden them to attend Anglo schools; consequently, these providers had virtually no formal education. Thus, although white providers had about a year more education on average than their black counterparts, the major educational distinction among ethnic groups is that between Hispanic and non-Hispanic caregivers.

Length of family day care experience is a commonly cited indicator of caregiver professionalism. Other things being equal, parents are inclined to choose the more experienced caregiver. However, experience is somewhat difficult to define. What should be included? The caregiver's experience in other day care settings? Her experience in raising her own family? Or only her experience in family day care? On closer inspection, it turns out that very few family day care providers have had any day care experience other than in family day care. For example, only 7.9% of study providers queried had worked in a day care center and an even smaller proportion had experience with other preschool or elementary school programs. Experience outside family day care does not therefore appear to be a useful indicator of caregiver qualifications. Measurement of the variation in experience gained in raising one's own family posed the opposite problem: not surprisingly, the vast majority of caregivers had children of their own. Because this measure does not vary across providers, it, too, is not a very useful measure of experience.

All the caregivers we interviewed had some experience in providing family day care, if only for a short period of time, but length of this experience varied substantially across providers. Among the caregivers interviewed, some had less than a month's experience and a large proportion (25%) had less than a year of experience. Fifty percent had 1 to 7 years of experience; the remaining 25% had been providing care for 7 to 36 years.

However, we found that the most important indicator of caregiver professionalism is training. Almost three-quarters of all sponsored caregivers have received some child care training, but this is true of less than one-third of all regulated providers and an even smaller proportion of unregulated providers.

Because of the enormous variety of the training that caregivers received, it proved difficult to develop a single measure of this training. Some caregivers attended weekly classes given by their system or local schools, whereas others attended a single seminar. Further, we had no way of objectively assessing, after the fact, the quality of the training received.

However, we were able to to capture information about caregivers' perceptions of the usefulness of their training. Their sentiments were mixed. Some providers felt that their experience in raising their own families taught them most of the skills necessary to provide child care and that training had done little to supplement this knowledge. On the other hand, many felt that the training program helped them substantially, especially by suggesting ideas for things to do and how to interact with children. Caregivers often emphasized that training had taught them specific skills, good nutrition, bookkeeping, basic first aid, educational games, and discipline techniques. Yet another group indicated that the supportive experience of meeting with other women and discussing the provision of family day care with professionals was the most helpful aspect of training, not necessarily the specific information taught by the instructor.

Given the varied nature of the training received and the range of responses to this training, we were surprised to find how useful training turned out to be. The findings of the analysis on the relationship of training to caregiver behavior is presented below.

Summary of Caregiver Characteristics

The previous section paints a picture of three groups of caregivers: young white mothers in their late 20s and 30s with their own young children at home; women in their 40s and 50s with at least one relative's child (often a grandchild) in care; and women in their 30s to 50s who care for the children of friends, neighbors, and others in the community but are not caring for their own or a relative's child. Whereas the first two groups tend to provide unregulated care, the last group of providers constitutes a large proportion of the regulated and sponsored caregivers.

The differences between younger and older providers extend, however, well beyond questions of their relationship to the children in care. The older caregiver tends to be more experienced but less educated than her younger counterpart and, if she is married, her husband also will have less education than the younger caregivers. Her husband is also most likely to be unemployed. Consequently, this older caregiver tends to have a lower total household income and earns a larger proportion of this income from child care.

In contrast, there is a younger, better-educated caregiver who has her own young children at home and does not provide care for her relatives. She is likely to be married and to have a husband who is employed and better educated than both herself and the husbands of older caregivers. Her total household income is generally higher and is not required to support the household.

Observations in Family Day Care Homes

In-home observations were conducted to answer such questions as the following: What kinds of experiences do children have in family day care and how they go about their daily activities? What kinds of things do caregivers do with children and are these activities appropriate given the ages of the children? What is the interplay between caregiver and child—for example, what kinds of behaviors do caregivers facilitate and control? How do children behave both in their interactions with other children and in their solitary play?

We were especially concerned with how the interaction patterns and the kinds of activities available for children in the family day care homes would be influenced by other characteristics of the home—the number of children present and their ages; caregiver characteristics such as age, education, experience and training; the regulatory status or administrative structure of the home; and so forth.

The observation data[3] were collected in two contexts within a home: in a natural situation as caregivers and children went about their normal daily activities and in experimentally structured situations where a common set of activities was presented in all homes. The former allowed comparison of homes based on observations of what the caregiver and children typically did during the day, and the latter allowed comparison of homes on the basis of a standardized set of activities. Observations were used to characterize the caregiver and child independently and to provide detailed information on the interactions between caregivers and children. The observations also provide an objective assessment of the family day care environment which can be used to supplement the caregiver's own report on her interactions with the children in her care.

In the natural situation, caregivers and children were observed as they went about their usual activities for approximately 2 hours during each of two mornings. Behavior was sampled every 20 seconds for periods of 5 minutes at a time. During each hour of observation the observer completed eight 5-minute segments.

The aspects of caregiver behavior covered included:

1. How the caregiver interacts with children—adult strategies likely to facilitate or restrict child activity, such as teaching, helping, conversing, controlling, or playing

---

[3]For a complete description of the history of the development of the system as well as the results of several reliability studies, see Stallings and Porter (1980).

2. The type of activity that the caregiver facilitates, restricts, or is otherwise involved in with the children
3. The caregiver's expression of positive, negative, or neutral feelings toward children
4. The caregiver's use of language in her interactions

The aspects of child behaviors covered included:

1. The child's activity
2. The person with whom the child is interacting
3. The child's participation in conversation
4. Child affect

Examples of child activities that can be coded include language, fine-motor activities, gross-motor activities, conversation, work, and watching television. In addition, such child behaviors as prosocial behavior, antisocial behavior, and distress can be recorded.

Observation Variables

For the analysis of caregiver and child behavior, observation variables were constructed from the codes on the instruments. Basic concepts from child development theory were used as a framework for the development of the child observation variables. A congruent set of observation variables was developed to describe adult behaviors.

The following list provides examples of adult behaviors and activities included in major observation variables:

1. *Adult involvement with children.* Adult involvement ranges from active involvement (teaching, playing, and participating in children's activities) to indirect involvement (supervising children) to no involvement (household chores and recreational activities).
2. *Adult facilitating behaviors.* With these behaviors the adult promotes or participates with children in prosocial, affectionate, and comfort-giving behaviors; language/information activities, fine-motor structured, fine-motor exploratory, and gross-motor activities; music, dance, and dramatic play; television; and physical needs activities.
3. *Adult control activities.* Adult control techniques range from positive routine control measures, for which explanations are given, to strict negative control measures.
4. *Adult affect.* Adult affect ranges from positive (laughing and smiling) to neutral (neither positive nor negative) to negative (angry, hostile, sad).

5. *Adult interactions with babies and older children.* Adult interacts with a baby or older child. This variable is included to account for the caregiver's interactions with children outside the age range of this study (12 to 59 months).

The following are examples of variables developed to describe child behavior:

1. *Persons with whom the child is interacting.* Child is engaging in an activity alone, with an adult, with a young child or group of children, with a baby or older child.
2. *Content of child's activities.* Child is engaging in prosocial, affectionate, and comfort-giving behaviors; language/information activities; fine-motor structured, fine-motor exploratory, and gross-motor activities; music, dance, and dramatic play; television; attending to physical needs or engaging in antisocial activities.
3. *Child's participation in a conversation.* Child initiates, receives, or responds to conversation or to task-related comments; child uses Spanish or English.
4. *Child's active engagement in an activity.*
5. *Child affect.* Child affect ranges from positive (laughing and smiling) to neutral (neither positive nor negative) to negative (angry, hostile, sad).

Quality of the Observation Data

Since the observation data systems used in the NDCHS were developed specifically for this research, there were no previous studies to establish their reliability. Accordingly, a series of reliability studies was conducted. The first study was designed to answer two related questions: Would white, black, and Hispanic observers perceive the same event in the same way? Did it make a difference if the person observed was of the same or different ethnicity? This study showed that ethnicity was not a factor in the accuracy and consistency with which observers coded behaviors of children and adults.

A second group of substudies was undertaken to determine how stable the observations were over time: from hour to hour, from morning to afternoon, across two adjacent days, and over a period of 4 weeks. In each case very high reliability was established for both adult and child observations. For nearly every type of behavior, reliabilities of 90% or better were reported.

In addition to the special substudies, observers were required to maintain 80% accuracy with the coding system. Observers were tested against a criterion videotape at the end of training and again during field operations. Several of the substudies also involved assessment of inter-observer reliability in the field whereby two observers coded activities in the same home simultaneously and the completed observations were checked for consistency. As a result of these reliability studies, the observation system was shown to be psychometrically sound and the data of consistently high quality.

Descriptive Analyses

One of the primary objectives of the observation component was to describe how caregivers and children spend their time. For example, we wanted to know what proportion of caregivers' time is spent in direct interaction with children and how that time is distributed among different types of behavior. How much teaching, playing, and helping is there? How often do caregivers facilitate and control the children's behavior? In what ways?

Because this was the first large-scale study of family day care to use this approach, there were no norms to indicate what the "typical" distribution of the caregiver's time should be. Patterns of similarity and variation found in the behavior of caregivers among sponsored, regulated, and unregulated homes help to develop an idea of what can be expected of caregivers in these settings.

The same is true for children's behavior. The observation component was designed to describe the proportion of children's time spent in direct interaction with the caregiver, with other children, and in independent activities. Within this broad context we wanted to know how their time was distributed in developmentally important ways. How often did children engage in cognitive, social, and physical activities? To what extent did they converse with adults and each other? What distinct behavioral patterns could be observed among children of different ages?

Caregiver Behavior

One of the most striking findings to emerge from the NDCHS is the high level of involvement with children exhibited by family day care providers. Overall, family day care providers spend nearly two-thirds of their day in child-related activities. On average, across all types of settings, ethnic groups and size of home, caregivers spend approximately half their time (46%) in direct interaction with children (Table 7; Figure 3). In

Table 7. Distribution of the Caregiver's Time[a]

Direct involvement with children	Percentage of time	
Interaction with 1- to 5-year-olds:		
Teach	13.9	
Play/participate	7.8	
Help	8.9	
Direct	3.7	
Converse	3.3	
Control	3.7	
	41.3	
Interaction with babies (< 1 year)	3.8[b]	
Interaction with school-aged children	1.0[b]	
Negative affect with any child[c]	0.3	
Total direct involvement		46.4
Indirect involvement with children:		
Supervise or prepare		16.5
Noninvolvement with children:		
Primary caregiver		
Converse with adults	6.3	
Recreation alone	7.8	
Housekeeping	19.4	
Out of range	1.3	
	34.8	
Secondary caregiver interaction	2.2	
Total noninvolvement		37.0
Grand total		99.9

[a] This picture is based primarily on morning observations and does not include periods in which the children are napping or eating or periods when more school-aged children are present.

[b] These figures may be misleading as they stand. These percentages were calculated for *all* homes, even though caregivers were observed to interact with babies in only 35% of all homes and with school-aged children in only 16% of all homes. Considering *only* homes in which babies are present, the caregiver spends about 11% of her time with babies. Considering *only* homes in which school-aged childred are present, the caregiver spends about 6% of her time with them.

[c] Negative affect occurred so infrequently that it could not be analyzed separately for each of the direct interaction variables but was instead aggregated into a single category of less than 0.3%.

addition, they spend another 17% of the day either supervising children or preparing for them.

Table 7 shows that 41.3% of the caregiver's time is spent interacting with the 1- to 5-year-old children in her care. (That is, 41.3% of the observations consisted of such interactions.) This is in line with previous research on family day care, which also demonstrated that most caregivers

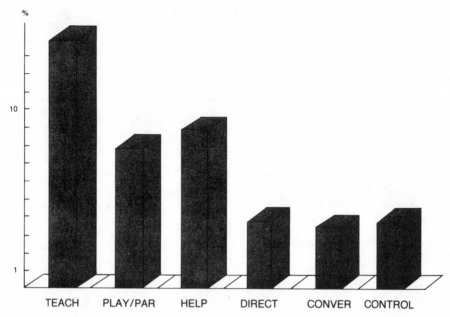

Figure 3. Histogram of Table 7—distribution of the caregiver's time: interaction with 1- to 5-year olds.

spend a substantial proportion of their time in contact with the children. It also reflects parents' statements about the nature of the care that their children receive. Furthermore, this time seems to be spent in appropriate ways; that is, it mirrors the needs of children in care as indicated by their ages. Figure 3, based on Table 7, illustrates that one of the most frequent interactions with children in the 1- to 5-year-old age range is teaching, which occupies 13.9% of the caregiver's time. In the remainder of caregiver/child interactions, play/participation and helping are about equal in frequency, respectively occupying 7.8% and 8.9% of caregivers' time. The amount of teaching and play in the homes in our study suggests that previous descriptions of family day care as lacking in stimulation for young children are not valid for our sample. Directing and controlling are substantially less frequent than other caregiver behaviors, each accounting for only 3.7% of the observed behaviors. Previous studies also found a minimal amount of restrictive behavior on the part of family day care providers.

Infants and school-aged children were found only in a subset of these homes. Whereas the observation instrument makes fine distinctions in the interactions of caregivers with 1- and 5-year-olds, their behavior with younger and older children is aggregated into coarser categories. We found that, averaged across all homes, the caregivers spent 3.8% of their time interacting with babies and 1% interacting with school-aged children.

Because negative affect was such an infrequent occurrence in family day care homes, it could not be analyzed separately for each of the interactions between caregivers and children noted above. Instead, all occurrences of negative affect were aggregated into a single measure. The reader may observe in Table 7 that even in the aggregate form, the caregiver demonstrated negative affect with the children in her care in only 0.3% of the observations.

On average, the caregiver spent slightly over half her time not actively involved with the children in her care. This time can be divided into two categories, indirect involvement and noninvolvement. Indirect involvement consists of supervising the children (without interacting but with the potential of interacting with the children) and making preparations directly related to their care. Together, these activities comprise 16.5% of the caregiver's time, leaving her apparently uninvolved with the children for approximately one-third of the time.

When the caregiver was not occupied with the children, she spent her time either talking to other adults (6.3%), entertaining herself by reading or watching television (7.8%), housekeeping (19.4%), or out or range of the observer (1.3%). Of course, even when she is not directly involved with the children, the caregiver can often respond to indications that something is amiss. In most cases she was in close physical proximity to the children, being out of observable range only 1.3% of the time.

The final category in Table 7 relates to secondary caregivers. In some of the homes, especially larger regulated and sponsored homes, some portion of the observations were taken up by helpers (secondary caregivers). On average, this constituted such a small proportion of the total observations (2.2%) that no useful analyses were feasible. Thus, these secondary caregivers were dropped in subsequent analyses.

Having described the distribution of the caregiver's time for the sample as a whole, we turn now to a consideration of similarities and differences in observed patterns of behavior for homes of different regulatory status. In fact, some of the most interesting study findings are implicit in comparisons of caregiver behavior across settings. Here we treat these comparisons in a purely descriptive manner, noting in which settings behaviors are relatively more frequent. The present discussion is consistent with the results of other analyses presented in subsequent sections and with the sense of family day care we have obtained through the caregiver interview process.

Table 8 and the accompanying two figures (Figures 4 and 5) illustrate the differences between observed caregiver behaviors and unregulated,

Table 8. Distribution of the Caregiver's Time by Regulatory Status

	Sponsored	Regulated	Unregulated
Direct involvement with children:			
Interaction with 1- to 5-year-olds			
Teach	17.0	12.8	12.1
Play/participate	8.6	7.3	7.3
Help	9.3	9.5	8.2
Direct	3.9	3.8	3.8
Converse	3.4	3.3	3.0
Control	3.6	3.8	3.5
Subtotal	45.8	40.5	37.9
Interaction with baby	3.4	5.3	2.5
Interaction with school-aged children	0.8	0.7	0.9
Negative emotional affect	0.2	0.2	0.4
Total direct involvement	50.2	46.7	41.7
Indirect involvement with children:			
Supervise and prepare	18.4	17.2	14.2
Noninvolvement with children:			
Converse with adults	5.5	5.8	6.8
Recreation alone	4.8	5.7	13.0
Housekeeping	17.9	17.8	22.0
Out of range	1.7	1.4	1.2
Subtotal	29.9	30.7	43.0
Total[a]	98.5	94.6	98.9

Activities facilitated:			
Language/information	10.6	8.4	7.8
Structured fine motor	6.1	3.1	3.5
Work	1.4	1.3	1.3
Physical needs	8.2	8.9	8.1
Dramatic play	1.1	0.8	1.2
Music/dance	2.1	0.7	0.4
Television	1.8	2.6	2.0
Exploratory fine motor	1.2	1.0	0.9
Gross motor	2.2	1.8	1.5
Total facilitation	34.7	28.6	26.7
Positive affect	6.0	5.6	4.6

[a]Recall that observations of helpers, averaging 2.2% overall, were deleted from the analysis. This accounts for total distribution of caregiver's time equaling less than 100%.

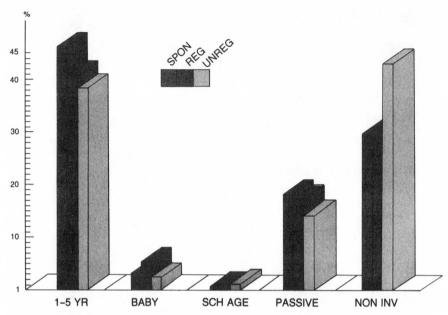

Figure 4. Histogram of Table 8—distribution of the caregiver's time by regulatory status.

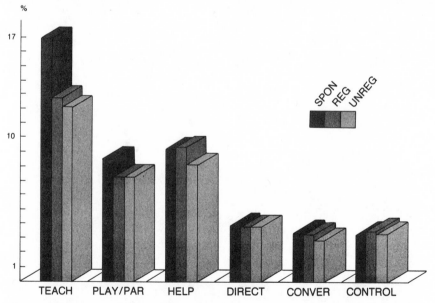

Figure 5. Histogram of Table 8—distribution of the caregiver's time by regulatory status: interaction with 1- to 5-year-olds.

regulated, and sponsored homes. Entries in Table 8, and in Table 7, are the percentages of observations that fall into each category, averaged across all the caregivers observed. Although all settings showed a substantial amount of caregiver/child interaction, the differences among settings are statistically significant. Unregulated homes showed the lowest level of caregiver interactions with 1- to 5-year-olds in care. Regulated homes showed a somewhat higher level of interaction, and sponsored homes showed by far the highest level. The differences between unregulated and regulated homes were generally small; half the difference in the level of interaction is in the frequency of helping behaviors, which account for 8.2% of the caregiver/child interaction in unregulated homes and 9.5% in regulated homes.

Sponsored homes, however, were substantially different in the amount of teaching that occurred. Whereas 12.1% of the caregiver's time in unregulated homes and 12.8% in regulated homes was spent in teaching, 17% of the caregiver's time in sponsored homes is spent in this manner—a very large difference. This is especially noteworthy in the light of other study findings indicating that many parents would prefer a day care environment that emphasizes teaching activities.

Expanding upon these differences among settings, the bottom portion of Table 8 is devoted to the activities that caregivers facilitate with children while they are interacting with them. This table shows that sponsored caregivers facilitated much more language/information, structured fine-motor activities, and music/dance activities. Also, there was somewhat more gross-motor activity in these homes and less watching of television. This implies a more preschool-like setting with structured activities for the children. On the whole, regulated and unregulated caregivers seem very different from sponsored caregivers but similar to one another.

On the other hand, regulated and sponsored caregivers were similar with regard to the time spent in supervision and preparation for children, whereas unregulated caregivers spent somewhat less time in these activities. Furthermore, unregulated caregivers spent substantially more time uninvolved with the children. Unregulated caregivers spend 43% of the time apart from the children, as opposed to about 30% for both regulated and sponsored caregivers. In unregulated homes, this means that, on average, 26 minutes of every hour were spent uninvolved with children, whereas only 18 minutes of every hour were spent in this manner in sponsored homes.

This set of findings suggests that the unregulated caregiver is somewhat less child-focused than the regulated caregiver and much less so than the sponsored caregiver. She spends more time than either attending both on her own needs and to those of her household while the day care children are present. The sponsored caregiver's added involvement with the children is apparent in several ways: there is more teaching, more play/participation, more supervision and preparation, and less housekeeping and solitary recreation. Further, when we look at the additional activities that sponsored caregivers facilitate—language/information, structured fine-motor, music/dance and gross-motor activities—we see behaviors that are often stressed in the child care training received by sponsored providers but by few regulated or unregulated providers. This suggests that caregiver training may make a difference. This impression is supported by the study's other data sources, including caregiver interviews and and observer summaries (recorded at the end of the observation sessions).

Finally, to put these findings into context, it is important to stress that observers and interviewers were consistently impressed by the quality of the care that they saw regardless of regulatory status of the home. Conclusions, therefore, about the relative frequency of behavior from one setting to another are not intended to imply that unregulated care is poor care. However, many parents may well feel that sponsored care provides important stimulation that is generally less available in other kinds of family day care.

Child Behavior

Whereas there is, in general, only one caregiver in each home, there are usually several children in care. Observations of children were divided among the younger children (1- to 3-year-olds) and the older children (3- to 5-year olds). Where possible, one child in each age range was observed in each home; however, not all age groups were represented in every home. Therefore, the number of children observed in each category is considerably less than the number of caregivers observed: 303 homes and caregivers were represented, but only 253 younger and 161 older children were observed.

Furthermore, because the children were grouped into such broad age spans and because they show rapid development during this age period, the variance in child behavior is often so large as to require multivariate statistical analyses to determine where there are actual differences in the behaviors between one care setting and another. The brief description of child behaviors that is presented here is intended only to buttress the description of caregiver and child interactions. For this purpose, we will discuss only the frequencies of behaviors for younger and older children, as this reinforces our sense that the observation system was responsive to the kinds of behavior one expects to see in children of these ages.

In the socioemotional domain, for example, one notes more affectionate behavior among the younger children as well as more distress, both typical of this age group. Older children demonstrate more prosocial behavior and more frequently control the behavior of a younger child, again as one might expect.

In the cognitive/linguistic domain, the older child exhibits more language/information activities, more dramatic play, more fine-motor structured activity, and more conversation with other young children. The younger child exhibits more fine-motor exploratory behavior alone. The most common activities in both age groups involved fine-motor skills such as puzzles, water play, or manipulating small toys—behaviors that were considerably more frequent than any other type. This picture is in contrast with some previous research that points to TV watching as the most frequent activity in family day care homes. Activities in the cognitive/linguistic domain were much more frequent than watching TV.

The the physical/motor domain, the younger child, as expected, has more physical needs to be met. The younger child also looks around, watches older children's activities, or otherwise monitors the environment more than does the older child.

Both younger and older children spend much of their time in independent activity—that is, not directly interacting with either the caregiver or another child. Younger children spend 62.6% of their time in this manner, whereas older children spend 51.9%—less than younger children but still more than half of their time. The younger children spend 14.7% of their time directly interacting with the caregiver, and older children spend 11.8% of their time in this way. There are many fewer direct interactions among the children, however. Younger children interact only 1.7% of the time with other children, and older children 5.1% of the time. Although it is generally agreed that the caregiver's interactions with children are of paramount importance to the children's family day care experience, the child's utilization of that large portion of time spent in independent activity is an equally important concern.

Multivariate Analyses

The descriptive profiles presented in the previous section set the stage for multivariate analyses of the observation data. The descriptive analysis asked: What was the process like in family day care homes? The multivariate analysis asks: How might differences in caregiver and child behavior by explained? The descriptive profile alone suggested that regulatory status of the home is strongly associated with differences in behavior; the multivariate analysis went further by examining the observation data simultaneously across multiple factors of interest, assessing the relative importance of each in describing caregiver and child behavior.

The simultaneous consideration of multiple factors afforded important advantages over a variable-by-variable examination of the observation data. The variables under consideration were, in addition to the design variables, a set of factors such as caregivers' qualifications or group size, which were not controlled in design but potentially related to caregiver and child behavior. Limiting the analysis to individual relationships between each variable and behavior would have been inappropriate—first, because the primary interest was in how the set of factors explained behavior and, second, because many of the factors were confounded (i.e., not independent of each other). For instance, if caregiver behavior were associated with both caregiver training and the regulatory status of the home, the fact that training and regulatory status are correlated means that these associations cannot be interpreted individually; the effects could not be attributed solely to either factor. Any given behavior might be due to either or both of these elements. Since many of the factors of interest were confounded in the study design and/or correlated in the real world, it was necessary to use techniques that could consider factors jointly and take into account the pattern of confounding. Multivariate analyses, though they could not completely disentangle related factors, did allow us to construct and test several different sets of factors which were selected to minimize confounding within a set.

Group Composition and Its Relationship to Caregiver Behavior

Group composition occupies a central place in most considerations of the nature of family day care environments. It was thus deemed essential that this study shed some light on the nature of the relationship between group size and the family day care routine. Observations provide an ideal way to examine these relationships.

Two aspects of group composition in the home were examined: the total number present and the ages of the children present. The number of children is a measure of caregiver burden as well as of potential attention for the individual child. One question was whether an increase in group size was associated with changing patterns of activities and interactions in the home. With respect to age mix, the question was whether particular age mixes were more burdensome than others or required different kinds of care and thereby influenced caregiver and child behavior.

The analyses showed that both aspects of group composition were strong determinants of the family day care environment. In fact, these measures of group composition showed the strongest and most consistent relationship with caregiver and child behavior among all the independent measures.

Total Enrollment and Caregiver Behavior. The caregiver's behavior with children was strongly related to the total number of children in the home. As the number of children in the home increased, interactions of virtually all types between the caregiver and individual children decreased. Thus, for example, the amount of teaching by a caregiver decreases as the number of children in care increases. At the same time, caregivers' interactions with groups of two or more children at a time increased. That is, as group size increased, the internal management of the home had to change; the caregiver refocused her attention from individuals to groups. In the process, individual caregiver/child interactions were diminished.

Total Enrollment and Child Behavior. The group-size relationships in the child-focused observations present a complementary pattern. In homes with more children present, children spend less time interacting with the caregiver but more time interacting with other children. Increased group size provides, from the child's point of view, more opportunities for peer interaction. This was true for both toddlers and preschoolers. For toddlers, larger groups were also spending time monitoring the environment (looking around or observings other's activities). Thus, although the caregiver and child observations in each home cannot be considered as two perspectives on the same scene, having been recorded on different days, they nevertheless present a consistent story regarding group size.

The question of whether increased group size has a negative effect on child behavior is a moot one, since there is no way to evaluate the relative benefits of interaction with peers, interaction with caregivers, and the time spent in independent activity, all of which are considered developmentally appropriate. Further, in larger homes, it is reasonable and probably effective for the caregiver to encourage more interactions among the children, more independent activities, and more group activities.

Age Mix and Caregiver Behavior. The strongest patterns for age mix concerned caregiver interaction with toddlers. The presence of a preschooler was associated with a significant decrease in all the caregiver's one-to-one interactions with individual toddlers. In effect, preschoolers were able to draw the caregiver's attention differentially when they were in care with younger children. On the other hand, caregiver interactions with individual preschool children were less strongly influenced by the presence of a toddler. In homes with a toddler, there was a decline in attention for preschoolers only in two types of "noncognitive" interactions with caregivers—play and work.

The effect of an infant in the home was seen almost exclusively in a few predictable ways. In homes with an infant present, caregivers tended to display more affection, provide more comfort, offer help more, and attend more often to physical needs. Thus, while the presence of an infant had little effect on the kinds or amounts of interaction between caregivers and the individual toddler or preschool child, it did appear to require some special behavior by the caregiver.

Further elaboration of the influence of an infant on interaction patterns was found in one of the subsample analyses. Homes were selected where there was at least one toddler and one preschooler present. In this sample, the presence of an infant in the home was associated with less cognitive activity (teaching, language/information, and structured fine-motor activity) and more helping and attention to physical needs. Thus, in homes where an infant's presence means that three age groups are represented, the presence of the infant appears to reduce certain positive kinds of caregiver interaction with older children.

It was difficult with our sample to examine the effect of school-aged children in the home on caregiver behavior because observations were conducted in the morning, when most school-aged children were away. Fewer than 30% of the homes had a school-aged child present during study observations. In this limited sample, the presence of a school-aged child was correlated with fewer cognitive activities for both toddlers and preschoolers and less attention to physical needs. These data should not be interpreted negatively, however, since the presence of a school-aged child in a family day care during the school day usually signals some exceptional event such as illness, which can be expected temporarily to place greater strain on the caregiver and other children.

Age Mix and Child Behavior. The effect of age mix was not as strong for child behavior as for caregiver behavior, but here again results formed a pattern consistent with the pattern for caregivers. For toddlers, the presence of a preschooler was associated with more monitoring of the environment and less interaction with the caregiver—results that parallel the picture presented in the caregiver data. Other results for toddlers were that the presence of a preschooler in the home was associated with more gross motor activity (which was more frequent among preschoolers than among toddlers) and more antisocial behavior. As with caregiver behavior, a toddler in the home had little effect on the behavior of preschool children.

The presence of an infant had few relationships to toddler behavior, and there were no effects on the behavior of preschool children. Although there were several effects for toddlers, there was no clear pattern. An infant was associated with more affection, more control of another child, and more time alone as well as less work and less exploratory fine-motor activity with another child.

Conversely, the presence of a school-aged child was related only to the behavior of preschool children. For preschoolers, presence of a school-aged child was associated with less language/information activity with the caregiver, less total interaction with the caregiver, and less music. One source of additional information about the effects of school-aged children in the home is the morning–afternoon reliability analayses of the observation instruments. Afternoon observations were conducted in a subsample of 12 homes. Since school-aged children were present in these homes, the data suggest how caregivers and younger children are affected by school-aged children. The data suggest that the presence of the additional older age group required a shift in the caregiver's attention aways from the younger children, especially the preschoolers. It was found that, compared with the morning observations, caregivers spent significantly more afternoon time interacting with school-aged children and less time interacting with preschoolers. Toddlers and preschoolers spent less time watching educational TV and more time watching noneducational TV.

Effects for Regulatory Status of the Home

The descriptive analyses showed consistent differences in caregiver behavior in sponsored homes compared to regulated and unregulated homes. The regression analyses confirmed these differences. Even with other independent measures accounted for, sponsored homes looked very different, with more cognitive teaching activities and less frequent caregiver behavior that did not involve children.

Caregiver Behavior. Caregivers in sponsored homes tended to engage more often in cognitive activities—teaching, language/information activities and structured fine-motor activities. In addition, sponsored homes more often have music activities. Caregivers in sponsored homes tended toward more supervision/preparation and less recreation alone, while the reverse pattern held in unregulated homes.

The pattern of effects for regulatory status suggests that sponsored homes look more center-like and less home-like. The reasons sponsored homes look different are probably multiple and complex. An important difference involves the caregivers themselves, who in sponsored homes more often had received some training. It is also likely that caregivers who have become affiliated with a sponsor have a different orientation toward their work than caregivers operating alone in that they are more inclined to perceive themselves as professionals. As an example, an attitude questionnaire was administered to caregivers in which they expressed their philosophies about child rearing, education, and related topics. In this interview, sponsored caregivers more often stressed the importance of the educational rather than the social environment. Such differences might explain the more structured environment in sponsored homes.

During the analyses, another possible explanation for the pattern of activities that distinguished sponsored homes was raised. It was pointed out that in the study sample, enrollment and regulatory status of the home are confounded; sponsored homes tended to be larger, which might account for a higher frequency of structured activities. To test this hypothesis, an analysis was conducted including only homes enrolling three or fewer children, thus eliminating the difference in size between sponsored and nonsponsored homes. In this sample, not only did the same differences hold but the results were stronger and involved a wider set of behaviors. In this special sample, the sponsored homes also tended to exhibit significantly more caregiver conversation with preschoolers, more helping, and less housekeeping. Thus it is possible to conclude that there are marked behavioral differences between sponsored and nonsponsored providers, and these differences are not attributable to the size of the sponsored homes.

Child Behavior. The effects of regulatory status on behavior were less strong and less systematic for the child variables. Results that were consistent with those for caregivers included the following: first, for both toddlers and preschool children, there was more structured fine-motor activity in sponsored homes; second, for toddlers, there was less interaction with the caregiver in regulated homes. The remaining effects for children were too scattered to interpret.

Effects for Caregiver Experience, Education, and Training

The effects of experience, education, and training were carefully analyzed because these caregiver characteristics are often used as surrogate measures of caregiver competence. Experience was quickly eliminated on the basis of the available data because there were too few significant relationships between experience and caregiver behavior; consequently, this variable did not distinguish caregivers from each other on the behavioral dimensions.

The remaining two variables required very careful analysis because each was strongly related to a variable used to design the study. Education was related to caregiver ethnicity: Hispanic caregivers had by far the lowest levels of educational attainment. Thus analyses of the observation data taken as a whole cannot clearly distinguish between the effects of education and those of ethnicity. To estimate the separate effects of caregiver education, analyses had to be conducted for each ethnic group separately to see whether the effects of education would be consistent for each group.

In a similar vein, whether or not a caregiver has received training is related to whether or not she is sponsored. Most sponsored providers are trained but most nonsponsored providers are not. Thus, to determine whether training itself makes a difference, it must be analyzed separately for sponsored, regulated, and unregulated caregivers. It is only by showing that training makes a difference for each of these groups that we can clearly conclude that training is beneficial.

Years of Education and Caregiver Behavior. Overall, more education was associated with more teaching, more language/information and prosocial activity, and less helping, directing, household work, attention to physical needs, and positive affect. Most of these relationships could be attributed to caregiver ethnicity as well, since nearly every measure of caregiver behavior related to education was also related to caregiver ethnicity. In order to help disentangle the effects of education and ethnicity, analyses were conducted for each ethnic group separately. The question was whether the same effects for education would be found for each group. Unfortunately, these analyses were not very helpful in separating out the effects of education and ethnicity, since the relationships between education and caregiver behavior varied across the ethnic groups. Education had little effect in the sample of black caregivers, it had the largest and most interpretable effects in the sample of Hispanic caregivers, and the effects in the sample of white caregivers were scattered.

Specifically, education among Hispanic caregivers was associated with more teaching, both cognitive and social, and less noneducational activity. Education was related to more teaching, play/participation, language/information, and prosocial activities; it was related to less conversation with adults, household work with preschoolers, directing preschoolers, and attention to physical needs. The larger effects for Hispanic caregivers, compared with white and black caregivers, may stem from the wider range of education that is represented in the Hispanic sample. The effects among white caregivers are consistent in tone with the results for Hispanic providers, but they are fewer in number. For white caregivers, education was related to less control, household work, directing, and exploratory fine-motor activities. Even the two significant effects among black caregivers were consistent with the above findings—more education was associated with less directing and less work with preschoolers.

Consistent results in the above analyses permit the limited conclusion that caregivers with more education are less likely to engage in household chores and less likely to direct children. Among Hispanic caregivers (or, perhaps, in any sample with a more extensive range of education, particularly at the lower end of the scale), higher education is also associated with more cognitive activities and encouragement of prosocial behavior. Thus, although education does appear to have some consistent relationship with caregiver behavior across ethnic groups, these relationships do not appear to be significant contributions to the family day care environment. Among Hispanics, it is quite possible that education makes a difference, but alternative hypotheses cannot be ruled out.

Years of Education and Child Behavior. The analyses of the child variables did not provide much support for any conclusions about caregiver education and ethnicity, since there were very few significant effects and those that were found were consistent with the caregiver findings. For toddlers, more education of caregiver was associated with less control. For preshool children, higher education was associated with more structured fine-motor activity.

Training and Caregiver Behavior. Although the effects of education on caregiver behavior are uncertain, the effects of training are strong and positive. This is perhaps the most encouraging of the study findings, for it means that an investment in caregiver training can have a beneficial impact on all kinds of caregivers. Thus the quality of the family day care environment can be enhanced by this means.

To disentangle the effects of training and sponsorship, effects for training were examined separately in sponsored homes, regulated homes, and unregulated homes. In sponsored homes, nearly 80% of the caregivers had some training—versus 30% in regulated homes and only 20% in unregulated homes. The question asked in this analysis was whether, when regulatory status was taken into account, trained caregivers behaved differently from untrained caregivers.

Analyses showed that there were consistent positive effects for training for each group of caregivers (see Table 9). The trained caregivers in regulated and sponsored homes looked similar. In these groups, training was associated with more teaching, helping, and dramatic play and with

Table 9. Caregiver Behaviors Associated with Training

	Sponsored	Regulated	Unregulated
More frequent behaviors:	Language/inform Structured fine-motor Music Dramatic play Teach Help	Dramatic play Teach Help Comfort	Comfort Positive affect
Less frequent behaviors:	Recreation alone	Supervise	Supervise Recreation alone

less activity that did not involve interaction with children. In sponsored homes, caregivers who had been trained also exhibited more structured teaching—more language/information and structured fine-motor activities. In both regulated and unregulated homes, training was associated with more comforting and less time away from the children.

Training and Child Behavior. There were few significant relationships between caregiver training and children's behavior. However, all these relationships were consistent with the findings for caregivers. Toddlers in homes with trained caregivers more often engaged in structured fine-motor activity, conversed less often with other children, and had to be controlled less often by the caregiver. For preschoolers, caregiver training was associated only with more music/dramatic activities.

Effects for Related Children in the Home

A final set of analyses was conducted to see whether caregivers behaved differently in homes that provided care for the caregiver's own child or a related child than in homes that provided care only to nonrelatives. Care of one's own child tended to occur in the homes of young, well-educated, white caregivers in unregulated homes. Nonresident relative care also tended to be provided by unregulated caregivers, but by older, less educated, nonwhite caregivers. If either type of home was shown to look different from other homes, it could be due to a number of characteristics of the home in addition to the type of child. In fact, for both types of home, the pattern of effects seemed as much attributable to the caregiver's situation as to the presence of a related child.

Care for One's Own Child. In general, homes where the caregiver's own child was present had fewer child-centered activities and less structured activity. More specifically, caregivers in these homes tended to engage in more housekeeping and control of antisocial behavior and less teaching, conversation with toddlers, play/participation, and TV. In general, there was less interaction between the caregiver and toddlers when the caregiver's own child was present. Looking at the child observation variables, the only noticeable effects were for preschoolers, and these effects were consistent with the caregiver findings. Presence of the caregiver's own child was associated with more time spent with other children, more exploratory fine-motor behavior with other children, more music activities, and more time reading books. One interpretation of these results is that homes where the caregiver's own child is present look more "homelike"—that is, the caregiver continues her own activities and less often initiates structured activities with the children. These homes also tended to be smaller, suggesting that this pattern may be less feasible in larger homes.

To disentangle the effects of the caregiver's own child in the home and the background characteristics of these caregivers, the presence of the caregiver's own child was examined within the sample of white unregulated caregivers (60% of this group cared for their own children). Even in this subsample of caregivers who shared a pattern of background characteristics, the effects of caring for their own children were significant. Caregivers who had their own child at home engaged in less teaching, conversation, and play with toddlers, and fewer language/information activities; they also engaged in more housekeeping and control of antisocial behavior.

Relative Care. Caregivers providing care to a relative's child (or children), like those who had their own child at home, tended to exhibit less cognitive teaching. These caregivers also showed less play/participation and helping, all of which suggests less interaction with children. At the same time, caregivers providing care to a relative's child exhibit more directing and do more household work. Comparable effects were found on the child variables. That is, for toddlers, relative care was associated with less language/information and less educational TV. For preschool children, it was associated with less language/information, less structured fine-motor activity, less attention seeking, more antisocial behavior with other children, and more prosocial behavior.

Conclusions

The observation system developed for the study proved to be very sensitive to the home process. It permitted the coding of noteworthy child and caregiver behaviors and allowed us to discern the effects on these behaviors of variables of policy and programmatic significance such as the caregiver's training, enrollment, age mix, and regulatory status.

In general, the observations showed family day care homes to be positive environments for children. It was observed that caregivers spent a considerable portion of their time in direct interaction with children, and the time spent with children seems to be appropriate to the needs of children of various ages. Caregivers rarely expressed any negative affect toward the children. The caregivers' homes were generally safe, homelike environments which were less structured and homogenous with respect to children's ages than day care centers.

Some of the most interesting implications of the study findings are based on comparisons among different types of family day care homes and among caregivers with differing degrees of preparation for child care. Specific examples of important differences found in such comparisons include the following:

1. On the whole, the types of activities in unregulated and regulated homes were similar to one another, but sponsored homes showed a different pattern, placing more emphasis on cognitive and expressive activities. These homes were more suggestive of a preschool environment. The differences in caregiver activities were generally small except for teaching behaviors. Teaching occurred almost 50% more often in sponsored homes, where it accounts for 17% of the caregiver's time, compared with 12.1% and 12.8% in unregulated and regulated homes respectively.

2. Caregiver training was also found to influence the pattern of activities in the family day care home. Caregivers who had some child care training tended to display more teaching, language/information activity, music/dramatic play, and comforting. This pattern of behaviors suggested more structured teaching on the part of trained caregivers. The patterns associated with training are very similar to those associated with sponsored home, referred to above. This remained true even after training and regulatory status were unconfounded.

3. Caregiver and child behaviors also tended to vary across homes with different group sizes and age mixes. As the number of children in the home increased, interactions of virtually all types between the caregiver and individual children decreased (with the exception of control activities). At the same time, caregivers' interactions with two or more children increased. Child-focused data also complemented the pattern of caregiver behavior which was observed: in homes with more children present, children spent less time interacting with the caregiver but more time interacting with other children.

4. The presence of the caregiver's own children or of a relative in care appears to affect the caregiver's behavior towards the children in care. In general, the homes where the caregiver's own child was present could be characterized as less formal, with more activities that were not centered on the children and that were less structured. This also tended to be true for caregivers who cared for a nonresident relative.

These observation data, while strongly suggestive of differences in caregiving style, should not by themselves be considered as the basis for evaluating the quality of care in different types of family day care homes. For example, the long-term effects on children of different emphases are not well established. It will be recalled that even though striking differences in the amount of time different groups of caregivers spent in particular kinds of activities were observed, all caregivers devoted a substantial portion of time to their overall involvement with the children. The patterns of differences that were found should, however, prove useful both in establishing guidelines for parents seeking specific activity patterns for their children and in informing policymakers of the probable effects of alternative family day care policies on home processes.

References

Bureau of Labor Statistics, U.S. Department of Labor. Personal communication concerning figures for March 1979.

Coelen, C., Glantz, F., & Calore, D. *Day care centers in the U.S.* Cambridge, Mass.: Abt Books, 1979.

Fosburg, S. *Family day care in the United States.* Washington, D.C.: U.S. Government Printing Office, 1981.

Fosburg, S. *Final report of the national day care home: Summary of findings* (Department of Health and Human Services Publication No. OHDS 80-30282). Washington, D.C.: U.S. Government Printing Office, 1981.

Rhodes, T., & Moore, J. Current patterns of child care use in the United States. In *National child care consumer study: 1975* (Vol. 2). Washington, D.C.: UNCO, Inc., 1975.

Stallings, J., & Porter, A. *National day care home study setting observation components: Final report.* Menlo Park, Calif.: SRI International, 1980.

Westinghouse Learning Corporation and Westat Research Inc. *Day care survey 1970.* Washington, D.C.: Westat, Research Inc., 1971.

CHAPTER 9

The Relationship between Parents' Beliefs about Development and Family Constellation, Socioeconomic Status, and Parents' Teaching Strategies

ANN V. McGILLICUDDY-DeLISI

Introduction

Many studies have indicated that children's performance on intelligence or achievement tests varies with family constellation factors such as number of children in the family, spacing between children, and the birth order of the child (Belmont & Marolla, 1973; Belmont, Stein, & Susser, 1975; Dandes & Dow, 1969; Davis, Cahan, & Bashi, 1976; Kellaghan & MacNamara, 1972; Kennett & Cropley, 1970; Marjoribanks, Walberg, & Bargen, 1975; Zajonc, 1976; Zajonc & Markus, 1975) as well as with socioeconomic status (SES) of the parents (Laosa, chapter 1; Lesser, Fifer, & Clark, 1965; Mumbauer & Miller, 1970; Thomas, 1971; Tulkin, 1968). In general it has been found that children from small families, families with large spacing between children, first-born children, and middle- or upper-class children perform better than other children on tests of intellectual ability.

Although these studies show that the family environment is an important factor in the cognitive development of children, such investigations have been criticized for failing to specify processes through which the environment affects the child (cf. Bronfenbrenner, 1979). That is, information about the types of activities or events in the home that might

ANN V. McGILLICUDDY-DeLISI ● Educational Testing Service, Princeton, New Jersey 08541. Research reported in this chapter was supported by NIH Grant R01 HD10686.

account for differences in children's abilities is not provided by such studies. The realization that we must obtain more specific descriptions of how family environments differ from one another led many investigators to study parents' child-rearing patterns (cf. Bradley, Caldwell, & Elardo, 1979; Campbell, 1970; Cicirelli, 1975, 1977; Elder, 1962; Elder & Bowerman, 1963; Laosa, 1980a; Marjoribanks, 1979; Sigel, see chapter 2).

Following this latter line of research, we began an investigation of parent teaching strategies in families that varied with respect to family constellation and education–income level of parents. We approached the problem of why children's scores on tests of intellectual ability vary with these two factors from the framework of distancing theory. Distancing theory proposes that children's representational thinking abilities are affected by teaching strategies that challenge the child to anticipate outcomes, reconstruct past events, and attend to transformations. Teaching strategies that present a maximum challenge for the child to engage in such mental activities vary in two ways. First, the use of inquiries rather than statements is presumed to place a greater demand on the child, since the child must attend and then become engaged in some internal representational processes in order to respond. Second, the content of the message from the teacher or parent may vary in the degree or type of internal representation that is required. For example, Sigel (chapter 2) describes strategies as placing either low-, intermediate-, or high-level mental operational demands on the child. Teaching strategies that place low-level mental operational demands on the child are those parental utterances that encourage a minimal amount of internal representation on the child's part (e.g., "Do you see that?" = demands that the child observe; "What is it?" = demands that the child label). High-level mental operational demands, on the other hand, focus on getting children to synthesize information internally, to propose and evaluate various alternatives. That is, the content of these types of parental utterances encourages the child to engage in more complex or higher-level mental processes.

When we began our first investigation of families, we proposed that the findings that linked SES, family constellation, and children's intellectual abilities were due to differences in parents' use of distancing teaching strategies. Our rationale was somewhat as follows. Within the context of distancing theory, the development of children's representational thinking abilities is enhanced by the parents' use of high-level distancing teaching strategies (e.g., inquiries and high-level mental operational demands). It is likely that parents vary from one another in their teaching styles, some parents naturally exhibiting a style that could be classified as high distancing and others as low distancing. Distancing strategies require more from the parent in the sense that posing a question, waiting for a response from the child, posing another question, and so on involves more time and attention from the parent than a simple declarative statement that offers information or facts to the child. In families with greater numbers of children or close spacing between children, parents may not have the freedom to engage in such teaching styles. As a result, the children in such families may not have been exposed to such high-level distancing during the history of the interactions with the parents and thus their representational abilities may not have been stimulated or challenged to the degree that is true for other children.

At this time we were working with an interview that required parents to tell us their preferred teaching strategies and to predict what they would actually do in a number of situations. We expected to find more discrepancies between preferred and predicted teaching strategies for parents with larger, more closely spaced families. Parents were asked to provide rationales for both preferred and predicted strategies. We found that parents' rationales did not focus so much upon constraints on their behavior due to demands of other children in the family as they did upon their view of how development occurs or the nature of children in general. As a result, we began to reformulate our hypotheses about why parents behave as they do with their children and why parental teaching strategies vary with factors like number of children in the family and SES.

Parents' Belief Systems as a Source of Teaching Strategies

Parents' verbalizations during this interview indicated that they have clear ideas about the nature of children and child development. The particular view or model of child development that was espoused varied from parent to parent; at times, the parents referred to specific incidents that were taken as "proof" of the particular orientation they were presenting to us. On the basis of these findings, we began to think that parents have evolved their own belief systems about children, which are similar to Kelly's (1955, 1963) system of Constructive Alternativism. Kelly's construct systems are actually broader in the domain to which they apply than parents' beliefs or constructs about children. For Kelly, each individual evolves a system of constructs through which reality is interpreted. One's behavior is dependent upon the nature of the construct system because reality, including other people, is in fact defined by these constructs. Different people have different systems because these constructs are built up on the basis of the individual's own experiences with other persons.

Constructs or beliefs that are specific to children can be seen as a source of parents' behaviors with their own children, similarly to Kelly's construct system as a source of behaviors whenever two individuals interact with one another. This formulation of parental belief systems led to a reconceptualization of how family members influence one another and why parents differ from one another in their teaching practices. Parents' beliefs about children and the ways development occurs were considered as a source of behaviors evidenced by adults during interactions with their children. This led us to question what types of factors might affect the content of belief systems, providing some explanation of why parents differ from one another in their teaching styles. That is, we wanted to know why some parents think that children develop knowledge or abilities in one manner— through their own experimentation, for example—while other parents believe in different processes, such as positive reinforcement or direct instruction from adults. There is some reason to think that family constellation and SES, among other factors, might affect the particular content of belief systems, creating differences between parents.

Differences between Parents' Beliefs

Kelly's personal construct systems are not static but are formed by processes of differentiation and integration as interactions with people and events affect their emergence and modification (Landfield & Leitner, 1980). From our perspective, parents' beliefs about children are also not formed into a closed system. Rather, beliefs are open to change as new or conflicting information is provided in the course of interactions with others. The individual's experiences as a parent have the potential for affecting beliefs in a variety of ways. For example, we have proposed that number, ordinal position, and sex of the children in the family can broaden beliefs to account for individual differences in development, differentiate beliefs to account for sex differences, and affect the parents' approach to later-born children (McGillicuddy-DeLisi, 1980). Number of children in the family is an important factor because the potential for disconfirmation of previously held beliefs is increased as the parent has the opportunity to compare different children in the family. If the first two children in the family differ from one another in terms of achieving developmental milestones, which is likely given the wide range of variability in development, this will provide discrepant or conflicting information about development to the parent. The belief system about development (1) may become broader in the sense that the development of both children will be incorporated as "normal," (2) may become differentiated with respect to sex differences in development if one child is a boy and one is a girl, (3) may change so as to ascribe a greater influence of genetics on all of development if the parent interprets the individual differences in one area as due to genetics, (4) may change so as to include the influence of siblings on development or differences in the environment of the home, and so on. Similarly, spacing between children may be an important factor. If two children are close in age as a result of near spacing, the discrepancies between abilities and/or developmental progress may be more apparent to the parent, thus posing a greater challenge to beliefs. In addition, the children's interactions with one another may vary with spacing (e.g., playing together as peers versus the older assuming a teacher or authority role with the younger), thus providing different experiential bases for parents with close versus far spacing between children.

The SES of the parents might also affect the content of parents' beliefs about development. If one considers SES as a descriptive factor that actually reflects a multitude of differences in life experiences, such differences should be associated with the information upon which parents construct their beliefs about children. For example, Bronfenbrenner (1958) has suggested that theories about children and development might filter down through the social classes. If this is true, parents from different SES backgrounds are exposed to different theories at the same point in time. Thus, parents from lower-SES backgrounds might be exposed to information about positive reinforcement derived from Skinner, while those from higher-SES groups are exposed to Piaget's ideas about knowledge tied to the child's own action. As a result, parents from different SES groups may reformulate their beliefs based on "expert" opinions that are very different from one another. In addition, the individual's life circumstances might affect the degree to which new information is assimilated and what types of experiences are likely to produce changes in beliefs. For example, Kohn (1969, 1976) has reported that parents from lower-SES groups value neatness and conformity, while middle-class parents value autonomy and independence. He suggests that it is not that middle-class parents do not value neatness but rather that this is taken somewhat for granted in the upper-SES groups. For a parent from a lower-SES background, success for their child is based on a different set of parameters, including neat personal appearance and "fitting in" as high priorities. With respect to beliefs about development, a similar discrepancy between social class groups may exist because parents focus on different developmental outcomes. For example, the amount of knowledge or information the child acquires may be seen as the end-point in development, or the ability to approach a problem creatively may be viewed as the outcome. Beliefs in developmental processes that lead to such end states are likely to differ. Finally, educational level or formal schooling of parents is linked to most indices of SES. In fact, Laosa

(1980b) has presented data indicating that differences in mothers' teaching styles that occur with SES and ethnic background can be largely attributed to years of schooling. It is possible that with more schooling, one is exposed to a greater variety of teaching styles, and such information could affect beliefs as well as the style of teaching that is adopted when interacting with children.

No doubt there are many other factors—such as experiences as a child in a family, beliefs of one's own parents, beliefs of one's spouse, and so on—that also affect the content of parents' beliefs about children and development. At this time, however, we choose to focus specifically upon family constellation and SES factors because these are the factors that have been linked in past research to differences in parents' teaching practices and in children's intellectual abilities.

An Investigation of the Role of Beliefs in the Family Environment

Parents' beliefs may be critical factors through which demographic characteristics such as family constellation SES, parental age, and so on affect parents' teaching strategies and ultimately the child's development. For example, Sigel's chapter in this volume focuses on how parents' teaching practices are related to children's problem-solving abilities on a variety of tasks. The data presented indicate that (1) parents with different family constellations and from different SES backgrounds differ from one another in the types and frequencies of teaching behaviors they use with their own child and (2) teaching behaviors of parents are related to children's scores on a battery of representational thinking tasks. These findings are consistent for the most part with Sigel's hypothesis that particular parental teaching strategies, called distancing strategies, are related to the development of children's representational thought. Thus, children of parents who do not use such strategies appear to be at a disadvantage with respect to development of representational abilities when they are compared with children whose parents do evidence distancing teaching styles

The question that remains open is why the parents in this sample differed from one another in the types of behaviors they evidenced when teaching their children. Why were working-class parents more likely than middle-class parents to ask questions that put a minimal demand on the child to represent during a story task (low-level questions)? Why were parents of an only child more likely to ask such questions than parents of three children? There are many possible explanations that can serve as after-the-fact rationales for each finding reported by Sigel. For example, parents of an only child may underestimate a pre-school-age child's abilities as opposed to parents of a pre-school-age child who has an older sibling. Parents of the latter type have had increased amounts and varieties of parenting experiences with preschoolers because two of their children have developed to or beyond this point. Postulation of parents' beliefs as mediating factors between SES/family constellation characteristics and parents' teaching strategies leads to a more elegant model of what affects parents' behaviors. The relationship between beliefs and teaching behaviors can be interpreted on theoretical grounds, increasing explanatory power concerning variability in beliefs. The relationship between SES, family constellation, and parental beliefs can be described in specific terms. Such information could prove to be invaluable to practitioners involved in parent education and intervention. With knowledge about sources of parental practices (beliefs, for example) that have been shown to vary with the individual's SES background and family constellation, the professional can choose to intervene at the level of beliefs—assuming that beliefs are more open to change than educational level or number of children—when attempting to alter family dynamics.

In summary, we propose that parents' beliefs about children and their development are critical factors through which family constellation and SES affect parental teaching practices. Within such a framework, parents' beliefs are a major source of parents' behaviors in interactions with their children. Parents from different SES backgrounds and with different family constellations are expected to differ from one another in their beliefs because the parent's own life experiences affect the content of the belief system. In the sections that follow, some findings about interrelationships among family constellation factors, SES, parents' beliefs and parents' teaching practices will be presented. Specifically, we will first look at beliefs of parents from different SES and family constellation groups in an effort to find and describe patterns of differences in beliefs. Second, we will look at relationships between beliefs and teaching behaviors in a manner that allows us to investigate whether beliefs are related to such behaviors above and beyond the factors of SES and family constellation.

Methods

The participants of the study were the same 120 two-parent families described in Sigel's chapter in this volume. To summarize the sample briefly, the families varied with respect to education–income level of the parents and number and spacing of children. Half of the families were characterized as working-class (no college experience/income below median for county of residence) and half as middle-class (college degree/income above median). Within this dichotomy, 40 families had an only child who was 3½ to 4½ years old (mean = 48.05 months; SD = 2.87) and 80 families had three children. The middle child in the three-child families was also 3½ to 4½ years old (mean = 48.09 months; SD = 3.56). Half of the three-child families had fewer than three years' spacing between the oldest and middle sibling (mean = 24.70 months; SD = 5.88) and half had greater than three years' spacing (mean = 45.18 months; SD = 9.58). An equal number of male and female target children made up each group. The oldest and middle children were of the same sex for 83% of the sample.

Mothers and fathers were interviewed individually to assess beliefs about the nature of child development. Each parent was also videotaped interacting with his or her pre-school-age child on a story task and on a paper-folding task. Manuals that describe the administration and coding procedures in detail are available from the author. Each measure will be briefly summarized below.

Parent Belief Interviews

The interview consisted of 12 vignettes that involved a 4-year-old and a mother or a father. Twenty-two sets of probes that focused on how children attain concepts and abilities stemmed from issues that were raised in each of the vignettes. For each set of probes, the initial question focused on whether or not the parent thought that 4-year-olds generally understand or have attained the ability in question. A series of questions that focused on how children attain concepts or abilities formed the latter part of each set of probes. For example, one vignette involved a child who was taking a bath and wondered if his metal spoon would float like his new boat. Probes accompanying this vignette were: "Do 4-year-olds understand which things float and which don't?" "How does a child (eventually) come to know which things float and which ones don't?" and "How does a child come to know why things float?" Similarly, another vignette involved a child who was playing with her toys instead of getting dressed to go to a movie she wanted to see. Probes included, "Does a 4-year-old understand time?" "How does a 4-year-old come to understand time?" "Are 4-year-olds able to plan?" and so on.

Parental responses were initially coded for frequency and intensity to 47 constructs of developmental states and processes which were summed across the 22 sets of probes. Twenty percent of the 240 interviews were scored by three coders. Range of agreement was from 91–100%, with a mean agreement of 94.35%. Correlational analyses of scores on each construct led to a reduction to 26 constructs of child development. Explicit definitions and examples of the constructs are included in the manual available from the author. A brief description of each construct is presented in Table 1. In addition, each parent's confidence in his or her expressed beliefs was rated on a Likert scale ranging from 1 (very uncertain) to 4 (very certain).

Table 1. Parental Belief Variables[a]

Construct	Brief definition
STATES	
Impulsivity:	Tendency to act on sudden spontaneous inclinations or incitement to unpremeditated action
Dependency:	Reliance on others for support, guidance, discipline, knowledge, etc.
Rigidity:	Thinking and affect that are stiffly set and unyielding
Positive affect:	Pleasant state marked by freedom from anxiety usually exists for the child
Negative affect:	An unpleasant internal state usually exists for the child
Conflict:	Child's involvement in internal struggles that result from incompatible needs, wishes, ideas
Creativity/ imagination:	Child's tendency to share notions that are new/original/ never before wholly perceived in reality
Readiness:	Necessary level of preparedness before children are capable of some experience, knowledge or action
Balance:	Tendency toward harmonious resolution of affective, social or cognitive components within the child or between the child and the environment
Stage:	A distinctive period or step in a progressive ordering of development
PROCESSES[b]	
Innate factors:	Characteristics that are inborn or developed through natural growth
Proximity/ exposure:	Existence of an object, event, or person in the child's presence
Structure of environment:	Organization that is inherent in circumstances, objects, persons, or events, therefore tending to influence/ determine activities and concepts of the child
Infusion:	Injection or thrusting of knowledge or skill into/onto children from an external source
Empathy/ contagion:	Imaginative fusion of child's inner state with that of another person
Direct instructions:	Process of conveying information through verbal presentation
Modeling/ identification:	Tendency to become similar to, incorporate traits of, or imitate another person

Continued

Table 1. (Continued)

Construct	Brief definition
Positive feedback:	Pleasant external consequence of a behavior that serves to motivate, provide information, or make behavior more likely to recur
Negative feedback:	An unpleasant external consequence of behavior that serves to motivate, provide information, or inhibit child behaviors
Observation:	Process of making a judgment/inference based on what is seen
Accumulation:	Increase in knowledge or skill that occurs through synthesis of multiple or repeated experiences
Experimentation:	Process through which an idea/behavior is applied to a situation, feedback received, idea/behavior modified, feedback received, etc.
Generalization:	Process whereby a behavior/idea obtains a general form applicable to many instances
Cognitive reorganization:	Drawing of underlying principles from objects/events and mentally integrating information to form concepts and ideas
Self-regulation:	Internal governing and controlling processes that produce systematic order and coordinated actions/behaviors

[a] A manual that provides elaborated definitions, coding rules, and examples is available from the author.
[b] Listed in descending order from a view of the child as less to more active in terms of internal mental processes.

Observations of Parents' Teaching Behaviors

Parent–child interactions on two tasks were videotaped through a one-way mirror. The tasks, instructions, and coding procedures are described in Sigel's chapter (see chapter 2). To reiterate briefly, for one task the parent was required to teach the child how to make a boat or an airplane by folding paper. For the other task the parent was asked to go through a story as he or she would at home. Parent behaviors were coded for distancing strategies (form of utterance and mental operational demand placed on the child), structuring and management behaviors (e.g., set task limits, power assertion), verbal emotional supports and feedback (e.g., approvals, corrections), and nonverbal emotional support and feedback behaviors (e.g., hugging, takeover). Child behaviors were coded for degree of engagement in the interaction, but these behaviors will not be addressed in the present paper. Five coders scored the videotapes. Range of agreement between pairs of coders for 20% of the tapes was 72–99% (mean = 86.54%).

Results and Discussion

Analysis of parents' beliefs focused on two separate but related questions. First, we wanted to know whether parents from the SES and family constellation groups differed from one another in the types of beliefs they espoused. Second, we addressed the question of whether or not beliefs are related to parents' teaching strategies after differences in such background factors are taken into account. Two different types of analyses were necessary to investigate these questions. Results concerning differences between groups of parents based on SES and family constellation will be addressed first, followed by results concerning relationships between parents' beliefs and teaching behaviors.

Differences in Parents' Beliefs: Family Constellation and SES Effects

In the introductory section it was proposed that the content of parents' beliefs about child development is affected by the individual's background and parenting experiences. If this is the case, one would expect that parents of an only child, for example, would posit different developmental processes than parents of three children. Analyses of variance (family constellation [3] $\times$ SES [2] $\times$ sex of parent [2] $\times$ sex of child [2]) were applied to the scores on each of the 26 construct variables and the confidence rating score in order to determine where differences between groups occurred. Scheffé tests were conducted on means involved in all significant main and interaction effects in order to obtain information about which groups differed from one another. Mothers' scores (mean number of references) on each of 17 belief variables for which differences between groups were obtained are presented in Table 2 by family constellation, SES, and sex of child. Fathers' scores are presented in the same manner in Table 3.

Many differences between groups were obtained. In some cases, the differences were straightforward (e.g., parents of an only child referred to some constructs of development more often than parents of three children). In other cases, differences between family constellation groups also depended on whether the parent was from a working-class or a middle-class background. Significant main effects (i.e., those straightforward differences between groups) will be presented first, followed by interaction effects that indicate several factors must be considered simultaneously.[1]

---

[1]In cases where both significant main and interaction effects were obtained, only the interaction effect is discussed. In addition, three four-way interactions reached the level of significance. These were not interpretable and are not discussed.

Table 2. Mean Number of References Made by Mothers to Selected Child-Development Constructs

Construct	Only child				3-Child, near spacing				3-Child, far spacing			
	Working class		Middle class		Working class		Middle class		Working class		Middle class	
	Girls	Boys	Girls	Boys	Girls	Boys	Girls	Boys	Girls	Boys	Girls	Boys
Absorption	5.90	3.60	2.80	4.20	2.40	4.60	2.40	4.00	3.00	4.80	5.20	3.00
Infusion	1.00	.90	.90	.60	.30	.90	.80	.70	.60	.20	1.40	.50
Positive feedback	4.60	5.20	4.10	5.80	4.70	4.20	6.30	6.00	4.60	2.50	3.60	4.70
Negative feedback	2.40	2.80	2.50	2.60	4.30	4.00	3.20	3.70	2.70	2.70	3.90	3.20
Direct instruction	11.90	10.90	10.40	7.50	9.50	5.60	9.50	7.50	8.10	9.60	7.70	7.70
Observation	2.20	3.20	2.50	3.30	5.20	2.80	2.00	1.80	2.30	2.00	3.60	3.90
Generalization	.40	.40	.30	.60	.50	.20	.20	1.20	.40	.70	.50	.40
Cognitive reorganization	0	.50	0	.90	.30	.30	.20	.40	0	0	.70	.40
Self-regulation	1.50	2.50	1.30	1.00	2.80	2.50	1.30	2.50	.90	1.40	3.40	3.20
Creativity	.70	1.00	2.50	1.70	1.70	2.50	1.10	2.40	1.00	1.90	.90	1.30
Readiness	3.40	4.40	6.20	3.80	5.60	3.40	6.60	5.30	3.70	4.70	4.60	5.90
Stage	1.20	1.70	2.40	2.70	1.80	1.50	2.20	2.10	1.60	1.80	1.70	3.00
Structure of environment	2.90	2.80	4.40	2.60	2.70	4.00	4.00	3.50	2.00	2.40	2.30	3.00
Conflict	.80	1.00	.60	.70	.70	.70	1.10	1.70	1.10	1.10	.50	1.10
Impulsivity	.80	1.20	1.50	1.30	1.00	2.10	1.90	1.80	1.80	2.00	1.30	1.00
Negative affect	1.00	1.10	1.40	1.10	1.40	.90	1.00	.80	1.00	.70	1.30	.40
Confidence in beliefs	1.90	2.80	2.30	3.20	2.90	2.40	3.10	2.30	2.00	2.60	2.50	3.20

Table 3. Mean Number of References Made by Fathers to Selected Child-Development Constructs

Construct	Only child				3-Child, near spacing				3-Child, far spacing			
	Working class		Middle class		Working class		Middle class		Working class		Middle class	
	Girls	Boys	Girls	Boys	Girls	Boys	Girls	Boys	Girls	Boys	Girls	Boys
Absorption	3.60	2.60	3.70	3.40	4.10	4.60	2.60	3.10	2.70	4.70	3.50	4.00
Infusion	.90	1.30	1.00	1.00	1.30	1.00	.90	1.30	1.50	2.30	.40	.80
Positive feedback	2.10	3.50	4.40	3.90	4.30	3.50	4.40	5.10	3.10	3.20	4.00	7.80
Negative feedback	2.20	2.90	4.20	3.30	3.10	3.20	3.70	4.80	4.10	3.20	4.60	4.40
Direct instruction	11.50	11.30	7.80	7.90	9.00	10.60	8.90	8.10	7.40	7.90	7.40	7.30
Observation	2.60	1.90	1.10	2.30	2.20	3.50	2.70	2.00	3.50	2.90	3.80	2.20
Generalization	.70	.50	.90	.30	1.30	.70	1.00	.90	.20	.80	1.80	.70
Cognitive reorganization	.20	.30	.30	.30	.20	0	.40	.70	0	.20	.70	1.70
Self-regulation	1.10	1.40	1.90	1.20	2.20	2.40	2.10	2.00	2.10	1.30	3.50	2.60
Creativity	1.70	1.20	2.40	2.00	1.60	2.10	1.30	1.90	1.30	1.70	1.40	1.50
Readiness	5.30	3.90	5.50	5.80	5.40	5.70	5.00	8.10	5.40	4.50	6.00	9.60
Stage	1.50	1.90	2.00	2.30	2.00	2.50	3.10	3.20	1.90	2.00	2.70	3.50
Structure of environment	2.00	3.70	3.70	4.10	2.70	3.30	4.20	4.40	2.70	2.90	3.50	3.70
Conflict	.80	1.10	1.40	.50	1.70	.20	1.50	.40	1.40	.80	1.30	.90
Impulsivity	1.30	1.10	1.10	1.30	2.00	2.90	1.90	1.50	1.80	1.80	.90	1.20
Negative affect	.70	.50	.70	.70	1.00	.40	.50	.60	1.00	.70	.90	.50
Confidence in beliefs	2.60	1.80	3.50	2.80	3.00	3.00	3.00	3.30	2.50	2.70	2.40	3.20

Parents from the three family constellation groups (only child vs. near spacing vs. far spacing) differed from one another on four belief variables or constructs.

1. Parents of an only child referred to *negative feedback* (an unpleasant consequence of behavior which serves to motivate or inhibit child behaviors) as a developmental process *less often* than parents of three children, regardless of spacing.
2. Parents of an only child referred to *direct instruction from adults* (verbal presentation of facts or information without implying involvement of processes internal to the child) *more often* than parents of three children with far spacing.
3. Parents of an only child referred to *self-regulation* (internal governing and controlling processes produce systematic order and coordinated actions/behaviors; process or mechanism through which equilibrium is achieved/maintained between internal and external states) *less often* than parents of three children regardless of spacing.
4. Parents of an only child referred to *impulsivity* (a tendency to act on sudden spontaneous inclinations or incitement to unpremeditated action) *less often* than parents of three children, regardless of spacing

These results indicate that the most salient feature distinguishing family constellation groups from one another is number of children. That is, parents of an only child tended to differ from parents of three children regardless of the spacing between children that existed in the three-child families. Any relationship that exists between family size and parental beliefs must be considered in terms of alternative directions of causality at this point. For example, parents of an only child posited direct instruction from adults as a process through which the child learns concepts more often than other parents; they also referred to self-regulation less often. It is possible that the parents of only children in this study planned to have an only child (or more than 4 years' spacing if the family was not yet complete) precisely because of their beliefs in the importance of direct instruction relative to self-regulatory processes. On the other hand, parents of three children may have observed that their second-born child developed similarly to their first-born in spite of the second-born's having received less direct instruction from the parents. Thus, the beliefs may either have existed prior to family constellation so that the family was planned in accordance with those beliefs or parental beliefs may have been affected by experience as a result of having more than one child.

Several differences between working-class and middle-class parents were also observed. Parents from the higher education–income groups referred to:

1. *Positive feedback more often* than working-class parents
2. *Readiness more often* than working-class parents
3. *Structure inherent in the environment more often* than working-class parents
4. *Stages more often* than working-class parents
5. *Direct instruction less often* than working-class parents
6. *Confidence in their beliefs more often* than working-class parents

These differences might indicate that middle-class parents are more aware of concepts (e.g., stage, positive reinforcement) inherent in currently popular theories of development and learning. In general, these constructs reflect a view of the child as an active processor who develops through his or her own interactions with a structured environment. Direct instruction, which was posited more often by parents from the lower education–income group, implies that adults must actively teach and socialize in order for the child to acquire a particular concept or skill.

Mothers and fathers also differed from one another in the types of developmental beliefs posited. Fathers referred to inferences based on observations, infusion directly from the environment, and readiness *more often* than mothers. They referred to negative affective states of the child *less often* than mothers did.

As mentioned at the beginning of this section, many of the differences between parents depended upon consideration of several factors at once. This was hardly surprising, since many previous investigations of children's intellectual abilities have reported that differences between family constellation groups (e.g., findings that scores of children from small families exceed those of children from large families) and more marked for lower-SES groups. In some cases, number of children in the family has been found to be related to children's intelligence scores only for lower-class families. Significant family constellation and SES interactions were obtained for four of the parent belief variables, indicating that parents as well as children differ from one another when these two factors are considered in conjunction.

1. Middle-class parents with far child spacing and working-class parents with near spacing referred to *self-regulatory processes more often* than parents in other SES-family constellation groups.
2. Middle-class parents with far spacing and working-class parents with near spacing posited *inferences based on observation* (process

of making a judgment based on sensory experience) as a developmental process *more often* than middle-class parents with an only child or with near spacing.

3. Middle-class parents with far spacing referred to *cognitive reorganization* (process of drawing underlying principles from objects/events and mentally integrating information to form concepts/ideas) *more often* than parents in all other groups.

4. Middle-class parents of an only child and working-class parents with near child spacing referred to children's *creativity and imagination* (forming a notion that is new or original or has never before been wholly perceived in reality) *more often* than all other groups.

Variation in parental beliefs with regard to differences in child spacing, as opposed to family size, appears to be important only when family constellation is considered in relation to SES. The similarity of middle-class parents with far child spacing and working-class parents with near child spacing in their more frequent references to self-regulatory processes and processes of inferences based on observations was not predicted *a priori*. It is interesting to note, however, that a discriminant function analysis applied to the six groups of children formed by considering family constellation and SES simultaneously yielded analogous results for children's problem-solving performance (cf. Sigel, McGillicuddy-DeLisi, & Johnson, 1980). That is, children from middle-class far-spacing and from working-class near-spacing families were similar to one another on the strongest function composed of cognitive assessment scores and were differentiated from the other four groups of children.

Similarity of parental beliefs for these two groups may be the result of different factors, although the impact on the children may be the same regardless of why parents believe what they do. Consider the following argument, for example. It has been hypothesized that middle-class parents would refer to processes included in more current developmental theories in accord with Bronfenbrenner's (1958) hypothesis that accessibility to expert opinion varies with social class. It is reasonable, therefore, to suppose that some of these middle-class parents who attend to such expert opinion might also rely on literature from experts that recommends far spacing between children. For example, a recent issue of *Baby Talk* (1977, vol. 44, p. 21) presented a column entitled "What do the experts say?" at the close of an article about the best time to have a second child. Burton White's position was summarized as "spacing less than three years is difficult for the baby, the mother and especially the slightly older child." Helen Smith's position was presented as a preference for 4-year spacing, and Lee Salk's for at least 3 years. Brazelton "recommends that a mother seriously evaluate her own stamina and patience. He warns that while two children under four can be difficult, two under two can be exhausting." Only one expert, Pomeranze, was presented as advocating 2-year spacing to provide companions and playmates for siblings. Thus, middle-class parents with far spacing may actually have planned their families to provide far spacing between birth intervals as a result of greater exposure to and reliance on expert opinion concerning both child development processes and family planning.

The beliefs of working-class parents of closely spaced children are not subject to such an interpretation and may arise from different considerations. On the basis of data concerning beliefs of parents from lower-SES backgrounds, Sutherland (1979) has suggested that, in lower—SES homes evidencing high degrees of density, parents are likely to espouse beliefs in self-regulation, independence, internal child processes, and internal locus of control in spite of other controlling (authoritative and authoritarian) aspects of parenting. Sutherland relates these findings to a concept of survival. That is, parents are constrained by the density of the family to such a degree that they must allow the child to develop on his or her own, to become self-sufficient, and to operate independently with a minimum of assistance from others either within or outside of the family.

When family constellation was considered in relation to either sex of the parent or sex of the child, differences between groups occurred for two belief variables:

1. Mothers of only children and with near spacing between children referred to *positive feedback* (pleasant external consequence of behavior, serving to motivate, provide information, or make behavior more likely to reoccur) as a developmental process *more often* than fathers in these same two family constellations.
2. Parents with near spacing between boys referred to *creativity and imagination more often* than parents in all other groups. In addition, parents of female only children made such references *more frequently* than parents of female children with far spacing.

Finally, there were two effects that involved family constellation, sex of the child, and SES; in one case, family constellation, sex of parent, and sex of child were involved in an interaction.

1. Middle-class parents with far spacing between daughters referred to *generalization* (process whereby a behavior or idea obtains a general form that is applicable to many situations outside of the specific

present instance) *more often* than parents of male only children and working-class parents with far spacing between daughters or near spacing between sons.

2. Working-class parents of a female only child and of sons with far spacing referred to *absorption* (taking in information without processing or transforming) *more often* than working-class parents with far spacing and middle-class parents with near spacing between daughters.

3. Mothers of a female only child expressed *less confidence* in beliefs than all other parents except mothers of far-spaced daughters. In addition, fathers of a female only child expressed *more confidence* than fathers of male only children.

To summarize thus far, the 23 significant effects indicate that parents' beliefs do vary with demographic or descriptive characteristics of the family. Family constellation and SES appear to be the most salient factors (as compared with sex of parent or sex of child, along which beliefs vary). Differences between parents of an only child versus parents of three children are relatively straightforward and suggest fundamental differences in the way these parents view child development. For parents of three children, development includes more factors internal to the child (references to self-regulation and impulsivity versus direct instruction) than for parents of an only child. These differences apparently occur regardless of the education-income level of the parents. With regard to spacing between children, however, no differences occur unless SES is considered in conjunction with this family constellation factor. In general, results support hypotheses that parents' beliefs about child development vary with the same characteristics (i.e., SES and family constellation) that have been shown to relate to children's intellectual ability. The question that remains is whether these beliefs are related to actual teaching strategies used by parents during interactions with their own child.

Relationships between Parent's Beliefs and Teaching Behaviors

The finding that parental beliefs vary with family constellation and socioeconomic status is interesting but would be of little importance if there were no relationship to parental practices or child outcomes. Sigel's chapter in this volume indicates that parental teaching strategies that are related to children's representational abilities also vary with family constellation and SES. Do parents' beliefs provide any information about ways in which individuals teach their child above and beyond characteristics such as SES and family constellation? That is, if we equated all the parents in this sample of 120 families on these factors, would beliefs be related to actual teaching practices?

In order to evaluate the relationship between parents' beliefs and teaching behaviors, four sets of stepwise regressions were conducted. In each case, family constellation, SES, and family interactions were forced into the analysis first, followed by belief variables.[2] As indicated in Sigel's paper, correlations between parents' teaching behaviors on the two observation tasks and correlations between mothers' and fathers' behaviors were low. Regression analyses were therefore conducted with task and sex of parent considered separately. Thus, the four sets of analyses conducted consisted of variables from (1) the mothers' behaviors during the story task, (2) mothers' behaviors during the paper-folding task, (3) fathers' behaviors during the story task, and (4) fathers' behaviors during the paper-folding task.

Results of analyses of the relationship between mothers' scores on belief variables and teaching behaviors observed during the story and paper tasks are presented in Table 4. A significant relationship between SES and mothers' teaching behaviors was obtained for six of the behavior variables (story: length of interaction, verbal approvals; paper: number of statements, number of questions, task structuring, helping intrusions). Family constellation was related to mothers' use of positive nonverbal supports and helping intrusions during the paper task. The multiple correlation between the interaction terms of SES and family constellation reached significance for number of low-level questions exhibited during the story

[2]In order to evaluate the relationship between parental beliefs and parental behaviors independently of effects of family constellation and SES, an analysis of covariance was conducted. In applying the general linear model to these data, the first task was to investigate the extent to which family constellation and SES correlated with parental behaviors (dependent variables). Tests for covariates involved testing for main effects separately in an equation that included the means of the dependent variables and testing the interaction of the covariates, with the interaction as an added term in the equation. The control variables (SES, family constellation, and interaction variables) and the explanatory variables (parents' belief scores) were then entered into a regression analysis in a stepwise fashion. This procedure was followed for each parental behavior variable in each of the two observation tasks. Thus, a multiple correlation indicating the magnitude of the relationship between parental beliefs and parental behaviors was produced after family constellation and SES were forced into the analysis. All multiple correlation coefficients were compared to zero-order coefficients for direction and significance of relationships. Differences in sign and/or significance occurred for only two of the obtained multiple correlation coefficients, and these variables were deleted from the results reported. One additional significant belief variable was deleted as a predictor because it failed to provide a minimum increment of at least three points in the multiple correlation coefficient.

Table 4. Multiple Correlations between Mothers' Behaviors on Two Tasks
and SES, Family Constellation, and Beliefs about Development

Story task		Paper-folding task	
Behavior	R^a		R
Time of interaction			
Control variables[b]		Control variables	
SES	.18[b]	SES	.13
Family constellation	.21	Family constellation	.22
Interaction terms	.22	Interaction terms	.30
Explanatory variables[c]		Explanatory variables	
Dependency	.30	Absorption	(-).35
Absorption	(-).35		
Self-regulation	.40		
Number of interaction units			
Control variables		Control variables	
SES	.10	SES	.09
Family constellation	.14	Family constellation	.17
Interaction terms	.18	Interaction terms	.26
Explanatory variables		Explanatory variables	
Dependency	.32	Absorption	(-).33
Balance	.40	Impulsivity	(-).38
Self-regulation	.46		
Absorption	(-).49		
Conflict	(-).52		
No mental operational demand (MOD)			
Control variables		Control variables	
SES	.17	SES	.12
Family constellation	.24	Family constellation	.14
Interaction terms	.28	Interaction terms	.19
Explanatory variables		Explanatory variables	
Experimentation	(-).38	Absorption	(-).26
Self-regulation	(-).43	Experimentation	(-).32
Low-level statements			
Control variables		Control variables	
SES	.06	SES	.02
Family constellation	.11	Family constellation	.09
Interaction terms	.13	Interaction terms	.22
Explanatory variables		Explanatory variables	
Accumulation	(-).39	Observation	.30
Self-regulation	.44		
Rigidity	.48		
Intermediate-level statements			
Control variables		Control variables	
SES	.01	SES	.07
Family constellation	.14	Family constellation	.12
Interaction terms	.18	Interaction terms	.15

Table 4. (Continued)

	Story task		Paper-folding task	
Behavior		R^a		R
Explanatory variables			Explanatory variables	
Readiness		$(-).26$		
High-level statements				
Control variables			Control variables	
SES		.09	SES	.12
Family constellation		.23	Family constellation	.17
Interaction terms		.26	Interaction terms	.19
Explanatory variables			Explanatory variables	
Negative affect		.35	Modeling/	
Dependency		.42	identification	.27
Low-level questions				
Control variables			Control variables	
SES		.14	SES	.07
Family constellation		.17	Family constellation	.11
Interaction terms		$.29^b$	Interaction terms	.12
Explanatory variables			Explanatory variables	
			Empathy/contagion	.32
High-level questions				
Control variables			Control variables	
SES		.05	SES	.14
Family constellation		.17	Family constellation	.15
Interaction terms		.18	Interaction terms	.21
Explanatory variables			Explanatory variables	
Accumulation		.32	Modeling/	
Conflict		.37	identification	$(-).29$
Total number of statements				
Control variables			Control variables	
SES		.02	SES	$.26^b$
Family constellation		.06	Family constellation	.27
Interaction terms		.11	Interaction terms	29
Explanatory variables			Explanatory variables	
Dependency		.22	Modeling/	
Accumulation		$(-).30$	identification	.35
Conflict		$(-).35$		
Total number of questions				
Control variables			Control variables	
SES		.03	SES	$.19^b$
Family constellation		.07	Family constellation	.19
Interaction terms		.14	Interaction terms	.23
Explanatory variables			Explanatory variables	
Accumulation		.30	Modeling/	

Continued

Table 4. (Continued)

Story task		Paper-folding task	
Behavior	R^a		R
		identification	(-).30
		Empathy/contagion	.36
Number lower-level MODs			
Control variables		Control variables	
SES	.15	SES	.05
Family constellation	.18	Family constellation	.11
Interaction terms	.25	Interaction terms	.13
Explanatory variables		Explanatory variables	
Self-regulation	.32	Empathy/contagion	.34
Accumulation	(-).37	Conflict	(-).38
		Absorption	(-).42
Number intermediate-level MODs			
Control variables		Control variables	
SES	.06	SES	.10
Family constellation	.09	Family constellation	.11
Interaction terms	.21	Interaction terms	.23
Explanatory variables		Explanatory variables	
Structure in environment	.29	Infusion	.30
Number high-level MODs			
Control variables		Control variables	
SES	.09	SES	.09
Family constellation	.15	Family constellation	.09
Interaction terms	.15	Interaction terms	.19
Explanatory variables		Explanatory variables	
Accumulation	.28		
Structuring task			
Control variables		Control variables	
SES	.04	SES	.22[b]
Family constellation	.19	Family constellation	.25
Interaction terms	.22	Interaction terms	.30
Explanatory variables		Explanatory variables	
Generalization	.29		
Innate factors	(-).35		
Child management			
Control variables		Control variables	
SES	.10	SES	.03
Family constellation	.16	Family constellation	.16
Interaction terms	.18	Interaction terms	.20
Explanatory variables		Explanatory variables	
Conflict	.34	Absorption	(-).27
Balance	.39	Modeling/	
Structure in environment	(-).44	identification	(-).33

Table 4. (Continued)

Story task		Paper-folding task	
Behavior	R^a		R
Verbal disapprovals			
Control variables		Control variables	
SES	.90	SES	.08
Family constellation	.15	Family constellation	.14
Interaction terms	.19	Interaction terms	.14
Explanatory variables		Explanatory variables	
Proximity/exposure	.29	Impulsivity	(-).24
Creativity	(-).36		
Correction			
Control variables		Control variables	
SES	.09	SES	.09
Family constellation	.16	Family constellation	.16
Interaction terms	.21	Interaction terms	.18
Explanatory variables		Explanatory variables	
Stage	.42	Experimentation	(-).32
Cognitive reorganization	.48	Dependency	.36
Positive affect	.52		
Informational feedback			
Control variables		Control variables	
SES	.03	SES	.02
Family constellation	.13	Family constellation	.03
Interaction terms	.17	Interaction terms	.13
Explanatory variables		Explanatory variables	
Creativity	(-).30	Positive feedback	.25
Self-regulation	(-).37		
Positive feedback	(-).42		
Observation	.47		
Readiness	.51		
Experimentation	(-).54		
Positive nonverbal supports			
Control variables		Control variables	
SES	.07	SES	.14
Family constellation	.14	Family constellation	.26[b]
Interaction terms	.25	Interaction terms	.30
Explanatory variables		Explanatory variables	
Readiness	.41	Modeling/	
		identification	.37
		Self-regulation	(-).42
Negative nonverbal supports			
Control variables		Control variables	
SES	.08	SES	.08
Family constellation	.12	Family constellation	.18
Interaction terms	.19	Interaction terms	.24

Table 4. (Continued)

Story task		Paper-folding task	
Behavior	R^a		R
Explanatory variables		Explanatory variables	
Creativity	.33	Negative affect	(-).31
Impulsivity	.40	Confidence in beliefs	(-).36
Innate factors	(-).44		
Attention getting			
Control variables		Control variables	
SES	.04	SES	.07
Family constellation	.13	Family constellation	.10
Interaction terms	.16	Interaction terms	.10
Explanatory variables		Explanatory variables	
Dependency	.31	Readiness	.37
Creativity	.36	Positive feedback	(-).43
		Dependency	.46
Diverting			
Control variables		Control variables	
SES	.13	SES	.00
Family constellation	.19	Family constellation	.12
Interaction terms	.20	Interaction terms	.16
Explanatory variables		Explanatory variables	
Proximity/exposure	(-).28	Creativity	.25
		Observation	.32
		Empathy/contagion	.37

[a]Negative relationships indicated by the sign of the F or t tests of significance are indicated in parentheses.
[b]R's for control variables that are significant at the .05 level.
[c]R's for all explanatory variables included in this table are significant at the .05 level.

task and takeover intrusions during the paper task. Significant multiple correlation coefficients between control variables (family constellation, SES, and interaction terms) and teaching behaviors are indicated in Table 4 by an asterisk. All multiple correlation coefficients listed for belief variables were significant ($p < .05$).

As indicated in Table 4, mothers' belief scores produced significant increments in the multiple correlation coefficient for nearly all the teaching behaviors that were assessed. Multiple correlations ranged from .26 to .54 for the story behaviors and from .15 to .46 for teaching behaviors evidenced during the paper-folding task. Thus, mothers' beliefs about how children develop were predictive of their teaching behaviors in two different contexts, even after SES and family constellation were taken into account.

In most cases, several belief variables were related to each teaching behavior variable after effects due to SES and family constellation were partialed out. These belief variables therefore produced significant increases or increments in the multiple correlation coefficient. The particular belief variables that produced significant increments depended on the type of parent teaching behavior under consideration (e.g., distancing versus emotional support behaviors) and the content of the interactions (i.e., story or paper task). For example, the length of time and number of interactions that occurred with mothers during the story task were larger when mothers believed children were dependent or self-regulating and shorter when they believed that children absorb knowledge in an automatic fashion. The relationship between such beliefs and duration of the task makes intuitive sense. If children are dependent on others to guide their behavior and development, mothers are likely to evidence more behaviors and take more time to ensure that the child understands the story. If the mother believes that processes internal to the child guide and control understanding, the child might set the pace of the interaction. If, on the other hand, children absorb information, teaching strategies need involve only presentation of the details of the story, which can be accomplished relatively quickly.

Mothers' beliefs that were related to types of distancing teaching behaviors (no mental operational demands through number of high-level mental operational demands) during the story task formed a pattern that was consistent with the theoretical underpinnings of distancing theory. Distancing theory rests on the assumption that children construct their own reality through the course of their own interactions with people, events, and objects (cf. Sigel, 1979). The use of questions and higher-level mental operational demands represents high-level distancing and was associated with beliefs that reflect a view of the child as an active processor for the most part. For example, mothers' belief that children develop concepts through their own accumulation of knowledge was positively related to their use of high-level questions, total number of questions, and number of high-level mental operational demands; accumulation was negatively related to low-level statements and number of low-level mental operational demands.

The mothers' beliefs that were related to emotional support behaviors (such as verbal disapprovals, positive nonverbal supports, negative nonverbal supports, attention getting) appear to involve the nature or state of the child rather than developmental processes accounting for progress. That is, beliefs about whether children are creative, impulsive, or dependent appear to be related to the mothers' use of such behaviors on both the story and paper tasks.

For the paper-folding task, for the most part, fewer belief variables produced significant increases in the multiple correlation coefficients. In

addition, beliefs that were predictive of teaching behaviors during the
paper task differed from those that were related to teaching behaviors
during the story task. For example, mothers' beliefs that children learn
through modeling and beliefs in children's empathic nature were most
often related to distancing strategies during the paper-folding task (cf.
Table 4; high-level statements, low-level questions, high-level questions,
number of statements, number of questions, and low-level mental operational demands).

Result of regression analyses on fathers' belief scores and teaching
behaviors are presented in Table 5. A significant relationship between SES

Table 5. Multiple Correlations between Fathers' Behaviors on Two Tasks and SES, Family Constellation and Beliefs about Development

Story task		Paper-folding task	
Behavior	R^a		R
Time of interaction			
Control variables[b]		Control variables	
SES	.05	SES	.02
Family constellation	.15	Family constellation	.05
Interaction terms	.27[b]	Interaction terms	.10
Explanatory variables[c]		Explanatory variables	
Absorption	(-).33	Experimentation	.29
		Absorption	(-).35
		Positive feedback	(-).40
		Confidence in beliefs	.44
		Impulsivity	.47
Number of interaction units			
Control variables		Control variables	
SES	.01	SES	.03
Family constellation	.14	Family constellation	.09
Interaction terms	.24	Interaction terms	.13
Explanatory variables		Explanatory variables	
Absorption	(-).30	Impulsivity	.35
		Absorption	(-).40
		Cognitive reorganization	.44
No mental operational demand (MOD)			
Control variables		Control variables	
SES	.05	SES	.14
Family constellation	.14	Family constellation	.20
Interaction terms	.17	Interaction terms	.21
Explanatory variables		Explanatory variables	
Modeling/		Self-regulation	.31
identification	(-).28	Observation	(-).36

Table 5. (Continued)

	Story task		Paper-folding task	
Behavior	R^a			R
Low-level statements				
Control variables			Control variables	
SES	$.18^b$		SES	.70
Family constellation	.20		Family constellation	.21
Interaction terms	.26		Interaction terms	.26
Explanatory variables			Explanatory variables	
			Infusion	.35
			Proximity/exposure	.41
Intermediate-level statements				
Control variables			Control variables	
SES	.02		SES	.12
Family constellation	.17		Family constellation	.12
Interaction terms	.24		Interaction terms	.16
Explanatory variables			Explanatory variables	
Generalization	.30		Modeling/	
Accumulation	(-).35		identification	.26
High-level statements				
Control variables			Control variables	
SES	.16		SES	.00
Family constellation	.26		Family constellation	.16
Interaction terms	.31		Interaction terms	.17
Explanatory variables			Explanatory variables	
Accumulation	(-).38		Observation	.29
Proximity/exposure	(-).43		Creativity/imagination	.36
Dependency	.46		Positive feedback	.40
Low-level questions				
Control variables			Control variables	
SES	.06		SES	.03
Family constellation	$.25^b$		Family constellation	.09
Interaction terms	.30		Interaction terms	.20
Explanatory variables			Explanatory variables	
Experimentation	.36		Positive affect	.32
Confidence in beliefs	(-).42		Absorption	.37
			Creativity/	
			imagination	(-).41
			Stage	(-).45
Intermediate-level questions				
Control variables			Control variables	
SES	.17		SES	.13
Family constellation	.18		Family constellation	.16
Interaction terms	.20		Interaction terms	$.30^b$
Explanatory variables			Explanatory variables	
			Generalization	.40

Continued

Table 5. (Continued)

Story task		Paper-folding task	
Behavior	R^a		R
High-level questions			
Control variables		Control variables	
SES	.02	SES	.10
Family constellation	$.25^b$	Family constellation	.14
Interaction terms	.29	Interaction terms	.18
Explanatory variables		Explanatory variables	
Structure in environment	$(-).34$	Stage	.38
		Absorption	$(-).43$
Number of statements			
Control variables		Control variables	
SES	.09	SES	.02
Family constellation	.13	Family constellation	.12
Interaction terms	.20	Interaction terms	.15
Explanatory variables		Explanatory variables	
Accumulation	$(-).28$	Accumulation	$(-).32$
Empathy/contagion	.33	Creativity/	
		imagination	.37
Number of questions			
Control variables		Control variables	
SES	.01	SES	.02
Family constellation	.06	Family constellation	.12
Interaction terms	$.25^b$	Interaction terms	.13
Explanatory variables		Explanatory variables	
		Positive affect	.27
		Accumulation	.33
Number of low-level MODs			
Control variables		Control variables	
SES	.16	SES	.00
Family constellation	$.32^b$	Family constellation	.10
Interaction terms	.32	Interaction terms	.18
Explanatory variables		Explanatory variables	
Negative affect	$(-).36$	Positive affect	.30
		Infusion	.40
		Proximity/exposure	.48
Number of intermediate-level MODs			
Control variables		Control variables	
SES	.13	SES	.06
Family constellation	.19	Family constellation	.11
Interaction terms	.26	Interaction terms	$.28^b$
Explanatory variables		Explanatory variables	
		Generalization	.38
Number of high-level MODs			
Control variables		Control variables	

Table 5. (Continued)

Story task		Paper-folding task	
Behavior	R^a		R
SES	.04	SES	.09
Family constellation	.29[b]	Family constellation	.17
Interaction terms	.34	Interaction terms	.19
Explanatory variables		Explanatory variables	
Structure in environment	(-).39	Stage	.38
		Absorption	(-).44
		Experimentation	.47
Structuring task			
Control variable		Control variables	
SES	.10	SES	.07
Family constellation	.13	Family constellation	.11
Interaction terms	.20	Interaction terms	.14
Explanatory variables		Explanatory variables	
Direct instruction	.30	Accumulation	(-).32
Experimentation	(-).36	Infusion	(-).37
Positive feedback	.41	Absorption	.41
Child management			
Control variables		Control variables	
SES	.03	SES	.21[b]
Family constellation	.19	Family constellation	.28
Interaction terms	.20	Interaction terms	.36[b]
Explanatory variables		Explanatory variables	
Balance	.31	Experimentation	.42
Innate factors	(-).35	Accumulation	.45
Verbal approvals			
Control variables		Control variables	
SES	.01	SES	.11
Family constellation	.07	Family constellation	.14
Interaction terms	.10	Interaction terms	.20
		Explanatory variables	
		Creativity/	
		imagination	(-).28
Verbal disapprovals			
Control variables		Control variables	
SES	.09	SES	.02
Family constellation	.15	Family constellation	.05
Interaction terms	.16	Interaction terms	.08
Explanatory variables		Explanatory variables	
Negative feedback	(-).29	Positive affect	.24
Impulsivity	.34		
Correction			
Control variables		Control variables	
SES	.03	SES	.14

Continued

Table 5. (Continued)

Story task		Paper-folding task	
Behavior	R^a		R
Family constellation	.12	Family constellation	.20
Interaction terms	.20	Interaction terms	$.32^b$
Explanatory variables		Explanatory variables	
Structure in environment	(-).29	Direct instruction	(-).41
		Readiness	.47
		Observation	(-).50
Information feedback			
Control variables		Control variables	
SES	.01	SES	.06
Family constellation	.06	Family constellation	.07
Interaction terms	.16	Interaction terms	$.24^b$
Explanatory variables		Explanatory variables	
Creativity	(-).24	Cognitive	
Modeling/identification	(-).30	reorganization	.33
Infusion	(-).35	Positive feedback	(-).39
		Observation	(-).43
Positive nonverbal supports			
Control variables		Control variables	
SES	.10	SES	.11
Family constellation	.16	Family constellation	.17
Interaction terms	.22	Interaction terms	.19
Explanatory variables		Explanatory variables	
Structure in environment	.36	Readiness	(-).27
Negative nonverbal supports			
Control variables		Control variables	
SES	.13	SES	$.20^b$
Family constellation	.16	Family constellation	.22
Interaction terms	.18	Interaction terms	.25
Explanatory variables		Explanatory variables	
Absorption	.28	Modeling/	
		identification	.33
		Readiness	.39
		Negative feedback	(-).43
Helping intrusions			
Control variables		Control variables	
SES	.13	SES	.02
Family constellation	.23	Family constellation	.06
Interaction terms	.29	Interaction terms	.14
Explanatory variables		Explanatory variables	
Experimentation	.37	Stage	.30
		Accumulation	(-).38
		Balance	.42
		Generalization	(-).46

Table 5. (Continued)

	Story task		Paper-folding task	
Behavior	R^a			R
Attention getting				
Control variables			Control variables	
SES	.01		SES	.11
Family constellation	.11		Family constellation	.12
Interaction terms	.15		Interaction terms	.14
Explanatory variables			Explanatory variables	
Negative affect	(−).25		Stage	.25
			Infusion	.31
Diverting				
Control variables			Control variables	
SES	.12		SES	.10
Family constellation	.20		Family constellation	.13
Interaction terms	.31^b		Interaction terms	.14
Explanatory variables			Explanatory variables	
			Observation	(−).23
			Balance	(−).30

^{a}Negative relationships indicated by the sign of the F or t tests of significance are indicated in parentheses.
^{b}R's for control variables that are significant at the .05 level.
^{c}R's for all explanatory variables included in this table are significant at the .05 level.

and paternal teaching practices was obtained for three variables (story: low level statements; paper: child management, negative nonverbal supports). Four of the teaching behavior variables varied with family constellation (story: low-level questions, high-level questions, low-level mental operational demands, and high-level mental operational demands); a significant relationship between SES–family constellation interaction terms and fathers' behaviors was obtained for 10 variables (story: length of interaction, out of contact, number of questions, reading, diverting; paper: intermediate-level questions, intermediate-level mental operational demands, child management, correction, informational feedback).

As was the case with results for mothers, fathers' belief scores did produce significant increments in multiple correlation coefficients after SES and family constellation factors were stepped into the regressions. Multiple correlations ranged from .10 to .46 for the story task and from .24 to .50 for the paper-folding behaviors evidenced by fathers. In general, then, fathers' beliefs were predictive of their teaching behaviors after relationships between demographic characteristics and fathers' behaviors were controlled.

The particular beliefs that were related to fathers' behaviors appear to vary with the content of the interaction (see story versus paper task), but a different pattern of results was obtained for fathers than was the case for mothers. For the story task, a belief that children absorb knowledge was most strongly related to length and number of units of the interaction. Although absorption also produced significant increments in the analysis of mothers' story behaviors, other belief variables (e.g., dependency, self-regulation, etc.) were also related to length and number of interaction units during the story for mothers. The relationships obtained for fathers' behaviors during the story task, in fact, resemble the findings for mothers during the paper task for these variables. That is, belief in absorption as a developmental process was the single best predictor of length of interaction on the paper task for mothers and length of interaction on the story task for fathers.

For fathers' behaviors during the paper-folding task, many belief variables produced significant increments for length and number of interaction units. For example, note that fathers' beliefs that children acquire knowledge through a process of experimentation and through positive feedback to the child and that the child is an impulsive being were positively related to length of interaction on the paper-folding task. Fathers' confidence in their beliefs and beliefs that children learn through absorption were negatively related to the length of the interaction during paper folding. These relationships also make intuitive sense. If a father behaves in accordance with his beliefs, the father–child interaction would be expected to last longer when the father allows the child to experiment and/or provides feedback to the child. Similarly, a father who simply conveys facts because he believes the child learns through absorption of information without processing it would take less time to complete the task. If a parent is confident that he understands how children learn and develop, then he can quickly proceed to teach the task, yielding the negative relationship between confidence and length of interaction. With regard to belief in an impulsive nature of the child, it is possible that fathers believe in such a construct because their children are indeed impulsive or easily distracted from the task at hand. If this is the case, teaching the child a particular task would be more time-consuming because of the need to continually get the child "back on the track."

With regard to fathers' distancing behaviors (no mental operational demand through number of high-level mental operational demands), more belief variables produced significant increments in the multiple cor-relation coefficient for behaviors evidenced during the paper task than during the story task. This pattern is the opposite of that obtained for mothers. However, the particular beliefs that were related to distancing behaviors did vary with the observational task, and in some cases there was consistency in types of relationships between beliefs and behaviors across mothers and fathers. For example, fathers' beliefs that children accumulate knowledge on their own was negatively related to intermediate and high-level statements as well as total number of statements evidenced during the story task. Recall that such a belief was negatively related to low distancing variables and positively related to high distancing variables in the analysis of mothers' behaviors during the story task.

The beliefs that were predictive of fathers' distancing teaching behaviors during the paper folding task differed from those that were related to mothers' behaviors during the paper task. Mothers' beliefs in modeling and empathy as developmental processes were most often related to their distancing behaviors during the paper task. For fathers, belief variables that reflect a view of the child as an active processor were related to high-level distancing. Those beliefs that reflect a more passive view of development, especially those indicating that knowledge exists external to the child initially, were predictive of low-level distancing behaviors. For example, beliefs in infusion, exposure, and absorption were related to low-level statements, low-level questions, and number of low-level mental operational demands evidenced by fathers during the paper task. Beliefs in stages and the creativity of the child were negatively related to use of low-level questions. These findings suggest that low-level distancing is related to the view that certain events occur in the presence of the child and an automatic process of absorbing or infusing that information occurs. If one believes that development occurs in this manner, the teaching of behaviors that focus on encouragement to observe, describe, label, and so on (i.e., low-level distancing) is consistent with such beliefs. Higher-level distancing, such as number of questions and number of high-level mental operational demands, was related to beliefs that include the child's own internal or overt behavior as mechanisms of development. Fathers who viewed the character of children as consisting of a positive nature and who saw development as a result of children's own accumulation of knowledge asked more questions during this task. Those fathers who expressed beliefs in stages of development and the child's own experimentation more often and beliefs in absorption less often were more likely to place high-level mental operational demands on the child. These patterns of relationships between beliefs and distancing teaching strategies are consistent with predictions based on distancing theory. That is, teaching behaviors that encourage children to propose alternatives and to anticipate, plan, and reach conclusions on their own (high-level distancing) were related to a view of the child that is consistent with the assumptions upon which distancing theory rests. These assumptions include the notion of stages as

well as feedback from the child's own action and active internal processes
that results in constructions of reality on the basis of interactions with the
environment (cf. Sigel, 1979). Thus, for the paper-folding task, the pattern
of relationships between teaching strategies and beliefs in the nature of
development was more consistent with distancing theory for fathers than
for mothers.

With respect to emotional support and feedback behaviors evidenced
by fathers, different beliefs were related to the use of such strategies on each
task. For example, beliefs in negative feedback were negatively related to
fathers' use of verbal disapprovals during the story task. This violates
predictions, since those fathers who referred to negative feedback less often
actually provided more negative feedback in the form of disapprovals more
often than other fathers. The relationship of fathers' beliefs in the
impulsive nature of the child and verbal disapproval behaviors does make
sense given that the father might use such disapprovals to attempt to
inhibit this impulsive predilection on the part of the child. On the paper
task, however, the best predictor of fathers' verbal disapprovals was a belief
in the child's positive affect. This implies that the father may feel freer to
evidence such disapprovals if he believes the child is basically a happy,
positive person. Thus, the fathers' use of disapprovals may stem from very
different sources depending on the context or task around which the
interaction occurs. Inspection of the belief variables that were predictive of
the remaining support and feedback behaviors reveals a similar pattern—
that is, different beliefs were related to such behaviors as were evidenced
during the two tasks.

To summarize the findings regarding relationships between parents'
beliefs and teaching strategies, beliefs were predictive of child-rearing
practices above and beyond factors of SES and family constellation. Thus,
there is some support for our hypothesis that there are factors internal to the
parent, such as beliefs, from which parents' child-rearing styles may
emerge. Information about such beliefs can help account for variation in
parents' teaching practices that ultimately affect the cognitive development
of the child. Inspection of the types of beliefs that did relate to particular
teaching practices revealed that there is, however, no one-to-one correspondence between beliefs and teaching behaviors. Patterns of beliefs that were
predictive of actual teaching behaviors appeared to be dependent on the
task the parent was teaching to the child, and patterns varied for mothers
versus fathers.

With respect to different patterns obtained across the story and paper
tasks, it was apparent that more belief variables were related to mothers'
teaching behaviors during the story task than during the paper task. That
is, more belief variables produced significant increments in the multiple

correlation between beliefs and behaviors when the story task rather than the paper-folding task was considered. Although differences in the number of belief variables that were related to behaviors were not so marked for fathers, the opposite trend appeared. A greater number of belief variables produced significant increments when the paper task rather than the story task was considered. In addition, the types of beliefs associated with a particular behavior appear to vary with the task.

Mothers' beliefs in accumulation of knowledge seemed to be most consistently and most strongly related to their distancing behaviors during storytelling, but mothers' lack of belief that children develop through modeling or identification were most often predictive of high-level distancing behaviors during the paper-folding task. This suggests that the task in which mothers are engaged with their child affects which beliefs and the teaching strategies that are likely to be evidenced. For example, the paper-folding task is more conducive to a demonstration or modeling teaching style than a story task is. If a parent believes that modeling is one means through which children acquire concepts or skills, that parent may be more likely to use modeling rather than distancing techniques when the the former are appropriate. During storytelling, however, beliefs in modeling as a developmental process may be irrelevant, since the task is more verbal and not clearly open to demonstration or modeling as a means to get the child to understand the story. As a result, the mother's teaching style during the storytelling task stems from other beliefs, such as beliefs in the child's own accumulation of knowledge.

The nature of the task is clearly not the single factor determining which beliefs will be related to particular teaching behaviors, however. Although mothers and fathers did not differ from one another in the frequency of their references to modeling as responsible for development and learning, fathers' beliefs in modeling were not related to their teaching behaviors during either task for the most part. In fact, belief in accumulation as a developmental process was related to fathers' distancing behaviors during the story task (cf. intermediate-level statements, high-level statements, total number of statements) and during the paper-folding task (cf. number of statements, number of questions). Thus, the relationship between this belief and distancing strategies was somewhat more consistent across tasks than was the case for mothers. This suggests that the belief–teaching behavior relationship is less susceptible to changes due to task parameters for fathers than it is for mothers. It is possible that mothers' beliefs about development are differentiated to take into account different aspects of a child's performance, while fathers' beliefs are more general, encompassing development in general. If this is the case, mothers might rely on different aspects of their belief systems to guide their teaching styles as they adapt their behaviors to different situational tasks or child demands. Fathers, on the other hand, would vary less in their teaching styles across different contexts because their beliefs about children and development are not differentiated in this manner. Analyses presented in Sigel's chapter support this notion. Although relationships between behaviors across the two tasks were infrequent and generally small, some distancing behaviors were significantly correlated across tasks for fathers but not for mothers.

Patterns of relationships between beliefs and parents' use of emotional support and feedback behaviors also appeared to vary with both task and sex of the parent. The degree to which mothers evidenced verbal disapprovals, positive nonverbal behaviors, negative nonverbal behaviors, and attention getting was related to beliefs that reflected their view of the nature or state of the child rather than developmental processes (e.g. beliefs in children's creativity, impulsivity, positive affect, dependency, readiness, and negative affect were related to these types of behaviors). However, the particular beliefs related to each of these behaviors varied depending on the task. For example, the mothers' use of negative nonverbal behaviors was related to beliefs in children's creativity and impulsivity for the story task, while beliefs in negative affective states of the child were most predictive of such behaviors evidenced during the paper-folding task. For fathers, beliefs related to child states were also related to these types of emotional support and feedback behaviors (e.g., creativity, impulsivity, positive affect, and readiness), but beliefs about developmental processes were also predictive of such behaviors. For example, beliefs in modeling and negative feedback as well as beliefs in readiness were related to fathers' use of negative nonverbal behaviors during paper folding. As was the case for mothers, the particular beliefs related to emotional support and to feedback behaviors varied with the task. Fathers' use of negative nonverbal behaviors during storytelling was related to beliefs in absorption rather than the beliefs listed above in relation to the paper-folding task. Thus, relationships between types of beliefs and parents' use of emotional support and feedback behaviors varied with the task the parent teaches the child. In addition, patterns appear to be dependent upon whether the mother or the father is the object of investigation.

Conclusions

Findings concerning differences between groups in parents' beliefs and concerning relationships between beliefs and teaching behaviors indicate that parent behaviors are neither random nor automatic responses to the child's behaviors in the strict behaviorist tradition. Rather, parents are thinking beings, organizing information about children as they develop as parents through the adult years themselves. Their beliefs about children and development can be viewed as both a source and an outcome of their parenting experiences. Differences in beliefs between parents of an only child and parents of three children, for example, could indicate that parents learned about children "on the job," so to speak. They believe in different developmental processes and view the child differently as a result of their experience of parenting only one child versus three children. The relationships between parents' beliefs and their behaviors while teaching their child even after family constellation and SES were controlled indicate, however, that parents' behaviors are probably not a result of simply being more or less experienced with preschool children. The fact that beliefs were related to teaching, support, and feedback behaviors above and beyond demographic characteristics provide support for our contention that beliefs are mediating variables between family constellation, SES, and parental practices. That is, one source of parents' behaviors with their children is the parents' beliefs about children in general, and it is the belief system of parents that is affected by background factors such as SES and number or spacing of children.

It is apparent, however, that a one-to-one correspondence between a particular belief or set of beliefs and a particular teaching style did not exist for the parents we studied. Beliefs that were related to one class of teaching behaviors (i.e., distancing strategies) varied depending upon the task the parent was teaching the child, especially for mothers. There was, in fact, no relationship between mothers' use of distancing behaviors across the two tasks (Sigel, McGillicuddy-DeLisi, & Johnson, 1980), indicating that mothers do not evidence a consistent teaching style across different types of tasks. Rather, they appear to adapt their styles of teaching to conform with the task demands. Thus, beliefs in cognitive processes such as accumulation of knowledge were related to teaching behaviors on the more verbal storytelling task, while beliefs in modeling were predictive of teaching strategies on the more structured paper-folding task, which involved production of a concrete, visible outcome. This "inconsistency" of teaching strategies across tasks or situations is actually a positive aspect of parental styles if one views the mother as flexible and capable of adapting her behavior in accordance with the types of performance demands on the child. The finding that different types of beliefs were related to teaching behaviors on the two tasks indicates that the sample of mothers varied both in beliefs and in teaching strategies available in their repertoires of possible behaviors. The task apparently influences what types of relationships between beliefs and behaviors will be observed, at least for mothers. For fathers, there were some low but significant relationships (i.e., r's $= .15-.25$) in frequency of distancing behaviors across tasks, and beliefs in internal cognitive processes such as accumulation were related to fathers' teaching strategies on both tasks. Thus, the belief–behavior relationship was less influenced by task and situational demands than was the case for mothers. This does not mean that fathers behave in accordance with their beliefs to a greater degree than do mothers but that similar beliefs are related to this class of behaviors across different teaching activities for fathers.

These patterns of differences, both in teaching behaviors and in belief–behavior relationships, suggest that the context of the parent–child interaction (i.e., the task being taught) is an important factor that is neglected in much of the parent–child literature. Different beliefs of parents appear to be related to particular behaviors as the task is varied, and mothers and fathers seem to differ from one another in the effect the task has upon the belief–behavior relationship. Mothers may have a more differentiated system of beliefs that takes into account the demands of the situation on the child, while fathers may adhere to a more global or general system regardless of external demands or circumstance. It is important, however, that beliefs do relate parents' behaviors in both cases. Conceptualization of constructs—such as beliefs as a link between a variety of factors including SES, family constellation and task demands, and parent practices—can clearly provide both descriptions and theoretical rationales for variability in parent behaviors that affect children's intellectual development.

References

Belmont, L., & Marolla, F. A. Birth order, family size and intelligence. *Science*, 1973, *182*, 1096-1101.

Belmont, L., Stein, Z. A., & Susser, M. W. Comparison of associations of birth order with intelligence test score and height. *Nature*, 1975, *255*, 54-56.

Bradley, R. H., Caldwell, B. M., & Elardo, R. Home environment and cognitive development in the first two years: A cross-lagged panel analysis. *Developmental Psychology*, 1979, *15*, 246-250.

Bronfenbrenner, U. Socialization and social class through time and space. In E. E. Maccoby, T. M. Newcomb, & E. L. Hartley (Eds.), *Readings in social psychology*. New York: Holt, 1958.

Bronfenbrenner, U. Contexts of childrearing: Problems and prospects. *American Psychologist*, 1979, *34*, 844-850.

Campbell, F. L. Family growth and variation in the family role structure. *Journal of Marriage and the Family*, 1970, *32*, 45-53.

Cicirelli, V. G. Effects of mother and older sibling on the problem solving behavior of the older child. *Developmental Psychology*, 1975, *11*, 749-756.

Cicirelli, V. G. Effects of mother and older sibling on child's conceptual style. *Journal of Genetic Psychology*, 1977, *131*, 309-318.

Dandes, H. M., & Dow, D. Relation of intelligence to family size and density. *Child Development*, 1969, *40*, 629-640.

Davis, D. J., Cahan, S., & Bashi, J. Birth order and intellectual development: The confluence model in the light of cross-cultural evidence. *Science*, 1976, *15*, 1470-1472.

Elder, G. H. Structural variations in the child rearing relationship. *Sociometry*, 1962, *25*, 241-262.

Elder, G. H., & Bowerman, C. E. Family structure and child rearing patterns: The effect of family size and sex composition. *American Sociological Review*, 1963, *28*, 891-905.

Kellaghan, T., & MacNamara, J. Family correlates of verbal reasoning ability. *Developmental Psychology*, 1972, *7*, 49-53.

Kelly, G. A. *The psychology of personal constructs*. New York: Norton, 1955.

Kelly, G. A. *A theory of personality*. New York: Norton, 1963.

Kennett, K. F., & Cropley, A. J. Intelligence, family size and socioeconomic status. *Journal of Biosocial Science*, 1970, *2*, 227-236.

Kohn, M. L. *Class and conformity: A study in values*. Homewood, Ill.: Dorsey, 1969.

Kohn, M. L. Social class and parental values: Another confirmation of the relationship. *American Sociological Review*. 1976, *41*, 538-545.

Landfield, A. W., & Leitner, L. M. (Eds.). *Personal construct psychology: Psychotherapy and personality*. New York: Wiley, 1980.

Laosa, L. M. Maternal teaching strategies in Chicano and Anglo-American families: The influence of culture and education on maternal behavior. *Child Development*, 1980, *51*, 759-765. (a)

Laosa, L. M. *The impact of schooling on interactions between parents and children*. Paper presented at the Conference on Changing Families, Educational Testing Service, Princeton, N.J., November 1980. (b)

Lesser, G. S., Fifer, G., & Clark, C. Mental abilities of children from different social class and cultural groups. *Monographs of the Society for Research in Child Development*, 1965, *30*, 1-115.

Marjoribanks, K. *Families and their learning environments: An empirical analysis*. London: Routledge & Kegan Paul, 1979.

Marjoribanks, K., Walberg, H. J., & Bargen, M. Mental abilities: Sibling constellation and social class correlates. *British Journal of Social and Clinical Psychology*, 1975, *14*, 109-116.

McGillicuddy-DeLisi, A. V. The role of parental beliefs in the family as a system of mutual influences. *Family Relations*, 1980, *29*, 317-323.

Mumbauer, C. C., & Miller, J. O. Socioeconomic background and cognitive functioning in preschool children. *Child Development*, 1970, *41*, 461-470.

Sigel, I. E. Consciousness raising of individual competence in problem solving. In M. W. Kent & J. E. Rolf (Eds.), *Primary prevention of psychopathology*, (Vol. III): *Social competence in children*. Hanover, N.H.: University Press of New England, 1979.

Sigel, I. E., McGillicuddy-Delisi, A. V., & Johnson, J. E. *Parental distancing, beliefs and children's representational competence within the family context* (ETS RB 80-21). Princeton, N.J.: Educational Testing Service, 1980.

Sutherland, K. Discussion of findings of the Parenting Resources Implementation Model (PRIMO) Project. Personal communication, November 15, 1979.

Thomas, E. C. Conceptual development in advantaged and disadvantaged kindergarten children. *Perceptual and Motor Skills*, 1971, *32*, 711-717.

Tulkin, S. R. Race, class, family and school achievement. *Journal of Personality and Social Psychology*, 1968, *9*, 31-37.

Zajonc, R. B. Family configuration and intelligence. *Science*, 1976, *192*, 227-236.

Zajonc, R. B., & Markus, G. B. Birth order and intellectual development. *Psychological Review*, 1975, *82*, 74-88.

CHAPTER 10

The Role of Categorization in the Socialization Process

How Parents and Older Siblings Cognitively Organize Child Behavior

MARGARET K. BACON and RICHARD D. ASHMORE

Introduction

Students of the socialization process have long recognized the central position of the family in the learning environment of the developing child. Cross-cultural studies, for example, have underlined the effect of variations in family structure on the experiences of children (cf. LeVine, 1970; Whiting & Whiting, 1975). Thus the extended family, the nuclear family, and the mother–child household are conceived as creating significantly different contexts for learning. Similarly, the agents of socialization available in the family unit constitute an important variable in socialization. These agents, or family members, who interact daily with the child may, of course, vary from one family to another along many dimensions (e.g., number, sex, age, personal characteristics).

Much has also been written on the subject of the parent–child interaction sequence. Most of this research has been based on the assumption that the interaction between the parent (usually the mother) and the child is a major factor in socialization. This interaction is usually seen as a kind of stimulus–response sequence in which the behavior of the parent influences or "shapes" the behavior (indeed, the enduring traits) of the child. More recent research has emphasized the child's role in eliciting

MARGARET K. BACON and RICHARD D. ASHMORE ● Rutgers—The State University, New Brunswick, New Jersey 08903. The collection and analysis of the data reported here and the preparation of this chapter were supported by National Institute of Mental Health grant 27737 (Margaret K. Bacon and Richard D. Ashmore, Co-Principal Investigators).

particular responses from parents (cf. Bell & Harper, 1977) and thus influencing the interaction process.

The data collected in socialization research have usually been organized in categories determined by the investigator. In general, two major techniques have been used. In many studies, parents have been asked how they handled various kinds of child behavior, which were labeled and defined by the investigator. The verbal responses of the parent have been used as an index of child-rearing practices (Sears, Maccoby, & Levin, 1957, is a classic example). The second approach has been based on direct observations of parent–child interaction. These have been coded in preselected categories, either at the time of observation or later (see Lytton, 1971, for a review). Both techniques involve an organization of the data base which has been imposed by the investigator.

Such methods of data collection disregard many important questions. What aspects of ongoing child activity do parents notice? How do they segment the behavior stream into meaningful units? What labels do they apply to these units? How do they organize them into categories and along dimensions consistent with the implicit theories of child behavior that they carry in their heads? How do they decide what is the proper socializing response? These perceptual–cognitive–decision processes mediate parental response to child behavior, yet very little is known about the nature of these processes or the factors which influence them.

Over the past several years we have been developing an approach to the study of socialization that focuses on the manner in which parents perceive and cognitively structure the child behavior they experience. In the working model that has guided our research, we have assumed that the cognitive activities of parents can be represented as a temporal sequence of somewhat separate but related processes. These include, for example, the focusing of attention on child behavior, the segmentation of the behavior stream into meaningful units or events, the categorization of the behavioral unit, and the decision regarding parental response. It is further assumed that this set of cognitive activities (termed *cognitive structuring*) is influenced by the parent's implicit theory of child behavior. These implicit theories resemble formal theories of developmental psychology. They identify important elements of child behavior, how these elements are interrelated, and the factors that cause or influence behavior. Such theories are presumably learned, in part, during the socialization of the parent. It is, therefore, predicted that implicit theories of child behavior will be influenced by various factors related to the background of the perceiving parent. Parents' implicit theories provide a cognitive frame of reference or set of schemata against which any given fragment of a child's behavior is seen and interpreted. The same fragment of behavior may be variously categorized according to the cognitive frame of reference against which it is experienced. For example, the same sequence of ongoing child activity may be called "fighting" or merely "horseplay," depending on the implicit theory of child behavior held by the observer.

A major purpose of this chapter is to uncover and describe the implicit theories of child behavior held by older siblings of early-school-age children. More specifically, we will explore the categorizations used by siblings to organize descriptions of behavior attributed to younger brothers and sisters. Before doing this, however, we will present in some detail an earlier study of how parents cognitively structure child behavior (Bacon & Ashmore, 1982). This "detour" is necessary for two reasons. First, our decision to study older siblings grew out of a hypothesis developed during the analysis and interpretation of the parents' data. The older siblings' and parents' categorizations will be compared in order to test this hypothesis and to explicate cognitive structuring and the factors influencing this process. Second, the methods of data collection and analysis are identical in the two studies. It is important to present these methods in detail, since they were developed in order to uncover and represent the schemata used by perceivers to organize perceived child behavior. At each stage in the research we sought to give parents and older siblings the greatest possible freedom to reveal their own implicit theories rather than assessing their willingness or ability to respond to our constructs.

Study 1

In Study 1 we sought to test the following proposition: Categorization of verbal descriptions of child behavior will vary as a function of the sex of the perceiving parent and the sex of the child to whom the behavior is attributed. In our approach to this question we developed a multistage procedure. In the first stage, which itself comprised several distinct steps, we derived a set of verbal descriptions of the social behavior of children in the age range 6 to 11. Next, an independent sample of parents sorted the verbal descriptions on the basis of similarity, which allowed computation of a distance measure between all possible pairs of descriptions. This distance measure was then used as input to multidimensional scaling and hierarchical clustering computer programs. In the final stage, ratings of the behavior descriptions in terms of psychological properties (made by another independent sample of parents) were used to interpret the structural representations produced by these computer programs.

All participants in our first study were white middle-class mothers and fathers who had at least one son and one daughter between the ages of 6 and

11. This sample was chosen so that all subjects would have experienced parenthood of both a boy and a girl of this age range. Some control was also provided by this sample selection for effects of variation in social class and race among parents and age differences among perceived children.

We began by eliciting from parents descriptions of child behavior for this age period. As noted above, in much of the research on socialization, parents have been asked how they respond to different kinds of child behavior described by the investigator. The assumption underlying such research seems to be that child behavior naturally comes in packages labeled something like *aggression* and *dependence*. What parents' labels might be for different groups of behavior has received little attention. Since we are interested in parental rather than investigator-described categories, every effort was made to elicit from parents descriptions of behavior in the parents' own words rather than ours. Accordingly, we devised a minimally structured interview in which mothers and fathers were encouraged to describe in their own words the behavior of children of this age. Their responses were tape-recorded.

The large number of descriptive words and phrases produced by these subjects was reduced by a series of steps. All sentences referring to child behavior were extracted. The 791 behavior descriptions resulting from this procedure were then judged by the two authors and two graduate students (one female, one male). All phrases or words referring to personality traits (e.g., "is competitive") or behavior not involved in social interaction (e.g., "picks nose") were eliminated. A single word or phrase was chosen to represent sets of descriptions judged to be similar in meaning—for example, "can talk self out of any situation" was chosen from a group that also included "can talk self out of a predicament" and "can talk self out of anything." Other groups of descriptions were reduced to the most general statement of the behavior in question—for example, "likes to build model airplanes," "likes to build tree houses," and similar specific statements became "likes to build things."

The remaining 195 behavior descriptions were typed in lists and submitted to a sample of parents who were asked to mark those that were not clear or were not descriptive of children of this age (i.e., 6 to 11). Parents in this sample were also asked to add to the list any additional behavior descriptions they thought should be included. Only a handful of items were suggested and even fewer were judged to be unclear or not applicable. The list of descriptions resulting from this procedure was reduced to 99 items (a limit imposed both by our respondents' patience and by the computer programs used to analyze the data). Since many of the items appeared evaluative in content, an attempt was made to obtain a rough balance of items which were positive, negative, and neutral or debatable kinds of behavior. The remaining 99 behavior descriptions were inserted into sentence frames, one for each sex of child. Thus, the phrase "is definitely a part of the conversation at dinner" yielded the two sentences: "A girl is definitely a part of the conversation at dinner" and "A boy is definitely a part of the conversation at dinner."

These descriptions of behavior in sentence form were presented to a sample of 40 pairs of parents who were asked to complete a sorting task. Each parent was instructed to put the sentences, which had been printed on small slips of paper, into piles so that items within the same pile would be similar in terms of how the parent would think, feel, or respond if the behavior were observed in the parent's own child. These very general instructions were used in order to allow the parent maximal freedom in categorizing the behavior descriptions. That is, the parent and not the investigator determined what basis to use in judging the similarity of the behavior descriptions. Parents did the task twice and were encouraged to sort the sentences differently on the second trial.[1] Half the parents sorted the sentences for girls and half for boys. In order to avoid making it obvious that we were interested in sex differences, each pair of parents sorted the sentences for the same sex of child. Thus, the Joneses sorted for a girl and the Smiths for a boy.

This sorting task provided a measure of psychological distance or dissimilarity between pairs of behavior descriptions. The disassociation measure (δ) of Rosenberg, Nelson, and Vivekananthan (1968) was used as an index of the psychological distance between pairs of sentences. This measure involves computing a "disagreement score" for each pair of sentences, representing the number of sorters who put the two sentences into different piles. The disagreement scores are converted into disassociation scores by means of a formula that takes into account both direct and indirect cooccurrence of items. The disassociation measure is based on the assumption that objects (in this case, behavior descriptions) that often occur together (direct co-occurrence) or with some third object (indirect co-occurrence) are psychologically similar or close, while objects that are

[1] Two sortings were obtained in order to get the most complete picture of the parents' cognitive structuring of the behavior descriptions. Rosenberg and Kim (1975) demonstrated that the single-sort method can bias structural representations if respondents ignore an obvious dimension. They found that many college students did not use sex when given just one chance to sort English kinship terms; this distorted the resulting scaling and clustering solutions in comparison with representations based on multiple sortings. Another possible problem is that a strong dimension might so dominate the attention of sorters that it obscures other cognitive distinctions. Both of these problems are minimized if respondents are given more than one opportunity to sort the objects (behavior descriptions in the present case) under study.

rarely sorted into the same pile are psychologically dissimilar or distant. The data at this stage consisted of a half matrix of measures of psychological relatedness between each pair of behavior descriptions. These measures of disassociation were analyzed separately according to the four conditions of sorting: mothers sorting for daughters (MoDa); fathers sorting for daughters (FaDa); mothers sorting for sons (MoSo) and fathers sorting for sons (FaSo). Within each condition, the results of the two sortings were analyzed separately.

In order to explore the nature of the cognitive structuring employed by parents, the data were subjected to multidimensional scaling and hierarchical clustering. Both techniques are designed to uncover underlying structure in similarities data. These methods are based on somewhat different assumptions and provide different forms of structural representation (cf. Rosenberg & Sedlak, 1972). The multidimensional scaling algorithm (Kruskal, 1967) produces a spatial representation of the data in one or more dimensions whereby the distance between the points is monotonically related to the psychological relatedness of the sentences as measured by the degree of disassociation. The program also computes a badness-of-fit measure, called *stress*, for each n-dimensional solution. Stress is measured in percentage terms, with 100% indicating no relationship between the input disassociation scores and the distances between objects in the configuration and 0% indicating a perfect monotonic relationship between input scores and scaled distances. In the hierarchical clustering analysis (Johnson, 1967, diameter method), input distances between items are used as a basis for partitioning the stimuli into a set of nonoverlapping clusters. The clustering is hierarchical in that a sequence is produced in which each succeeding cluster represents a merging of clusters from the preceding level. Each successive level of clustering is produced when an increasingly larger distance is taken as the criterion for including stimuli in the same cluster. The clustering process begins with each item in its own cluster ($\delta = 0$) and concludes when all items have been merged into a single cluster.

Inspection of the results of the multidimensional scaling and hierarchical clustering suggested that parents might have been making use of the following seven categorizations in their response to the sorting task:

1. Behavior that Should be Encouraged versus Behavior that Should be Changed
2. Good versus Bad Social behavior
3. Mature versus Immature behavior
4. Hostile/Aggressive versus Not Hostile/Aggressive behavior
5. Normal versus Problem behavior
6. Typical versus Not typical behavior

7. Behavior that Shows versus Behavior that does not Show Sexual
   Interest

In order to provide some test of these hypothesized cognitive structures, an independent sample of couples was asked to rate (using a seven-
point scale) each of the 99 behavior descriptions on three of the seven scales
(randomly grouped and ordered). Each behavior description (as applied to
a son or daughter) was rated on each property. The mean rating of each
behavior description for each of the four conditions of rating (i.e., MoDa,
FaDa, MoSo, FaSo) on each property was then calculated. The properties
were then fitted to the multidimensional scaling configurations by means
of linear multiple regression (see Rosenberg & Sedlak, 1972, for details). In
an analogous manner, each of the seven psychological properties was fitted
to the eight tree diagrams produced by the hierarchical clustering program
(see Rosenberg & Jones, 1972, for details).

The results of this first study have been detailed elsewhere (Bacon &
Ashmore, 1982) but can be summarized in part here. Considerable evidence
was found to support the basic hypothesis that parental categorization of
verbal descriptions of child behavior (of 6- to 11-year-old children) varies
with the sex of the perceiving parent and the sex of the child to whom the
behavior is attributed. Stated more concretely, mothers often categorized
the same behavior description differently than fathers did, and mothers and
fathers often categorized the same behavior description differently when it
was attributed to a daughter than when attributed to a son.

In addition to these sex differences in cognitive structuring, there was
one outstanding area of agreement: the existence of a strong evaluative
dimension. This appeared in both methods of analysis and for all eight
sortings (two sortings for two sexes of parent for two sexes of child). As can
be seen in Table 1, the stress values ranged from 7.8% to 11.4% for the
parents' one-dimensional configurations. These values are quite low,
indicating that the parents' categorizations of the 99 behavior descriptions can be adequately represented by a single dimension. That there is a
small but appreciable reduction in stress in the two-dimensional configurations but little improvement in the quality of fit in higher dimensions suggests that the sorting data might best be accounted for by one
powerful dimension and the hint of a second. (Hereafter the discussion of
the multidimensional scaling results will refer to the two-dimensional
configurations.) The identification of the dominant dimension as evaluative was indicated by the content of the verbal descriptions and their
location along this dimension as well as by the angles between and the
multiple R's for the properties. For example, items such as "hits parents"
and "torments a pet" tended to occur at one end of this dimension in
opposition to items such as "has good manners in public" and "likes to

Table 1. Stress Values (in Percentages) for the Five-through One-Dimensional Configurations for Study 1 (Parents) and Study 2 (Older Siblings)[a]

Dimensionality of configuration	Study 1 (Parents)										Study 2 (Older Siblings)									
	Mother-daughter (MoDa)		Father-daughter (FaDa)		Mother-son (MoSo)		Father-son (FaSo)		Average		Female-sister (FeGi)		Male-sister (MaGi)		Female-brother (FeBo)		Male-brother (MaBo)		Average	
	1st Sort	2nd Sort	1st Sort	2nd Sort	1st Sort	2nd Sort	1st Sort	2nd Sort	1st Sort	2nd Sort	1st Sort	2nd Sort	1st Sort	2nd Sort	1st Sort	2nd Sort	1st Sort	2nd Sort	1st Sort	2nd Sort
Five	3.8	3.4	3.0	2.7	3.2	2.2	4.1	2.5	3.5 (4.0)[b]	2.7 (3.0)	2.9	4.9	4.6	9.4	4.5	4.9	4.9	5.4	4.2	6.2
Four	4.2	4.4	3.6	3.4	4.2	2.7	4.6	3.0	4.2 (5.1)	3.4 (4.0)	3.7	6.6	5.5	10.8	6.0	6.7	6.5	6.7	5.4	7.7
Three	5.4	5.5	4.8	4.8	5.3	3.4	5.8	3.9	5.3 (6.6)	4.4 (5.5)	7.0	9.5	6.6	13.9	7.9	11.0	8.2	8.7	7.4	10.8
Two	6.8	7.6	6.1	5.9	6.5	4.6	8.7	4.9	7.0 (8.9)	5.8 (7.8)	8.8	14.1	10.9	18.8	12.8	17.8	11.9	13.6	11.1	16.1
One	10.2	10.4	10.4	10.6	11.1	7.8	11.4	8.0	10.8(14.4)	9.2(12.2)	16.0	25.4	20.3	27.5	19.3	28.2	17.5	21.8	18.3	25.7

[a] Stress is measured in percentage terms, with 100% indicating no relationship between the input disassociation scores and the distances between objects in the configuration and 0% indicating a perfect monotonic relationship between input scores and scaled distances.
[b] Values in parentheses are averages based on eight 10-subject subsamples, two for each of the four basic conditions (see footnote on page 311).

help around the house" at the other end. Between these extremes were such items as "messes up the house while playing" and "puts away toys after playing with them," which are apparently judged as less extreme on a continuum of disapproved versus approved behavior.

Inspection of the angles between the fitted axes (in the two-dimensional configurations) revealed that three of the properties were so closely aligned as to be virtually indistinguishable. These were Encourage-Change, Good-Bad Social Behavior, and Mature-Immature. The angles between these axes fall between 0° and 34° in all eight conditions, with an average angle of 12.1°. Further, these properties have the highest multiple R's, indicating that they fit the configurations best. These three properties were, therefore, identified as major components of the evaluative dimension (for this sample of parents and this sample of behavior descriptions).

In interpreting the evaluative dimension, we have considered the degree of emphasis on such a dimension as a variable in itself. We expect that cross-cultural variations in evaluative emphasis occurs. Such cultural variations might be a function of differences in belief systems and role expectations. Parents, for instance, may vary in the degree to which they believe that the behavior of children is malleable. Those who believe that child behavior can be "shaped" may be more inclined to view social behavior in an evaluative frame of reference than those who believe that the behavior of children is predetermined at birth by genetic or supernatural influences. Similarly, parents may differ in their perception of their role as parents. Thus, they may vary considerably, both cross-culturally and within a given cultural group, in the degree to which they feel responsible for the socialization of their children. We would assume that parents who rank high on this felt responsibility would be more inclined to view child behavior in an evaluative frame of reference than those who rank low. If this is true, then it might be expected to follow that parents would be more evaluative of the behavior of their own children than they would be of the neighbors' children. It might also be expected that parents in nuclear families, where responsibility is concentrated in the biological parents, might tend to see the behavior of their children in a more evaluative light than parents in an extended family, where the responsibility is diffused among many adults. And we would predict that mothers, who have primary responsibility for child rearing, would be more motivated than fathers to evaluate their children's behavior. Our first study produced evidence that seemed to support the latter hypothesis. For example, when asked to rate the behavior descriptions on a continuum of Good-Bad Social Behavior, mothers rated more items at the extremes of the scale than fathers did.

The argument that degree of felt responsibility is positively associated with evaluative emphasis also suggests that parents would be more evaluative than older siblings in viewing the behavior of children. This reasoning was assessed in our second study. Here we tested the following hypothesis: Older siblings of 6- to 11-year-old girls and boys are less inclined to organize the behavior descriptions within an evaluative frame of reference than are mothers and fathers of children of this age.

Study 2

In Study 2, college students with a younger sibling in the 6- to 11-year age range were asked to sort the same behavior descriptions that the sample of parents had sorted; 20 male and 20 female students participated in this task. Half the male and half the female older siblings sorted the sentences for sisters and half for brothers, resulting again in four conditions of sorting: females sorting for sisters (FeGi) and brothers (FeBo) and males sorting for each sex of sibling (MaGi and MaBo). The results of the sorting task were converted to measures of disassociation as described for the first study, and these, in turn, were subjected to multidimensional scaling and hierarchical clustering. Only the results of the former will be presented in this chapter.

The multidimensional scaling analysis yields evidence that supports our hypothesis. As already indicated, the "stress," or badness-of-fit, figures showed that the parents' data could be adequately represented by a single dimension and possibly best represented by one strong dimension plus a tentative second. This powerful dimension for the parents' data was identified as evaluative in nature. In contrast with the parents' tendency toward unidimensional cognitive structuring, the stress figures for the older siblings' data reveal a quite different pattern (see Table 1). These data cannot possibly be accounted for by a single dimension. The stress values in one dimension range from 16.0% to 20.3% for the first sortings and from 21.8% to 28.2% for the second sortings. There is in all conditions a significant improvement in the quality of fit in two dimensions and some further improvement in the three- and four-dimensional representations. Thus, the stress figures indicate that there are definitely two and possibly three dimensions involved, with the hint of a fourth. This is particularly true for the second sortings. In fact, the difference between the parents and older siblings is clearest when both the first and second sortings are considered for each sample. On the first sorting, the parents are more unidimensional than the older siblings (i.e., the one-dimension stress values for parents are low in an absolute sense and are lower than those for older siblings). On the second sorting, parents become more unidimensional (i.e., the stress values decrease), but the older siblings become markedly less unidimensional (i.e., the stress values increase to such an extent that a one-dimensional configuration definitely cannot account for the sorting-task data).

Comparison of the stress values for the scaling solutions in the two studies suggests, then, that our sample of older siblings did not emphasize an evaluative dimension in their response to the sorting task as strongly as the parents did.[2] This does not mean that the "good versus bad" distinction was unimportant to older siblings. Rather, it was simply a less indispensable part of their approach to the sorting task. The evaluative dimension quite adequately, though not completely, accounted for the parents' sorting data on both the first and second sortings (hence, the relatively low stress values in one dimension), but this was not the case for older siblings. They showed somewhat higher stress values than parents on the first sortings, and they were considerably less unidimensional in their second sortings of the behavior descriptions (hence, the relatively high stress for the one-dimensional solutions based on the second sortings). In sum, parents appeared to emphasize an evaluative continuum on both sortings; older siblings, when given a second opportunity to categorize the behavior descriptions, seemed to employ an alternative strategy that was not so strongly dominated by the "good versus bad" distinction.

Although the pattern of stress values is complex, it does provide evidence that supports our hypothesis. We have suggested that the crucial factor operating in the difference in evaluative emphasis between parents and older siblings is one of felt responsibility. On the other hand, it is possible that the mediating factor operating is merely one of age. Perhaps the tendency for white middle-class subjects to categorize verbal descrip-

---

[2] Since the scaling solutions in Study 1 are based on 20 sorters and those in Study 2 on 10, it is possible that the lower stress values for parents are due to the larger number of sorters. In order to test this possibility, the 20 subjects in each of the parents' conditions were randomly partitioned into two groups of 10. For each data set, the disassociation measure was calculated and used as input to the multidimensional scaling computer program. For each condition the stress values for the 10-subject subsamples were somewhat higher than the values based on 20 subjects. This can be seen in the average stress values reported in Table 1. When the parent and older-sibling samples are "equated" in terms of number of subjects per condition, the differences in stress values for the first sortings are reduced. The quality of fit remains better for parents, but the difference between the two samples is not as great as when the parents' scaling is based on 20 subjects. For the second sortings, however, the gap between parents and older siblings remains quite large even when the parents' solutions are based on 10 subjects. The stress figures for older siblings are approximately twice the size of those for parents. And the average quality of fit for the parents' 10-subject subsamples in one dimension (i.e., 12.2%) is actually better than the average goodness of fit for older siblings in two dimensions (i.e., 16.1%).

tions of behavior in an evaluative way increases with age. The samples of
parents and older siblings also differ in other ways. For example, relatively
few (10%) of the latter group had younger siblings of both sexes, while all
the parents had both a son and a daughter in the age range 6 to 11. Our
findings indicate that parents and siblings differ in degree of evaluative
emphasis. We believe that degree of felt responsibility is the most plausible
explanation.

The Categorization of Verbal Descriptions of Child
Behavior by Older Siblings and by Parents

In this section we will consider some of the cognitive structures used by
siblings in categorizing the verbal descriptions of child behavior and
compare them with the parents' data. We inspected the multidimensional
scaling and hierarchical clustering data for the siblings and hypothesized
that these subjects might be making use of the following categorizations in
their cognitive organization of the behavior descriptions:

1. Behavior the Should be Encouraged versus Behavior that Should be
   Changed
2. Good versus Bad Social Behavior
3. Good Friend versus Not Good Friend
4. Not Hostile/Aggressive versus Hostile/Aggressive Behavior
5. Not Sissy versus Sissy
6. Not Loner versus Loner

To facilitate comparison with the parents' data, the properties
Normal–Problem and Shows Sexual Interest–Does Not Show Sexual
Interest were also included. Another sample of older siblings was asked to
rate the behavior descriptions on the eight properties. (As a further aid to
comparison of the two studies, an independent sample of mothers and
fathers rated the 99 items on the scale Not Sissy–Sissy.) The mean ratings on
these properties were then fitted to the multidimensional scaling solutions
as in our first study. In general, the hypothesized properties fit the
configurations very well (see Table 2). The multiple R's were all highly
significant ($p < .001$) except for the Not Loner–Loner and Shows Sexual
Interest properties.[3] As can be seen in Table 2, the multiple R's for the

---

[3] The low multiple R's in both Study 1 and Study 2 indicate that the Shows Sexual Interest
property is not a bipolar cognitive continuum for either parents or older siblings in
responding to behavior descriptions attributed to early-school-age boys and girls. Thus,
this property will not be discussed below.

Table 2. Multiple R's between Eight Properties and the One- through Three-Dimensional Configurations for the Eight Conditions of Sorting in Study 1 (Parents) and in Study 2 (Older Siblings)[a]

Study 1 (Parents)

Property	Mother-daughter First			Mother-daughter Second			Father-daughter First			Father-daughter Second			Mother-son First			Mother-son Second			Father-son First			Father-son Second		
	1d	2d	3d	1d	2d	3d	1d	2d	3d	1d	2d	3d	1d	2d	3d	1d	2d	3d	1d	2d	3d	1d	2d	3d
Encourage	.93	.93	.93	.93	.93	.93	.94	.94	.94	.92	.93	.93	.93	.94	.94	.96	.96	.96	.94	.94	.94	.96	.97	.97
Good social behavior	.95	.95	.95	.94	.94	.94	.96	.96	.96	.95	.95	.96	.92	.93	.93	.94	.94	.95	.95	.95	.95	.95	.95	.95
Mature	.90	.90	.90	.91	.91	.91	.91	.91	.92	.90	.90	.91	.89	.91	.91	.91	.90	.91	.91	.91	.92	.90	.90	.90
Not hostile/aggressive	.90	.91	.91	.87	.91	.92	.85	.88	.89	.86	.91	.91	.84	.91	.91	.86	.89	.92	.84	.89	.89	.81	.91	.94
Normal	.82	.83	.85	.83	.84	.88	.84	.85	.86	.83	.83	.86	.84	.86	.88	.79	.79	.89	.73	.76	.84	.71	.72	.76
Typical	.65	.67	.76	.65	.66	.71	.61	.62	.64	.60	.62	.64	.60	.71	.74	.51	.51	.72	.44	.52	.74	.42	.45	.57
Not sissy	.78	.78	.79	.78	.78	.79	.85	.85	.85	.84	.85	.85	.81	.81	.82	.81	.81	.85	.71	.71	.74	.73	.74	.75
Shows sexual interest	.44	.48	.49	.39	.44	.45	.49	.52	.56	.48	.55	.57	.56	.56	.56	.51	.51	.58	.39	.44	.49	.36	.41	.45

Study 2 (Older Siblings)

Property	Female-girl First			Female-girl Second			Male-girl First			Male-girl Second			Female-boy First			Female-boy Second			Male-boy First			Male-boy Second		
	1d	2d	3d	1d	2d	3d	1d	2d	3d	1d	2d	3d	1d	2d	3d	1d	2d	3d	1d	2d	3d	1d	2d	3d
Encourage	.90	.92	.93	.79	.87	.87	.87	.88	.89	.83	.85	.86	.90	.91	.92	.85	.87	.90	.87	.89	.89	.85	.87	.87
Good social behavior	.85	.89	.91	.74	.83	.84	.88	.88	.89	.86	.85	.86	.88	.87	.89	.85	.88	.88	.86	.88	.87	.84	.86	.86
Good friend	.70	.76	.77	.66	.76	.77	.84	.86	.86	.85	.85	.85	.84	.85	.86	.74	.81	.86	.92	.93	.93	.87	.87	.87
Not hostile/aggressive	.77	.81	.81	.74	.74	.74	.82	.82	.83	.81	.82	.83	.65	.68	.68	.66	.65	.67	.88	.88	.91	.82	.84	.84
Normal	.77	.78	.81	.69	.72	.74	.75	.74	.75	.73	.73	.74	.69	.68	.78	.69	.71	.77	.42	.61	.57	.40	.57	.63
Not sissy	.65	.69	.71	.60	.65	.66	.83	.83	.85	.80	.82	.83	.76	.76	.81	.71	.77	.82	.48	.60	.61	.48	.63	.65
Not loner	.45	.64	.67	.29	.67	.68	.58	.59	.60	.63	.64	.67	.37	.38	.43	.30	.37	.55	.30	.49	.52	.28	.50	.54
Shows sexual interest	.34	.35	.50	.23	.25	.30	.02	.12	.23	.02	.08	.11	.25	.41	.38	.22	.24	.24	.27	.43	.38	.21	.27	.31

[a] All multiple R's except those in italics are significant at $p < .001$.

sibling sample are consistently smaller in magnitude than those for the parent sample. In this connection it is important to note that the number of subjects who rated the items on the various properties was different for the two samples. In the parent sample, 7 to 10 mothers and fathers rated the behavior descriptions for each of the properties; for the sibling sample, the number of raters was 5. This difference could well account for the difference in the size of the R's since a small number of raters would be expected to produce less reliable mean ratings.

In considering each of the hypothesized cognitive structures or schemata, four types of data will be presented: multiple R's, angles, extreme direct ratings, and extreme projections. The first two types of evidence pertain to each spatial configuration as a whole. The "multiple R provides a quantitative estimate of the degree to which a property actually corresponds to a dimension in the trait [behavior description] space" (Rosenberg & Sedlak, 1972, p. 246). The angles between vectors indicate the relation between properties when fitted to a particular multidimensional scaling configuration. (In the present case, the two-dimensional configurations.) Angles near zero or 180° mean that the two properties are highly related, while angles near 90° indicate that the cognitive distinctions represented by the properties are orthogonal or unrelated.

Extreme direct ratings and extreme projections will also be reported. An item was considered to be extreme on the direct rating task if it received a mean of less than 2.0 or more than 6.0 on the 1-to-7-point rating scale. Items with projections of ±1.00 onto the fitted axes in the two-dimensional configuration were taken to be extreme. Extreme items were looked at in two ways. First, we simply counted the number of behavior descriptions with extreme ratings and extreme projections. The number for each condition of rating or sorting is presented in Tables 4 and 5. These "counts" provide an index of the utility of each property. It is assumed that a relatively large number of extreme items indicates that the property is useful in cognitively organizing the behavior descriptions. Second, we inspected the specific items with extreme ratings or projections for each property. This provides insight into how parents and older siblings implicitly define the particular property labels that we provided. For example, the meaning of Sissy to parents and older siblings is suggested by the content of the behavior descriptions with extreme ratings (6 or more) and extreme projections (+1.00 or more) for the Not Sissy–Sissy property. The extreme mean ratings and extreme projections, of course, are not independent types of evidence, since the property fitting is based on the ratings. They are, however, complementary rather than redundant. The direct rating task requires the respondent to make a conscious judgment about each of the behavior descriptions. The behavior descriptions with extreme mean ratings, then, are those that a sample of socializers consciously agree are clearly at one end or the other of the rating scale. The extreme projections, while depending on the ratings, are also determined by the sorting-task data. In the sorting task, perceivers used their own definitions of similarity between items rather than making conscious decisions about the behavior descriptions in terms of provided scales.

Except for the multiple R's, it is not possible to assign probability values or confidence limits to the findings we report. It is, thus, important to be cautious in interpreting and generalizing our results. We regard this research as primarily an attempt to explore the cognitive structuring of child behavior by adults and to generate rather than test hypotheses.

The Evaluative Dimension

The multiple R's for the older sibling sample were generally highest for the three properties Encourage-Change, Good-Bad Social Behavior, and Good Friend versus Not Good Friend. For the first two properties they ranged from .83 to .92. The multiple R's for Good Friend-Not Good Friend were also very high (.81 to .93) except for the Female–Girl condition, where they were .76 for both the first and second sortings. (These values are for the two-dimensional solutions. Since two dimensions provide an adequate and parsimonious representation of the older siblings' data, and in order to facilitate comparison with the parents' data, only the two-dimensional configurations will be discussed.) Inspection of the angles between the vectors for the three properties also reveals a strong convergence (1° to 34° separation, average angle = 9.2°; see Table 3), indicating that these properties probably constitute three components of a strong single dimension. Examination of the positioning of items along this dimension again, as with parents, identifies it as an evaluative continuum. For example, in Figure 1, which presents the two dimensional solution for the MaBo2 condition, Good Friend-Not Good Friend and Encourage-Change run from the upper right to the lower left corner of the configuration. (The vector for Good-Bad Social Behavior is not plotted, since it is separated from that for Encourage-Change by only 1°.) It can be seen that items such as "likes to help" appear at one end of the dimension (at the top of the figure) in opposition to such items as "picks fights" and "spits at other kids" at the other end (at the bottom of the figure); items representing moderately good (e.g., "likes to build things") and moderately bad (e.g., "puts off doing things") behavior fall nearer to the center of the configuration.

Further evidence regarding the evaluative dimension may be found in

Table 3. Angles (in Degrees) between Fitted Axes for Seven Properties in the Two-Dimensional Configurations for the Eight Conditions of Sorting in Study 2 (Older Siblings)[a]

Female-girl / Male-girl

Property	E	GSB	GF	NH/A	N	NS	NL	Property	E	GSB	GF	NH/A	N	NS	NL
Encourage		8	15	64	4	8	39	Encourage		9	5	23	26	37	13
Good social behavior	3		7	71	11	0	31	Good social behavior	4		14	14	17	28	23
Good friend	8	5		79	18	7	24	Good friend	1	5		28	31	42	9
Not hostile/aggressive	43	46	52		60	71	102	Not hostile/aggressive	23	19	24		3	14	37
Normal	12	15	21	31		11	42	Normal	23	19	24	0		11	40
Not sissy	3	6	11	40	9		31	Not sissy	34	30	35	11	11		50
Not loner	35	32	27	78	47	38		Not loner	19	22	17	42	42	53	

Female-boy / Male-boy

Property	E	GSB	GF	NH/A	N	NS	NL	Property	E	GSB	GF	NH/A	N	NS	NL
Encourage		22	34	58	15	34	9	Encourage		1	3	11	42	36	46
Good social behavior	10		12	36	6	13	30	Good social behavior	16		4	12	41	35	45
Good friend	15	5		24	18	1	42	Good friend	16	14		8	45	39	50
Not hostile/aggressive	22	12	7		42	23	67	Not hostile/aggressive	45	44	30		53	47	57
Normal	8	2	7	14		19	24	Normal	43	45	59	88		6	5
Not sissy	22	12	6	1	14		43	Not sissy	38	40	54	83	5		10
Not loner	10	21	26	33	19	32		Not loner	50	52	66	95	7	12	

[a] The values above the diagonal are for the first sorting; those below the diagonal are for the second sorting.

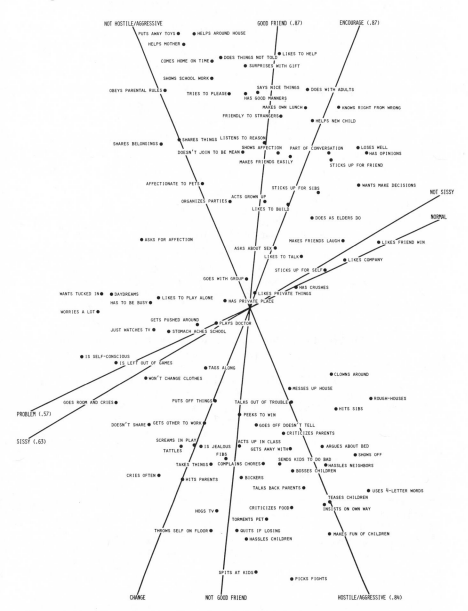

Figure 1. Two-dimensional configuration of the 99 behavior descriptions for the MaBo2 condition, showing best-fitting axes of the Not Hostile/Aggressive–Hostile/Aggressive, Not Good Friend-Good Friend, Encourage-Change, Normal-problem, and Not Sissy-Sissy properties. (Each number in parentheses is the multiple correlation between projections on the axis and the property values.)

the analysis of the direct ratings. In our first study, there was a definite tendency for mothers to assign extreme ratings (at both the positive and negative ends of the properties) to more behavior descriptions than fathers did. Also, on the evaluative properties, daughters were, on the whole, given more extreme ratings than sons by both fathers and mothers. As noted above, the sex-of-parent effect was interpreted as indicating that mothers are more inclined to view child behavior as clearly good or bad than fathers. This, in turn, was explained as due to mothers' greater felt responsibility for the behavior of their children. Regarding the second finding, it was speculated that, in terms of social behavior, girls may be judged more strictly than boys.

Neither the sex-of-perceiver nor the sex-of-target effect obtained in Study 1 is replicated in the older-sibling sample (see Table 4). The sex-of-perceiver effect is reversed, though the differences are not large, for the Good-Bad Social Behavior and Good Friend-Not Good Friend properties. That is, older brothers tended to rate more items at the extremes of these properties than did older sisters. The sex-of-target effect is consistently reversed. Although some of the differences are small, the male child (i.e.,

Table 4. Number of Behavior Descriptions with Extreme Mean Ratings on Nine Properties[a]

Property	Study 1 (parents)				Study 2 (older siblings)			
	MoDa	FaDa	MoSo	FaSo	FeGi	MaGi	FeBo	MaBo
Encourage	27	22	16	7	14	13	27	20
Change	23	7	11	16	18	18	26	25
Good social behavior	27	21	16	4	21	23	24	27
Bad social behavior	13	6	3	3	2	8	5	12
Mature[b]	9	10	12	6				
Immature[b]	9	5	10	3				
Good friend[c]					5	12	8	22
Not good friend[c]					10	12	12	15
Not hostile/aggressive	49	29	33	53	23	14	17	35
Hostile/aggressive	2	0	5	5	4	4	0	8
Normal	17	12	31	7	10	23	36	7
Problem	1	1	3	0	0	0	2	0
Not sissy	59	10	44	55	0	45	31	9
Sissy	0	0	0	0	0	3	0	0
Not loner[c]					11	4	9	5
Loner[c]					1	1	2	0

[a] Extreme mean ratings are 1.9 or less and 6.1 or more. The rating scales ran from 1 to 7.
[b] Mature-immature was used only in Study 1.
[c] Good friend–not good friend and not loner–loner were used only in Study 2.

younger brother) drew more extreme ratings than the female child (i.e., younger sister) in all possible comparisons.

That the sex-of-perceiver effect noted in Study 1 is not replicated in Study 2 suggests that the crucial factor is not sex *per se*. That is, it is not simply that females use the extremes of the evaluative dimensions more than do males. Although various interpretations are possible, we believe that the mediating factor is role relationship. The mother role carries with it more felt responsibility than the father role, while the older-sister and older-brother roles do not differ in this respect. This explanation, of course, is intended for this particular sample of parents and older siblings only. In fact, we would expect that in many societies older brothers and sisters would differ greatly in responsibility for the care of younger siblings, with females generally having greater responsibility.

The opposing sex-of-child effects obtained for the two samples are interpreted as follows. Another way of stating the speculation that parents judge girls' social behavior more strictly than boys' is that parents may allow boys a wider range of acceptable behavior, that is neither extremely good or bad but simply acceptable. The parents' relative lack of setting limits for young boys may contribute to making boys' behavior more diverse and perhaps more unpredictable. Thus, younger brothers might be harder for older siblings to live with than younger sisters. As a consequence, behavior descriptions attributed to boys are more often judged by siblings as extremely good or extremely bad. That this pattern is strongest for the Encourage-Change property suggests that siblings feel little boys to be more in need of some kind of "guidance" (encouraging and changing) than girls are.

The number of items at the extremes of the fitted axes for the Encourage-Change and Good–Bad social Behavior properties is presented in the top four rows of Table 5. Here the number of items projecting at the extremes of both of these dimensions is consistently larger for the parents than for the siblings. This seems to provide further evidence that parents are more inclined to view child behavior in an evaluative frame of reference than are siblings. There were no sex-of-perceiver or sex-of-perceived effects for either sample in terms of the number of items with extreme projections onto the fitted axes for the evaluative properties.

Evidence regarding the content of the "good-bad" distinction is found in both the direct ratings for the evaluative properties and in the projections onto the fitted axes for these properties. While there are differences between the extreme mean ratings and extreme projections and across the various conditions in the two studies, there is remarkable convergence in the present data regarding the implicit definition of "good" and "bad" child behavior. At the positive end, the following items have

Table 5. Number of Behavior Descriptions with Extreme Projections on the Fitted Axes for Eight Properties[a]

Property	Study 1 (parents)								Study 2 (older siblings)							
	MoDa		FaDa		MoSo		FaSo		FeGi		MaGi		FeBo		MaBo	
	1st	2nd	1st	2nd	1st	2nd	1st	2nd	1st	2nd	1st	2nd	1st	2nd	1st	2nd
Encourage	23	27	21	23	16	23	20	23	13	12	17	18	19	12	13	19
Change	17	20	18	19	19	24	18	25	13	5	16	15	10	17	12	10
Good social behavior	24	24	21	22	13	17	26	19	13	12	16	18	19	11	12	20
Bad social behavior	17	21	23	21	18	18	22	24	6	4	18	15	14	17	12	11
Mature[b]	23	25	21	23	6	26	24	26								
Immature[b]	17	21	20	19	16	24	21	26								
Good friend[c]									8	8	18	18	15	10	14	17
Not good friend[c]									0	2	13	15	16	17	15	14
Not hostile/aggressive	14	0	0	0	0	0	0	0	4	14	15	14	8	6	15	15
Hostile/aggressive	19	7	14	12	1	5	8	0	17	19	20	15	14	17	18	15
Normal	22	18	20	23	4	27	0	0	17	15	15	14	20	10	0	1
Problem	16	18	17	20	13	24	10	18	15	16	20	15	12	17	7	1
Not sissy	20	17	21	23	20	21	24	21	13	13	15	12	15	7	0	1
Sissy	20	18	23	19	21	25	21	21	6	7	19	15	16	17	8	3
Not loner[c]									0	3	12	16	17	12	0	1
Loner[c]									0	1	7	7	10	13	1	1

[a] Extreme projections are ± 1.00 on fitted axis.
[b] Mature–immature was used only in Study 1.
[c] Good friend–not good friend and not loner–loner were used only in Study 2.

extreme mean ratings and extreme projections for Encourage-Change and Good-Bad Social Behavior[4] (the two evaluative properties used in both Study 1 and Study 2): "says nice things to people," "shares things," "surprises parent with gift," "offers to help mother," "likes to help." The behavior descriptions that are consistently extreme at the "bad" end of the evaluative dimension describe "hostile/aggressive" actions (e.g., "spits at other kids"). This categorization will be discussed in the next section.

Hostile/Aggressive Behavior

The multidimensional scaling results indicate that the distinction we have labeled "not hostile/aggressive versus hostile/aggressive" played a significant role in the responses of the older siblings to the sorting task. The fit of the Hostile/Aggressive property to the configurations was quite good except for the two Female-Boy conditions (see Table 2). Thus, the older siblings—except possibly for females responding to behavioral descriptions attributed to a younger brother—clearly organized the behavioral descriptions along a continuum from "not hostile/aggressive" to "hostile/aggressive." This is consistent with the results from our initial study except that there was little variation across conditions in the quality of fit for parents (i.e., the multiple R's were uniformly high, ranging only from .88 to .91).

Although there are many possible reasons for the somewhat lower fit of the Hostile/Aggressive property in the Female-Boy conditions, the obtained pattern is consistent with Maccoby and Jacklin's (1974, p. 238) conclusion that there is a "tacit assumption that girls will not be aggressed against." Females may experience less direct hostility or open aggression from their brothers (especially younger brothers) than they do from their sisters or than do boys from siblings of either sex. This interpretation centers on the negative or "hostile/aggressive" end of the dimension. While the relatively low fit of the Hostile/Aggressive property in the FeBo condition could be due to elements at any point along the continuum, our focus on such behaviors seems warranted in light of the direct ratings. In the FeBo condition, not one item received a mean rating above 6.0 and only five items received a mean rating above 5.0, while the numbers were considerably higher in the other three conditions (see Table 4). Thus, whatever the explanation, the FeBo condition is distinctive from the others in terms of not having verbal descriptions of child behavior categorized as extremely "hostile/aggressive."

---

[4] Similar results are found for Mature-Immature and Good Friend-Not Good Friend.

Insight into the meaning of the categorization of child behavior as "not hostile/aggressive versus hostile/aggressive" is provided by inspection of the relation in the two-dimensional configurations of the Hostile/Aggressive vector to those for the three evaluative properties. Here the pattern for older siblings is quite different from that for parents. In our initial investigation we found that the fitted axes for the Hostile/Aggressive property and those for the three evaluative properties were separated by smaller angles for mothers (average angle was 40°) than for fathers (average angle was 61°). No such sex-of-perceiver effect was obtained for older siblings. The average angles between Hostile/Aggressive and the three evaluative properties in the second study were: FeGi, 71°, 47°; MaGi, 22°, 22°; FeBo, 39°, 14°; MaBo, 10°, 40°. Two related aspects of this pattern stand out. First, evaluation and Hostile/Aggressive are most nearly orthogonal in the Female–Girl condition. Second, there is marked disagreement between female and male perceivers about the evaluation of hostile/aggressive behavior in a younger sister. While females apparently regard "not hostile/aggressive–hostile/aggressive" and "good–bad" as somewhat unrelated distinctions for girls, older brothers see them as closely related.

The relatively small angles between Hostile/Aggressive and the evaluative properties in the MaGi conditions may reflect sex stereotypes and their attendant expectations. Older brothers probably do not expect girls (in this case, younger sisters) to behave aggressively or demonstrate hostility; if they do, such behavior is clearly disapproved. Further, and perhaps more significantly, older male siblings may categorize as "hostile/aggressive" certain actions when done by a girl but not when done by a boy. The behavior descriptions with extreme projections onto the "hostile/aggressive" end of the Hostile/Aggressive vector provide evidence of such a tendency. There are five items that have extreme projections in either MaGi1 or MaGi2 but not in either of the MaBo conditions: "bickers," "roughhouses," "argues with parents about going to bed," "sometimes acts up in class," and "hits brothers and sisters." These behavior descriptions involve assertiveness and seem to be part of the traditional male sex role (as adapted to an early school age boy). That such behavior is differentially perceived suggests that when girls intrude into the masculine domain, their actions are viewed by their older brothers as "hostile/aggressive." This may inhibit the development of assertiveness in females.

The relatively large angles between Hostile/Aggressive and the evaluative properties in the FeGi conditions suggest that older females may be consciously or nonconsciously rejecting cultural sex stereotypes that proscribe female aggressiveness. Or they may identify as "hostile/aggressive" some behavior descriptions that are not clearly "bad." Again, the extreme projections indicate that this is the case. The following three items are extremely "hostile/aggressive" in one of the two sortings for females responding to a girl but not in any of the other three basic conditions: "does not like to share belongings," "likes to see how much she can get away with," and "screams in play." They appear to represent indirect forms of "aggression," and older female siblings may view these as part of the way girls express hostility and aggressiveness.

In order to explore further the content of "hostile/aggressive behavior as perceived by older siblings, the same procedure was followed as for the evaluative properties. We identified the behavior descriptions with extreme projections onto the Hostile/Aggressive vector and also those with high mean ratings on this property. Inspection of the items with extreme projections yielded both similarities and differences when compared with the results of Study 1. In that investigation, the following behavior descriptions were identified as "hostile/aggressive" (on the basis of the hierarchical clustering and direct ratings) regardless of sex of parent or sex of child: "sends younger children to do bad things," "hassles neighbors," "torments a pet," "spits at other kids," "picks fights," "hassles other children," "makes fun of other children," and "hits parents." These same items ("hits parents" is an exception) have consistently extreme projections (i.e., seven of eight conditions) onto the Hostile/Aggressive vector for the sibling sample. They also received consistently extreme mean ratings by older siblings. ("Sends younger children to do bad things," "hassles neighbors," "torments a pet," "spits at other kids," and "hits parents" received means of 5.1 or higher (with 7 = Hostile/Aggressive) in all four conditions; "picks fights" and "hassles other children" in three conditions; and "makes fun of other children" in two.) Thus, there is agreement across variations in sex and role of perceiver and sex of target that these items are "hostile/aggressive." Such agreement would probably extend across other variations in attributes of perceiver and perceived and may be part of an American cultural pattern. Whether this would be true in other cultures is not certain.

In addition to this agreement, there are differences between parents and older siblings in the implicit definition of "hostile/aggressive" child behavior. These differences are easily interpreted in terms of differences in role relationship. Older siblings apparently regard the following behaviors as more definitely "hostile/aggressive" than do parents: "likes to tease small children" (extreme projections in 8 of 8 conditions for older siblings but only 4 of 8 for parents), "hits brothers and sisters" (6 vs. 3), "sometimes takes things that belong to others" (6 vs. 3), "hogs TV" and "bosses other children" (7 vs. 2), and "insists on own way" (5 vs. 0). These behaviors are more likely to involve directly or be associated with negative outcomes for a sibling than for a parent of a child emitting the behavior. Thus, it is not surprising that older siblings are more prone to code such actions as "hostile/aggressive" than are parents.

Normal versus Problem Behavior

As was true for parents, the Normal-Problem property fit the older siblings' multidimensional scaling configurations well, although again the multiple R's were lower than for both the evaluative properties and Not Hostile/Aggressive–Hostile/Aggressive. The multiple R's ranged from .72 to .78 when perceivers responded to a younger sister. The quality of fit was somewhat lower in the FeBo conditions (.68 and .71) and still lower in the MaBo conditions (.61 and .57). Thus, older siblings appear to have used a schema that might be labeled "normal versus problem" in doing the sorting task. This schema may have been less salient when older siblings— especially males—responded in terms of a younger brother than a younger sister (see below, however).

The angles separating the Normal-Problem vector from the fitted axes for the evaluative properties are generally small, with some differences being a function of the perceiving sibling (see Table 3). Male older siblings tended to see Normal–Problem as more unrelated to "good–bad" than did females. And this difference was most pronounced when the target child was a boy. The average angles between the three evaluative properties and Normal-Problem were as follows: FeGi, 11°, 16°; MaGi, 25°, 22°; FeBo, 13°, 6°; MaBo, 43°, 49°. This pattern is not identical with that obtained for parents. In our initial study there was a sex-of-child effect, with Normal-Problem closer to the evaluative dimension for daughters than for sons. There is, however, an interesting convergence: For both parents and older siblings, the male perceiver-male perceived conditions (i.e., FaSo and MaBo) have the largest angles separating Normal-Problem and the evaluative properties. That is, fathers and older brothers agree that variations in judgments about "normal-problem" and "good-bad" are closely related for girls but less so for boys.

The relationship between Normal-Problem and Not Hostile/Aggresive–Hostile/Aggressive for older siblings is in striking contrast to that for parents. In the first study, the angles for these two properties were more nearly orthogonal in the MoSo and FaDa than in the MoDa and FaSo conditions. This cross-sex effect was actually somewhat reversed for older siblings (see Table 3). For older siblings, the cognitive judgments regarding "normality" and "hostility" were more unrelated when a same-sex child was the target. And this was particularly true for male perceivers who apparently regard "normal versus problem" and "not hostile/

aggressive-hostile/aggressive" as equivalent in a younger sister but as relatively unrelated when categorizing the behavior of a younger brother. This latter finding is particularly interesting when considered in conjunction with the angles involving the evaluative properties and the multiple R's. The Normal-Problem property does not fit the MaBo conditions as well as the other conditions, but it appears to be a more unique dimension since it is more nearly orthogonal to both the "good-bad" and "not hostile/aggressive-hostile/aggressive" distinctions.[5]

In Study 2, those behavior descriptions that have extreme projections onto the "problem" end of the Normal-Problem vector are, for the most part, the same items that fell near the "hostile/aggressive" end of the fitted axis for Hostile/Aggressive. This was also true for the parent sample, thus suggesting that both groups of perceivers agree that "hostile/aggressive" child behavior is clearly "problem" behavior. There was an exception to this general pattern in both samples; the exception occurred in the FaSol and MaBo2 conditions. In FaSol, the hierarchical clustering revealed a "problem-but-not-hostile" grouping of descriptions that was considered more of a problem than the cluster of "hostile/aggressive" items. The items in the "problem-but-not-hostile" grouping in FaSol also appear to be important in defining the Normal–Problem fitted axis in MaBo2. As can be seen, this vector runs from right to left across Figure 1. The "problem" end of the axis is anchored by items at the left-center of the figure, such as "goes to room and cries," "cries often," and "is left out of others' games," all of which appeared in the FaSol "problem-but-not-hostile" cluster. The extremely "hostile/aggressive" behavior descriptions, on the other hand, are at the lower right corner of the figure. These behaviors range from clearly a "problem" (e.g., "hits parents") to somewhat "normal" (e.g., "hits brothers and sisters"). In sum, both older brothers and fathers, while agreeing with older sisters and mothers that hostile/aggressive actions are a problem, also have a problem category for boys that they regard as of equal importance. This category comprises problem behavior that is not hostile.

There are some differences between parents and older siblings in the categorization of behavior descriptions as a problem. Parents appear to regard the following behavior descriptions as more clearly a "problem" than do older siblings: "hits parents" (extreme projections in 8 of 8

---

[5] This uniqueness may, in fact, contribute to the lower fit of the Normal–Problem property. Since Evaluation and Hostile/Aggressive are strong dimensions, they account for a considerable amount of variation in the distances between the 99 points. This may leave little variation to be accounted for by fitted axes that tend to be orthogonal to these strong dimensions. (In Figure 1 it can be seen that the variation from the top to the bottom of the figure is much greater than that from the left to right.)

conditions versus 5 of 8 for older siblings), "uses four-letter words" (5 vs. 2), "talks back to parents" (5 vs. 2), "throws self on floor" (5 vs. 0), and "goes off and doesn't tell parent" (5 vs. 1). As with the differences noted in the categorization of child behavior as "hostile/aggressive," these differences make sense in light of the different relationship between perceiver and perceived for the two samples. All of these behaviors would be experienced as a problem by parents with respect to one or more of their role relationships with their children—as direct target of hostility (e.g., "hits parents"), as socializer (e.g., "uses four-letter words"), and as protector (e.g., "goes off and doesn't tell parent").

Sissy Behavior

When the Not Sissy-Sissy property was fitted to the scaling solutions, the multiple R's indicated a good fit for both samples (see Table 2). For parents, they ranged from .71 to .85. For the older sibling sample, the multiple R's were lower and indicated a definite cross-sex effect. The quality of fit was better in the FeBo and MaGi conditions than in the MaBo and FeGi conditions.

The angles separating Not Sissy-Sissy from Normal-Problem are small in all eight conditions of sorting for the older sibling sample (from 5° to 19°). As a consequence, the relation of Not Sissy-Sissy to the evaluative properties and to Hostile/Aggressive parallels that for Normal-Problem. The "not sissy versus sissy" distinction is related to "good-bad" (i.e., relatively small angles in all conditions), although this is less true for male perceivers, particularly when they are responding to behavior descriptions attributed to a boy. Thus, sissy behavior for older siblings is problem behavior, and it is disapproved, though not so strongly by male perceivers. Perhaps older male siblings were less likely than their female counterparts to view sissy behavior in an evaluative sense because they know better what it feels like to be called a "sissy."

For parents the pattern of angles involving Not Sissy-Sissy is similar though certainly not identical to that for older siblings. The Sissy and Problem vectors are separated by small angles except in the FaSo conditions. There are also small angles between Not Sissy-Sissy and the three evaluative properties. In sum, parents agree with older siblings that sissy behavior is a problem (though this is less the case for fathers responding in terms of a son) and behavior that is disapproved. The biggest difference between the two samples is in the way in which male perceivers categorize sissy behavior in a boy. Fathers regard "sissy" as more definitely bad than a problem, while the reverse is true for older male siblings. This may be due to differences in empathy and felt responsibility. Older brothers may respond to a young boy's sissified actions primarily on the basis of empathy (thus viewing it as a problem but not necessarily bad). A father, while empathizing with his son, may feel that he is more responsible for the boy's socialization and that sissified behaviors are clearly not acceptable and should be changed.

The parents' direct ratings for the Not Sissy–Sissy property yielded some unexpected results. As can be seen in Table 4, parents seemed to avoid rating any of the behavior descriptions as extreme in the direction of sissy. Not a single item received a mean rating of greater than 6.0 (see Table 4), and only one mean was greater than 5.0. If the cutoff point is lowered to 4.0, mothers still avoid making this rating (MoDa, 1; MoSo, 0). Fathers, on the other hand, so rate 12 items for girls but only 3 for boys.

Older siblings also seemed reluctant to rate behavior descriptions as extremely "sissy," but this reluctance was less than that observed for parents. As can be seen in Table 4, only three items received mean ratings of 6.1 or greater. If the cutoff point is lowered to 4.0, the following numbers of items are rated in the direction of "sissy": FeGi, 23; MaGi, 18; FeBo, 11; MaBo, 6. This resembles the parents' pattern. Few items are given extreme ratings (i.e., over 6.0). Even if the criterion is lowered to the scale midpoint, the number of "sissy" items remains small, especially when the target is a boy. Apparently, being called a "sissy" is a very bad thing for a child, especially for a boy.

It is difficult to use the present data to determine how adults implicitly define the word *sissy*. Very few items received extreme means in the direction of "sissy" on the direct rating task. And, the meaning of *sissy* in terms of extreme projections is somewhat obscured because the hostile/aggressive behaviors used in this research are regarded by the present samples as *extremely* bad and *extremely* problem. Thus, the extreme projections onto any axis that is close to Normal-Problem and the evaluative properties—as is Not Sissy-Sissy—will include these items at the negative end. There is, however, a hint of what parents and older siblings might regard as sissified behavior in a 6- to 11-year-old child. On the direct rating task, "tattles" and "quits the game if things don't go right at the beginning" received means of 4.1 or greater in all four older-sibling conditions and two of the four parent conditions. Thus, a "sissy" might cognitively overlap with two other possible categories which might be labeled "tattletale" and "quitter."

Since it is only in the MaBo2 condition that "sissy" tends to be orthogonal to evaluation, it is only in this condition that the extreme projections show what the content of "sissy" might be independent of general evaluation. The behavior descriptions with the most extreme projections onto the "sissy" end of the Not Sissy-Sissy fitted axis in this condition are (in order of extremity): "is self-conscious in public," "goes to room and cries," "cries often," "does not like to share belongings," "is left out of others' games," "throws self on floor," "hits parents," "worries a lot," "hogs TV," "tattles," "won't change clothes if another person is present," "wants to be tucked in," "spits at other kids," and "quits the game if things don't go right at the beginning." These items include being a "tattletale" and a "quitter" and there is also considerable overlap with the "problem-but-not-hostile" grouping discussed above.

Even though these findings must be regarded as quite tentative, they represent a significant addition to our understanding of the concept "sissy." There is surprisingly little research directly relevant to this topic (see, however, Hartley, 1959). Maccoby and Jacklin (1974, p. 328) were able to find two studies, both of which investigated parents' reactions to preschool children engaging in sex-inappropriate activities (e.g., a boy wearing a dress or playing with a doll). The present findings suggest that adults view certain styles of behavior (e.g., to tattle, to quit, to cry, to be self-conscious and dependent) as unmanly and hence "sissy" even in a young boy.[6] It is significant also that the direct-rating-task data suggested that being a "quitter" and a "tattletale" indicated "sissiness" for a girl as well as a boy. Although this may not be borne out by subsequent research, it is possible that *sissy* may not be a term solely for boys and may have a somewhat different meaning when assigned to a girl.

Loner Behavior

The Not Loner-Loner property did not fit the multidimensional scaling configurations very well. The multiple R's in two dimensions ranged from .37 to .67. They were lower for a male target child, particularly as perceived by an older sister. This suggests that older siblings were able to organize the behavior descriptions along a Not Loner-Loner continuum, but the fit with the configurations—especially for females responding to a boy—was less close than with the preceding properties.

Examination of the angles between the fitted axes for Not Loner and the three evaluative properties yields a consistent pattern. In six of the eight conditions (i.e. FeGi, MaGi, and FeBo, both first and second sortings), Not

---

[6] Studies of parents' responses to sex-inappropriate behavior do not consistently find such behaviors to be disapproved. For example, Rothbart and Maccoby (1966) found that parents were more permissive of dependency and aggressiveness in the opposite-sex child.

Loner and the evaluative vectors are separated by relatively small angles (i.e., 9° to 42°, mean of 24°). In contrast, the angles in the MaBo condition tended somewhat more toward independence (i.e., 45° to 66°, mean of 52°). This suggests that for both sexes of older-sibling "loner" behavior is evaluated negatively for girls (as bad social behavior, behavior to be changed, and not-good-friend behavior). For younger brothers, however, older siblings disagree. "Loner" behavior for older sisters is perceived negatively. Such behavior is viewed somewhat independently of evaluation by older brothers.

The relationship between the Not Loner-Loner vector and that for Normal–Problem indicates a sex-of-target child effect (see Table 3). For both sexes of older siblings, the two vectors are much more in the the direction of convergence for brothers than for sisters. In the MaBo condition they nearly coincide. Apparently older siblings—especially males—feel that being a "loner" is not necessarily a problem for girls but is definitely a problem for boys.

The Not Loner-Loner association with the Not Sissy-Sissy continuum is revealed in the following angles (averaged over the first and second sortings) between the vectors: FeGi, 35°; MaGi, 52°; FeBo, 38°; MaBo, 11°. These angles indicate that, for the female-girl or female-boy and male-girl conditions, there was some association between the Loner and Sissy properties. For males looking at brothers, however, the association is very close. For male siblings, younger brothers who are "loners" are "sissies"; they go together and both are a "problem."

The direct ratings yield further evidence of similarities and differences as a function of sex of perceiver and sex of perceived. As is clear in Table 4, very few behavior descriptions received extreme "loner" ratings (i.e., above 6.0) in any of the four basic conditions. If the cutoff point for identifying "loner" items is reduced to 5.0, sex differences are revealed: FeGi, 13; MaGi, 10; FeBo, 9; MaBo, 2. Even at this level, older male siblings seem unwilling to rate behaviors as "loner" in a young boy. If it is noted that Loner and Problem are separated by quite small angles in the MaBo conditions, this finding may indicate that older male siblings have an attitude of empathy or protectiveness, which reflects itself in an unwillingness to apply to a younger brother a label that they regard as pejorative.

In terms of content, only two items—"is left out of others' games" and "does not like to share belongings"—were rated as extremely "loner" by both sexes of older sibling for both female and male target children. These were the only two items with mean ratings over 5.0 in the Male-Boy condition. The items added by males for girls are "just sits and watches television," "quits the game if things don't go right at the beginning," "torments a pet," "hits parents," "likes to play alone," "goes off and doesn't tell parent," "hassles neighbors," and "spits at other kids." Males seem to rate as "loner" behavior actions that might lead to or result from ostracism of a girl by her peers.

In the MaGi and FeBo conditions, the items with the most extreme projections at the "loner" end of the fitted axis for the Not Loner-Loner property were primarily "hostile/aggressive" (e.g., "spits at other kids"). For both of the Female–Girl sortings and for MaBo2, the extreme "loner" projections were not "hostile/aggressive" behavior descriptions. Rather, they were items that also had extreme projections in the direction of "problem" and "sissy" behavior (e.g., "cries often," "is left out of others' games"). In the MaBo1 condition, the extreme "loner" projections included "hostile/aggressive" and "problem" behavior (e.g., both "spits at other kids" and "cries often").

Discussion

A major focus of this chapter has been on older siblings as part of the social environment of the early-school-age child. Siblings as caretakers have been repeatedly described in the ethnographic literature (e.g., Rogoff, Sellers, Piorrata, Fox, & White, 1975) but have received much less attention in analyses of child rearing in western industrial societies (cf. Weisner & Gallimore, 1977). Increased attention to the significant role of siblings as socializers has become evident during the last decade (e.g., Rheingold, 1969; Sutton-Smith & Rosenberg, 1970; Whiting & Whiting, 1975; Bank & Kahn, 1977). As with socialization research involving parents, however, most work with siblings has involved self-report and observational data that have been structured and organized by the investigator. (A research strategy unique to the assessment of sibling effects is to compare the personality and behavior of children in different family configurations; e.g., Koch, 1955; Sutton-Smith & Rosenberg, 1970). Our approach has been quite different: we have attempted to uncover and represent the way in which older siblings cognitively structure child behavior as one possible determinant of their socializing influence.

The present study of older siblings follows directly on Study 1, and both derive from our conceptualization of the role of the cognition of the socializer in the adult–child interaction sequence. Thus, Study 1 investigated the effect of variations in the sex of the perceiving parent and the sex of the perceived child. Our working model also predicts that the cognition of socializers is related to the role relationship between the socializing agent and the child. Thus, parents would be expected to cognitively organize child behavior in a different way than teachers or, as was tested in Study 2, in a different way than older siblings.

The present study received further impetus from one of the findings of our initial investigation of parents' categorization of child behavior. Although a strong evaluative dimension was found for both mothers and fathers, there was some evidence that mothers tended to use the extremes of the dimension more than fathers. This suggested that mothers might be emphasizing the "good-bad" distinction to a greater extent than fathers. This difference in evaluative emphasis was interpreted in terms of felt responsibility, since—for the white, middle-class, suburban American couples that we studied—the mothers could be assumed to have much greater responsibility for child rearing than the fathers. This interpretation led to the more general hypothesis that the degree of evaluative emphasis in cognitive structuring of child behavior is a positive function of degree of felt responsibility for the child and child rearing. The study of older siblings was in part a test of this hypothesis. It was predicted that older siblings would evidence less evaluative emphasis in organizing descriptions of child behavior than parents to the extent that the older-sibling role carries with it less responsibility for child care and socialization than does the parent role.

Major Findings

We will now review some of our major findings, organizing this review will be as follows. We first present aspects of the cognitive structuring of child behavior that hold across differences in the characteristics of the perceiver and of the perceived. Next, we discuss variations in the categorization of child behavior. These variations will be reported in terms of three general factors specified by our working model as influencing cognitive structuring: (1) characteristics of the perceiver (here, sex), (2) characteristics of the perceived (here, sex), and (3) nature of the role relationship between perceiver and perceived (here, parent versus older sibling).

General Aspects of Adult Categorization of Child Behavior

There are two sets of findings that did not vary appreciably across the independent variables used in Study 1 and Study 2. The first pertains to the relative importance of the psychological properties and their organization in the adult perceiver's overall cognitive structure for interpreting observed child activity. The second general finding involves the response of parents and older siblings to the direct rating task.

For both parents and older siblings, the pattern of multiple R's indicates that evaluation is the primary dimension, since the evaluative properties have the highest multiple R's relative to the full set of properties. Thus, regardless of differences in role relationship, sex of perceiver, or sex of perceived, evaluation is the most central cognitive categorization for the interpretation of the social behavior of early-school-age children. This is, of course, congruent with the considerable body of research using the semantic differential (cf. Osgood, May, & Miron, 1974) and with multidimensional scaling investigations of implicit theories of personality (cf. Kim & Rosenberg, 1980).

The present findings are a contribution to the socialization literature in two related ways. First, they suggest an obvious point but one seldom discussed in research on the socialization process: Adults view child behavior in an evaluative frame of reference. It is likely that this tendency is accentuated in the white middle-class American samples we have studied (see Bacon & Ashmore, 1982). We expect substantial variation among adults in evaluative emphasis; differences between parents and older siblings in this regard are discussed below. Second, we have identified some of the components of the general "good-bad" continuum for viewing child behavior. Three of these involve judgments about the behavior itself (i.e., Good-Bad Social Behavior, Mature-Immature, Good Friend-Not Good Friend), while the fourth refers to the proper response by the socializer to the behavior (i.e., Behavior Should be Changed vs. Encouraged). Future research might fruitfully be aimed at identifying other components of "good-bad" and to investigating differences between perceivers in the content and organization of the evaluative dimension. For example, we suspect—though our data do not allow a test of this suspicion—that Mature-Immature is not as salient a cognitive distinction for older siblings as for parents. This hunch is based on the fact that in white middle-class American families it is the parents who are held accountable—by themselves and others—for "developing the child into a competent, social, and moral person" (Gecas, 1976, p. 33), and "mature versus immature" is a continuum that marks the progress or lack of progress being made in this developmental process.

Although the picture is not quite as clear as that for the central position of evaluation, there is evidence that Hostile/Aggressive–Not Hostile/Aggressive, Normal-Problem, and Not Sissy-Sissy are important cognitive continua in the categorization of child behavior. It is important, however, to qualify this conclusion by noting that the labels for these dimensions were provided by us. Both parents and older siblings were able to rate the behavior descriptions in terms of these labels and the ratings accounted for significant aspects of the scaling configurations. We are not certain, however, that these are the best labels for representing how parents spontaneously cognitively structure observed child behavior.

There was also agreement within the older-sibling sample that Not Loner–Loner is not a major dimension in the overall cognitive structure for the organization of child behavior. This finding, however, does not mean that this property taps an unimportant cognitive distinction. The poor fit to the configurations can be traced to two factors. First, the sample of behavior descriptions did not include items that might better have defined this property. Since we have focused on the *social* behavior of early-school-age children, we do not have very many items that refer to solitary activities. Second, Not Loner-Loner may account for parts of the overall structure but not be a continuous bipolar dimension. More specifically, older siblings may recognize the cognitive category "loner" but not necessarily regard this as one end of a complete bipolar continuum that is useful for thinking about children's behavior.

Across all conditions of rating, there were only a very small number of items that were rated as extreme in the direction of Hostile/Aggressive, Problem, and Sissy. In part, this is due to the procedure used to derive the 99 behavior descriptions. We began by asking the parents of "normal" children to describe what children in the 6- to 11-year-old age period do. This approach focuses attention on typical behaviors and thus may underrepresent the more extreme (and less frequent) actions that a parent would view as "hostile/aggressive," "problem," or "sissy." We believe, however, that the small number of extreme ratings at the negative end of these three rating scales is also due to conscious and nonconscious avoidance of such responses by raters. While conscious distortion of response in order to present a "socially desirable" image of self to the researcher is possible, we believe that most of the distortion was non-conscious and resulted from a fairly widespread belief (at least in American society) that children should not be given pejorative labels. If true, this interpretation would also apply to much of the extant socialization literature which is based on interviews and questionnaires. The sorting task used in the present research is much less obtrusive, and one potentially fruitful direction for future work on socialization would be to develop other less reactive approaches.

Sex-of-Perceiver Effects in the Categorization of Child Behavior

If a sex-of-perceiver effect is defined as similarity of response within sex-of-perceiver groups and dissimilarity between sex-of-perceiver groups, there are few such effects in our data. That is, there are not many instances where female perceivers (regardless of role relationship or sex of perceived) are similar in cognitive structuring and are different from male perceivers.

Stated yet another way, the effect of perceiver sex on the categorization of child behavior depends on, or interacts with, role relationship and sex of perceived. Unfortunately, there is not much socialization research with which to compare this finding. As Maccoby and Jacklin (1974) and Block (1979b) have pointed out, the large majority of such studies have involved only mothers. (The father has, of course, drawn greater attention in recent years; e.g., Booth & Edwards, 1980; Lamb, 1976, 1979). And even more rare are studies that assess child-rearing practices or views across both sex and role relationship. Our findings suggest such research is needed if we are to obtain the most comprehensive picture of the "socialization environment" of the developing child.

Sex-of-Perceived Effects in the Categorization of Child Behavior

Sex-of-perceived effects are almost as rare in our data as those for perceiver sex. This does not mean that boys and girls are not differentially socialized (cf. Block, 1979a,b). Rather, how the behavior of young children is interpreted depends not simply on the sex of the child but also on the sex of the perceiver and the role relationship. Further, these three factors seem to interact with one another in shaping categorization of child behavior. Thus, to the extent that differences in cognitive structuring are reflected in behavior toward the child, the process of sex-role socialization is likely to be highly complex.

There is, however, one hint of a sex-of-perceived effect, and we feel it is an important one. Across sex of perceiver and role relationship there is a tendency for boys to receive fewer extreme "sissy" ratings than girls. Although other explanations are possible, we believe this reflects a widely held belief that "sissy" is a very negative label to attach to a young boy and as such is to be avoided when possible.

Same-Sex and Cross-Sex Effects in the Categorization of Child Behavior

Of the many effects that depend on the sex of both the perceiver and the perceived, only three—all involving males as perceivers and boys as targets—will be discussed. First, both fathers and older brothers agree that Normal-Problem and "good-bad" are relatively unrelated in viewing the behavior of a boy. For male perceivers "normal" and "good" behavior in a young boy may be distinguished because they regard some "bad" behaviors as extensions of the male sex role (e.g., "hits brothers and sisters" may be seen as an aspect of defending oneself). Mothers may not evidence this distinction because (1) the boy's learning of the male role may be less salient for them (see, however, Lambert, Hamers, & Frasure-Smith, 1979; Block, 1979a), and (2) they must more often cope with bad behavior (cf. Newson & Newson, 1976). Second, while there is agreement across all conditions that "hostile-aggressive" behavior is "problem" behavior, fathers and older siblings distinguish a second type of problem behavior in a boy. These behaviors are not hostile-aggressive and there is considerable overlap with behaviors viewed as indicative of being a "sissy." That fathers distinguish a "sissy-problem" type of behavior in a boy is consistent with the conclusion of Maccoby and Jacklin (1974) that fathers are very concerned about sex-inappropriate behavior in a son. Our findings suggest that this concern is shared by older male siblings. (As already noted, however, male siblings appear to take less evaluative view of "sissy" behavior in a younger brother.) Third, the male–boy condition stands out in the older-sibling sample with regard to the Not Loner-Loner property. The angles between Not Loner-Loner and the evaluative properties are relatively large in this condition, while the angles with Sissy are quite small. Further, very few items are rated as extreme in the direction of Loner in the MaBo condition. As noted above, this may reflect empathy on the part of the older brother.

Effects of Role Relationship on the Categorization of Child Behavior

Two types of findings are relevant to role relationship effects. First, there are results for which the parent conditions are similar to one another and are different from the older-sibling conditions. Second, there is indirect evidence of role relationship effects where the patterns of data are different in the two samples.

The most outstanding direct role relationship effect concerns evaluative emphasis. As noted above, there is agreement across variations in sex and role relationship that evaluation is the most central (of the psychological properties measured) categorization of child behavior. There is, however, evidence supporting our prediction that parents are higher in "evaluative emphasis" than are older siblings.

The evidence regarding this prediction will now be reviewed. This review is organized in terms of the various possible meanings of the concept "evaluative emphasis." Each of these meanings is phrased in terms of a question. First, can the overall cognitive structuring of child behavior be reduced to a single evaluative continuum? The stress values indicate that parents are much more unidimensional in the cognitive structuring of the behavior descriptions than are older siblings. For parents, the relations among the 99 items are quite well accounted for by the single dimension which is evaluative in nature. This is not the case for older siblings. Their cognitive organization of the behavior descriptions cannot be reduced to a single continuum, particularly when given two opportunities to sort the behavior descriptions. Additional dimensions (or categorizations or schemata) are necessary in order to account for the sorting data adequately. Thus, for both parents and older siblings, evaluation is the most central dimension; but parents emphasize this distinction to a greater extent than older siblings.

Second, to what extent are schemata regarding child behavior perceived in an evaluative framework? The answer to this question is in the angles separating the evaluative dimension from other properties. There are three what we will term "content properties" common to both studies: Not Hostile/Aggressive-Hostile/Aggressive, Normal-Problem, Not Sissy-Sissy. These are cognitive continua that are not clearly good-bad distinctions in denotative terms. The angles between the fitted axes for these properties and those for the two evaluative properties used in both studies (i.e., Good-Bad Social Behavior, Encourage–Change) are not smaller in the parent sample than in the older sibling sample. In fact, the differences tend to be in the other direction. For example, the largest difference was for the angle between Encourage-Change and Not Hostile/Aggressive-Hostile/Aggressive; the average angle (averaging over all eight conditions in each study) was 59° for parents but only 36° for older siblings. Such averages obscure rather wide differences between conditions. The point to be made here is simply that the angles did not reveal any greater tendency on the part of parents than older siblings to assimilate the content distinctions (at least those that were assessed in the two studies) to an evaluative frame of reference.

Third, to what degree do perceivers use the extremes of the evaluative dimension? In terms of the direct ratings, there is no evidence of greater evaluative emphasis by parents than by older siblings. At the "encourage" end of Encourage-Change and the "bad" end of Good-Bad Social Behavior, parents and older siblings do not differ in the number of extreme ratings. Older siblings actually give more extreme ratings than parents for behavior "to be changed" and "good social behavior." Although this finding is clearly at variance with our basic prediction, it is important to note that the direct rating task is quite obtrusive; thus the ratings are subject to both conscious and nonconscious biases. The number of extreme projections in the two samples are clearly in line with the prediction of greater evaluative emphasis. For both ends of the Good-Bad Social Behavior and Encourage-Change vectors there are considerably more extreme projections in Study 1 than in Study 2. This finding, however, is not independent of the "stress" values. The extremity of projections depends on the overall distribution of points in a configuration, and the parents' solutions are much more unidimensional; the older siblings, on the other hand, tend toward a somewhat more circular distribution in the two-dimensional configurations. Thus, the greater number of extreme projections for parents reflects their tendency to "stretch" the points out along the single continuum rather than utilize alternative classifications of the items.

This review of the evidence regarding evaluative emphasis yields two major conclusions. First, "evaluative emphasis" is a complex concept. Second, parents do emphasize evaluation more than older siblings in the sense that "good-bad" is a more indispensable construct for them than for older siblings. This raises the question of what are the implications for socialization of this differential evaluative emphasis. If it is assumed that evaluative emphasis is somehow communicated to the child, then it is important to inquire how it is experienced by the child. If the actions of the child are responded to primarily within an evaluative framework, the child may experience this as socialization pressure (i.e., pressure to behave in a socially acceptable manner) or as a kind of interference with freedom. This, in turn, might shape perceptions of and attitudes toward the socializers and external events. In the present case, it may lead children to view parents more than older siblings as putting demands on them or interfering with them. As noted in introducing the concept, evaluative emphasis is not conceptualized as referring only to differences between parents and older siblings. Individual differences among parents and among older siblings are expected. And differences between cultural groups are predicted. Assuming that such differences exist, it seems evident that, for a growing child, an environment where nearly every act is responded to in some evaluative manner is quite different from one where a wide range of behavior is accepted without comment.

There are five major instances where the pattern of data is different for the parent and older sibling samples and suggests that role relationship may account for the difference. First, mothers provided more extreme direct ratings on the evaluative properties than fathers, but in Study 2, older male siblings gave slightly more extreme "good" and "bad" ratings than older female siblings. As noted above, we see this as suggesting that the difference in evaluative emphasis is not due to sex of perceiver *per se* but to differences between the maternal and paternal roles. This is consistent with the considerable body of research indicating that the mother has primary responsibility in the family for child care and socialization (cf. Gecas, 1976).

Second, in the parent sample, the angles between Normal–Problem and the evaluative properties are smaller when the behavior of a daughter is being judged, but the analogous sex-of-perceived effect does not occur for older siblings. Parents see "being normal" and "being good" as going together in a daughter and as somewhat unrelated in a son. And at the other end of the continua, a daughter who misbehaves is a "problem," while "bad" behavior by a son is not necessarily a "problem." That Normal-Problem and evaluation are more unrelated for sons than daughters is related to the tendency for parents to regard sons as more "difficult" (cf. Maccoby & Jacklin, 1974). We believe this pattern is futher related to several of the differences in parents' reports of child-rearing practices obtained by Block (1979a). Parents expressed a greater punishment orientation in their responses to sons than daughters (since sons "normally" engage in some "bad" behavior) and more warmth and physical closeness and trust for daughters than sons (since daughters are "normally good").

Third, parents—but not older siblings—assign more extreme ratings on the evaluative properties to girls (daughters) than to boys (sons). On the surface this seems to contradict the fairly consistent finding that boys receive more positive and negative feedback from parents than do girls (cf. Block, 1979b; Maccoby & Jacklin, 1974). We believe, however, that the two results are complementary. If parents expect girls to be good (as the angles between Normal-Problem and evaluation suggest), then they will not need to use feedback either to promote good behavior or to suppress bad behavior. And if bad behavior is not expected in a girl, it is possible that ratings of a girl doing something bad will be more extreme than the same action when attributed to a boy. This "contrast effect" explanation, however, does not account for why daughters receive more extreme ratings at the positive end of the evaluative properties. Here it would be predicted that boys, for whom good behavior is not expected, would receive more extreme ratings.

Fourth, the vectors for Hostile/Aggressive and those for the evaluative properties were closer for mothers than fathers, but the parallel sex-of-perceiver effect did not occur for older siblings. That mothers more so than fathers view hostile–aggressive behavior in an evaluative frame of reference is consistent with the already noted point that mothers are required to cope with problem behavior. In addition, the mother role requires more prolonged contact with children, and hostile–aggressive child activity may simply make this contact more unpleasant for mothers (see Bacon & Ashmore, 1982). Whatever the interpretation, the present finding is consistent with Lambert and his colleagues' (1979) finding across 10 national groups that fathers were "more lenient than mothers in coping with a six-year-old's displays of temper or disputes with a guest" (p. 335).

The fifth and final role relationship effect concerns the Sissy property. The angles involving this property suggest that fathers see "sissy" behavior as more "bad" than a "problem," while just the reverse is true for older male siblings. As noted above the finding for fathers is consistent with research indicating that fathers are very concerned about sex-inappropriate behavior in a son. The present results suggest that fathers are not only concerned but see the sissified actions as "bad social behavior," "immature," and "behavior to be changed." This view may stem from the father's perceived responsibility to prepare his son to be a man. Unmanly behavior is simply not acceptable and must be changed. The older male sibling, not having this responsibility, may more easily identify with the younger brother and view the "sissy" behavior as clearly a "problem" but not so clearly "bad."

Future Directions

We conclude by noting two general directions that research guided by our working model might fruitfully take . First, as the preceding review of major findings makes clear, the categorization of child behavior by socializers is quite complex. All three of the factors we studied (i.e., sex of perceiver, sex of perceived, and parent versus older-sibling role relationship) were associated with differences in the cognitive structuring of the 99 behavior descriptions. More importantly, "main effects" for these factors were rare. Most often differences in categorization depended on two or even all three of the factors under study. We believe that the picture is even more complex than the present findings suggest. Two observations illustrate this point and suggest directions for future research.

1. We have here treated the parent and older-sibling roles as static concepts. Obviously they are not. Nash and Feldman (1980), for example, found that mothers'—but not fathers'—responsiveness to babies varied as a function of the age of the mothers' own children. This suggests that the mother role varies with the stages of the family life cycle.
2. We have "kept constant" a number of factors that, on the basis of our working model, should influence cognitive structuring. All perceivers were white, middle-class Americans and all targets were in the 6- to 11-year age range. Within American society we would expect social-class differences in the perception of children and their behavior (e.g., Kohn, 1969; Lambert et al., 1979), and it is likely that social class will "interact" with sex of perceived (e.g., Paige, 1978; Lambert et al., 1979). And our model predicts differences between cultures in the cognitive structuring of observed child activity.

A second general direction would involve integration of the present type of research with work on parental values and other cognitive–affective variables. It is even more important to know how parental cognitive structuring is reflected in parents' behavior toward children. Integration of these lines of research is obviously necessary if we are to understand how the family and other learning environments influence the developing child.

Acknowledgments

We thank Frances K. Del Boca and Robin M. Uili for their comments on an earlier draft of the manuscript and Victoria K. Burbank, who had primary responsibility for gathering the data from older siblings. We also thank Audrey Puskas and Joan Olmizzi for typing assistance.

References

Bacon M. K. & Ashmore, R. D. *How mothers and fathers categorize descriptions of social behavior attributed to daughters and sons.* Manuscript submitted for publication, 1982.

Bank, S., & Kahn, M. D. Sisterhood–Brotherhood is powerful: Sibling subsystems and family therapy. In S. Chess & A. Thomas (Eds.), *Annual progress in child psychiatry and child development.* New York: Brunner/Mazel, Inc., 1977.

Bell, R. Q., & Harper, L. V. *Child effects on adults.* Hillsdale, N.J.: Lawrence Erlbaum, 1977.

Block, J. H. Another look at sex differentiation in the socialization behavior of mothers and fathers. In J. Sherman & F. L. Denmark (Eds.), *Psychology of women: Future directions of research.* New York: Psychological Dimensions, 1979. (a)

Block, J. H. *Personality development in males and females: The influence of differential socialization.* Paper presented at the Annual Convention of the American Psychological Association, New York, September, 1979. (b)

Booth, A., & Edwards, J. N. Fathers: The invisible parent. *Sex Roles,* 1980, *6,* 445–456.

Gecas, V. The socialization and child care roles. In F. I. Nye (Ed.), *Role structure and analysis of the family.* Beverly Hills, Calif.: Sage, 1976.

Hartley, R. E. Sex-role pressures and the socialization of the male child. *Psychological Reports,* 1959, *5,* 457–468.

Johnson, S. C. Hierarchical clustering schemes. *Psychometrika,* 1967, *32,* 241–254.

Kim, M. P., & Rosenberg, S. Comparison of two structural models of implicit personality theory. *Journal of Personality and Social Psychology,* 1980, *38,* 375–389.

Koch, H. L. Some personality correlates of sex, sibling position, and sex of sibling among five and six year old children. *Genetic Psychological Monographs,* 1955, *52,* 3–50.

Kohn, M. L. *Class and conformity.* Homewood, Ill.: Dorsey, 1969.

Kruskal, J. B. *How to use MDSCAL, a multidimensional scaling program (version 3).* Unpublished manuscript, Bell Telephone Laboratories, Murray Hill, N.J., May 1967.

Lamb, M. E. (Ed.), *The role of the father in child development.* New York: Wiley, 1976.

Lamb, M. E. Paternal influence and the father's role: A personal perspective. *American Psychologist,* 1979, *34,* 938–943.

Lambert, W. E., Hamers, J. F., & Frasure-Smith, N. *Child-rearing values: A cross-national study.* New York: Praeger, 1979.

LeVine, R. Cross cultural study in child psychology. In P. Mussen (Ed.), *Carmichael's manual of child psychology,* (Vol. 2). New York: Wiley, 1970.

Lytton, H. Observation studies of parent–child interaction: A methodological review. *Child Development*, 1971, *42*, 651–683.

Maccoby, E. E., & Jacklin, C. *The psychology of sex differences*. Stanford, Calif.: Stanford University Press, 1974.

Nash, S. C. & Feldman, S. S. Responsiveness to babies: Life-situation specific sex differences in adulthood. *Sex Roles*, 1980, *6*, 751–758.

Newson, J., & Newson, E. *Seven year olds in the home environment*. New York: Wiley, 1976.

Osgood, C. E., May, W. H., & Miron, M. S. *Cross-cultural universals of affective meaning*. Urbana, Ill.: University of Illinois Press, 1975.

Paige, K. E. Sources of sex inequality: Family, schools, personality. In S. Golden (Ed.), *Work, family roles and support systems*. Ann Arbor, Mich., Center for Continuing Education for Women, 1978.

Rheingold, H. L. The social and socializing infant. In D. A. Goslin (Ed.), *Handbook of socialization theory and research*. Chicago: Rand McNally, 1969.

Rogoff, D., Sellers, M. J., Piorrata, S., Fox, N., & White, S. Age of assignment of roles and responsibilities to children: A cross-cultural survey. *Human Development*, 1975, *18*, 353–369.

Rosenberg, S., & Jones, R. A. A method for investigating and representing a person's implicit theory of personality: Theodore Dreiser's view of people. *Journal of Personality and Social Psychology*, 1972, *22*, 372–386.

Rosenberg, S., & Kim, M. P. The method of sorting as a data-gathering procedure in multivariate research. *Multivariate Behavioral Research*, 1975, *10*, 489–502.

Rosenberg, S., Nelson, C., & Vivekananthan, P. S. A multidimensional approach to the structure of personality impressions. *Journal of Personality and Social Psychology*, 1968, *9*, 283–294.

Rosenberg, S., & Sedlak, A. Structural representations of implicit personality theory. In L. Berkowitz (Ed.), *Advances in experimental social psychology* (Vol. 6). New York: Academic Press, 1972.

Rothbart, M. K., & Maccoby, E. E. Parents' differential reactions to sons and daughters. *Journal of Personality and Social Psychology*, 1966, *4*, 237–243.

Sears, R. R., Maccoby, E. E., & Levin, H. *Patterns of child rearing*. Evanston, Ill.: Row Peterson, 1957.

Sutton-Smith, B., & Rosenberg, B. G. *The sibling*. New York: Holt, 1970.

Weisner, T. S., & Gallimore, R. My brother's keeper: Child and sibling caretaking. *Current Anthropology*, 1977, *18*, 169–180.

Whiting, B. B., & Whiting, J. W. M. *Children of six cultures: A psycho-cultural analysis*. Cambridge, Mass.: Harvard University Press, 1975.

CHAPTER 11

Learning to Do Things without Help

NICHOLAS ZILL and JAMES L. PETERSON

As children grow up, their learning encompasses far more than the traditional academic skills of 'readin,' 'ritin,' and 'rithmetic.' Among these others are domestic skills—like shopping, making beds, and cooking; mechanical skills—using tools, operating toys or household appliances, building and repairing things; and social skills—such as dealing with peers and taking care of younger children. A lot of this learning takes place not in schools but rather in the family. But there has been relatively little research about the role of parents and siblings as modelers, teachers, and encouragers of these practical and social skills.

There are a number of reasons for an interest in the development of practical skills. One is the need to broaden our understanding of the intergenerational transmission of individual and group differences in socioeconomic status. Research findings have consistently shown the relationship of parents' education, occupation, income, and race to some aspects of child development (e.g., Bradley, Caldwell, & Elardo, 1977; Clarke-Stewart, 1977; Marjoribanks, 1977; Trotman, 1977). However, much of this research has focused on a narrow range of criterion measures, namely IQ scores or closely related academic achievement measures. There are good reasons for this focus in terms of predicting school success. But there is also reason to believe that competencies and work habits that start taking shape in childhood and are only weakly correlated with IQ have a bearing on adult functioning in the job market and in everyday life.

In a related set of interests, feminist reformers have focused attention

NICHOLAS ZILL and JAMES L. PETERSON ● Child Trends, Inc., Washington, DC. 20036. The analyses described in this report were supported by a grant to Child Trends, Inc., from the Foundation for Child Development. The Foundation also sponsored the collection of data in the National Survey of Children.

on sex-role development in childhood. They have done so in the belief that inequalities between women and men in education, employment, income, and creative accomplishment result not only from the discriminatory practices of institutions in our society but also from limiting aspects of the traditional female role itself. It may be easier now than in earlier times for a woman to become a surgeon, an airline pilot, or an orchestra conductor. But that will not mean much if most girls aspire only to be nurses, stewardesses, and second violinists. Much of the socialization through which sex roles are developed involves the differential acquisition of social and practical skills. Hence many feminists seek to challenge conventional socialization practices and to teach girls—and boys—that they are "free to be...you and me." What effect are these efforts having on children growing up amid the "sex-role revolution?" Are significant shifts toward more egalitarian treatment of sons and daughters occurring in American child-rearing practices?

Finally, in what has been called the "new home economics," researchers have begun to examine the household as a producer of goods and services, from meals cooked and houses cleaned to vegetables grown and children reared (Schultz, 1974). In this productive process, children are not only the object of services (child care, education, etc.), but are also producers themselves. Children do a considerable amount of work at home. The amount and nature of this work is intimately tied to the practical skills they develop.

Until recently, we have not had much systematic data about how children from different family backgrounds vary in their ability to perform specific practical tasks at different ages. Adaptive behavior inventories like the Vineland Social Maturity Scale (Doll, 1953, 1965) and the Adaptive Behavior Scale (American Association on Mental Deficiency, 1974) have been applied primarily to the assessment of the mentally retarded. Data concerning the motor and social development of normal children have been more plentiful with respect to pre-school-age children (e.g., Frankenburg, Dick, & Carland, 1975) than to those who are older.

The situation has been improved by the advent of the National Assessment of Educational Progress (NAEP) and specifically by the Career and Occupational Development Assessment. This federal program periodically measures the acquisition of practical skills in national samples of 9-, 13-, and 17-year-olds and in young adults (NAEP, 1976, 1977a). Although the program is a big step forward, it has its limitations. The ages assessed are widely spaced and only a few basic child and family characteristics are recorded along with the skill assessments.

The purpose of this report is to present data measuring practical skills in a national sample of elementary school children, to demonstrate by comparison that this measure behaves differently from an established measure of intellectual development, and to describe the relationship of a number of family background characteristics to practical skill level in children.

Methods

The Sample

This analysis is based on data collected in the Foundation for Child Development's 1976 National Survey of Children (Zill, 1983). The survey covered a broad range of indicator data describing the circumstances and conditions of children in the United States.

The survey was based on a national (the coterminous United States) probability sample of households containing one or more children aged 7-11. (See Table 1.) Of 2,193 households found to be eligible from household screenings, 1,747 or 80% agreed to participate in the study. Up to two eligible children were included from each household. If more than two were eligible, two were selected using random procedures. Black families were oversampled and weights were developed to correct for this oversampling, for the undersampling of children from households with more than two eligible children, and for other minor discrepancies between sample and census estimates of the distribution of the population by age, sex, race, and area of residence.

Data Collection and Measures

Data were collected through personal interviews with the children and their parents in the fall of 1976 and by mailed questionnaires completed by their teachers the following spring. All together, 2,279 children were interviewed, and school information was obtained on 1,682 or 73% of these children. The personal interview followed a completely structured format and consisted primarily of closed-ended questions. The wording of some of the principal questions discussed in the text is given in Tables 2 and 3. The principal dependent variable is a measure of the child's level of practical skill development.

Parents were read a series of 14 practical tasks, requiring varying degrees of skill and maturity, and asked whether or not the child had ever done each one by himself or herself, without anyone's help. The specific tasks were derived largely from questions in the NAEP Career and

Table 1. Number and Percentage Distribution of U.S. Children
(Aged 7-11) in FCD Survey

	Unweighted number of cases	Weighted percentages[a]
Type of community		
Giant central cities (1 million plus)	267	12.1
Large central cities (250,000-999,999)	206	10.7
Medium central cities (50,000-249,999)	109	7.4
Affluent suburbs	318	11.5
Other suburban areas	796	27.0
Small towns (outside SMSAs)	320	13.5
Extreme rural areas	285	17.8
	2,301	100.0
Ethnic group of child		
Nonminority	1,639	80.0
Black	558	14.5
Hispanic	84	4.7
Other	20	0.8
	2,301	100.0
Number of children in family		
One	137	5.9
Two	698	30.0
Three	604	26.3
Four	349	15.4
Five	219	10.5
Six	114	4.9
Seven or more	167	7.0
	2,288	100.0
Parent educational attainment (more educated parent)		
Grade school only	175	7.3
Some high school	406	15.4
High school graduate	942	43.7
Some college	361	16.9
College graduate	381	16.7
	2,265	100.0
Family income (1975)		
Less than $5,000	339	11.6
$5,000-$9,999	474	21.1
$10,000-$14,999	525	25.2
$15,000-$24,999	667	31.2
$25,000 and over	250	10.9
	2,255	100.0

[a]Percentage distributions calculated with missing data cases excluded.

Table 2. Items in Family Activities Index

"I will read a list of family activities. For each activity, please tell me if you have done it recently, or if you wanted to do it but just didn't have the time or couldn't affort it right now, or whether you didn't do it for some other reason during this time. How about: . . ."	Percentage of children whose parents report that they have done it
In the last month	
Took the family to the movies	23
Took the family out to dinner	65
Bought toys or games for your child(ren)	64
Went out for an evening without your child(ren)	54
Bought new clothes for your child(ren)	85
Went with your child(ren) for a whole morning or afternoon in a park	26
In the last week	
Played a game with your child(ren)	63
Helped you child(ren) with schoolwork	83
Did things with your child(ren) around the house, such as build or make things, cook, or sew	80

Occupational Development Assessment (NAEP, 1977b). However, in NAEP the questions were asked of children rather than of parents. Among the tasks on the list were such domestic chores as washing dishes, changing sheets on a bed, baby-sitting, baking a cake or pie, ironing clothes, and cooking a complete meal for the family—all considered "women's work" in the preliberation era. Also on the list were construction and repair jobs conventionally assigned to the "home handyman": putting batteries in a flashlight or toy; painting some object other than a picture; buiding something out of wood with real tools; fixing a bicycle, wagon, or roller skates; and making a model.

A summary score for each child was developed based on the proportion of tasks that he or she was reported to have done without help. While more refinement in the measurement of skill level might be obtained by incorporating data on the frequency and quality of performance as well as on whether or not each task had ever been accomplished, these additional measures were not available from the survey. The effects of age and sex were removed by subtracting the mean proportion of tasks completed by children of the same age and sex as the child and dividing the resulting difference by the standard deviation for children in that sex–age group. All

Table 3. Sex Differences in Practical Accomplishments,
U.S. Children Aged 7–11, 1976

| | Percentage of children aged 7–11 reported to have done task without help | | |
	Girls $n = 1,136$	Boys $n = 1,129$	Difference[a]
Tasks that girls accomplish earlier than boys			
Wash dishes	92	68	24
Bake a cake or pie	42	16	26
Iron clothes	41	16	25
Change sheets on a bed	72	52	20
Write a letter and mail it	73	56	17
Baby-sit	46	31	15
Cook a complete meal for the family	19	11	8
Tasks that boys accomplish earlier than girls			
Make a model, like a model car, boat, or airplane	18	69	51
Build something out of wood with real tools, like a hammer and saw	34	75	41
Fix a bicycle, wagon, or roller skates	31	70	39
Put batteries in a flashlight or toy	81	94	13
Paint some object other than a picture	71	80	9
Tasks that both sexes accomplish at about the same ages			
Shop at a store by himself/herself	74	78	4[ns]
Set the time on a clock or watch	68	71	3[ns]

[a]All differences are significant at $p < .01$ unless indicated by [ns].

deviation scores were converted into standard scores with a mean of 50 and a standard deviation of 10[1].

Group differences in the practical skills index across children from different family backgrounds were then examined. Families were classified according to community of residence, parent educational attainment, family income, family size, ethnic group, and a family activities score based on parent reports of things that the family had done together in the last month.

The communities in which the survey families resided were classified into seven categories ranging from central cities to rural areas. Central cities were categorized by size as "giant" (1970 population of 1 million or more); "large" (population 250,000-999,999); or "medium" (population of 50,000-249,999). Suburban communities within Standard Metropolitan Statistical Areas (SMSAs) were categorized as "affluent suburbs" (communities where, according to census figures, 60% or more of the households had incomes at or above three times the official poverty level in 1970) or as "other suburban areas." Communities outside of SMSAs were divided into those within "small towns" and those in "extreme rural areas." The percentage distribution for this and each of the other background variables, as estimated by the FCD sample, is shown in Table 1.

The number of years of education completed by the child's more educated parent was used to summarize the family education level. (When the child was living with one parent only, information about the nonresident parent's educational attainment was obtained if the separation or divorce had occurred within the previous 5 years.) Years of education were grouped into five categories: grammar school only; some high school; high school graduate; some college; and college graduate or more.

Parent respondents in the survey were asked to report the family's total income before taxes in 1975, using a set of 13 income classes similar to those employed in the U.S. Census Bureau's Current Population Survey. Parent reports of family income were available for 95% of the children in the

---

[1] Psychometric analyses of the practical skills items have been carried out by Howard Wainer of the Bureau of Social Science Research. He has found that the reliability of a summary index based on the 14 items is satisfactory, having a value of approximately .70 as estimated by Kuder-Richardson Formula 20. Furthermore, the reliability estimate shows little variation when calculated for four different subgroups of children: black boys, black girls, nonminority boys, and nonminority girls. Wainer has also found that the items fulfill the requirements of the Rasch Model (Rasch, 1966) reasonably well, although the scoring of individual items has to be adjusted for differences in item difficulties for boys as opposed to girls. This suggests that there is a single underlying dimension along which the items can be arrayed and that individual children can properly be assigned developmental scores along the same continuum.

survey. When the parents refused to report or said they did not know the total family income, the interviewer was asked to make an extimate of the family's income using the same response categories. If the interviewer supplied such an estimate, it was included in the analysis. As with parent education, family income was grouped into five broader categories for the analyses reported here: less than $5,000, $5,000-$9,999, $10,000-$14,999, $15,000-24,999, and $25,000 or more.

The number of children in the family was coded in seven categories ranging from only child to seven or more chidren.

Black families were oversampled in the FCD survey in order to provide data on appproximately 100 black children at each year of age. Thus, the sample contained 558 black children instead of the 333 that would be expected on a straight probability basis. Weights were applied in analyzing the data to compensate for this oversampling.

Hispanic families were not oversampled. Conclusions drawn about Hispanic children must be tempered not only by the small number of these children in the sample (84 cases) but also by the fact that, because of budgetary limitations, a Spanish-language version of the questionnaire was not fielded. Hence, the Hispanic families in the survey were representative only of Hispanic Americans who had some proficiency in English.

Attempting to show developmental differences in children from various family backgrounds will not tell us what the families actually *do* (or do not do) to nurture the development of practical skills in their children. A more direct measure of parent–child interaction was derived from a series of nine questions to the parent respondents in the FCD survey. These questions concerned specific things that the parent had done with or for the children in the last month (e.g., took the family to the movies, took the family out to dinner, bought toys or games for the children, etc.) or in the last week (played a game with the children, helped the children with schoolwork, did things with the children around the house).

For each activity in the list, the parent was asked to tell "if you have done it recently." The family activities index was constructed by simply adding up the total number of "have done" items reported by each parent. The index had an overall mean of 5.4 with a standard deviation of 1.8. Only 2% of the parents reported that they had done all nine of the activities in the list and less than 1% said that they had done none of them. The specific items that made up the family activities index and the percentage of parents who said they had done each activity are shown in Table 2.

For purposes of comparison with the results for the practical skills index, these same background variables were used to predict the child's score on a more traditional measure of intellectual development: an abbreviated version of the Peabody Picture Vocabulary Test that was administered to each child as part of the household interview. The raw vocabulary test scores were also adjusted for age (but not sex) and converted into standard scores with a mean of 50 and a standard deviation of 10. There was a significant but relatively weak positive relationship between the vocabulary score and the practical skills index ($r = .23, p < .01$).

Methods of Analysis

The relationships of these background variables to the practical skills index and the Peabody Test were examined both separately and jointly by means of multiple classification analysis (Andrews, Morgan, & Sonquist, 1967), a form of multiple regression analysis using categorical predictors.

Two measures of the degree of association between variables were used. *Eta*, the unadjusted correlation ratio, measures the proportion of the total sum of squares of the dependent variable explainable by the independent variable, using the categories given. *Beta*, the adjusted correlation ratio, adjusts *eta* for the simultaneous effects of all the other independent variables entered in the model. This measure is analogous to the standardized regression coefficient (Andrews *et al.*, 1967, p. 22). Comparison of these two statistics shows how much of a variable's raw effect may be attributed to its association with other independent variables.

Findings

Age and Sex Differences in Practical Skills

Almost all the individual items making up the practical skills index showed distinct differences in the percentage of sons and the percentage of daughters who were reported to have accomplished the tasks without help, and all the differences were in the direction expected from sex-role stereotypes (see Table 3 and Appendix figures). Only the tasks of setting the time on a clock or watch and of shopping at a store did not show significant differences between the sexes.

Girls were more likely than boys to have performed housecleaning, cooking, and child care tasks on their own. More than 2½ times as many daughters as sons were reported to have baked a cake or ironed clothes. More than 90% of elementary school-age girls had washed dishes without help, nearly three-quarters had changed sheets on a bed, and almost half had some baby-sitting experience—all substantially more than the equivalent percentages for boys in elementary school.

The differences between boys and girls are even greater, though in the opposite direction, when it comes to the mastery of construction or repair skills. While most sons are acquiring "Mr. Fix-It" skills at relatively early ages, a majority of daughters are still lacking most of these skills by the end of grammar school. Only a third of grammar school girls in the United States had ever built something out of wood using a hammer, saw, or other real tool by comparison with the three-quarters of boys who had done such woodwork. When her bicycle, wagon, or roller skate breaks down, a girl is less likely to fix it herself; more than twice as many boys as girls had done such a repair job. Comparatively few girls had ever been given a model car, boat, or airplane to construct. Less than one daughter in five had built a model versus seven out of ten sons, nearly a fourfold difference. The

Table 4. Prediction of Vocabulary Test Score from Family Characteristics (Multiple Classification Analysis)

	Predicting vocabulary skills from each characteristic separately	Predicting vocabulary skills from seven characteristics simultaneously
Predictors	Eta[a]	Beta[b]
Parents' education level	.36[g]	.24[g]
Ethnic group	.26[g]	.14[g]
Family size	.20[g]	.12[g]
Family income	.29[g]	.11[g]
Sex of child	.12[g]	.10[g]
Community size and type	.18[g]	.09[g]
Family activities score	.18[g]	.05
		$R = .43^{c}$
		$R^2 = .18^{dg}$
Unweighted $n = 2,232$		Percentage variance explained = 19.3%[e]

[a] Eta is the correlation ratio unadjusted.
[b] Beta is the correlation ratio adjusted for effects of other predictors.
[c] R is the multiple correlation coefficient corrected for degrees of freedom.
[d] R^2 indicates the proportion of variance in the dependent variable explained by all predictors together after correcting for degrees of freedom.
[e] Percent Variance Explained is the percentage of variance explained with no correction for degrees of freedom.
[f] $p < .05$.
[g] $p < .01$.

Table 5. Prediction of Practical Skills Index from Family Characteristics
(Multiple Classification Analysis)

Predictors	Predicting practical skills from each characteristic separately	Predicting practical skills from six characteristics simultaneously
	Eta	Beta
Family activities score	$.28^b$	$.25^b$
Parents' education level	$.22^b$	$.16^b$
Family size	$.07$	$.10^b$
Community size and type	$.10^b$	$.09^b$
Ethnic group	$.11^b$	$.05$
Family income	$.15^b$	$.05$
		$R = .33$
		$R^2 = .11^b$
Unweighted $n = 2,249$		Percentage variance explained $= 12.0\%$

Note: See Table 4 for explanation of entries.
[a] $p < .05$.
[b] $p < .01$.

difference between the sexes even shows up with such simple tasks as
putting batteries in a flashlight or toy or painting some object other than a
picture. Although a majority of girls had done these things, the numbers
who had was still significantly smaller than that for boys.

As would be expected of any developmental measure, the proportion of
children ever having accomplished each task rises with age (see Appendix
figures). This is true of both boys and girls, although the rate of
improvement with age varies by sex of child within some of the tasks (e.g.,
baby-sitting, baking a cake, making a model, and fixing a bicycle, wagon,
or roller skates).

In the following analyses relating the family background characteristics to practical skills and vocabulary levels, the age–sex-adjusted
summary score over all 14 tasks was used for each child. These analyses are
summarized in Tables 4 and 5.

Community Size and Type

The practical skills index showed less association with community
type (eta = .10, $p < .01$) than did the vocabulary scores (eta = .18, $p < .01$).
There was nearly a 6-point difference between the average vocabulary score

of children in affluent suburbs (mean = 53.3) and that of children in rural small towns (mean = 47.5) or giant central cities (mean = 47.4). The average vocabulary scores of children in the other types of communities were of intermediate value and did not differ significantly from one another.

When parent education, family income, ethnic group, and the other characteristics of the families residing in the different types of communities were controlled by means of multiple classification analysis, the variation in vocabulary scores attributable to community of residence was substantially reduced (beta = .09, $p < .01$). Large central cities (those with populations under a million) came out best and rural small towns came out worst, but there was less than a 4-point difference between them. The other community types did not differ from one another on the adjusted mean vocabulary scores.

For the practical skills index, affluent suburbs once again came out best (mean = 52.3) in terms of the raw means. But other suburban areas (mean = 49.5) fell at the bottom of the list, along with rural small towns (mean = 49.2). When the practical skills means were adjusted for the characteristics of the families living in the different neighborhood categories, other suburbs and small towns remained at the bottom of the list. Children in large and giant central cities came out at the top on the basis of the adjusted mean scores. However, the largest difference between community types was only slightly more than 2 points (beta = .09, $p < .01$).

In short, variations in children's scores from one type of community to another on both the vocabulary test and the practical skills index had more to do with the characteristics of the families residing in the communities than with the size or type of community as such.

Parent Educational Attainment

Of the family characteristics examined, parent education was the best predictor of the child's score on the picture–vocabulary test (eta = .36, $p < .01$), and the second best predictor of the child's score on the practical skills index (eta = .22, $p < .01$). The relationship between parent educational attainment and the child's vocabulary score was essentially linear, with more than a full standard deviation separating the mean vocabulary score of children in the highest parent education category (mean of children of college graduates = 55.2) from those in the lowest education category (mean of children of grade school dropouts = 43.5). When parent education was entered into a multiple classification analysis along with the other family characteristics, the strength of the relationship between education and vocabulary score was reduced somewhat (beta = .24, $p < .01$). However, there was still a difference of nearly three-quarters of a standard deviation in vocabulary score between the top and bottom parent education categories.

The relationship between parent education and children's scores on the practical skills index was generally positive but not as strong as the relationship with vocabulary score. Moreover, the highest average score was not attained by children of college graduates (mean = 51.5), but by children whose parents had some college but no degree (mean = 53.8). These children scored nearly 9 points higher on the practical skills index than did children whose parents had only a grade school education (mean = 45.3). When other family characteristics were taken into account, this spread was reduced to 6 points, but the correlation between parent education and practical skills remained significant (beta = .16, $p < .01$), and the curvilinear shape of the relationship was maintained.

The specific tasks that correlated most strongly and positively with parent education were writing a letter and mailing it, painting some object other than a picture, building something out of wood, and setting the time on a clock or watch. On the other hand, the tasks of changing sheets on a bed and ironing clothes actually showed a slight negative correlation with parent education. Children of better-educated parents were less likely to have done these things without help than were children of parents with little education.

Family Income

When the children's vocabulary test scores were predicted from each of the family characteristics separately, family income was the second best predictor, coming after education (eta = .29, $p < .01$). There was nearly a full standard deviation spread between the mean vocabulary scores of children in the lowest (mean = 44.9) and highest (mean = 54.3) family income categories. However, the predictive power of income was substantially diminished (beta = .11, $p < .01$) when it was combined with the other family characteristics in a multiple classification analysis. This indicates that poverty or affluence is less important as a determinant of a child's intellectual development than are other family factors, such as parent education and family size, with which family income is associated. When these other correlated factors were controlled, the spread in vocabulary scores between the highest and lowest income categories was reduced to little more than a 3-point difference.

Family income displayed less of a relationship to children's scores on the practical skills index (eta = .15, $p < .01$) than to their vocabulary scores. The spread in mean scores from the bottom (mean = 46.7) to the top (mean = 52.6) income categories was just under 6 points. There was practically no difference, however, among the middle three categories. When the other family characteristics were taken into account, the effect of family income was reduced to just over a 1-point spread (beta = .05, ns).

The pattern of relationships between family income and the individual tasks in the practical skills index was much like that noted for parent education. That is, children from low-income families were less likely than children from more affluent families to have written a letter or to have set the time on a clock. But they were more likely to have ironed clothes or to have changed sheets by themselves.

Family Size

Children from larger families tended to have lower vocabulary scores than children from small families (eta = .20, p < .01; see Table 4 and Figure 1). There was more than a 9-point difference between the mean vocabulary scores of only children (mean = 54.6) and of children in families with seven or more children (mean = 45.2). However, families with large numbers of children also tended to have lower parent education and income levels.

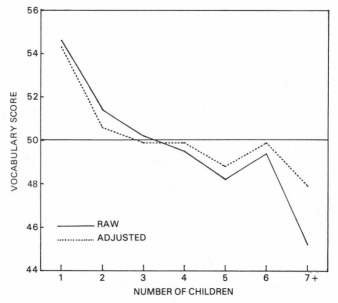

Figure 1. Mean vocabulary test score of children by number of children in family, U.S. children aged 7–11, 1976.

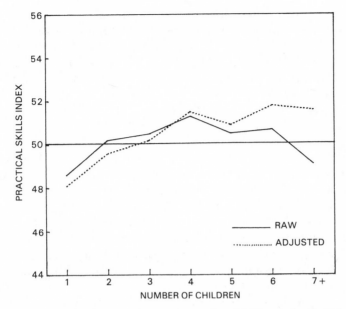

Figure 2. Mean practical skills score of children by number of children in family, U.S. children aged 7–11, 1976.

When these and other family characteristics were taken into account, the effect of family size on vocabulary score was diminished (beta = .12, $p < .01$). Nevertheless, there was still a 6-point spread in the adjusted vocabulary scores from family size 1 to family size 7. Only children remained significantly superior in average vocabulary performance to children in all other familiy sizes—even those in family size 2.

Only children did not come out so well with respect to practical skills development. When the association between family size and the practical skills index was examined separately, a weak and bow-shaped relationship between the variables was observed (eta = .07, ns; see Table 5 and Figure 2). Only children and children from the largest families showed lower mean scores than children from intermediate-sized families. In this case, however, controlling for education, income, and the other family characteristics served to bring out a positive and generally linear relationship between family size and practical skills development (beta = .10, $p < .01$).

Ethnic Group

The family situation of many black and Hispanic children in the United States is very different from that of most nonminority children.

Fifty-six percent of the black children in the survey came from homes where the most educated parent did not have a high school diploma. The same was true of 48% of the Hispanic children but of only 16% of the nonminority children. Nearly three-quarters of the black children were living in families with 1975 incomes below $10,000; so were nearly half of the Hispanic children. Among nonminority children, the comparable proportion was 24%. The average family size was larger among black families. Nearly 54% of the black children in the survey were growing up in families with four or more children. This was true of less than 35% of the nonminority children in the survey. Hispanic families were slightly larger, with 39% in families with four or more children.

Given the socioeconomic characteristics of many minority families and the relationships noted above, it is to be expected that children from these families would not do as well on the vocabulary test as children from nonminority families. For Hispanic children, there was the additional factor that English may not have been the principal language spoken in the home. When the vocabulary test results were analyzed by ethnic group, there was more than a 6-point difference (eta = .26, $p < .01$) between the average vocabulary score achieved by nonminority children (mean = 51.4) and that attained by black children (mean = 44.8) or Hispanic children (mean = 45.1).

When parent education, income, number of children, and other family characteristics were statistically controlled, ethnic differences in vocabulary scores were reduced to just over a 3-point difference for black children and just over a 4-point difference for Hispanic children by comparison with nonminority kids. However, the child's ethnic group remained a significant predictor of vocabulary test performance—the second best predictor in the multiple classification analysis (beta = .14, $p < .01$). (Similar results have been obtained by Edwards & Grossman, 1979, analyzing data from Cycle II of the Health Examination Survey with respect to black and white children's scores on the vocabulary and block design subtests of the Wechsler Intelligence Scale for Children and on the Wide Range Achievement Test.)

Turning to the practical skills index, black children had a lower average score on this (mean = 47.6) than did nonminority children (mean = 50.8), but the difference (eta = .11, $p < .01$) was not as large as that found with the vocabulary test. When other family characteristics in a multiple classification analysis were controlled, ethnic differences were virtually eliminated (beta = .05, ns). Just over 1 point separated black and nonminority children when the mean scores were adjusted for family activity level, parent education, and so on. The practical skills development reported by parents of Hispanic children (mean score = 50.7) was equivalent to that reported for nonminority children. Adjustments for other family characteristics actually made the average Hispanic score slightly higher than the adjusted score for nonminority children.

The magnitude and even the direction of the differences between black and nonminority children showed considerable variation across the individual tasks that contributed to the practical skills index. Black children did not differ from nonminority children on tasks like washing dishes, shopping at a store, baby-sitting, fixing a bicycle, or cooking a meal for the family. And there were more black children than nonminority children who had ironed clothes (47% versus 24%) or changed sheets on a bed (74% versus 59%). But fewer black children than nonminority children had learned how to set the time on a clock or watch (55% versus 73%), and a smaller proportion of black children had ever written a letter and mailed it without help (47% versus 68%). Black children were also behind non-minority children in learning how to put batteries in a flashlight or toy, how to paint some object other than a picture, and how to build something out of wood with real tools.

Family Activities

Correlates of Family Activity Level

The family activities score displayed an intuitively sensible set of relationships with the other family characteristics. The level of family activities was most closely related to parent educational attainment (eta = .35, $p < .01$), with more educated parents reporting a greater number of recent activities with the family than did less educated parents. Family income was also positively related to family activity level (eta = .31, $p < .01$). Not surprisingly, lower-income parents reported fewer of those activities that cost money, namely taking the family out to dinner, going out for an evening without the children, buying new clothes for the children, and buying toys or games for the children. Family size was negatively related to family activities (eta = .21, $p < .01$), primarily because larger families were less apt to have gone out to dinner, to the movies, or to a park together. Parents in large families were also less likely than parents in small families to have purchased new toys or games for their children.

Black parents reported fewer family activities, on the average (mean = 4.5), than did nonminority parents (mean = 5.6). However, the effect of parent education level on family activities was more pronounced among black families (eta = .42) than among nonminority families (eta = .26). The size of the difference between black and nonminority families diminished as parent education increased until, at the college graduate level, there was no difference at all in average activities scores. Although Hispanic families had lower parent education and income levels than nonminority families, the average number of family activities reported by Hispanic parents (mean = 5.3) did not differ significantly from the nonminority average.

Finally, there was a slight negative relationship between the age of the subject child and the family activities score (eta = .09, $p < .05$). This is probably because as children get older they are more likely to do things with peers or on their own. Consequently, the frequency of parent–child interaction and the number of activities performed by the family as a whole decreases.

Family Activities and the Child's Vocabulary Score

The family activities score showed a positive and fairly linear relationship to the child's vocabulary score (eta = .18, $p < .01$), but the association was not as strong as that between parent education and vocabulary score. When parent education and other family characteristics were controlled in the multiple classification analysis, the relationship between family activities and vocabulary performance was virtually eliminated (beta = .05,ns). This suggests that family activities and children's vocabulary proficiency may simply covary rather than being causally related.

Family Activities and the Development of Practical Skills

A different picture emerged when the family activities index was used as a predictor of practical skills development. Taken individually, the family activities score was more closely related to the child's score on the practical skills index (eta = .28, $p < .01$) than were any of the other family characteristics. There was a difference of more than 17 points between children from families in the lowest family activities category (mean practical skills score = 39.0) and children in the highest family activities category (mean = 56.2). The family activities score remained the leading predictor of practical skills when all the family characteristics were combined in a multiple classification analysis (beta = .25, $p < .01$).

When the component items in the family activities index were examined separately, the items showing the best correlations with practical skills development were those that dealt most directly with parent–child interaction. Thus, the leading three items were: "did things with your children around the house," "took the family out to dinner," and "played a

game with your children." But the next best correlation was with a different
type of item, namely: "went out for an evening without your children."

Discussion

Sex-Role Socialization

Sex differences found in the acquisition of practical skills clearly
demonstrate the persistence of role stereotypes. All the differences were not
only in the direction one would expect from these stereotypes but also large
and significant. Perhaps women's liberationists should take heart from the
findings that two-thirds of the 7- to 11-year-old boys learned to wash dishes,
more than half had changed sheets on a bed, and nearly a third had done
baby-sitting at least once. But it is apparent that, as of 1976, girls in the
United States were still expected to learn to handle these household
responsibilities at an earlier age than boys, and they were less likely to be
allowed to get away with *not* mastering such domestic skills at all.

One explanation for the persistence of striking sex differences in the
acquisition of practical skills is that the changes that are being wrought by
the women's movement had not yet penetrated to the children of "middle
America" at the time of the survey. Perhaps future cohorts of girls and boys
will show some truly dramatic changes in their practical accomplishments.
It remains for future national surveys of children to establish whether or
not this is true.

If the prediction is valid, we should expect that children of better-
educated and higher-income parents in the present survey would show less
stereotyping than the children of parents with less education and lower
incomes. This was clearly the case with respect to survey questions to
children themselves regarding their attitudes about a woman President:
boys and girls from relatively affluent or highly educated families were
more favorably disposed toward the possibility of a female President. But
this was not the case with respect to children's liking or disliking typically
"feminine" activities like sewing or cooking or typically "masculine"
activities like boxing or woodwork (see Zill, 1983).

When it comes to the acquisition of practical skills, there was certainly
a positive main effect of parental education on the skill development of
both boys and girls. But there was only limited evidence of an education-
sex interaction effect whereby the accomplishments of boys and of girls
became more similar in families with higher education and income levels.

To illustrate, Figure 3 shows the percentages of sons and daughters
reported to have baked a cake or pie without help as the function of their

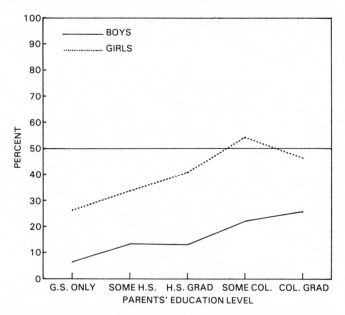

Figure 3. Percentage of children who have baked a cake or pie, by parent educational attainment and sex of child, U.S. children aged 7–11, 1976.

parents' education level. The proporation of boys who have baked a cake clearly goes up with rising parent-education levels; from 6% of boys with a parent who has only had a grade school education to 26% of the sons of college graduates (eta = .17, $p < .01$). But the proportion of girls who have baked a cake also rises with parent education levels, and in roughly parallel fashion: from 26% among daughters of grade school dropouts to 46% among daughters of college graduates (eta = .16, $p < .01$). Note that boys at the highest parent-education level were equivalent to girls at the lowest parent-education level in their likelihood of having learned baking skills.

There was more evidence of convergence on the task of building something out of wood with real tools (see Figure 4). The proportion of sons who have done this shows an increase from 61% at the grade school level to 79% at the college graduate level (eta = .11, $p < .05$). The increase among daughters is more dramatic: from 14% at the grade school level to 48% among daughters with college-educated parents (eta = .22, $p < .01$). Daughters of college graduates were as likely to have built something out of wood as to have baked a cake or pie. Nevertheless, girls at the highest parent-education levels were substantially below boys at the lowest parent-education level in terms of their woodworking accomplishments. And sons

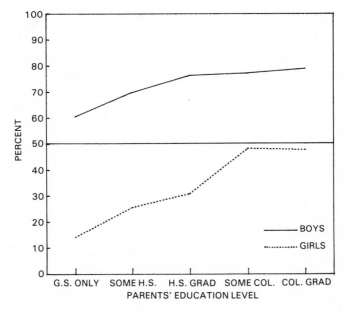

Figure 4. Percentage of children who have built something out of wood with real tools, by parent educational attainment and sex of child, U.S. children aged 7-11, 1976.

of college graduates were much less likely to have baked a cake than to have built something out of wood. The sex-role revolution obviously has a way to go.

Family Background and Practical Skills Development

The findings presented in this report suggest—although they do not prove—that the intergenerational transmission of practical skills is at least partly mediated through the family environment. After sex differences were controlled, the measure of family activities was the best predictor of the child's development of practical skills. This was not only the case when each predictor was considered alone but also when all other predictors were taken into account. It was noted that among the items in the family activities score, "went out for an evening without your children" was among those correlating most strongly with practical skills. This suggests that parents may foster the development of practical skills by leading active lives of their own as adults as well as by direct instruction of the children and participation in shared activities. Active families where parents do things with their children—but where children are also expected to make some accommodation to adult demands and requirements—appear to be best for nurturing practical skills in children.

Well-educated, affluent families are more likely to provide their children with this kind of active environment than are poorly educated, low-income families. This appears to be at least part of the reason why children from higher-SES families tend to be more advanced in their overall development of practical skills than are children from lower-SES families. When the level of family activities was controlled, the relationship between practical skills and parent education was reduced, and that with family income was essentially eliminated. Ethnic differences in overall skill development were also greatly reduced when family activity level was controlled.

At the same time, it was apparent that the development of at least certain practical skills was related to economic necessities. Although the overall skills index was unrelated to income once other factors were taken into account, it was noted that children from low-income families were more likely to have ironed clothes or changed sheets by themselves. Low-income families are less likely to have labor-saving equipment in the home or to purchase household services in the market, meaning that a greater amount of household production, such as laundry, must be accomplished by household members, including children.

Likewise, family size showed a positive relation to practical skills once other background factors were taken into account. For obvious practical reasons, parents in large families would tend to make more demands upon their children to help with household chores and child care. Indeed, the individual tasks that showed significant positive correlations with family size were changing sheets, baby-sitting, ironing clothes, fixing a bicycle, and shopping at a store. It may also be that older children in large families help to teach these skills to the younger children. Thus, although children with a number of brothers or sisters seem to be slower in acquiring vocabulary knowledge, they appear to be more mature in terms of domestic responsibility and child care skills than are children from small families.

Family Background and Vocabulary Development

If the family environment plays an important role in the development of children's vocabulary skills, the level of family activities does not appear to be a significant element in the process. The family activities score was moderately associated with vocabulary development when it was considered alone. But it was reduced to insignificance when other factors, especially the parents' education level, were taken into account.

There are, of course, several possible explanations for the failure of the family activities index to be more predictive of the child's vocabulary development than were parent education and other "distal" characteristics of the family. It may be that the index is not a particularly good measure of those aspects of parent–child interaction that help to build a child's vocabulary. Or it may be that what parents *did* with their children during the preschool years is more important as far as vocabulary development is concerned than is the level of family interaction during the grammar school years. Other investigators have developed home environment inventories (Bradley *et al*., 1977; Trotman, 1977) and measures of parental "press for achievement" (Marjoribanks, 1977) that seem to predict to IQ scores better than the family activities index related to vocabulary scores in the present study. However, the home environment measures tend to be highly similar for different siblings in the same family and do not, therefore, account for the considerable degree of within-family variation in children's IQ scores. This and other limitations of existing studies have led Willerman (1979) to argue that "we know less than we think about the environmental causes of intellectual differences" (p. 923).

One reason why the practical skills index showed a stronger relationship to family activities than did vocabulary scores may be that the practical skills measure is not purely a measure of the child's abilities. It can be argued (see Jensen, 1980, pp. 684–685) that the practical skills items have as much to do with what parents permit, encourage, or make children do as with what the children themselves can or cannot do. This is not necessarily a drawback as far as studies of learning in the family are concerned.

In addition, both the practical skills index and the family activities score were based on reports by the parent respondent (in most cases, the same parent responded to both sets of questions). The questions were in two different and widely separated sections of the interview, but they were similar in format (i.e., the questions were worded so that positive responses served to increase the scores on both indices). Thus, it may be that some of the association between the two measures is attributable to shared method variance or common response bias. It would be desirable to confirm and extend the relationship in future studies where family activities and the development of practical skills are measured independently.

The contrasts between the two measures of child development examined here are intriguing. They differed not only with respect to the strength of their relationships with family activities but also, and markedly, in their relationships with family size. Although both measures were positively related to the parents' education level, the relationship with vocabulary development was linear whereas that with practical skills was curvilinear at the top. The reversal in the trend at the highest education level may indicate that college-graduate parents, while more likely than less educated parents to encourage their children in intellectual and arts-and-crafts pursuits, are less likely to make maturity demands as far as domestic chores are concerned.

All in all, these findings suggest that conclusions about the kinds of variables which are important for child development will depend on the particular dependent measure of development being considered. Those who wish to understand the family as a learning environment would do well to broaden their focus and examine measures of child development that go beyond the customary IQ and scholastic achievement scores.

ACKNOWLEDGMENTS

The authors wish to thank the editors, Ann McGillicuddy-DeLisi and other members of the ETS Conference on The Family as a Learning Environment for their helpful comments.

Computer programming assistance was provided by Robert Patrick, Richard C. Roistacher, and the late Gunnar Gruveaus. Michelle Chibba and Georgene Murray helped to prepare the tables and graphs.

References

American Association on Mental Deficiency. *Adaptive Behavior Scale: Manual.* Washington, D.C.: The Association, 1974.

Andrews, F., Morgan, J., & Sonquist, J. *Multiple classification analysis.* Ann Arbor, Mich.: The Institute for Social Research, 1967.

Bradley, R. H., Caldwell, B. M., & Elardo, R. Home environment, social status, and mental test performance. *Journal of Educational Psychology*, 1977, *69*, 697–701.

Clarke-Stewart, A. *Child care in the family.* New York: Academic Press, 1977.

Doll, E. A. *The measurement of social competence.* Minneapolis: Educational Test Bureau, 1953.

Doll, E. A. *Vineland Social Maturity Scale: Manual of directions* (rev. ed.). Minneapolis: Educational Test Bureau, 1965.

Edwards, L. N., & Grossman, M. The relationship between children's health and intellectual development. In S. Mushkin & D. Dunlop (Eds.), *Health: What is it worth?* New York: Pergamon Press, 1979.

Frankenburg, W. K., Dick, N. P., & Carland, J. Development of preschool-aged children of different social and ethnic groups: Implications for developmental screening. *Journal of Pediatrics*, 1975, *87*, 125–132.

Jensen, A. R. *Bias In Mental Testing.* New York: The Free Press, 1980.

Marjoribanks, K. Socioeconomic status and its relation to cognitive performance as mediated through the family environment. In A. Oliverio (Ed.), *Genetics, environment, and intelligence.* Amsterdam: Elsevier, 1977.

National Assessment of Educational Progress. *The first national assessment of career and occupational development: An overview.* Report No. 05-COD-00. Denver, Col.: Education Commission of the States, 1976.

National Assessment of Educational Progress. *An assessment of career development: Basic work skills.* Report No. 05-COD-02. Denver, Col.: Education Commission of the States, 1977. (a)

National Assessment of Educational Progress. *What students know and can do: Profiles of three age groups.* Denver, Col.: Education Commission of the States, 1977. (b)

Rasch, G. An item analysis which takes individual differences into account. *British Journal of Mathematical and Statistical Psychology,* 1966, *19,* 49–57.

Schultz, T. W. *Economics of the family.* Chicago: University of Chicago Press, 1974.

Trotman, F. K. Race, IQ, and the middle class. *Journal of Educational Psychology,* 1977, *69,* 266–273.

Willerman, L. Effects of families on intellectual development. *American Psychologist,* 1979, *34,* 923–929.

Zill, N. *American children: Happy, healthy, and insecure.* New York: Doubleday-Anchor, 1983, in press.

Appendix

Percentage of children who have accomplished specific tasks without help, by age and sex of child, U.S. children, 1976.

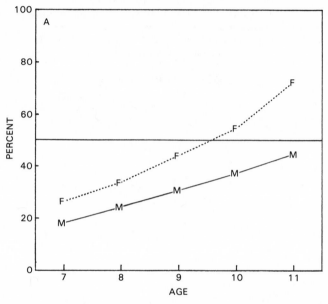

Figure A. Baby-sit.

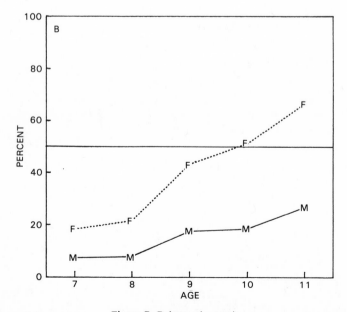

Figure B. Bake a cake or pie.

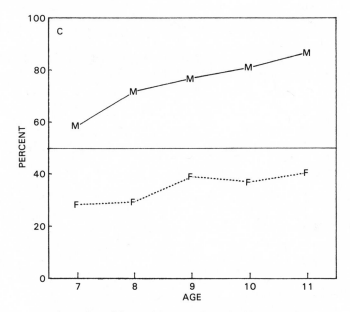

Figure C. Build something out of wood with real tools.

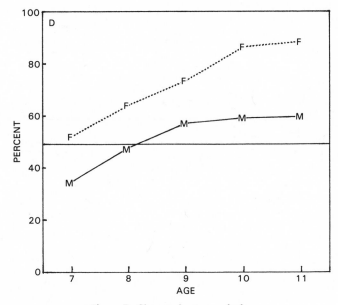

Figure D. Change sheets on a bed.

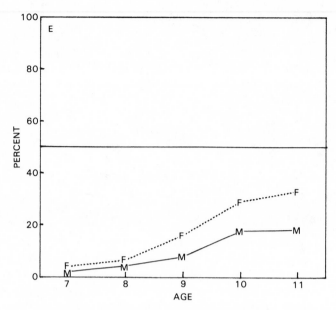

Figure E. Cook a complete meal for the family.

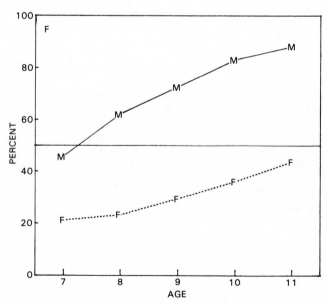

Figure F. Fix a bicycle, wagon, or roller skates.

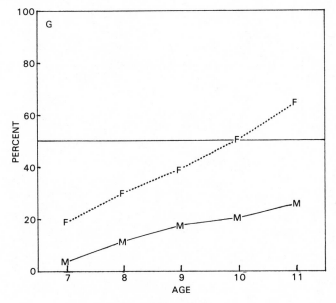

Figure G. Iron clothes.

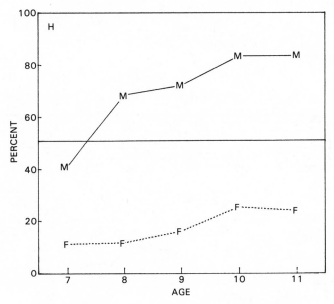

Figure H. Make a model, like a model car, boat, or airplane.

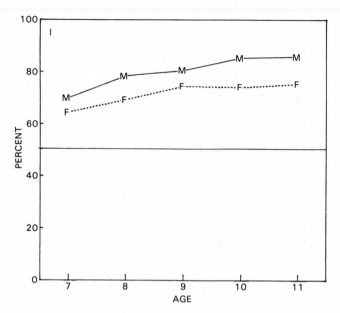

Figure I. Paint some object other than a picture.

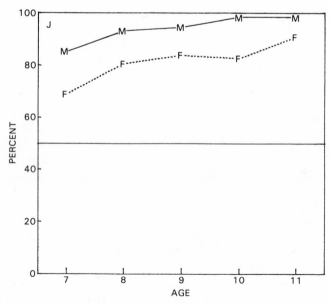

Figure J. Put batteries in a flashlight or toy.

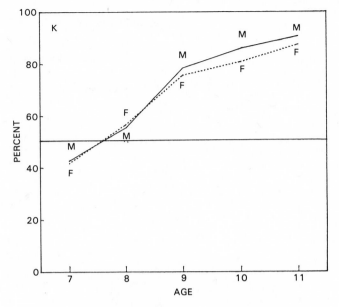

Figure K. Set the time on a clock or watch.

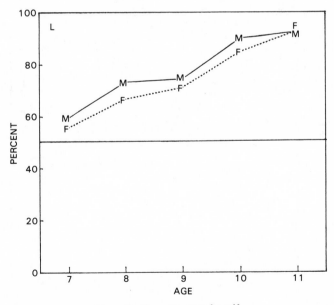

Figure L. Shop at a store by self.

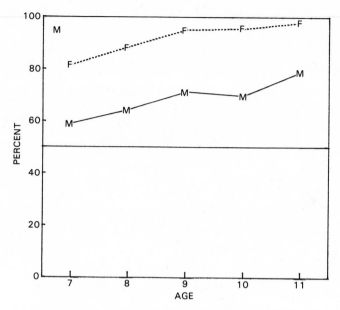

Figure M. Wash dishes.

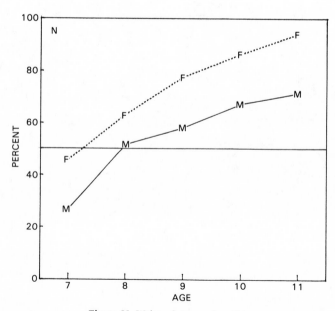

Figure N. Write a letter and mail it.

Author Index

Subject Index